THE COMIC BOOK GUIDE TO
GROWING FOOD

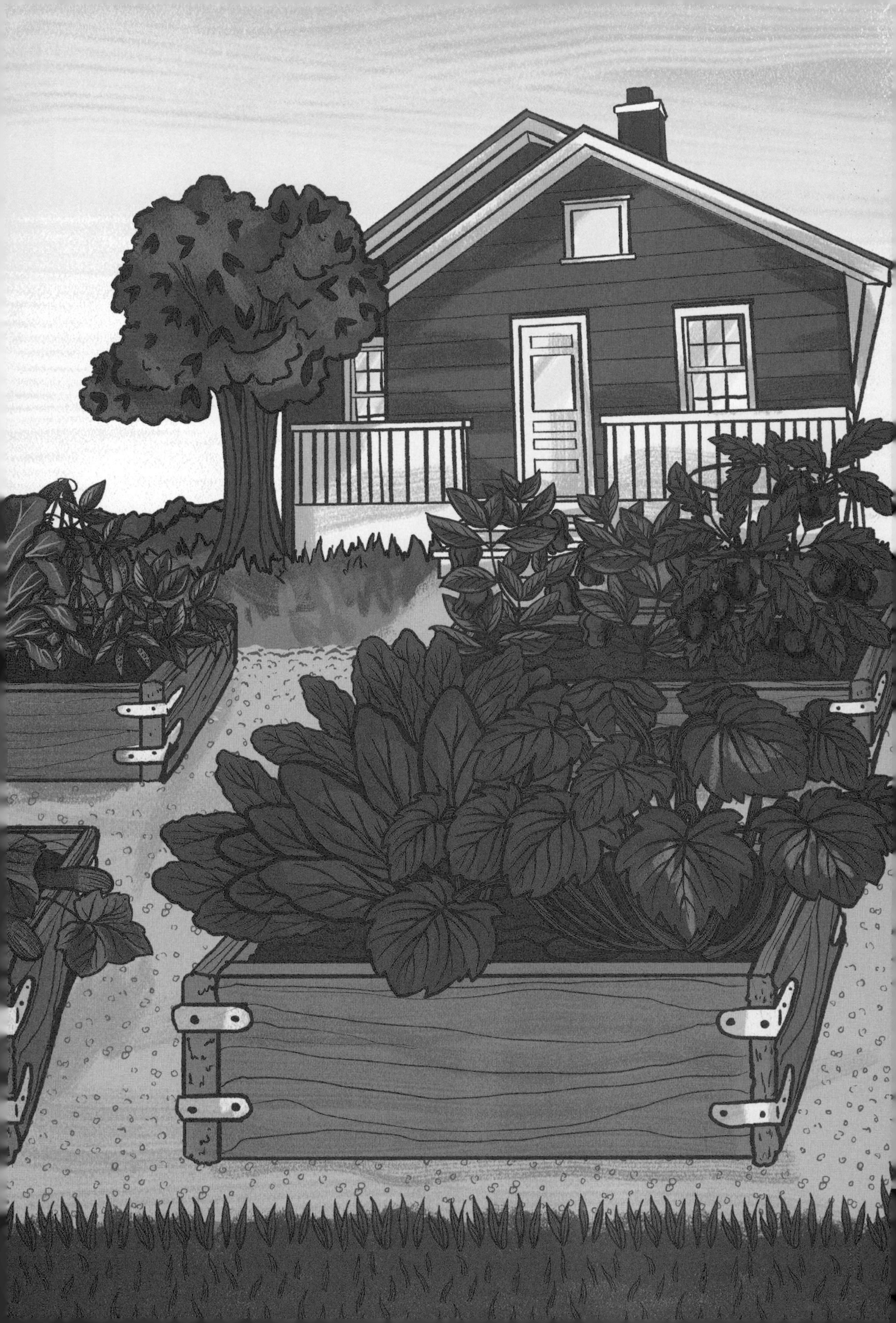

THE COMIC BOOK GUIDE TO GROWING FOOD

STEP-BY-STEP VEGETABLE GARDENING FOR EVERYONE

JOSEPH TYCHONIEVICH

ART, COLORS, AND LETTERS BY
LIZ ANNA KOZIK

TEN SPEED PRESS
California | New York

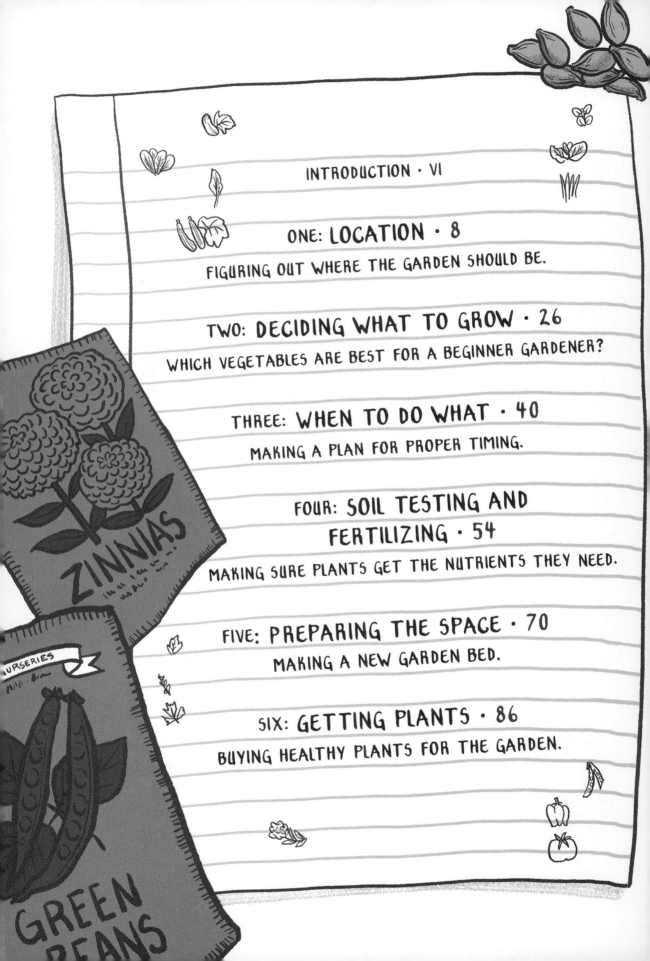

ZINNIAS

URSERIES

GREEN
BEANS

INTRODUCTION

MY NAME IS MIA. I SPENT MY DAYS AT WORK, WRITING CODE, AND EATING PREMADE CRAP FROM THE FROZEN FOODS AISLE.

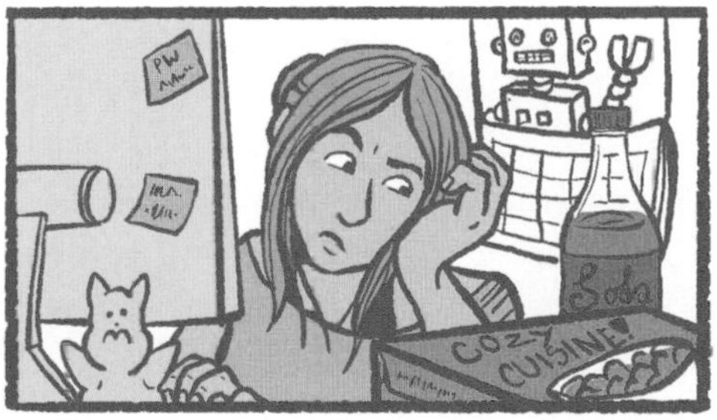

COZY CUISINE!
Soda

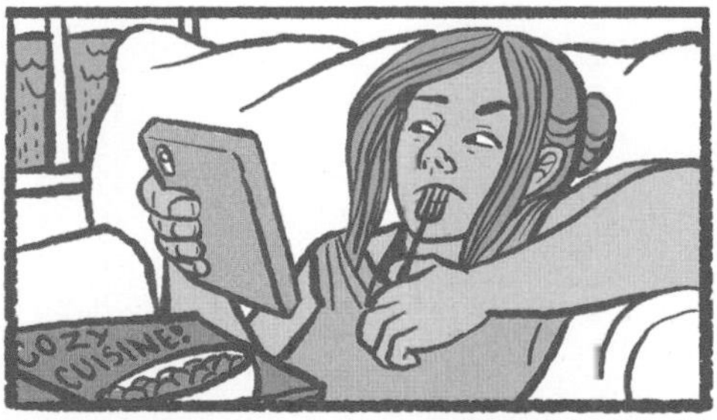

COZY CUISINE!

THEN I'D GO HOME TO ANOTHER FROZEN DINNER AND SIT WATCHING TV, IGNORING AND BEING IGNORED BY MY FRIENDS.

THEN EVERYTHING CHANGED...

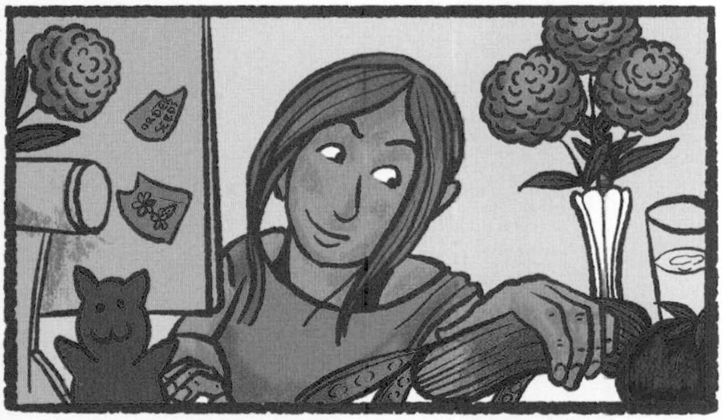

NOW WORK IS FULL OF FLOWERS AND THE FRESHEST, MOST DELICIOUS PRODUCE I'VE EVER EATEN.

AND I COME HOME TO MORE FLOWERS, VEGETABLES, AND, BEST OF ALL, A PLACE THAT FRIENDS AND NEIGHBORS LIKE TO VISIT AND HANG OUT IN.

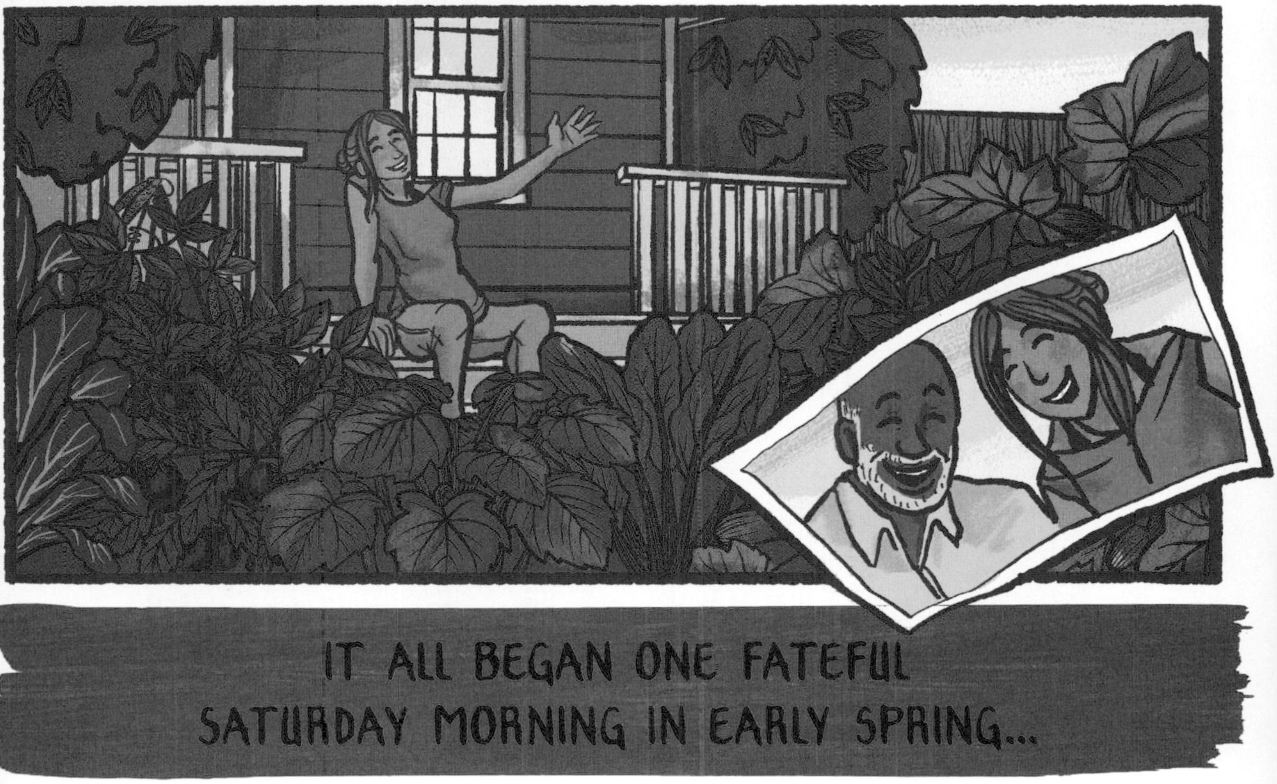

IT ALL BEGAN ONE FATEFUL SATURDAY MORNING IN EARLY SPRING...

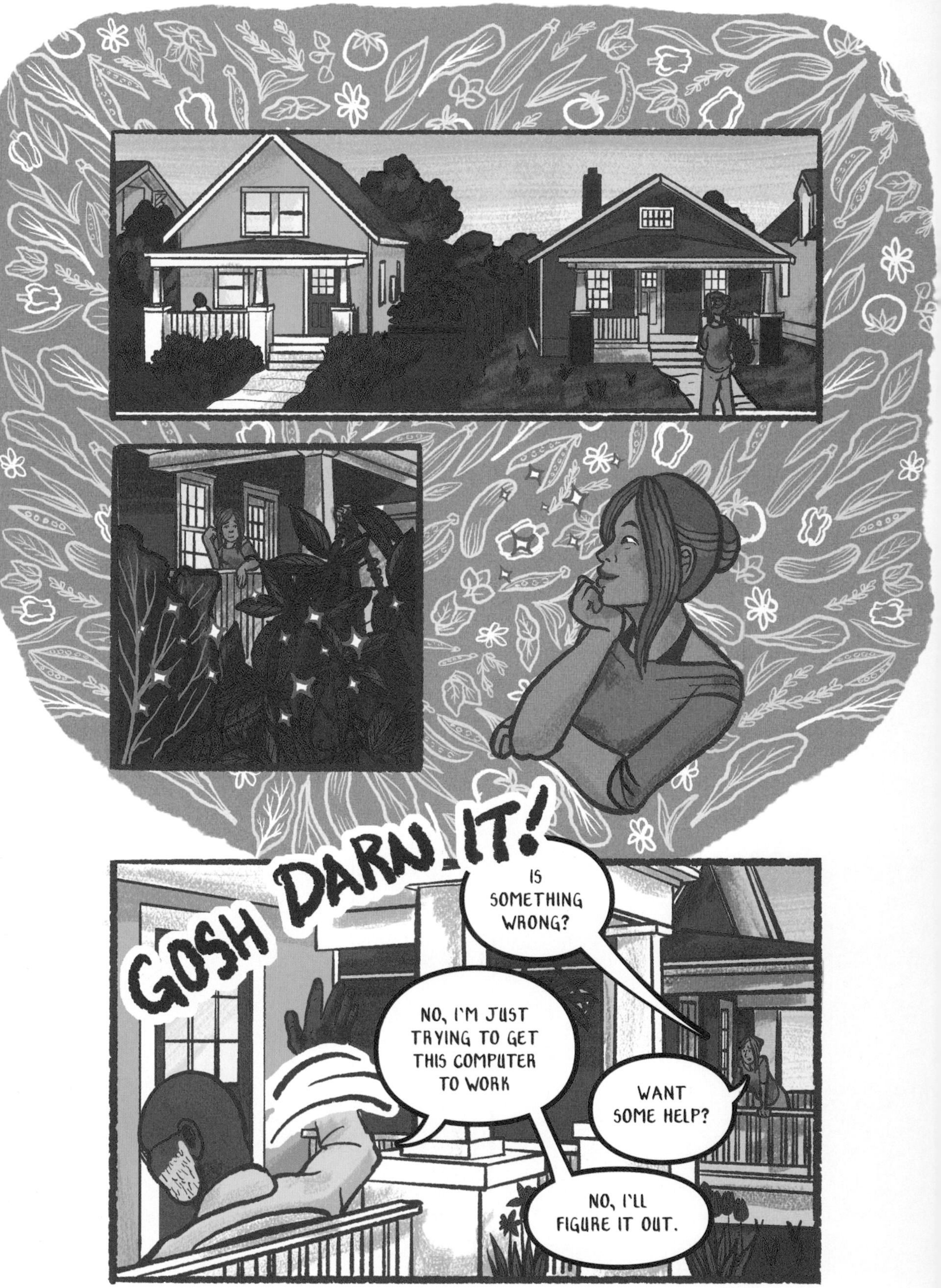
GOSH DARN IT!
IS SOMETHING WRONG?
NO, I'M JUST TRYING TO GET THIS COMPUTER TO WORK
WANT SOME HELP?
NO, I'LL FIGURE IT OUT.

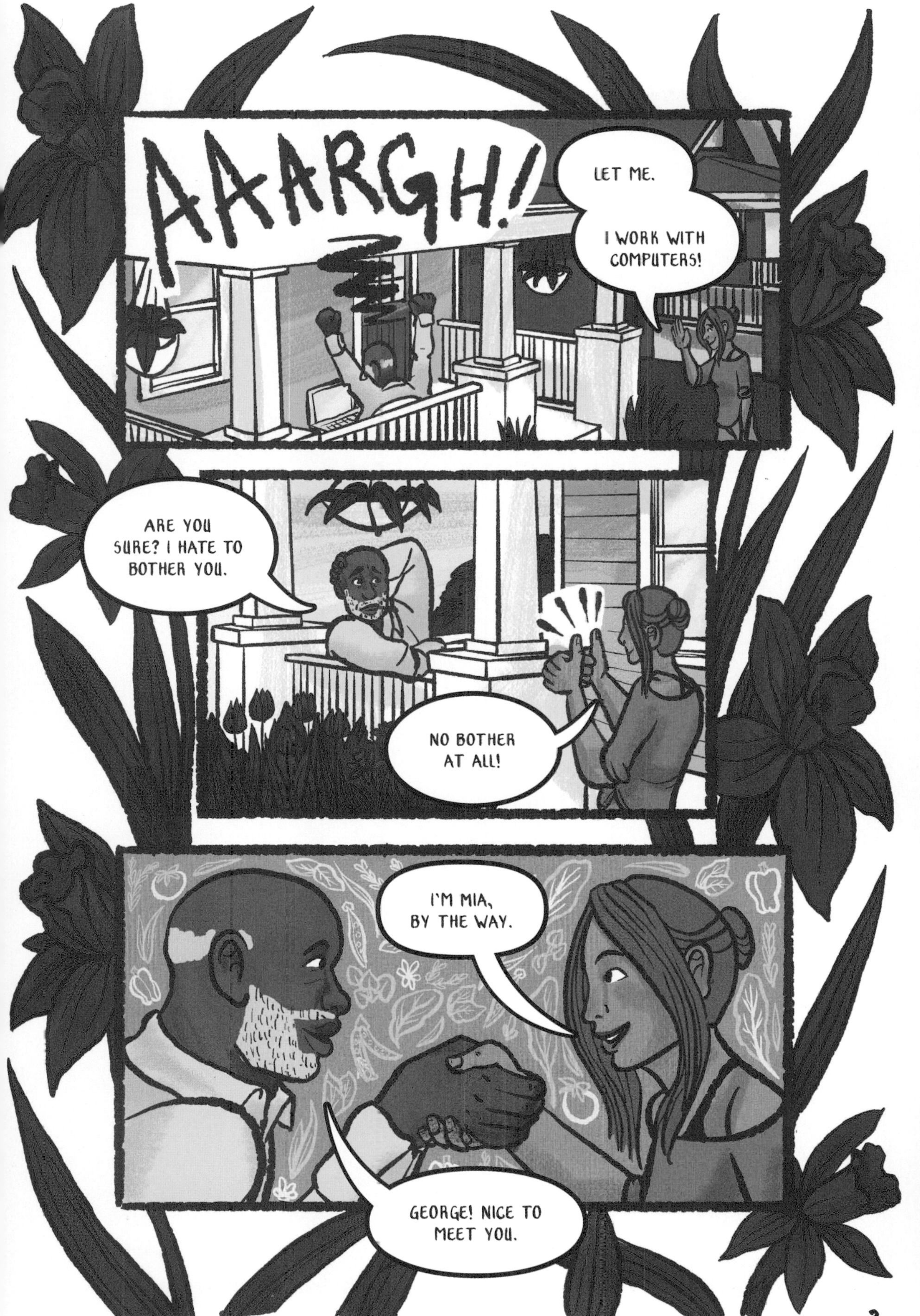
AAARGH!
LET ME.
I WORK WITH COMPUTERS!
ARE YOU SURE? I HATE TO BOTHER YOU.
NO BOTHER AT ALL!
I'M MIA, BY THE WAY.
GEORGE! NICE TO MEET YOU.

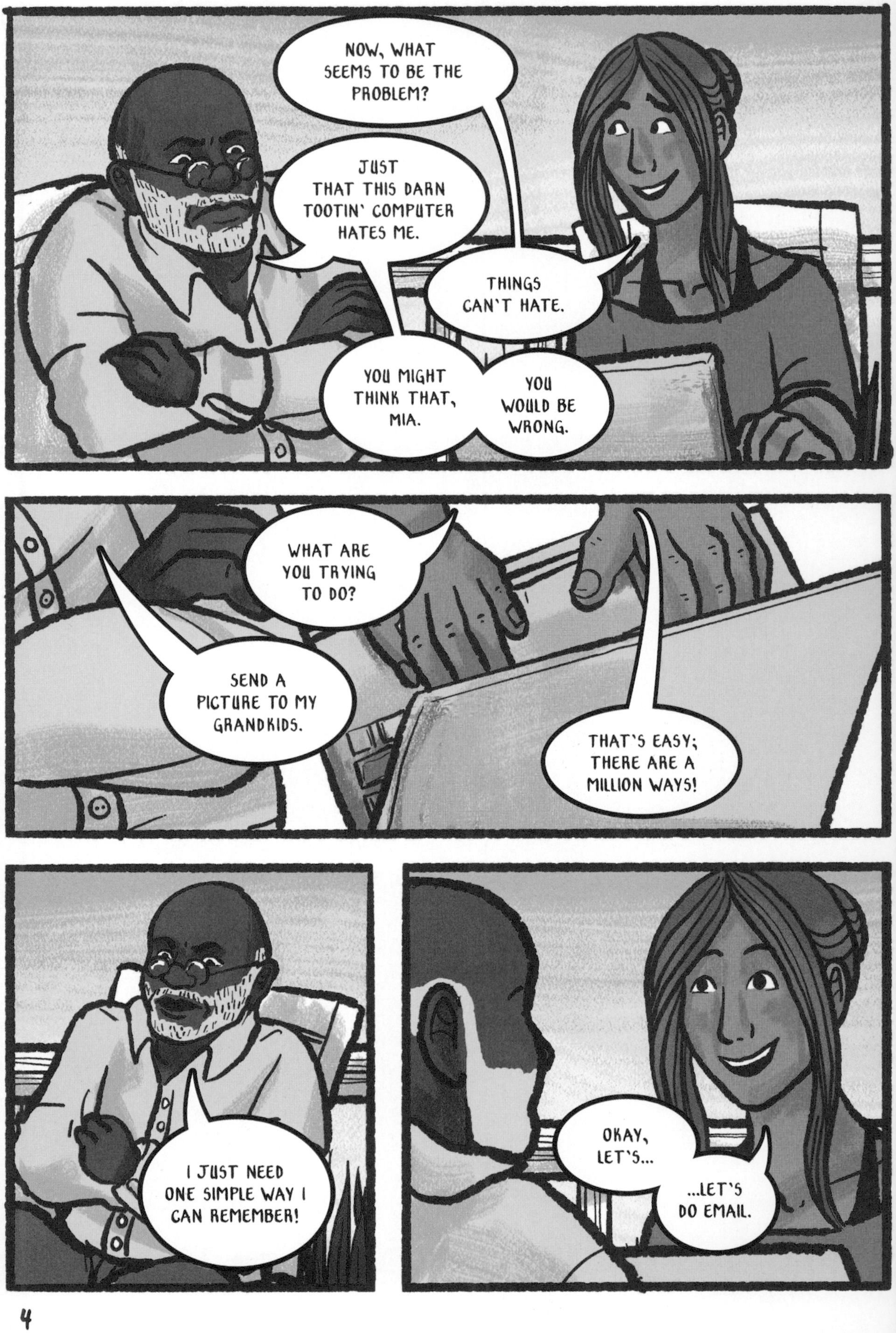
NOW, WHAT SEEMS TO BE THE PROBLEM?
JUST THAT THIS DARN TOOTIN' COMPUTER HATES ME.
THINGS CAN'T HATE.
YOU MIGHT THINK THAT, MIA.
YOU WOULD BE WRONG.
WHAT ARE YOU TRYING TO DO?
SEND A PICTURE TO MY GRANDKIDS.
THAT'S EASY; THERE ARE A MILLION WAYS!
I JUST NEED ONE SIMPLE WAY I CAN REMEMBER!
OKAY, LET'S...
...LET'S DO EMAIL.

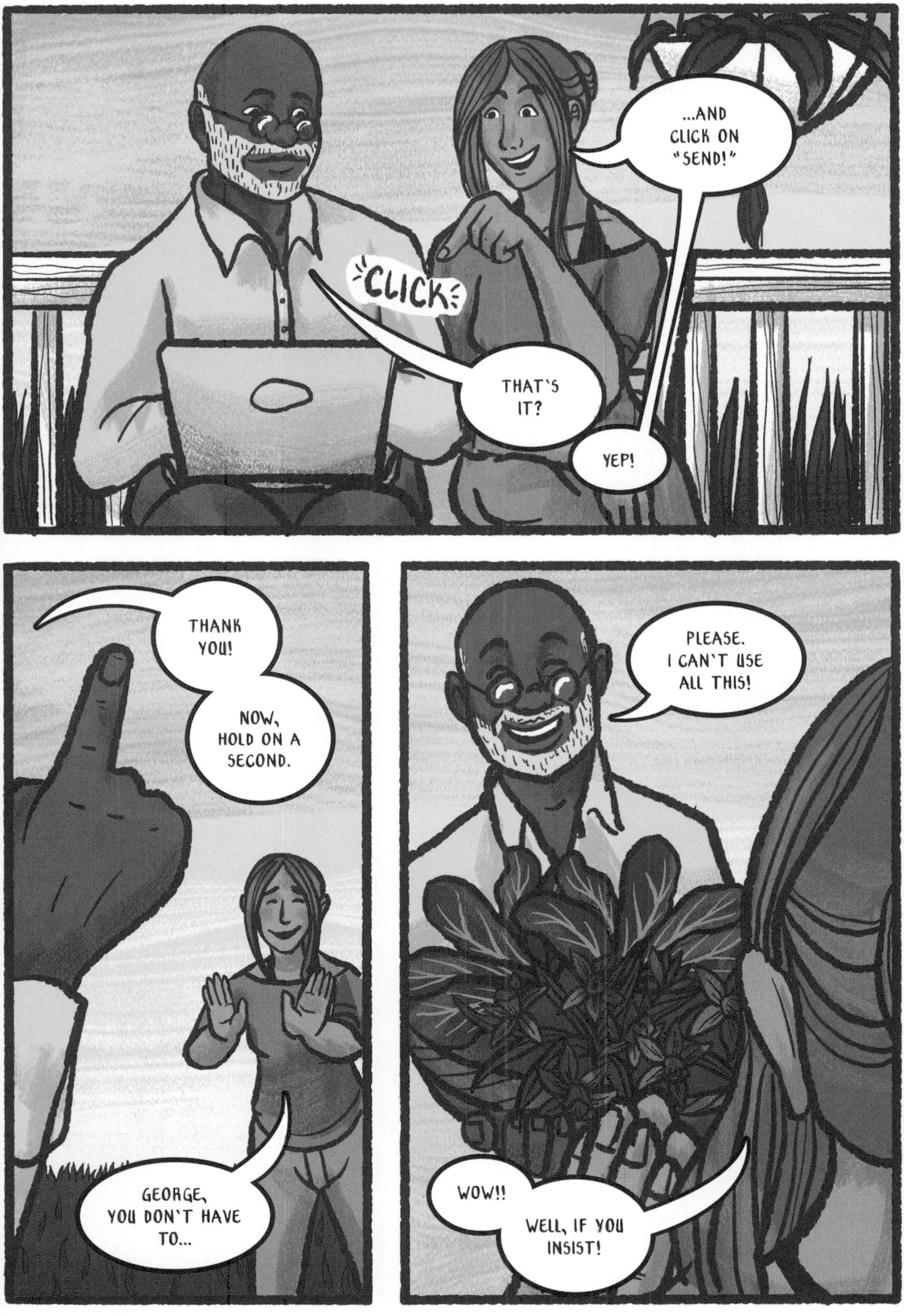
...AND CLICK ON "SEND!"
CLICK
THAT'S IT?
YEP!
THANK YOU!
NOW, HOLD ON A SECOND.
GEORGE, YOU DON'T HAVE TO...
PLEASE. I CAN'T USE ALL THIS!
WOW!!
WELL, IF YOU INSIST!

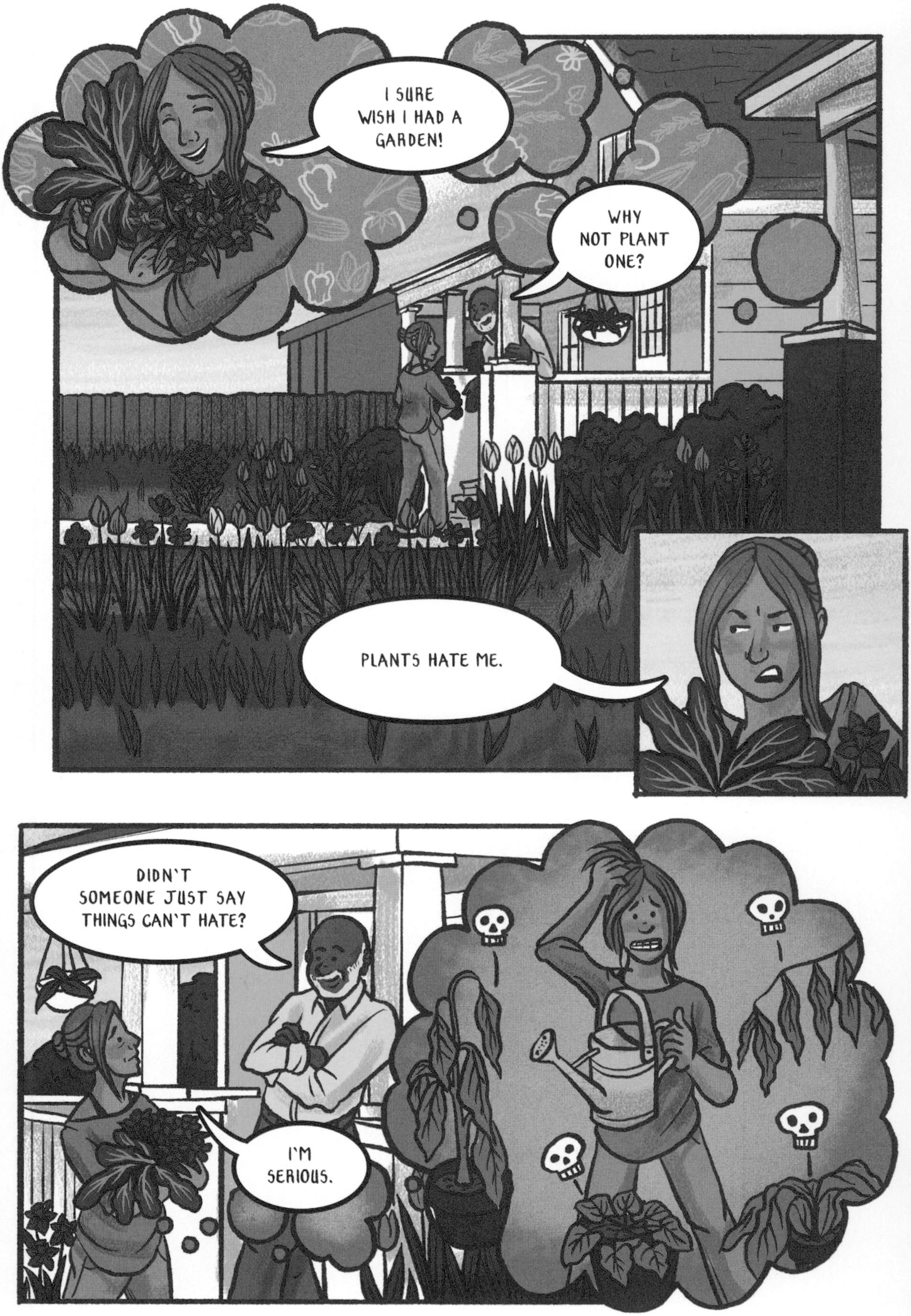
I SURE WISH I HAD A GARDEN!
WHY NOT PLANT ONE?
PLANTS HATE ME.
DIDN'T SOMEONE JUST SAY THINGS CAN'T HATE?
I'M SERIOUS.

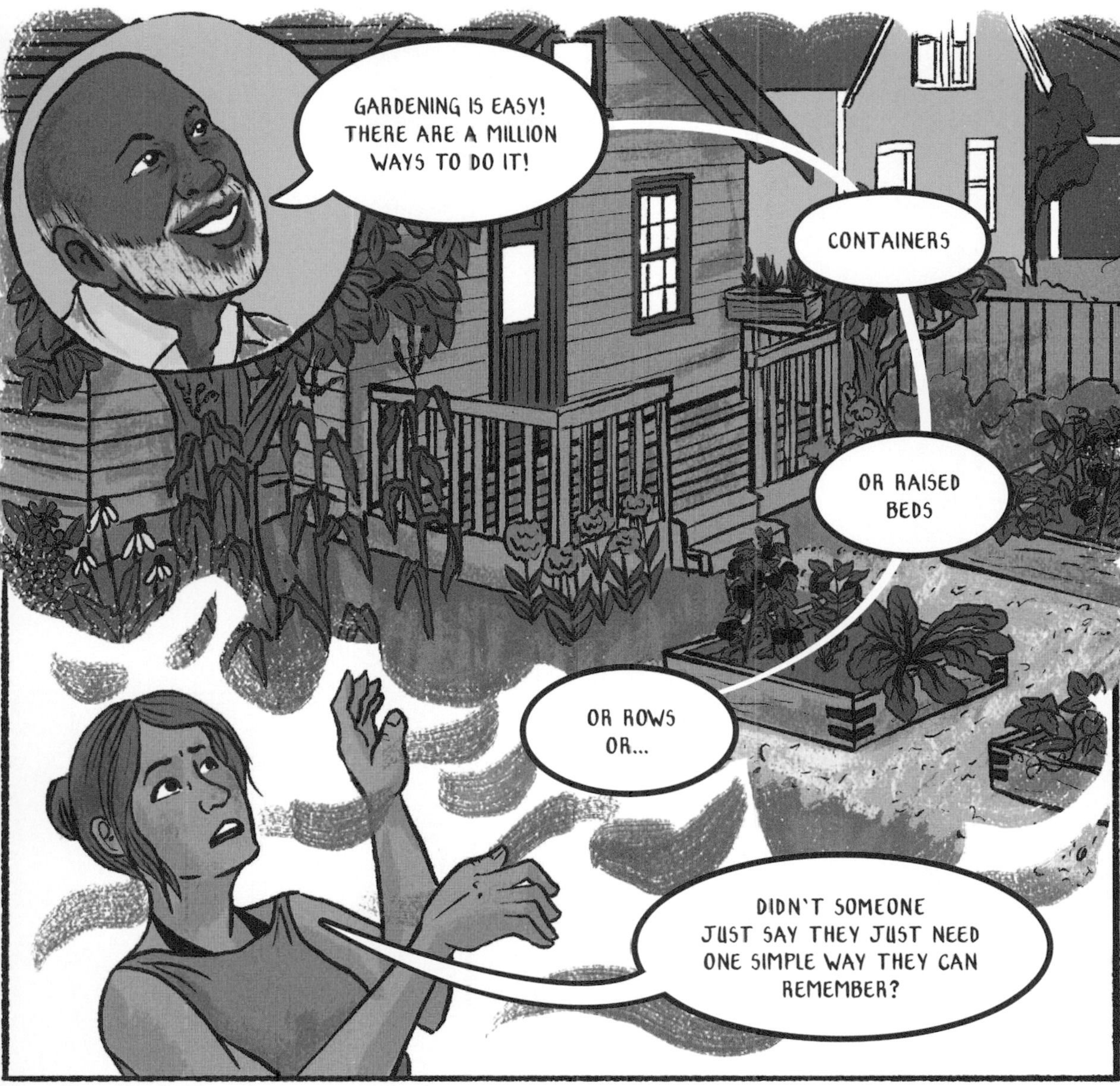
GARDENING IS EASY! THERE ARE A MILLION WAYS TO DO IT!
CONTAINERS
OR RAISED BEDS
OR ROWS OR...
DIDN'T SOMEONE JUST SAY THEY JUST NEED ONE SIMPLE WAY THEY CAN REMEMBER?

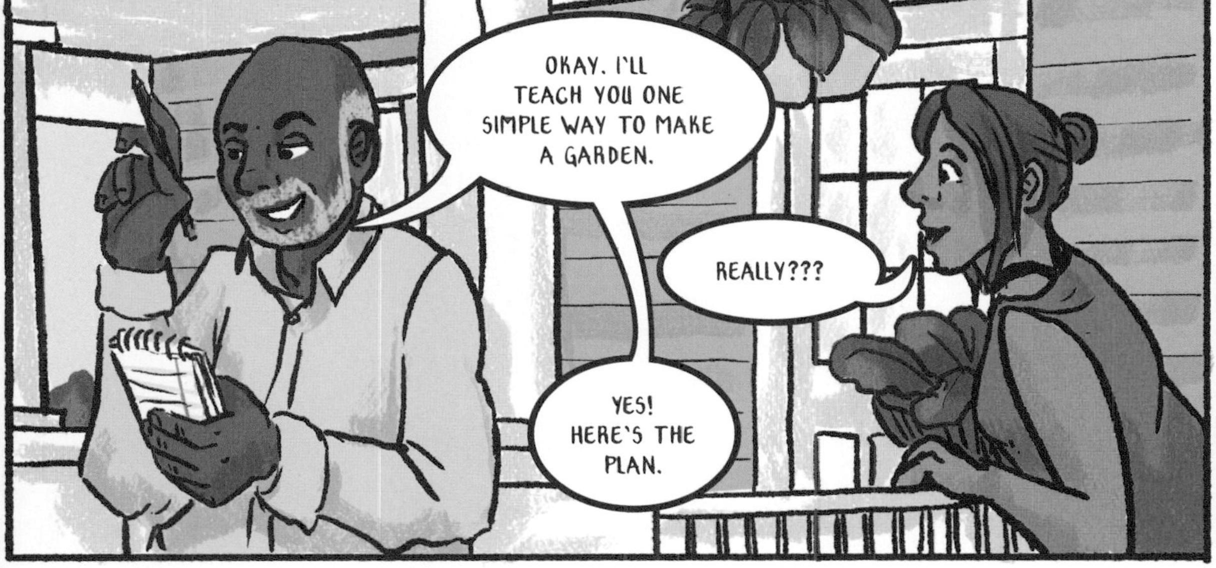
OKAY. I'LL TEACH YOU ONE SIMPLE WAY TO MAKE A GARDEN.
REALLY???
YES! HERE'S THE PLAN.

ONE:
LOCATION

FIGURING OUT WHERE
THE GARDEN SHOULD BE.

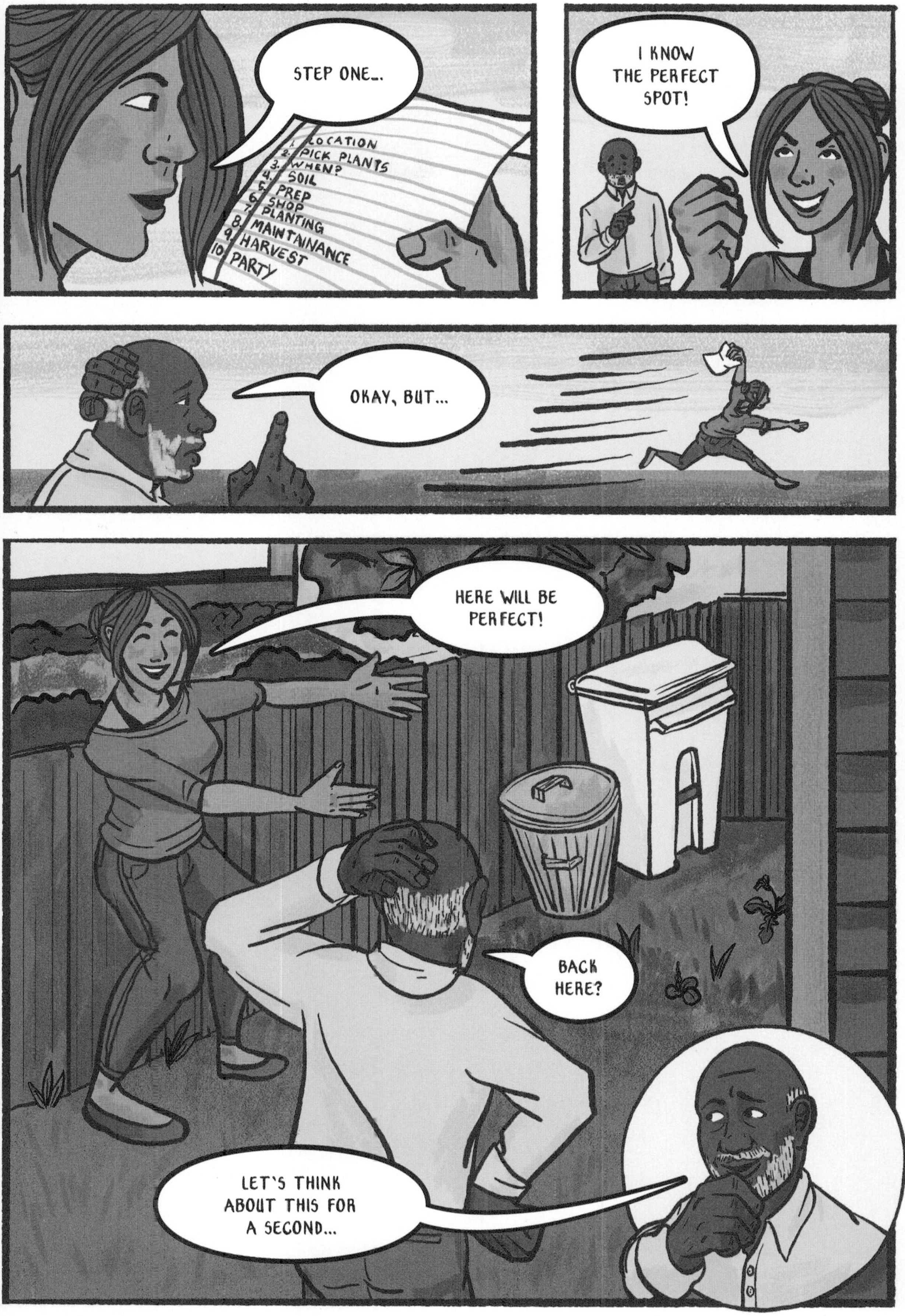
STEP ONE...
1. LOCATION
2. PICK PLANTS
3. WHEN?
4. SOIL
5. PREP
6. SHOP
7. PLANTING
8. MAINTAINANCE
9. HARVEST
10 PARTY
I KNOW THE PERFECT SPOT!
OKAY, BUT...
HERE WILL BE PERFECT!
BACK HERE?
LET'S THINK ABOUT THIS FOR A SECOND...

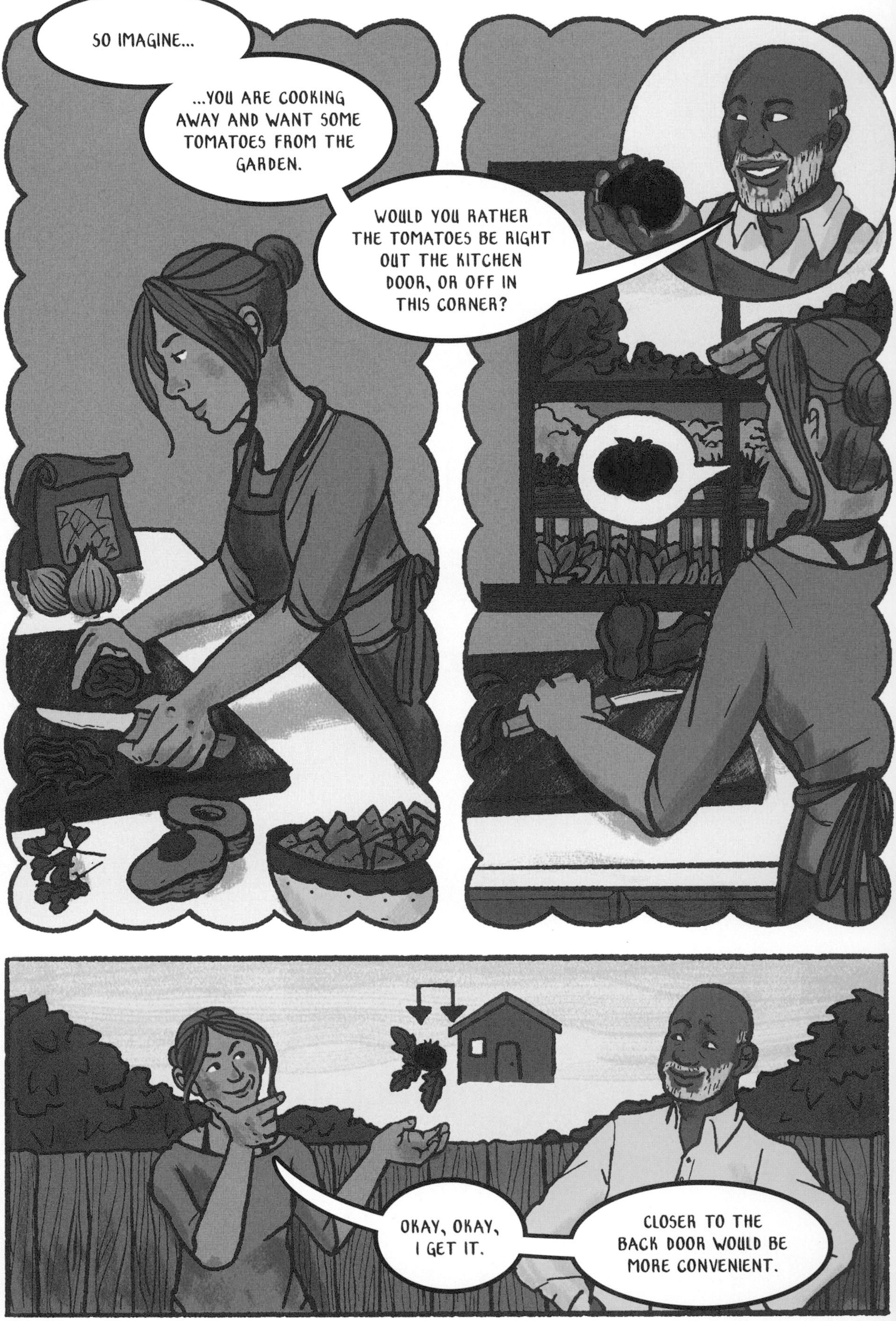
SO IMAGINE...
...YOU ARE COOKING AWAY AND WANT SOME TOMATOES FROM THE GARDEN.
WOULD YOU RATHER THE TOMATOES BE RIGHT OUT THE KITCHEN DOOR, OR OFF IN THIS CORNER?
OKAY, OKAY, I GET IT.
CLOSER TO THE BACK DOOR WOULD BE MORE CONVENIENT.

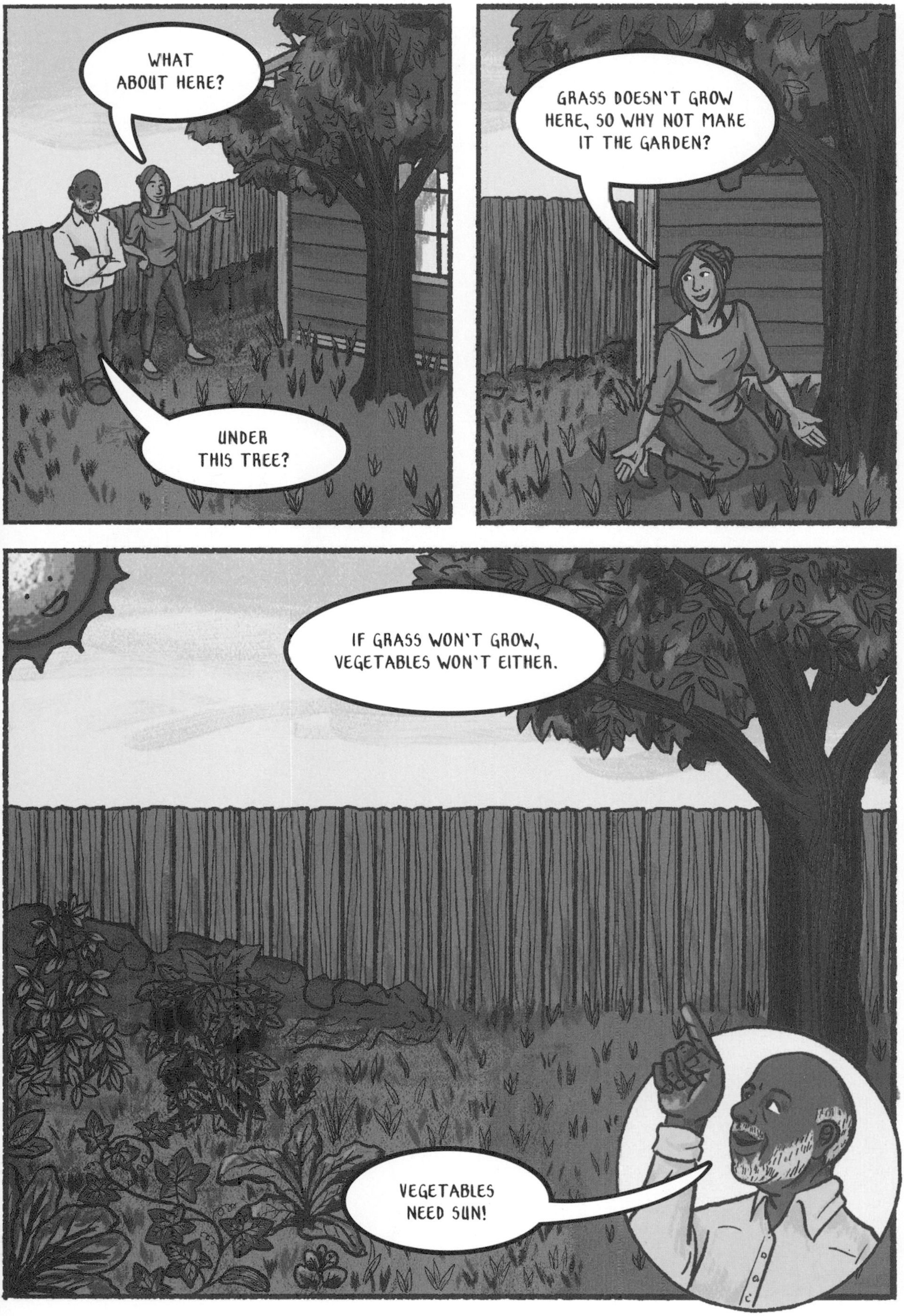
WHAT ABOUT HERE?
UNDER THIS TREE?
GRASS DOESN'T GROW HERE, SO WHY NOT MAKE IT THE GARDEN?
IF GRASS WON'T GROW, VEGETABLES WON'T EITHER.
VEGETABLES NEED SUN!

HOW MUCH SUN DO YOU NEED?

RULE OF THUMB:
6 HOURS DIRECT, UNFILTERED SUNLIGHT A DAY.

IF YOU LIVE
IN A HOT DESERT,
LESS IS OKAY.

IN A COOL, CLOUDY
CLIMATE, MORE SUN
IS BEST.

APPROVED CHEAT SHEET

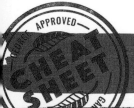

HOW MUCH SUN DO YOU HAVE?

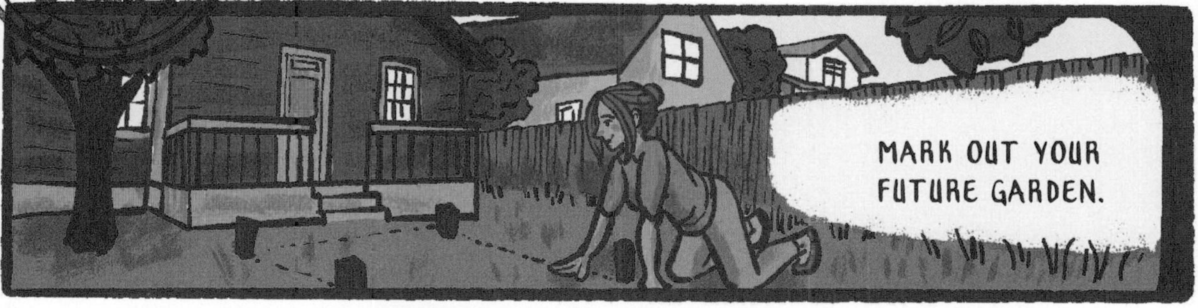
MARK OUT YOUR FUTURE GARDEN.

WATCH DURING THE DAY TO SEE HOW MUCH SUN IT GETS.

FOR EXAMPLE:

8:00 A.M.

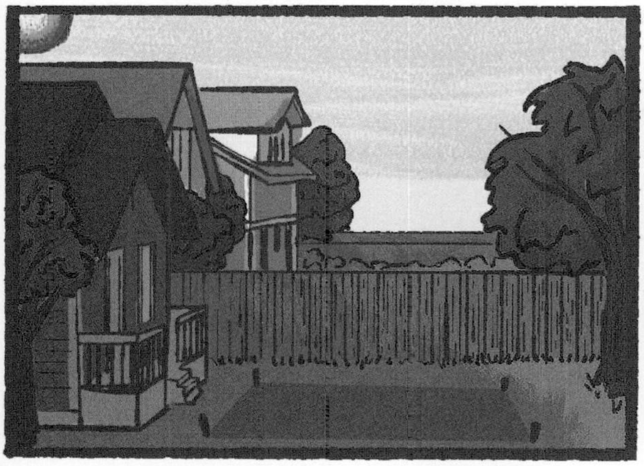

10:00 A.M.

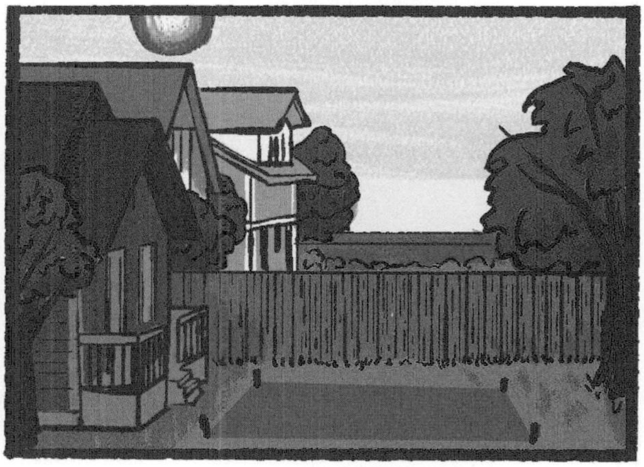

4:00 P.M.

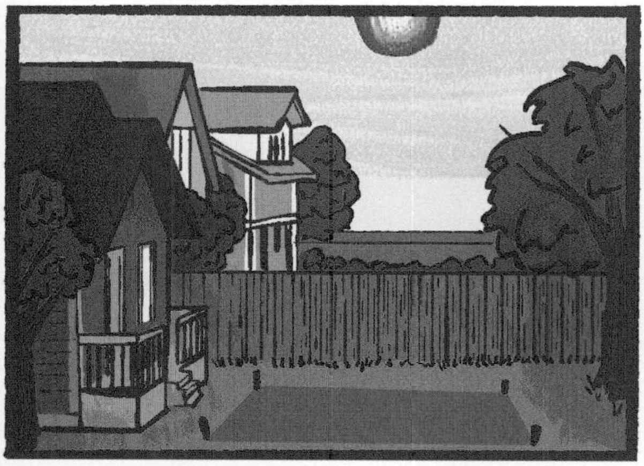

6:00 P.M.

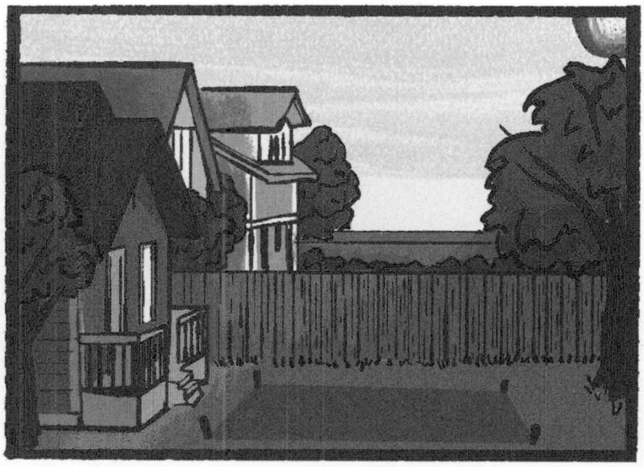

IN MIA'S YARD,

FULL SUN FROM 10 TO 4 = 6 HOURS = GOOD TO GO!

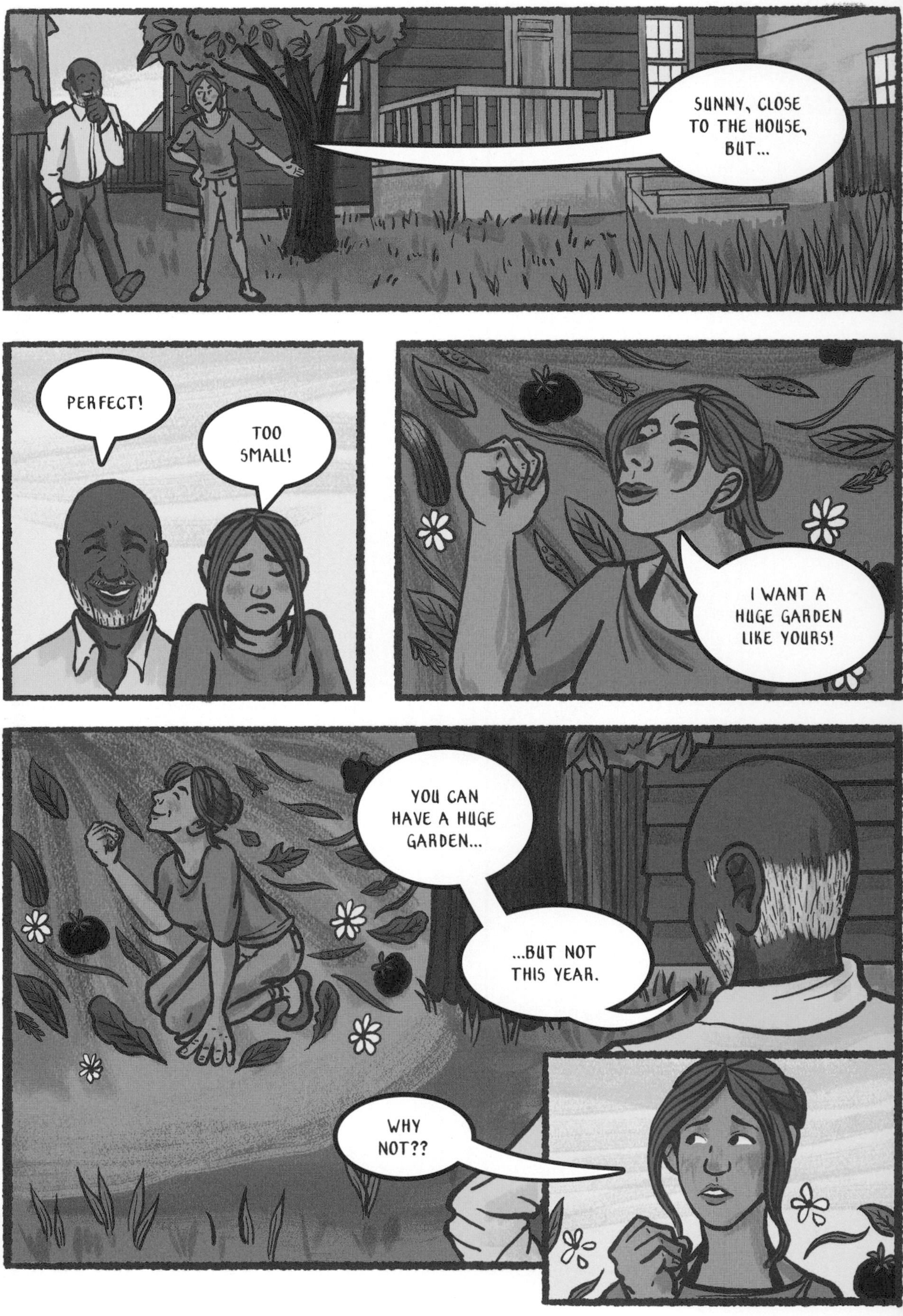
SUNNY, CLOSE TO THE HOUSE, BUT...
PERFECT!
TOO SMALL!
I WANT A HUGE GARDEN LIKE YOURS!
YOU CAN HAVE A HUGE GARDEN...
...BUT NOT THIS YEAR.
WHY NOT??

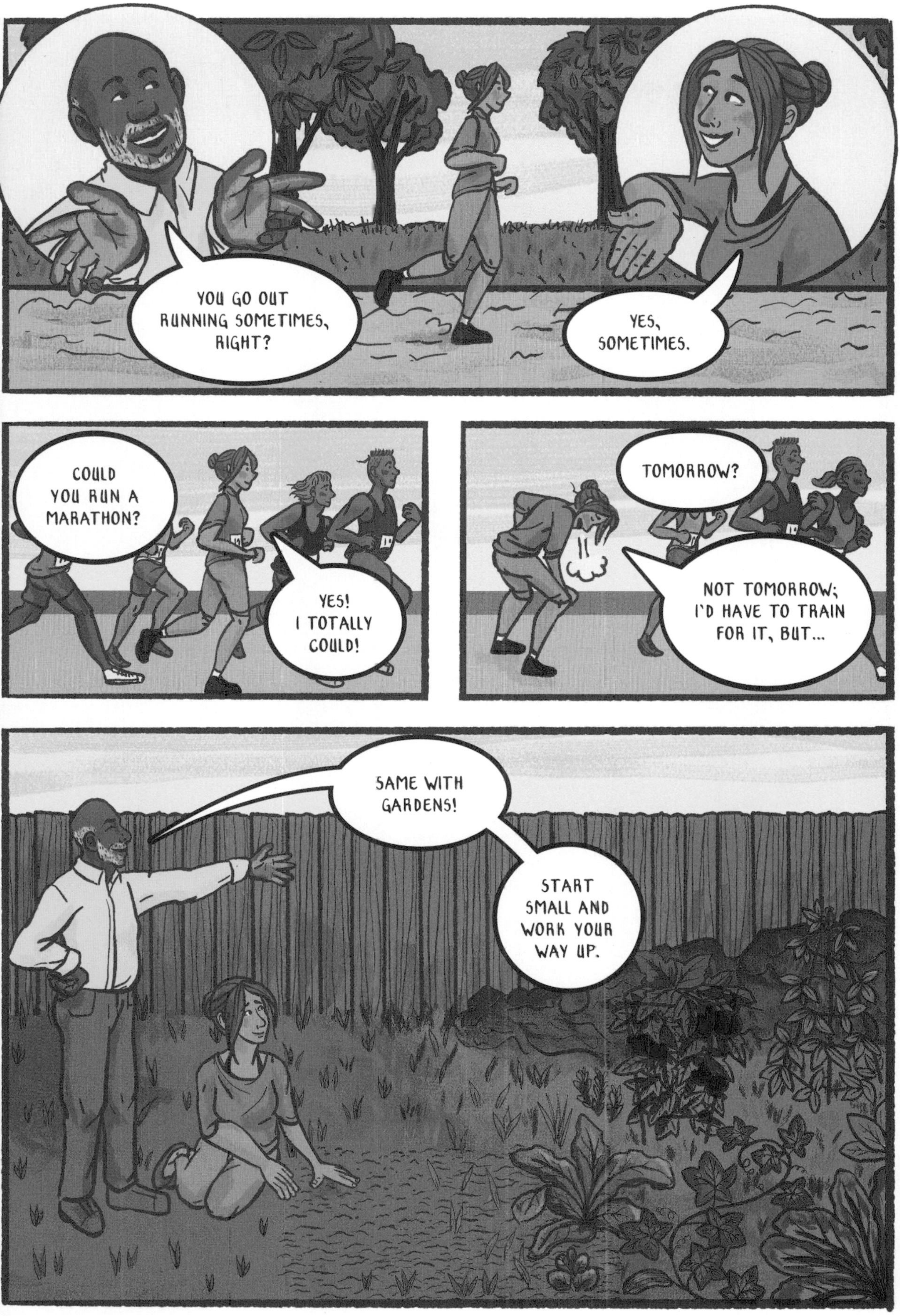
YOU GO OUT RUNNING SOMETIMES, RIGHT?
YES, SOMETIMES.
COULD YOU RUN A MARATHON?
YES! I TOTALLY COULD!
TOMORROW?
NOT TOMORROW; I'D HAVE TO TRAIN FOR IT, BUT...
SAME WITH GARDENS!
START SMALL AND WORK YOUR WAY UP.

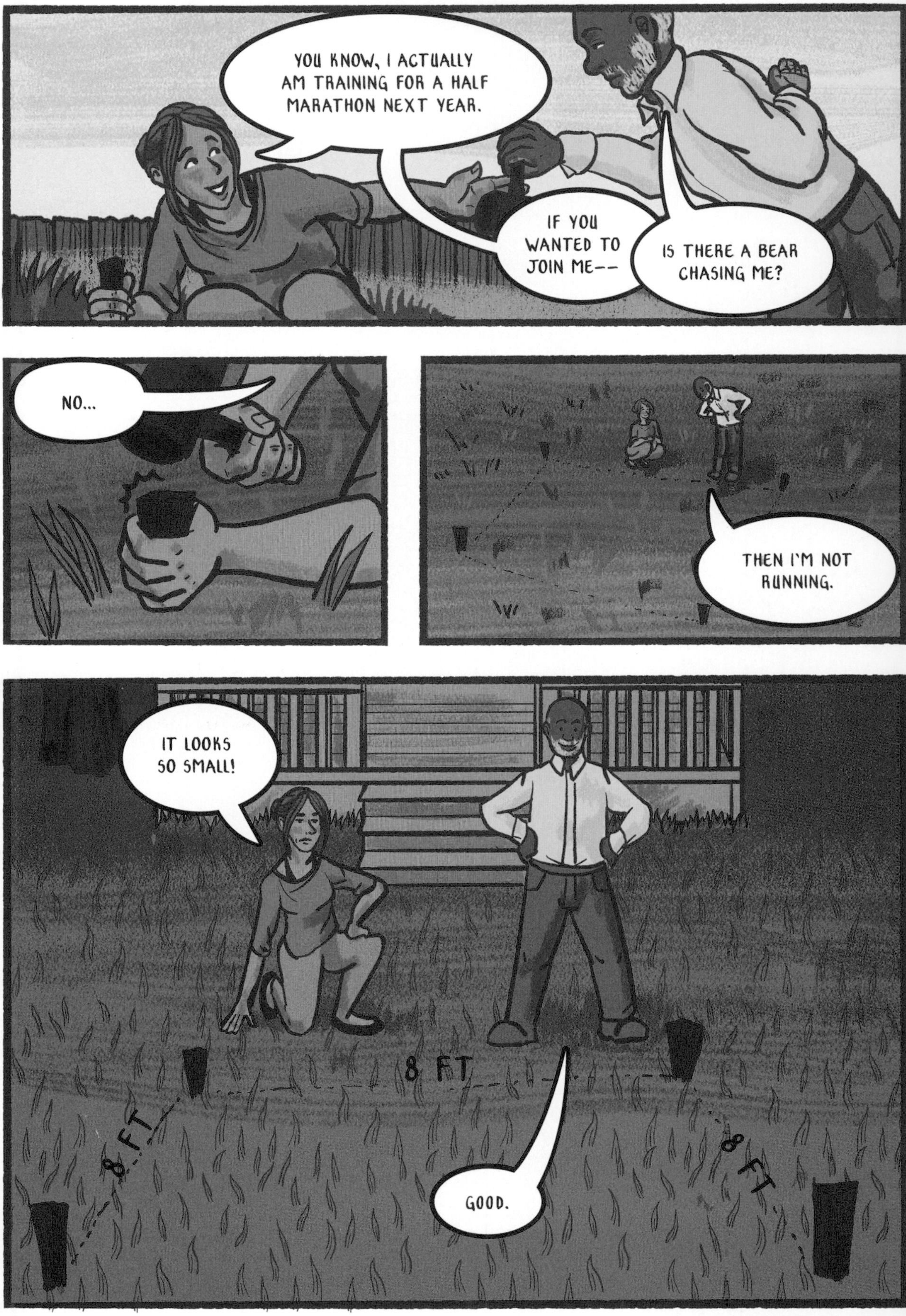
YOU KNOW, I ACTUALLY AM TRAINING FOR A HALF MARATHON NEXT YEAR.
IF YOU WANTED TO JOIN ME--
IS THERE A BEAR CHASING ME?
NO...
THEN I'M NOT RUNNING.
IT LOOKS SO SMALL!
8 FT
8 FT
8 FT
GOOD.

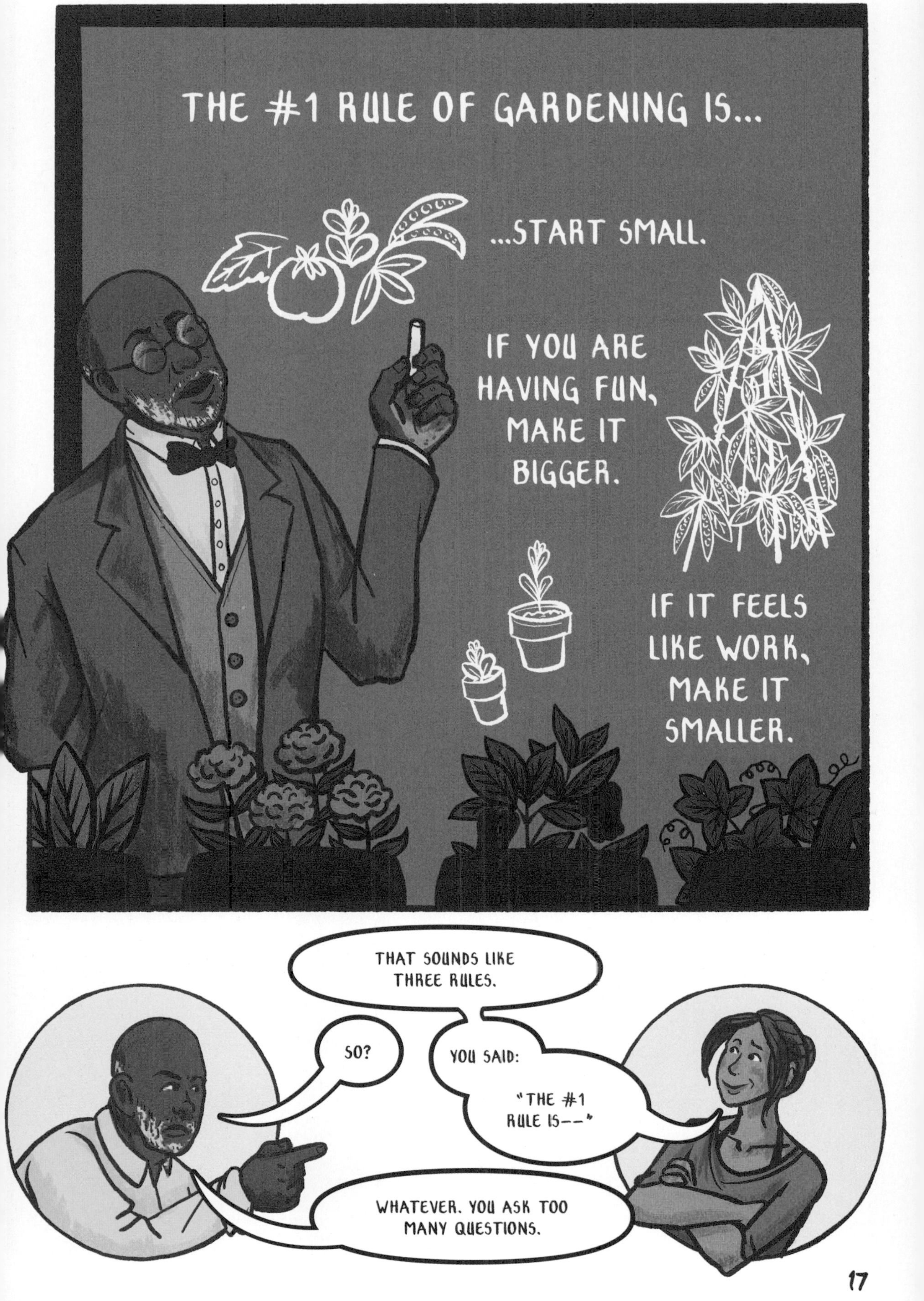
THE #1 RULE OF GARDENING IS...
...START SMALL.
IF YOU ARE HAVING FUN, MAKE IT BIGGER.
IF IT FEELS LIKE WORK, MAKE IT SMALLER.
THAT SOUNDS LIKE THREE RULES.
SO?
YOU SAID:
"THE #1 RULE IS--"
WHATEVER. YOU ASK TOO MANY QUESTIONS.

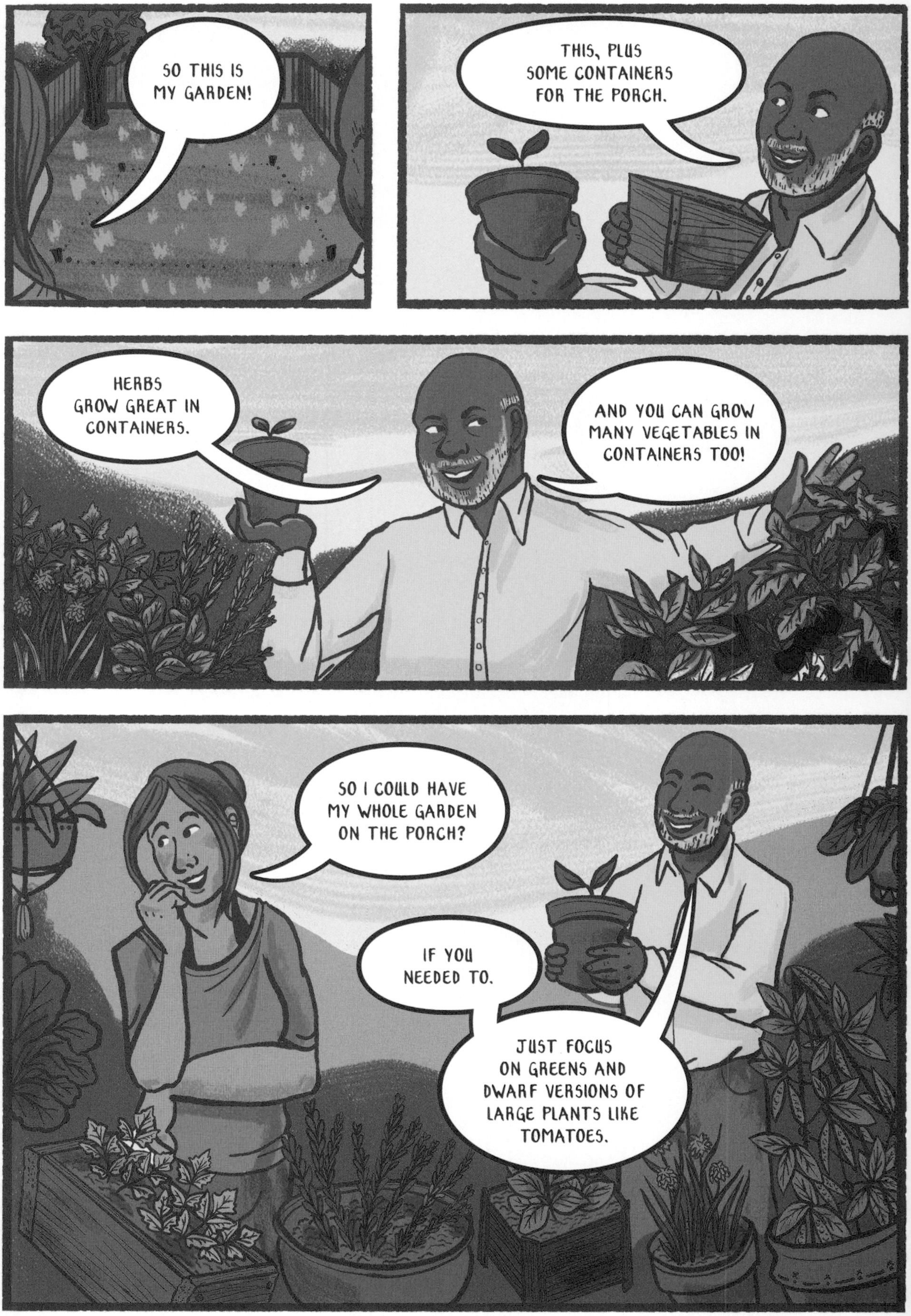
SO THIS IS MY GARDEN!
THIS, PLUS SOME CONTAINERS FOR THE PORCH.
HERBS GROW GREAT IN CONTAINERS.
AND YOU CAN GROW MANY VEGETABLES IN CONTAINERS TOO!
SO I COULD HAVE MY WHOLE GARDEN ON THE PORCH?
IF YOU NEEDED TO.
JUST FOCUS ON GREENS AND DWARF VERSIONS OF LARGE PLANTS LIKE TOMATOES.

GEORGE APPROVED CHEAT SHEET GARDEN TIPS

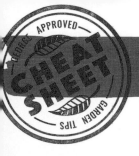

GROWING FOOD IN CONTAINERS

MANY VEGETABLES CAN BE GROWN IN CONTAINERS ON A PORCH, PATIO, OR EVEN A FIRE ESCAPE. THE BEST CHOICES ARE PLANTS THAT STAY NATURALLY SMALL OR DWARF VERSIONS OF LARGER VEGETABLES.

SMALL PLANTS TO TRY:

HERBS
BASIL
CHIVES
MINT
OREGANO
PARSLEY
ROSEMARY
THYME

GREENS
KALE
SWISS CHARD

DWARF VARIETIES OF LARGER VEGETABLES
BELL PEPPER 'CUPID'
GREEN BEANS (ANY DESCRIBED AS A "BUSH" VARIETY)
HOT PEPPERS (MANY VARIETIES)
TOMATO 'TIDY TREAT', 'SWEET SCARLET DWARF', OR 'TUMBLING TOM'

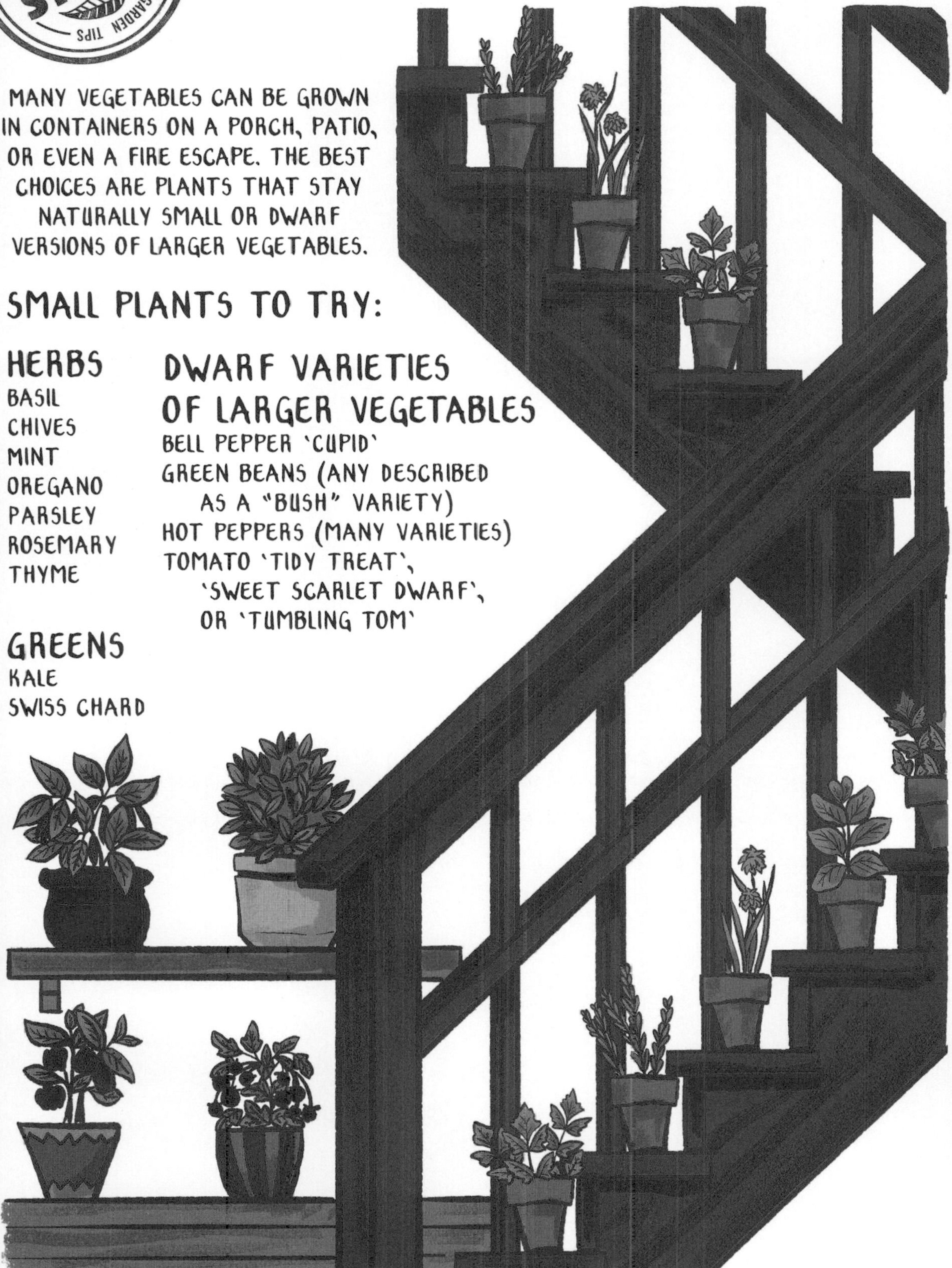

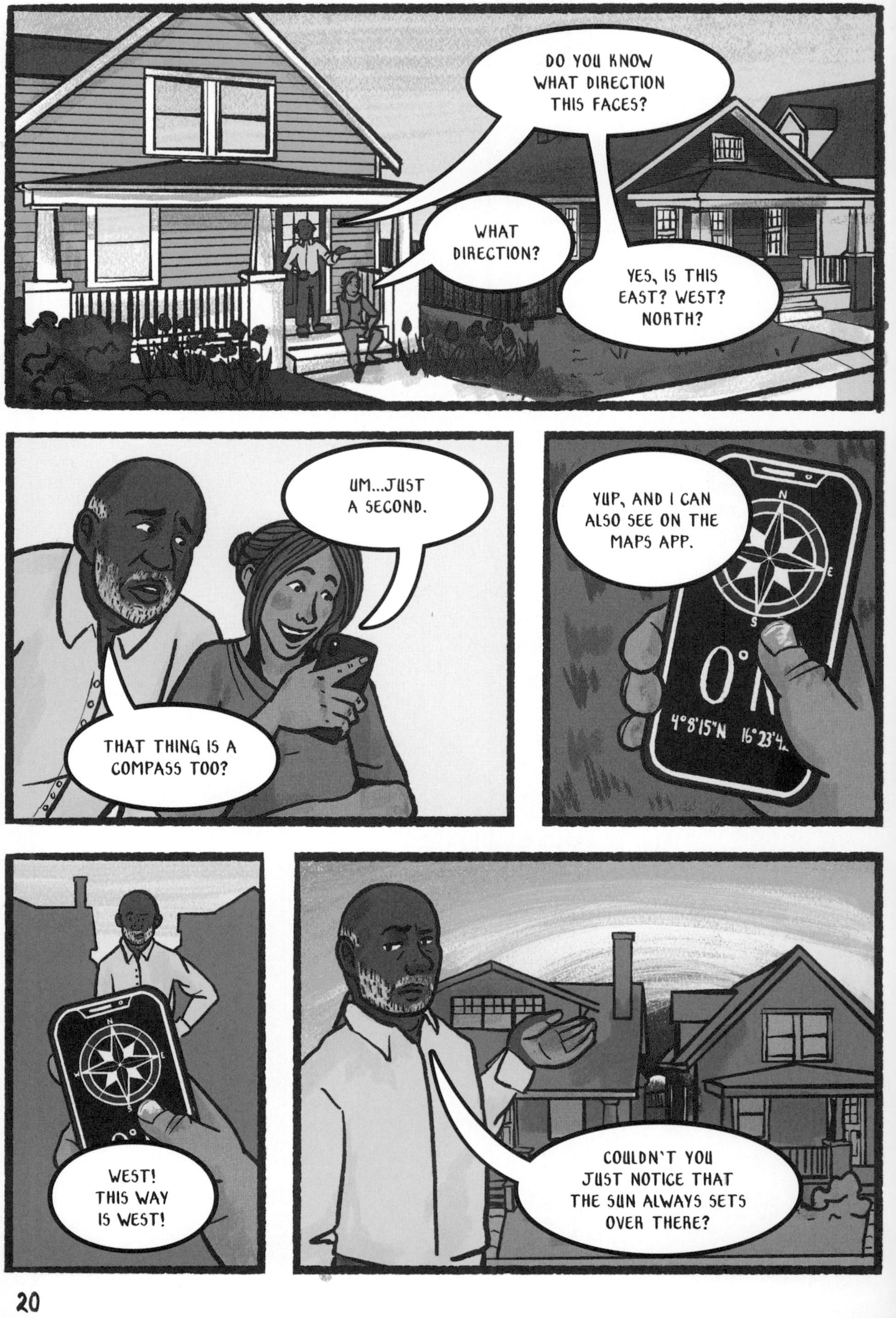
DO YOU KNOW WHAT DIRECTION THIS FACES?
WHAT DIRECTION?
YES, IS THIS EAST? WEST? NORTH?
UM...JUST A SECOND.
THAT THING IS A COMPASS TOO?
YUP, AND I CAN ALSO SEE ON THE MAPS APP.
4°8'15"N
WEST! THIS WAY IS WEST!
COULDN'T YOU JUST NOTICE THAT THE SUN ALWAYS SETS OVER THERE?

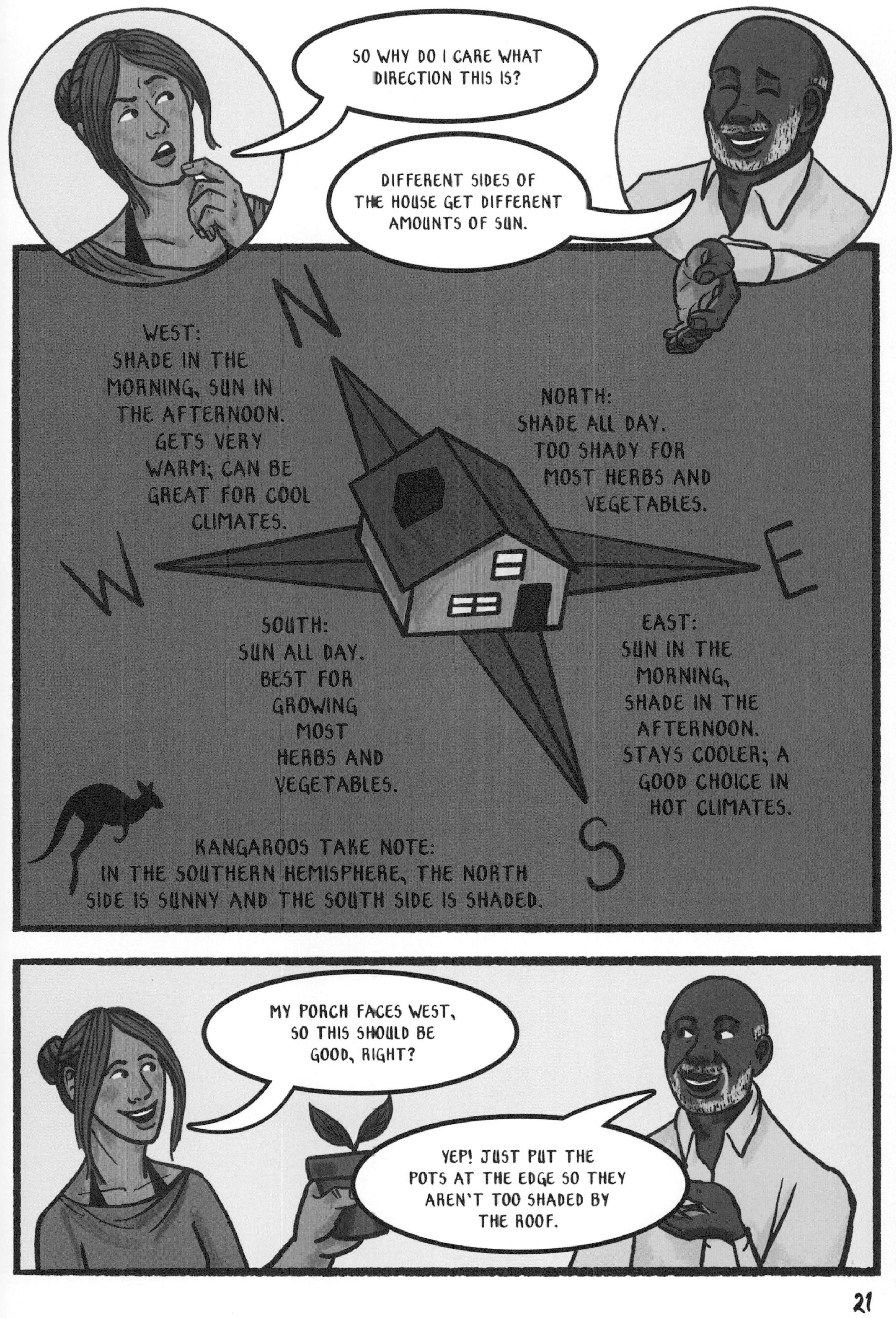
SO WHY DO I CARE WHAT DIRECTION THIS IS?
DIFFERENT SIDES OF THE HOUSE GET DIFFERENT AMOUNTS OF SUN.
N
W
E
S
WEST: SHADE IN THE MORNING, SUN IN THE AFTERNOON. GETS VERY WARM; CAN BE GREAT FOR COOL CLIMATES.
NORTH: SHADE ALL DAY. TOO SHADY FOR MOST HERBS AND VEGETABLES.
SOUTH: SUN ALL DAY. BEST FOR GROWING MOST HERBS AND VEGETABLES.
EAST: SUN IN THE MORNING, SHADE IN THE AFTERNOON. STAYS COOLER; A GOOD CHOICE IN HOT CLIMATES.
KANGAROOS TAKE NOTE: IN THE SOUTHERN HEMISPHERE, THE NORTH SIDE IS SUNNY AND THE SOUTH SIDE IS SHADED.
MY PORCH FACES WEST, SO THIS SHOULD BE GOOD, RIGHT?
YEP! JUST PUT THE POTS AT THE EDGE SO THEY AREN'T TOO SHADED BY THE ROOF.

I DON'T HAVE A SUNNY SPOT!

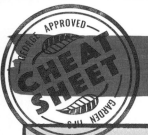

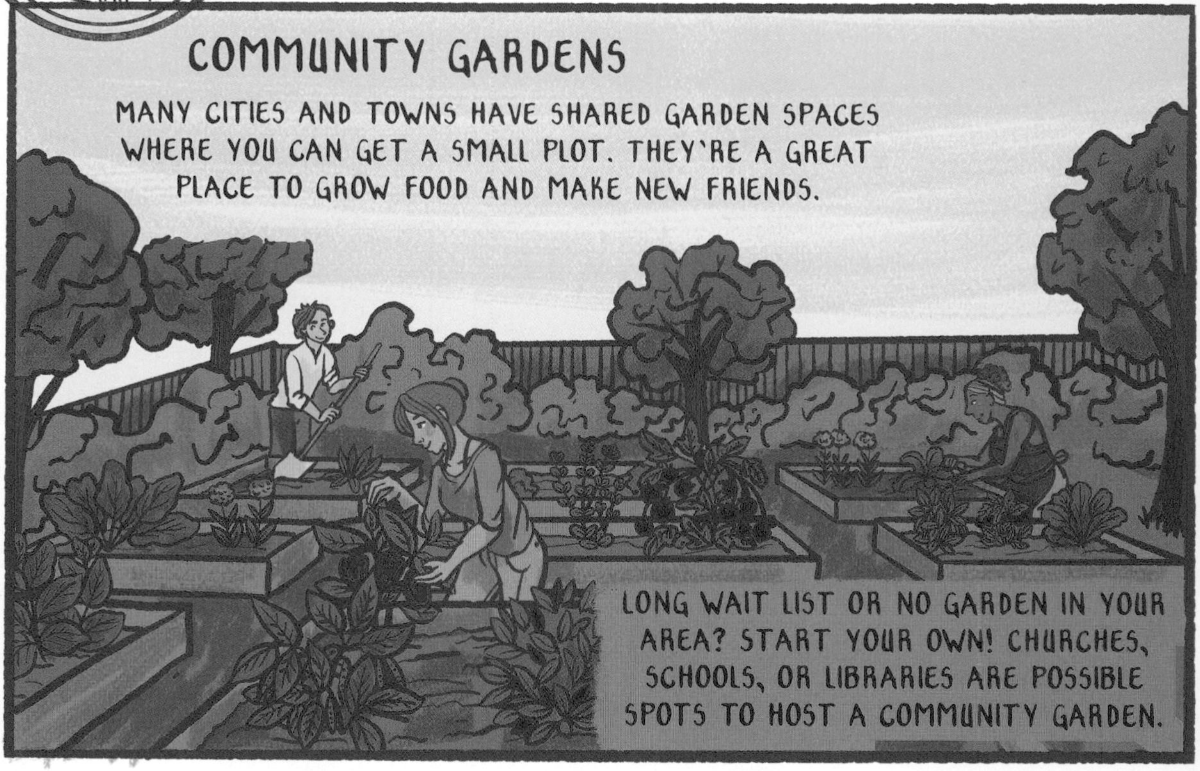
COMMUNITY GARDENS
MANY CITIES AND TOWNS HAVE SHARED GARDEN SPACES WHERE YOU CAN GET A SMALL PLOT. THEY'RE A GREAT PLACE TO GROW FOOD AND MAKE NEW FRIENDS.
LONG WAIT LIST OR NO GARDEN IN YOUR AREA? START YOUR OWN! CHURCHES, SCHOOLS, OR LIBRARIES ARE POSSIBLE SPOTS TO HOST A COMMUNITY GARDEN.

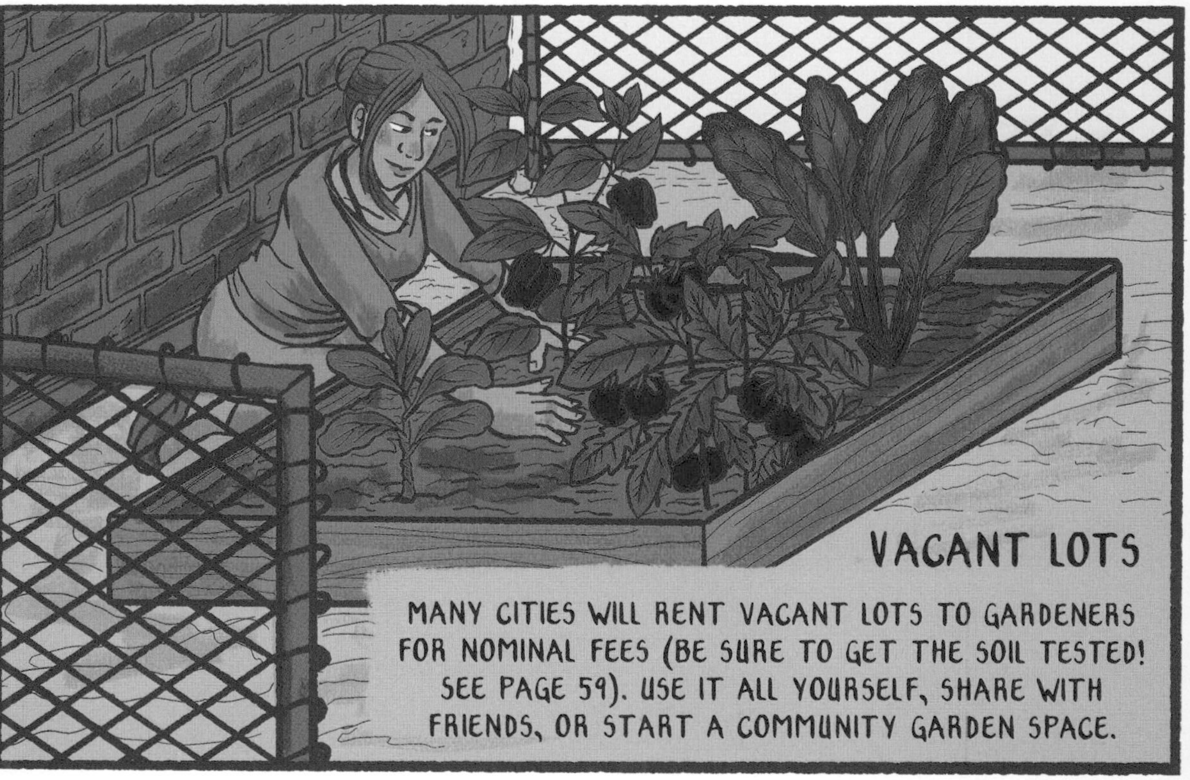
VACANT LOTS
MANY CITIES WILL RENT VACANT LOTS TO GARDENERS FOR NOMINAL FEES (BE SURE TO GET THE SOIL TESTED! SEE PAGE 59). USE IT ALL YOURSELF, SHARE WITH FRIENDS, OR START A COMMUNITY GARDEN SPACE.

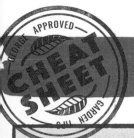

I DON'T HAVE A SUNNY SPOT!

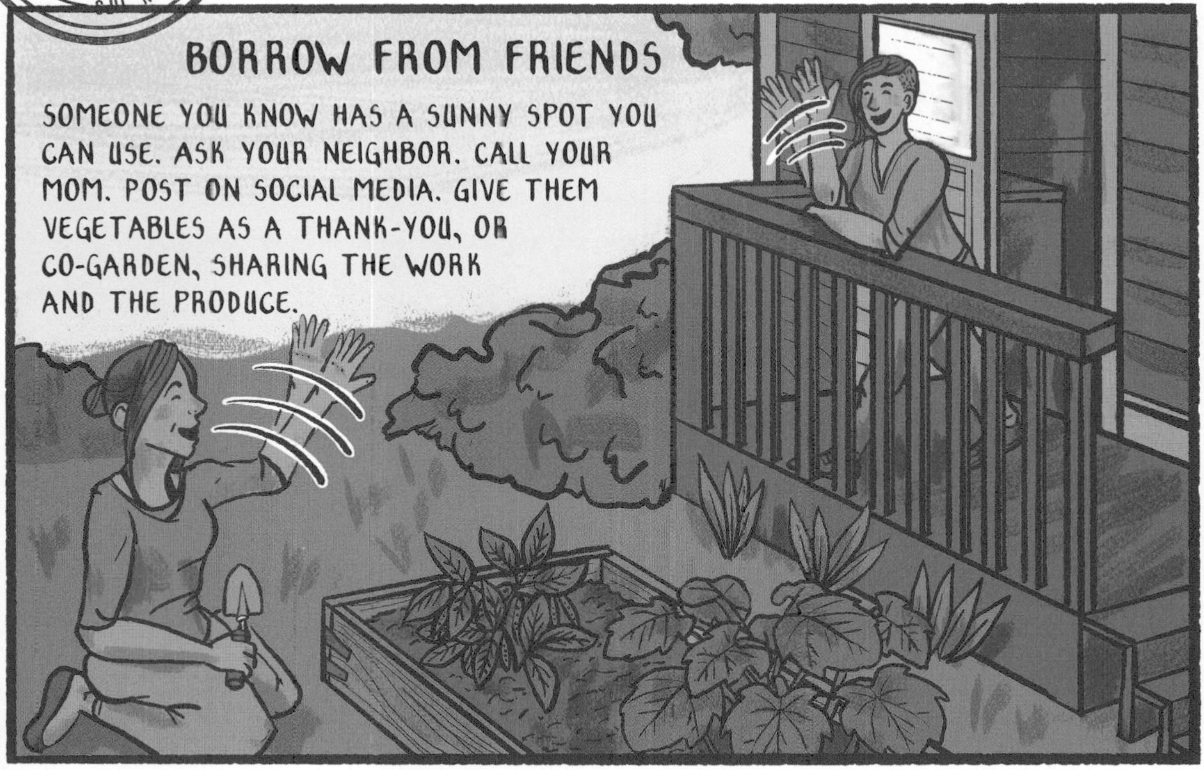
BORROW FROM FRIENDS
SOMEONE YOU KNOW HAS A SUNNY SPOT YOU CAN USE. ASK YOUR NEIGHBOR. CALL YOUR MOM. POST ON SOCIAL MEDIA. GIVE THEM VEGETABLES AS A THANK-YOU, OR CO-GARDEN, SHARING THE WORK AND THE PRODUCE.

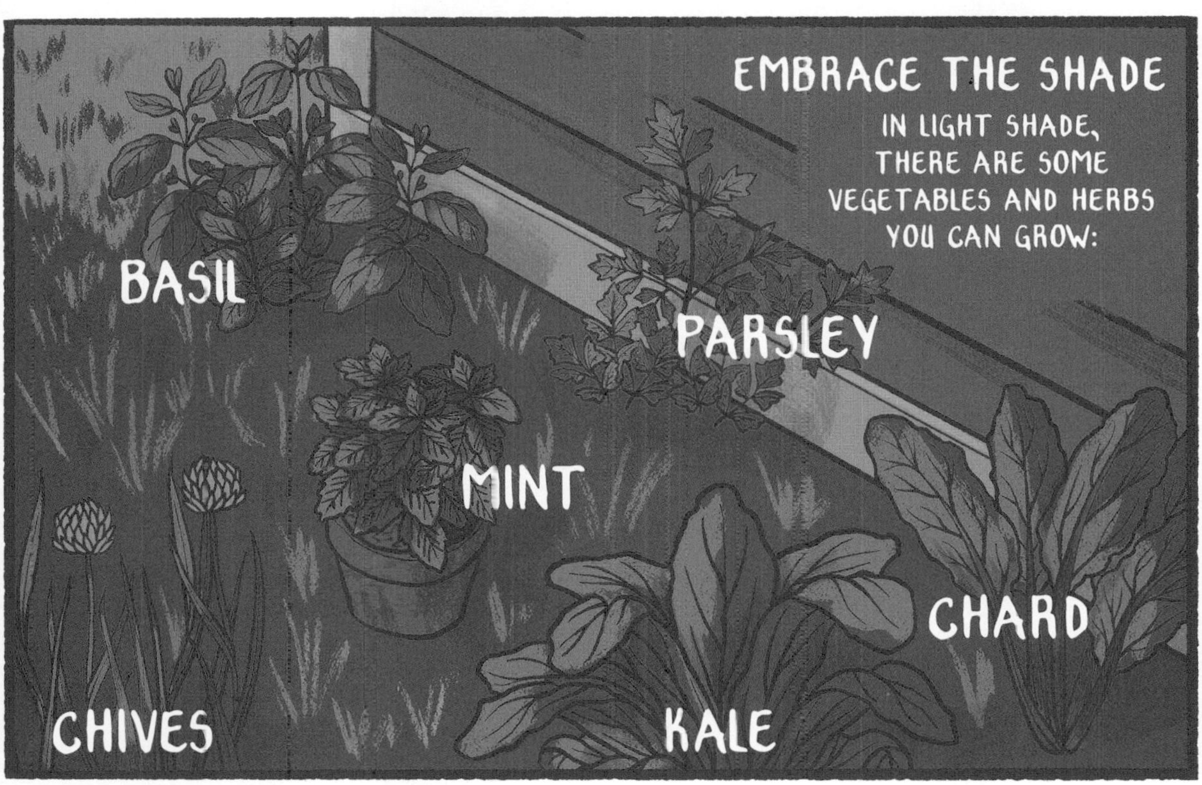
EMBRACE THE SHADE
IN LIGHT SHADE, THERE ARE SOME VEGETABLES AND HERBS YOU CAN GROW:
BASIL
PARSLEY
MINT
CHARD
CHIVES
KALE

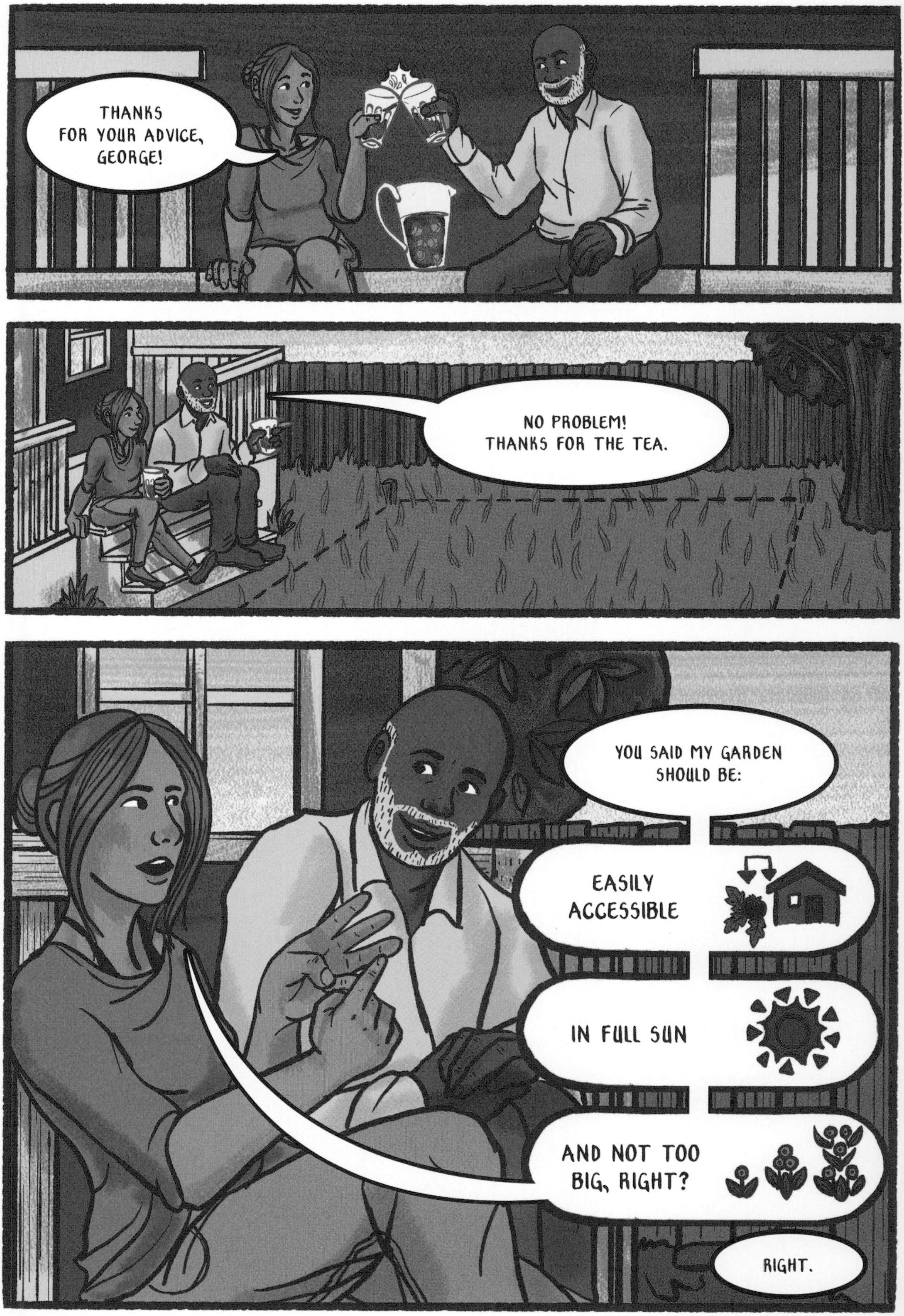
THANKS FOR YOUR ADVICE, GEORGE!
NO PROBLEM! THANKS FOR THE TEA.
YOU SAID MY GARDEN SHOULD BE:
EASILY ACCESSIBLE
IN FULL SUN
AND NOT TOO BIG, RIGHT?
RIGHT.

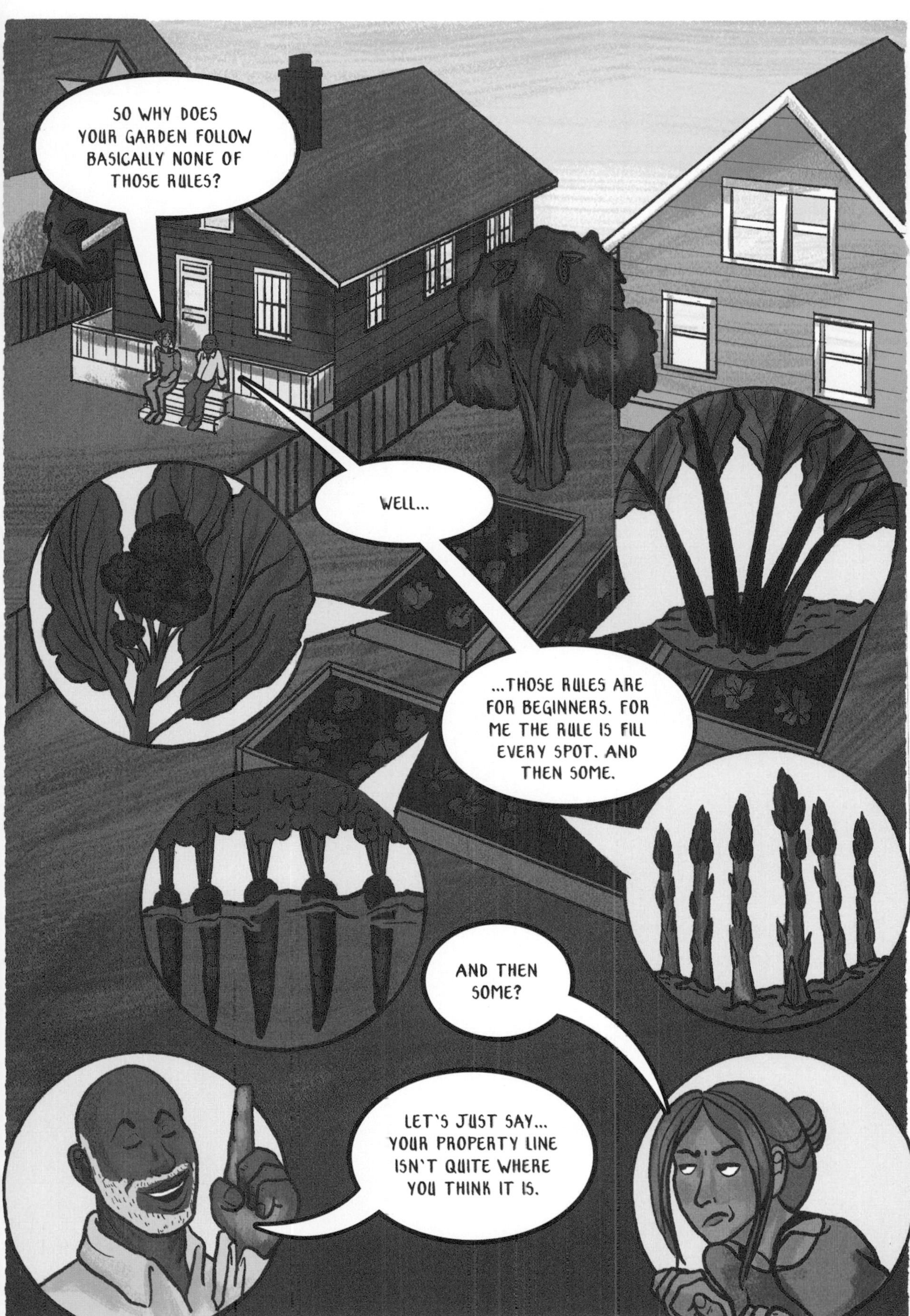
SO WHY DOES YOUR GARDEN FOLLOW BASICALLY NONE OF THOSE RULES?
WELL...
...THOSE RULES ARE FOR BEGINNERS. FOR ME THE RULE IS FILL EVERY SPOT. AND THEN SOME.
AND THEN SOME?
LET'S JUST SAY... YOUR PROPERTY LINE ISN'T QUITE WHERE YOU THINK IT IS.

TWO:
DECIDING WHAT TO GROW

WHICH VEGETABLES ARE BEST FOR A BEGINNER GARDENER?

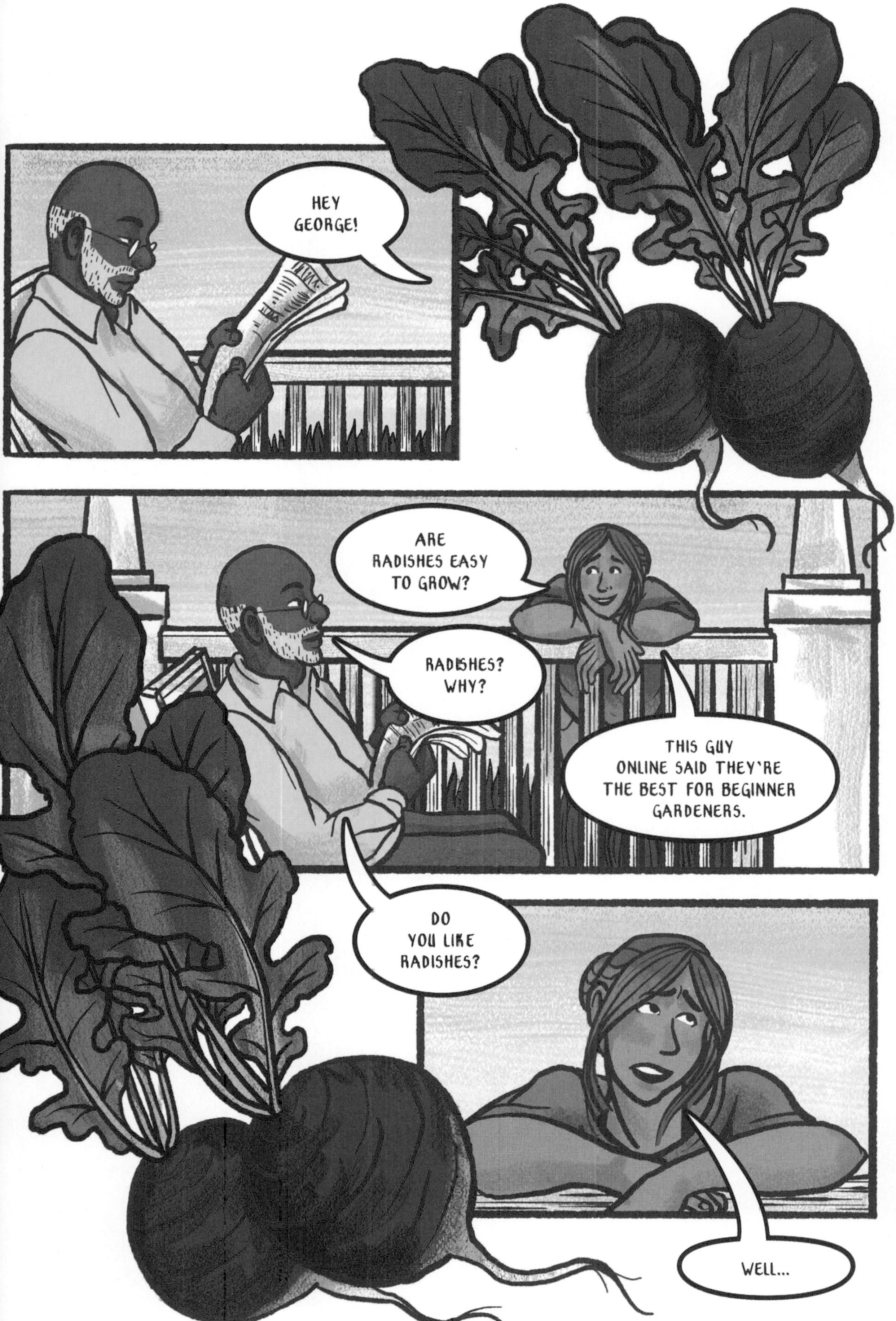
HEY GEORGE!
ARE RADISHES EASY TO GROW?
RADISHES? WHY?
THIS GUY ONLINE SAID THEY'RE THE BEST FOR BEGINNER GARDENERS.
DO YOU LIKE RADISHES?
WELL...

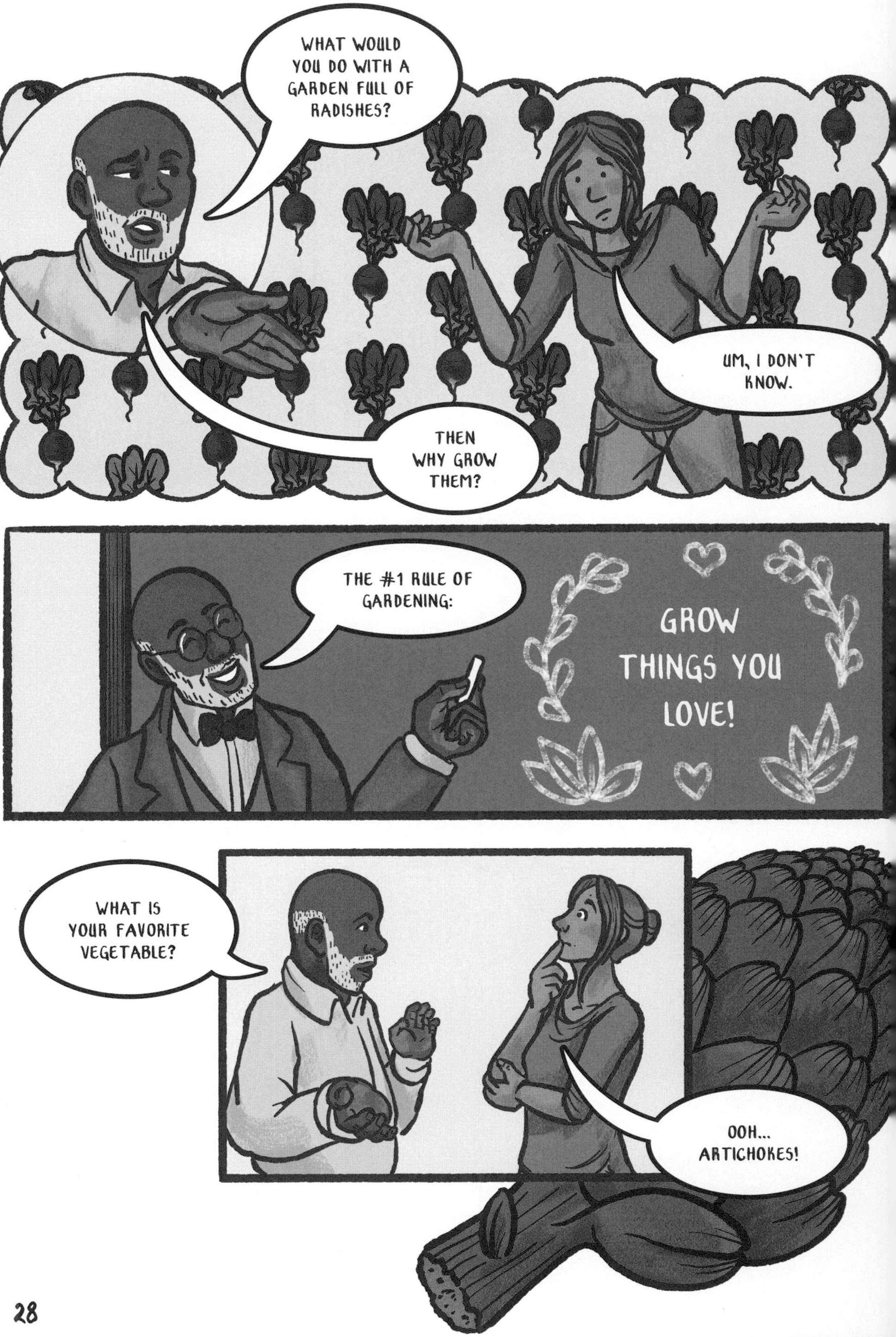

WHAT WOULD YOU DO WITH A GARDEN FULL OF RADISHES?
UM, I DON'T KNOW.
THEN WHY GROW THEM?
THE #1 RULE OF GARDENING:
GROW THINGS YOU LOVE!
WHAT IS YOUR FAVORITE VEGETABLE?
OOH... ARTICHOKES!

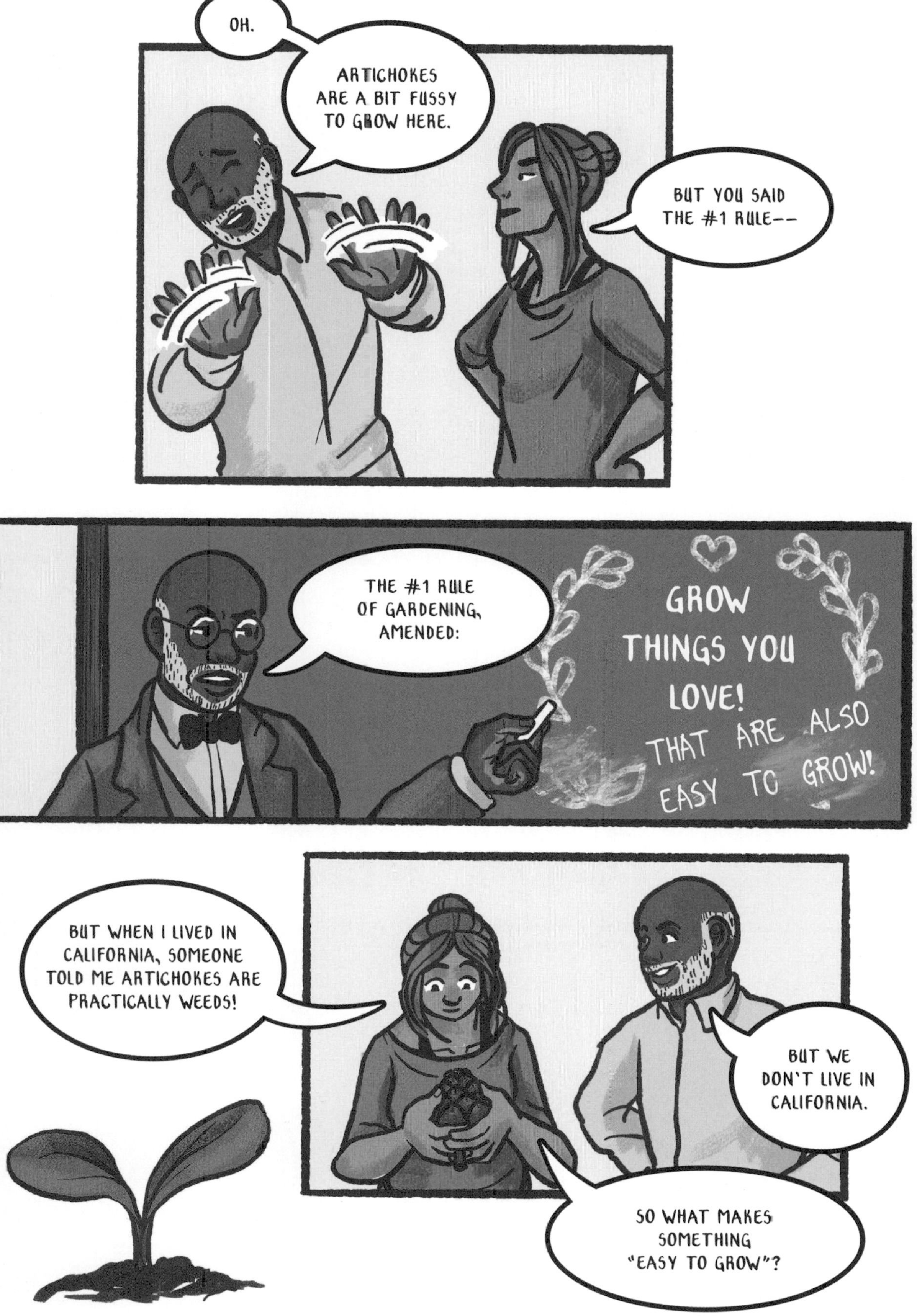
OH.
ARTICHOKES ARE A BIT FUSSY TO GROW HERE.
BUT YOU SAID THE #1 RULE--
THE #1 RULE OF GARDENING, AMENDED:
GROW THINGS YOU LOVE!
THAT ARE ALSO EASY TO GROW!
BUT WHEN I LIVED IN CALIFORNIA, SOMEONE TOLD ME ARTICHOKES ARE PRACTICALLY WEEDS!
BUT WE DON'T LIVE IN CALIFORNIA.
SO WHAT MAKES SOMETHING "EASY TO GROW"?

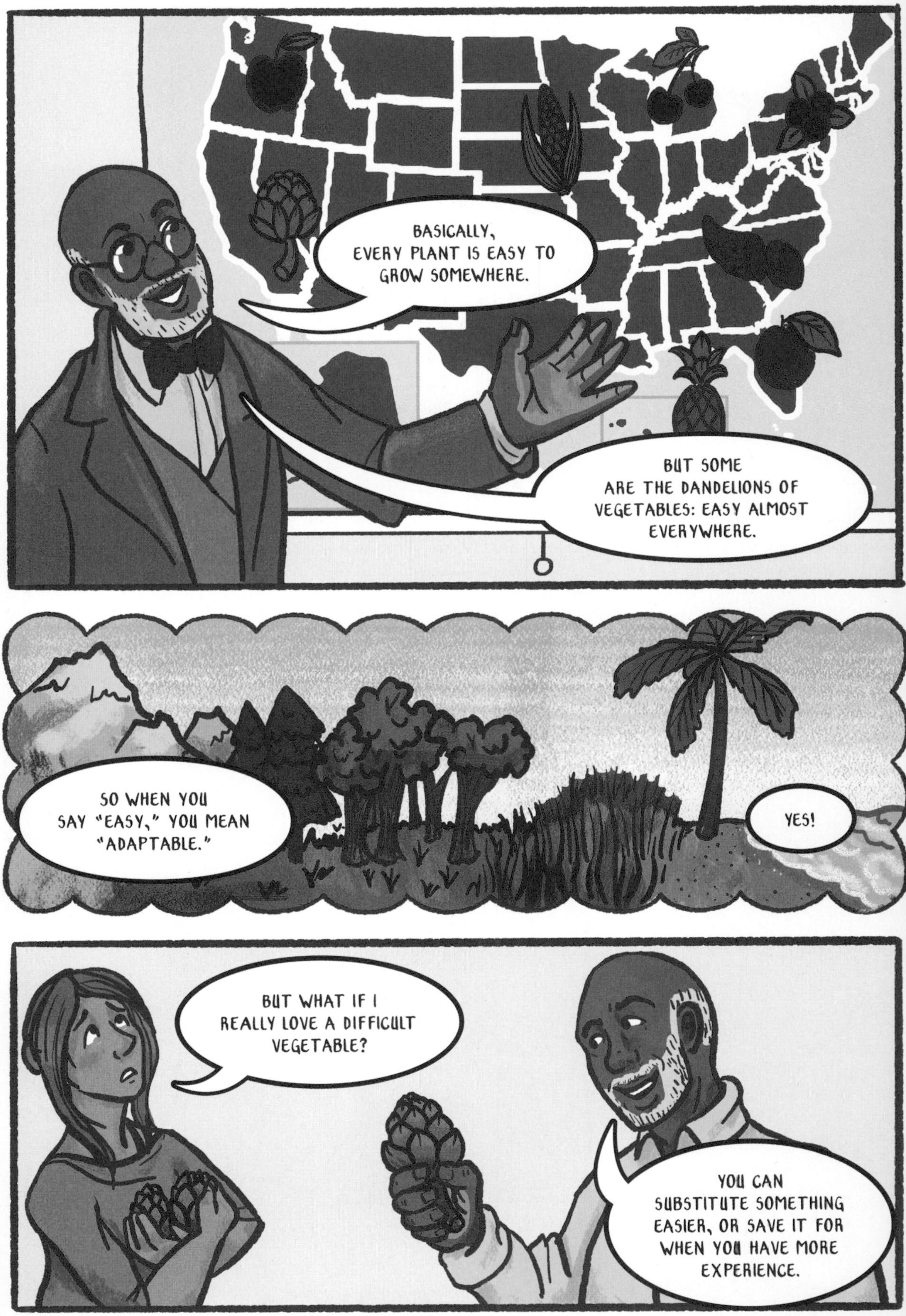
BASICALLY, EVERY PLANT IS EASY TO GROW SOMEWHERE.
BUT SOME ARE THE DANDELIONS OF VEGETABLES: EASY ALMOST EVERYWHERE.
SO WHEN YOU SAY "EASY," YOU MEAN "ADAPTABLE."
YES!
BUT WHAT IF I REALLY LOVE A DIFFICULT VEGETABLE?
YOU CAN SUBSTITUTE SOMETHING EASIER, OR SAVE IT FOR WHEN YOU HAVE MORE EXPERIENCE.

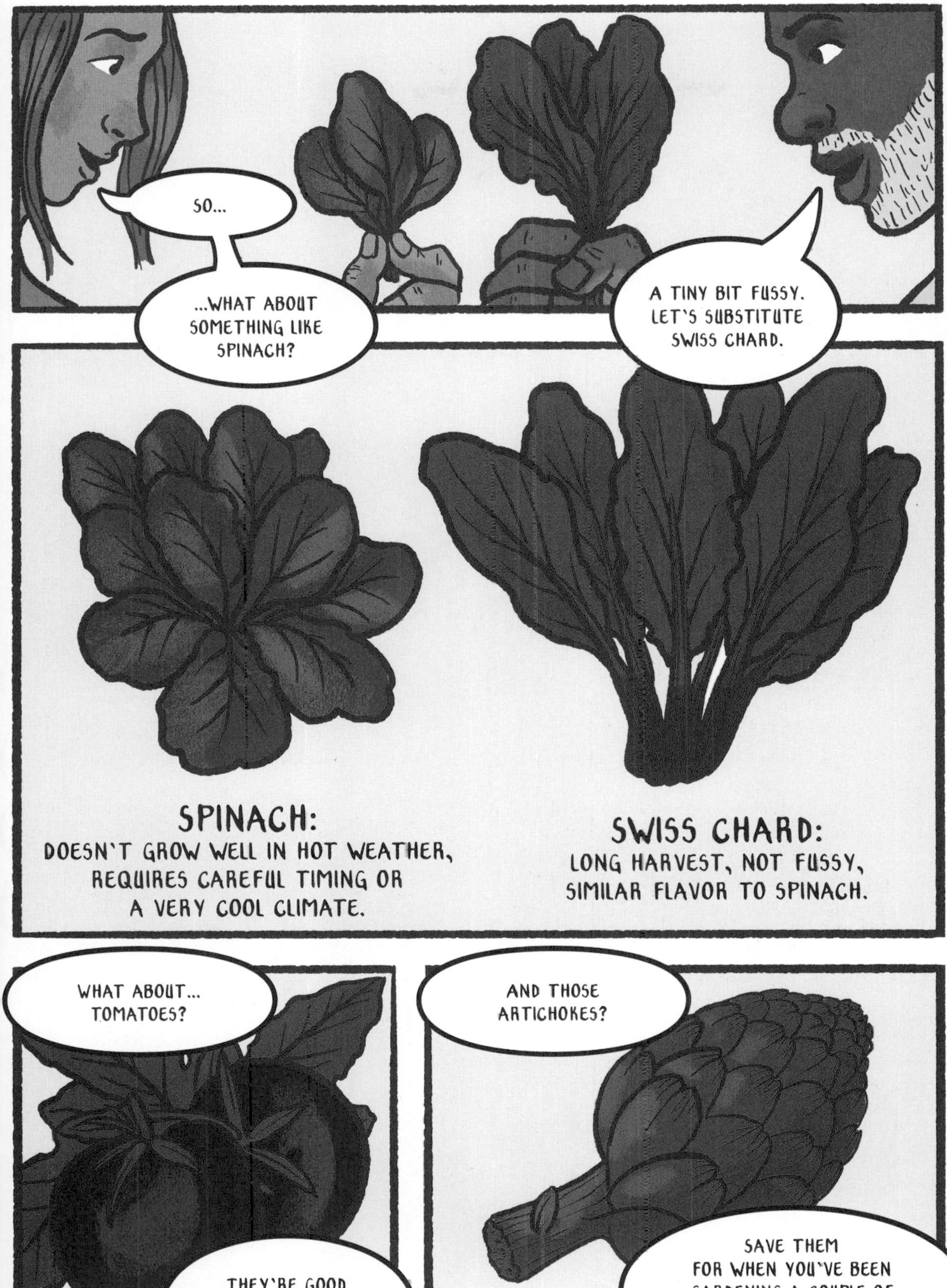

SO...
...WHAT ABOUT SOMETHING LIKE SPINACH?
A TINY BIT FUSSY. LET'S SUBSTITUTE SWISS CHARD.
SPINACH:
DOESN'T GROW WELL IN HOT WEATHER, REQUIRES CAREFUL TIMING OR A VERY COOL CLIMATE.
SWISS CHARD:
LONG HARVEST, NOT FUSSY, SIMILAR FLAVOR TO SPINACH.
WHAT ABOUT... TOMATOES?
THEY'RE GOOD TO GO! EASY ALMOST EVERYWHERE.
AND THOSE ARTICHOKES?
SAVE THEM FOR WHEN YOU'VE BEEN GARDENING A COUPLE OF YEARS AND KNOW WHAT YOU ARE DOING.

GEORGE APPROVED
CHEAT SHEET
GARDEN TIPS

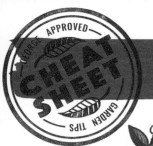

EASY-TO-GROW VEGGIES

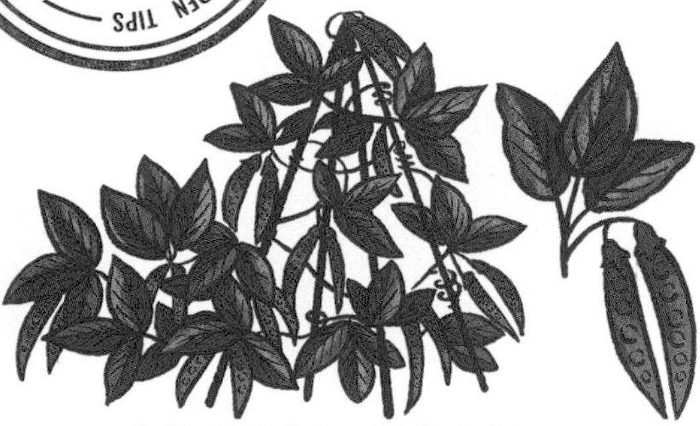

GREEN BEANS

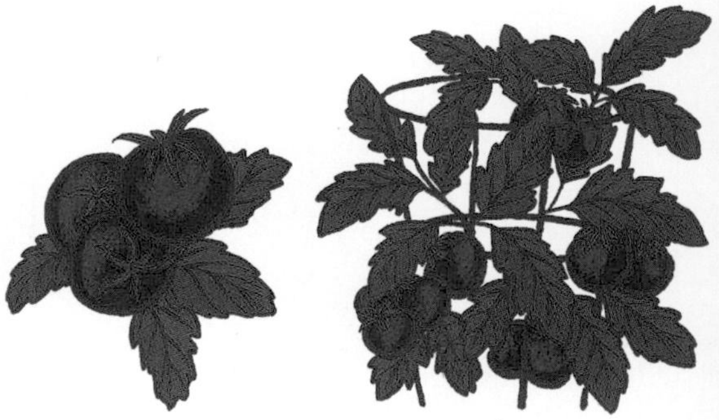

TOMATOES

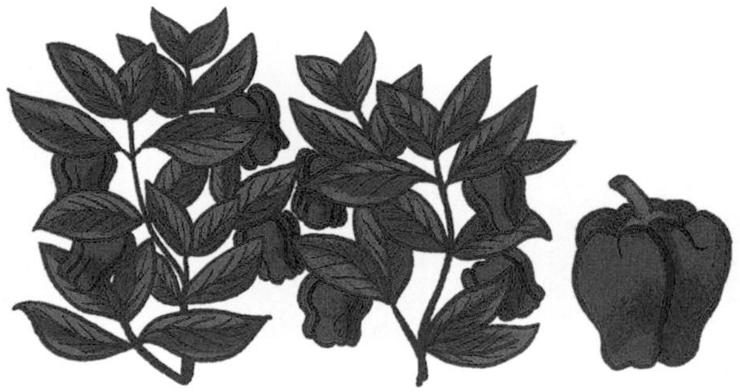

PEPPERS

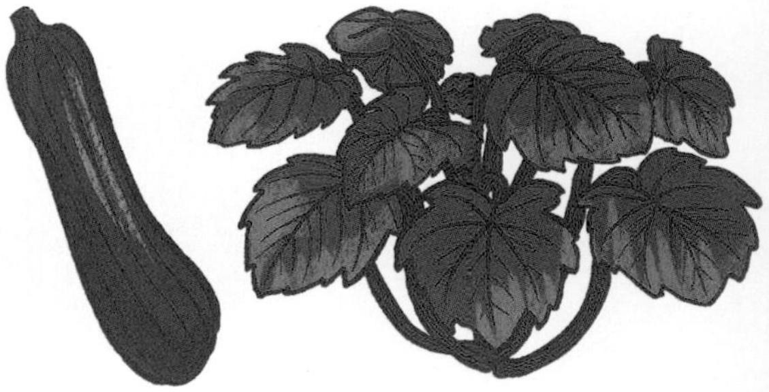

ZUCCHINI

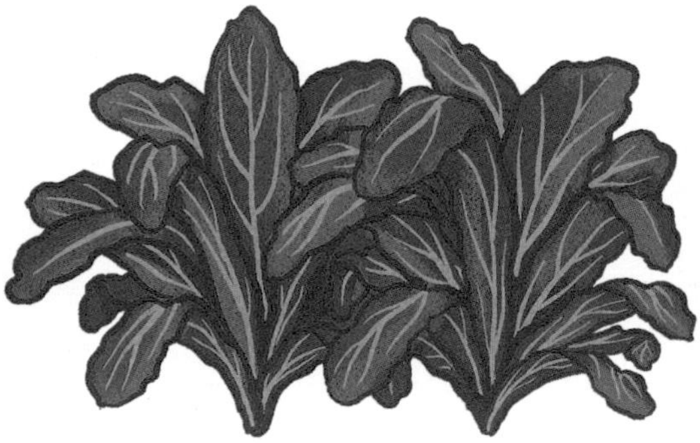

KALE

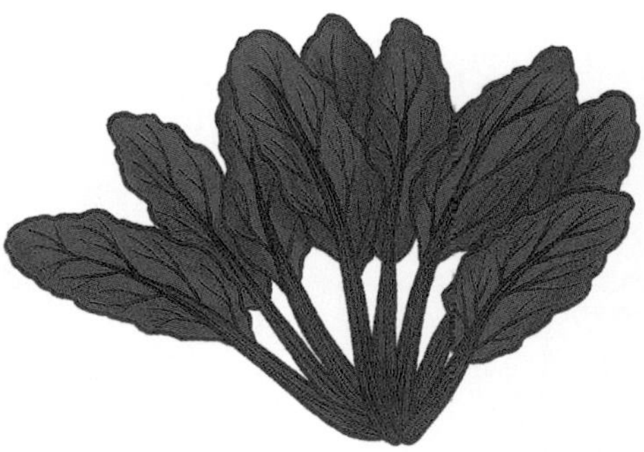

SWISS CHARD

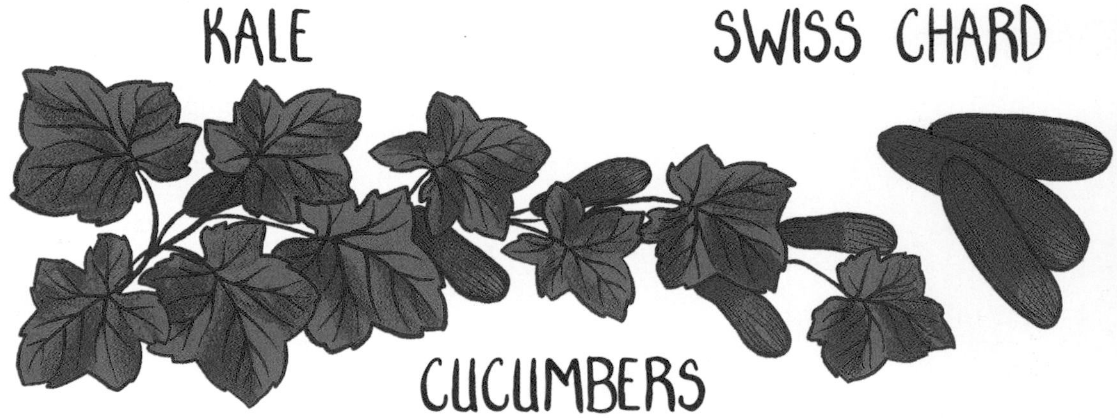

CUCUMBERS

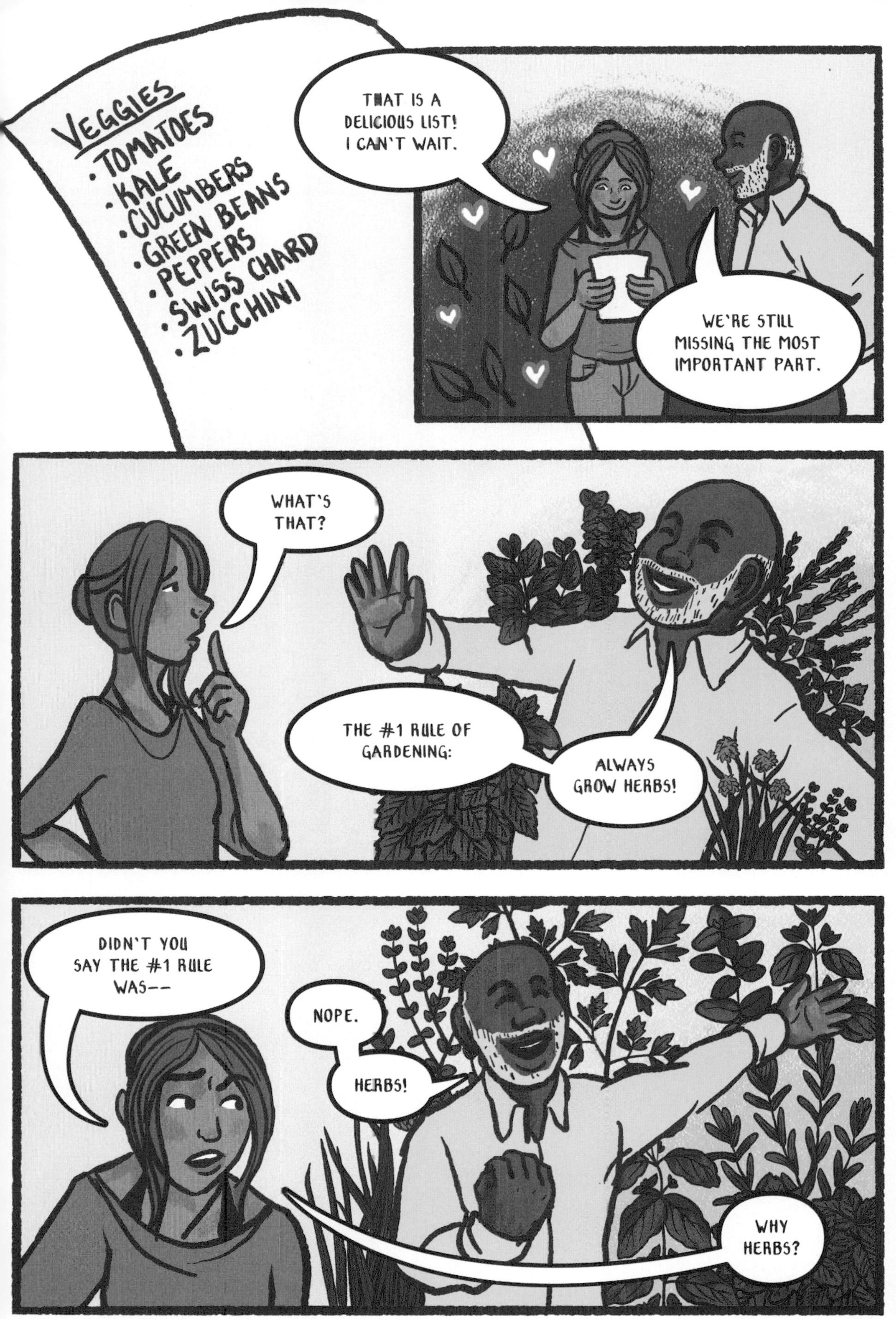
VEGGIES
• TOMATOES
• KALE
• CUCUMBERS
• GREEN BEANS
• PEPPERS
• SWISS CHARD
• ZUCCHINI
THAT IS A DELICIOUS LIST! I CAN'T WAIT.
WE'RE STILL MISSING THE MOST IMPORTANT PART.
WHAT'S THAT?
THE #1 RULE OF GARDENING:
ALWAYS GROW HERBS!
DIDN'T YOU SAY THE #1 RULE WAS--
NOPE.
HERBS!
WHY HERBS?

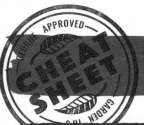

WHY GROW HERBS?

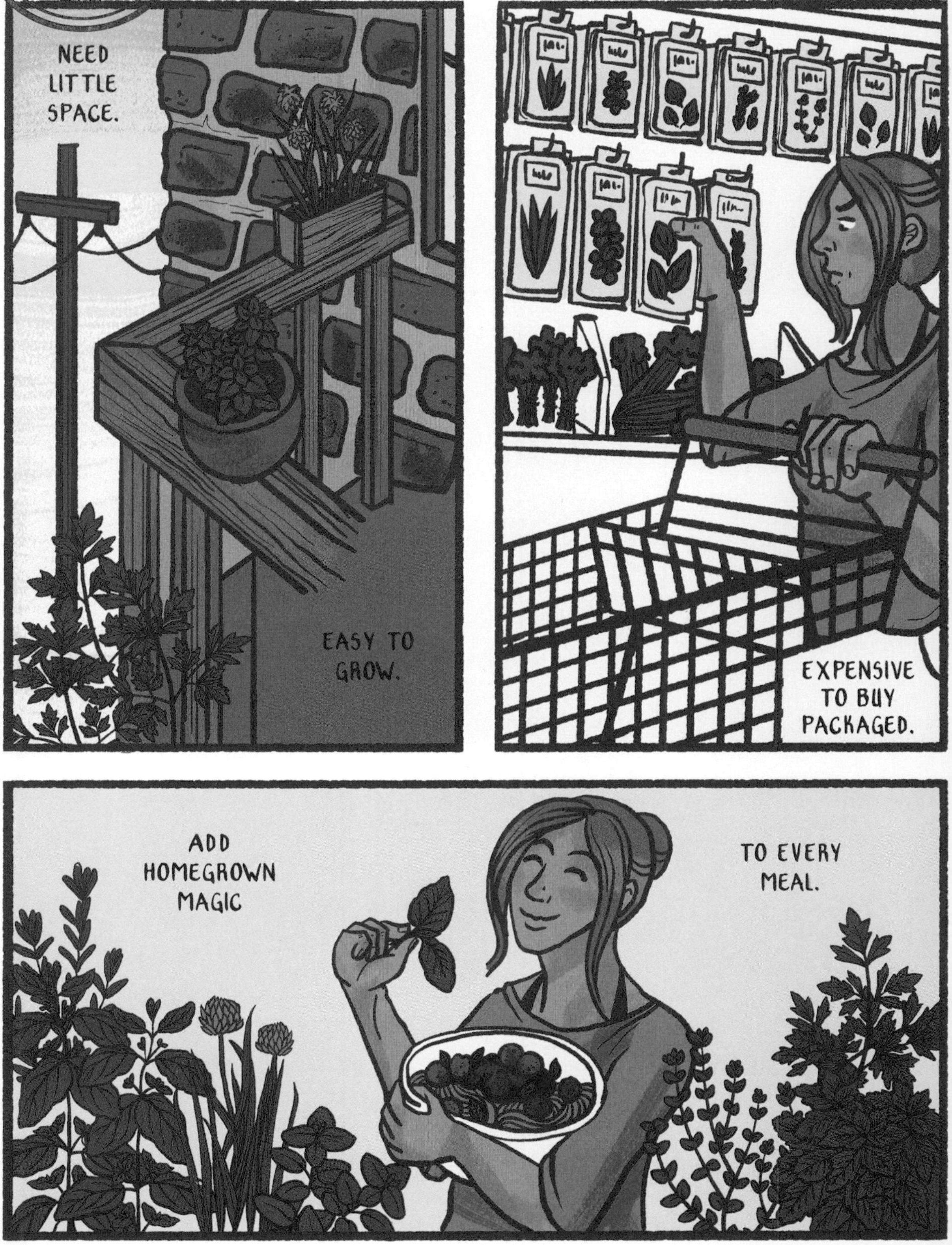
NEED LITTLE SPACE.
EASY TO GROW.
EXPENSIVE TO BUY PACKAGED.
ADD HOMEGROWN MAGIC
TO EVERY MEAL.

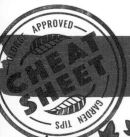

HERBS TO GROW

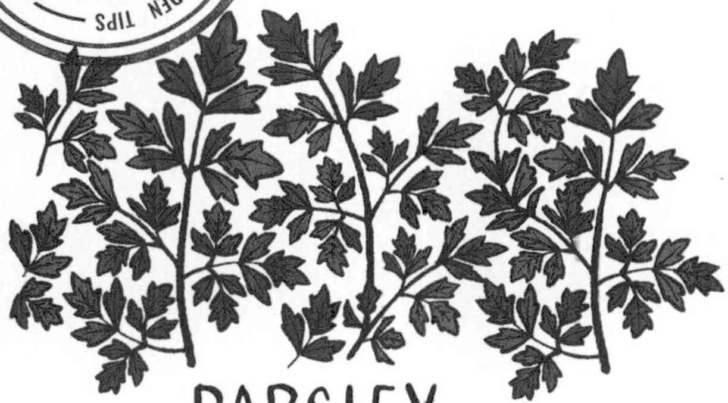
PARSLEY

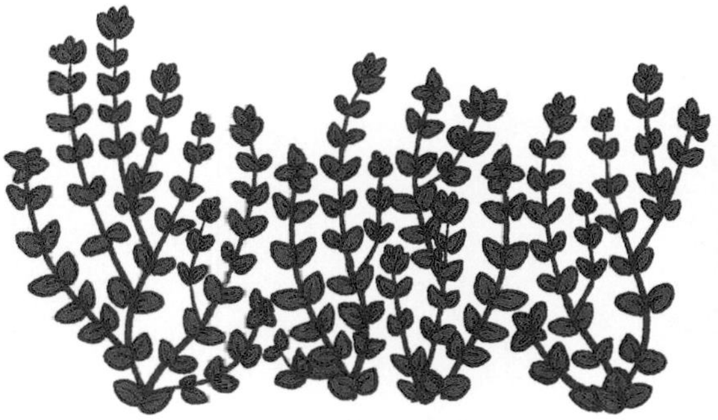
THYME

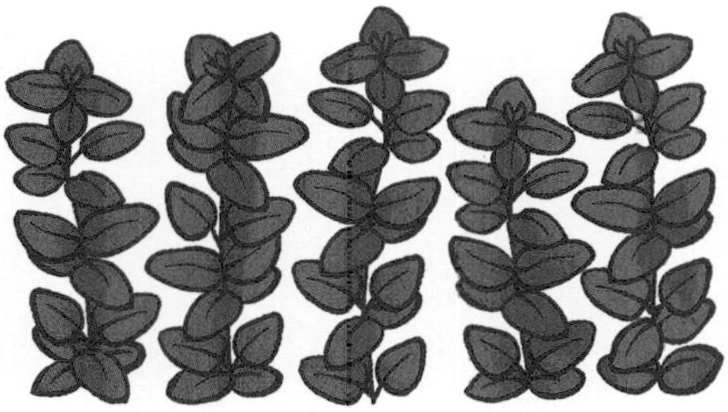
OREGANO

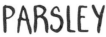

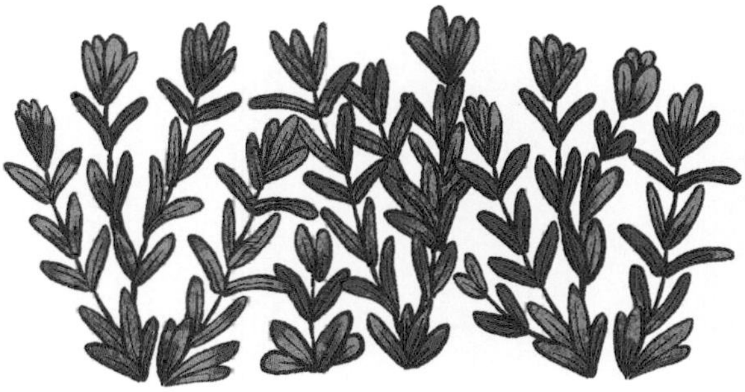
ROSEMARY

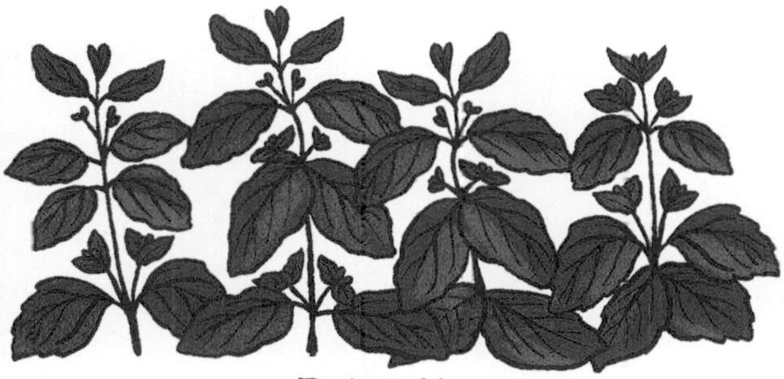
BASIL

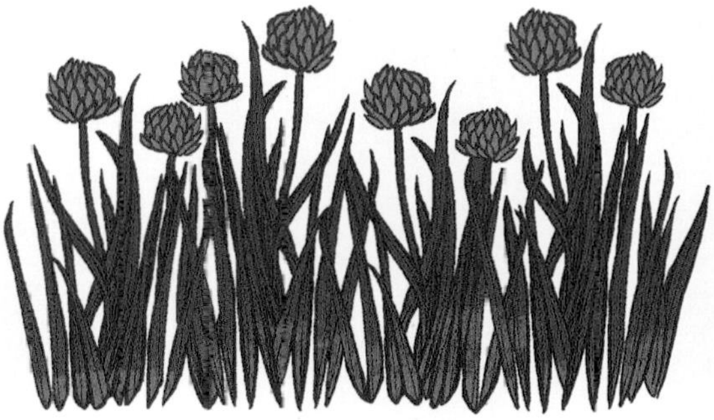
CHIVES

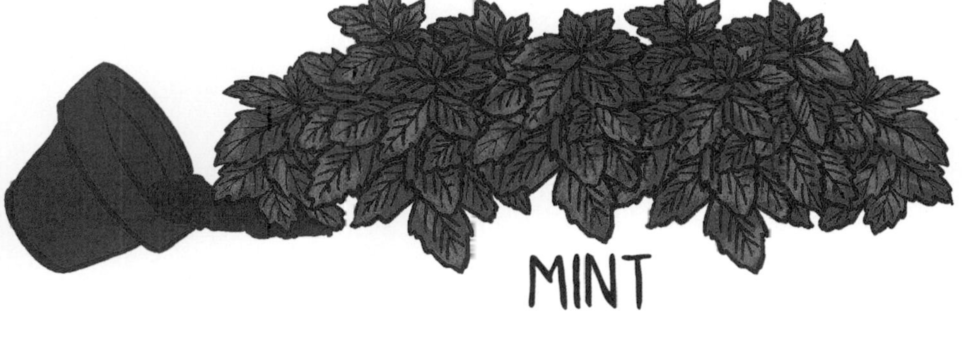
MINT

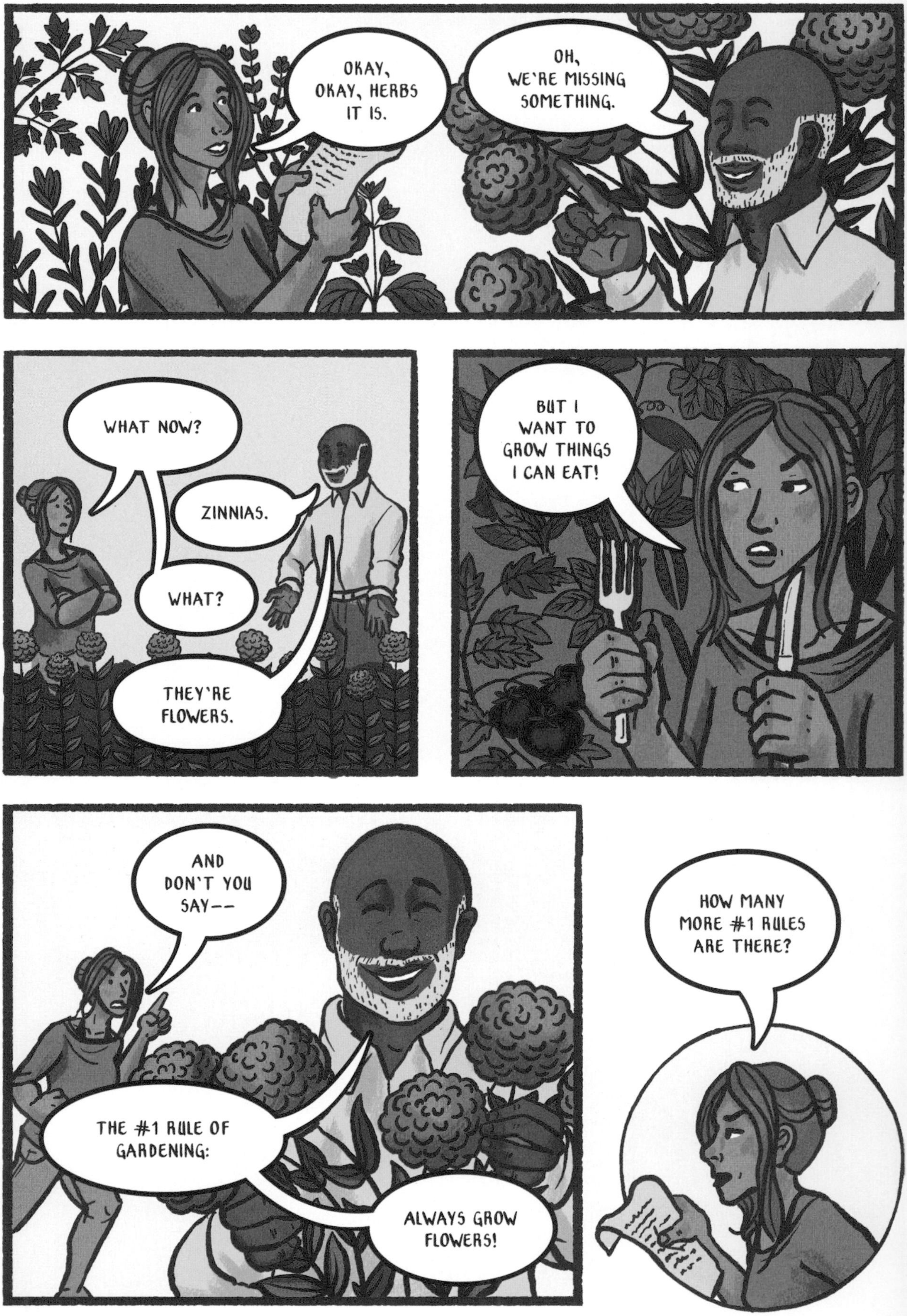
OKAY, OKAY, HERBS IT IS.
OH, WE'RE MISSING SOMETHING.
WHAT NOW?
ZINNIAS.
WHAT?
THEY'RE FLOWERS.
BUT I WANT TO GROW THINGS I CAN EAT!
AND DON'T YOU SAY--
THE #1 RULE OF GARDENING:
ALWAYS GROW FLOWERS!
HOW MANY MORE #1 RULES ARE THERE?

WHY GROW FLOWERS?

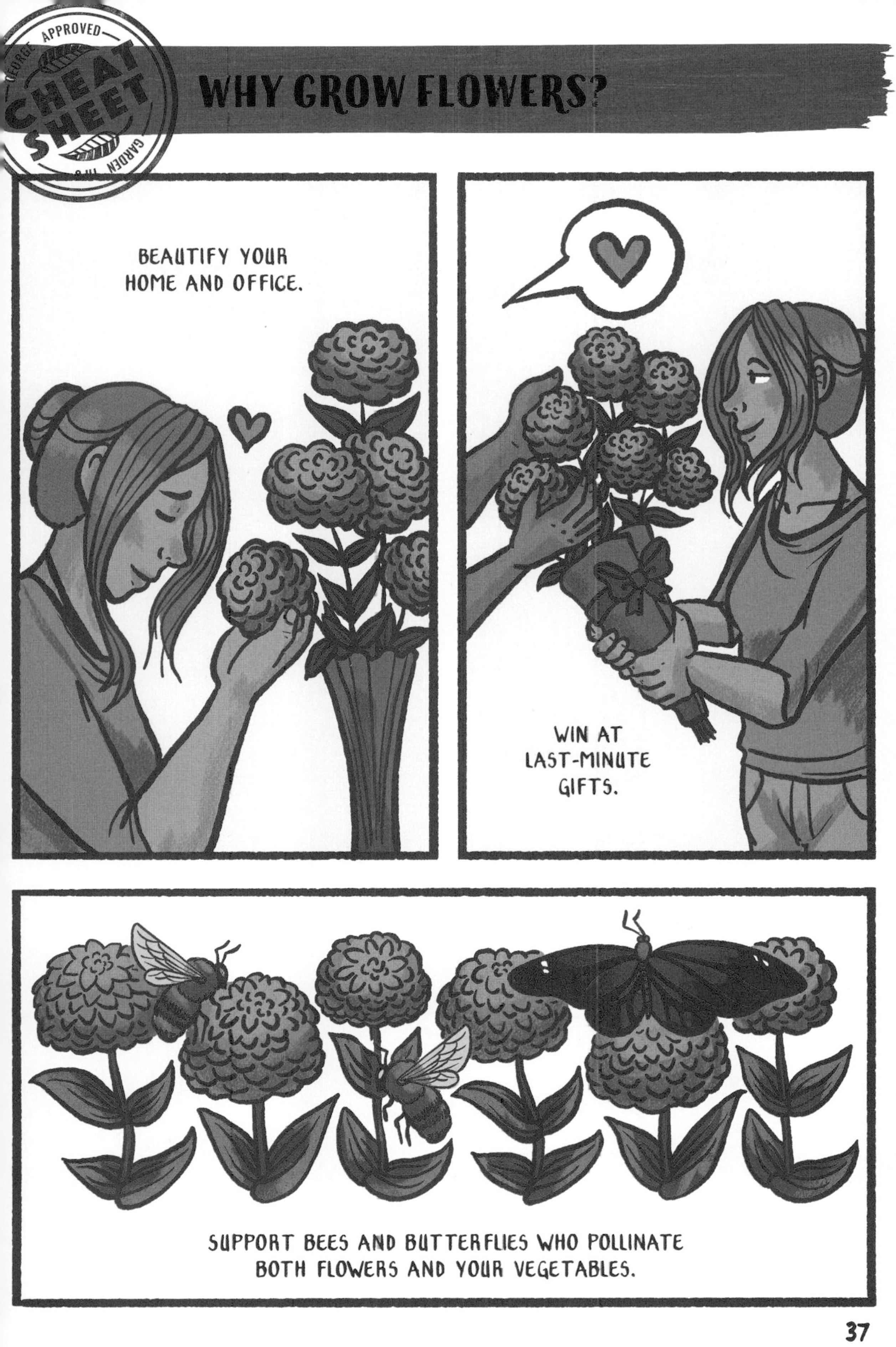

BEAUTIFY YOUR HOME AND OFFICE.
WIN AT LAST-MINUTE GIFTS.
SUPPORT BEES AND BUTTERFLIES WHO POLLINATE BOTH FLOWERS AND YOUR VEGETABLES.

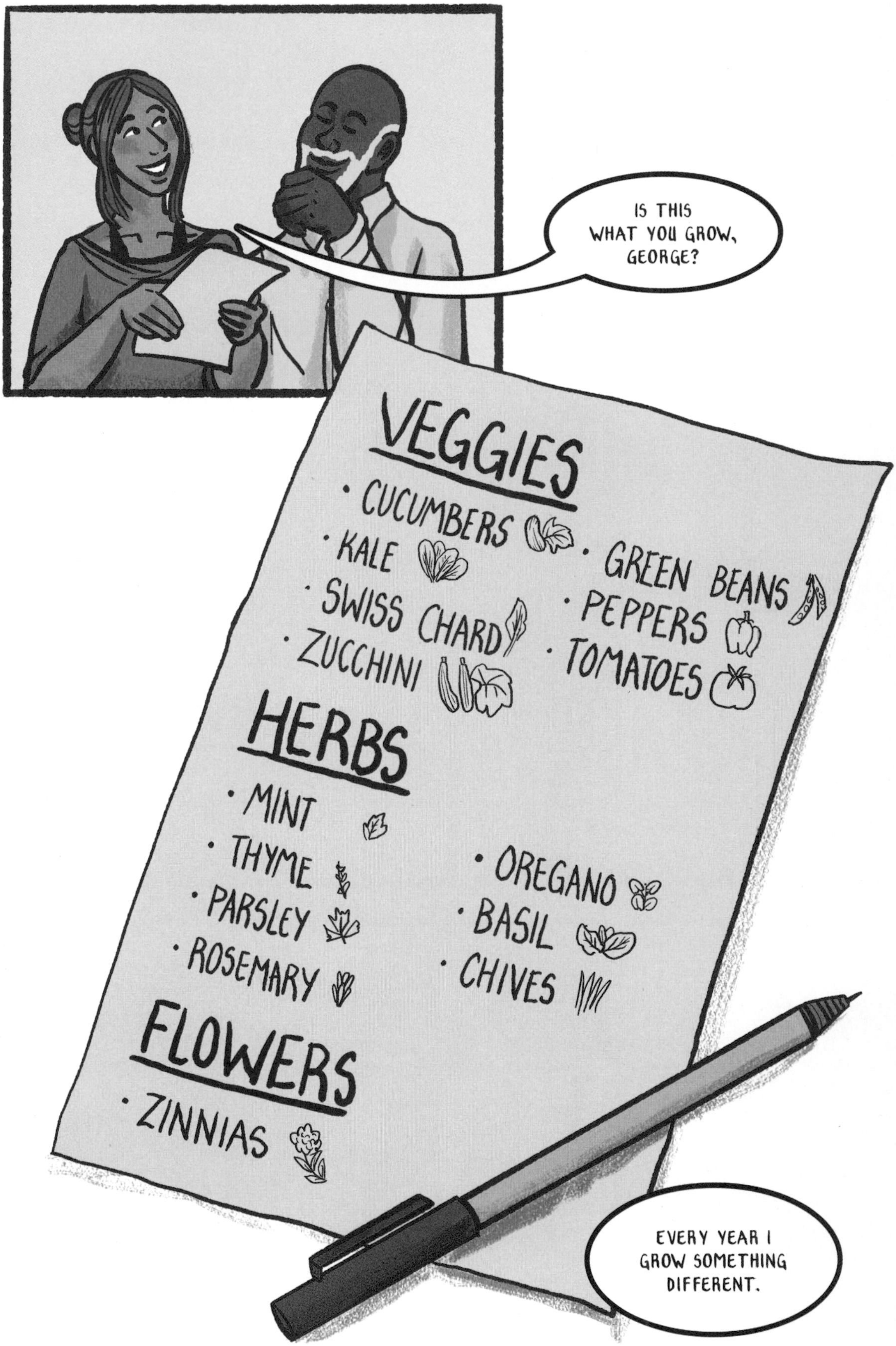
IS THIS WHAT YOU GROW, GEORGE?
VEGGIES
· CUCUMBERS
· KALE
· SWISS CHARD
· ZUCCHINI
· GREEN BEANS
· PEPPERS
· TOMATOES
HERBS
· MINT
· THYME
· PARSLEY
· ROSEMARY
· OREGANO
· BASIL
· CHIVES
FLOWERS
· ZINNIAS
EVERY YEAR I GROW SOMETHING DIFFERENT.

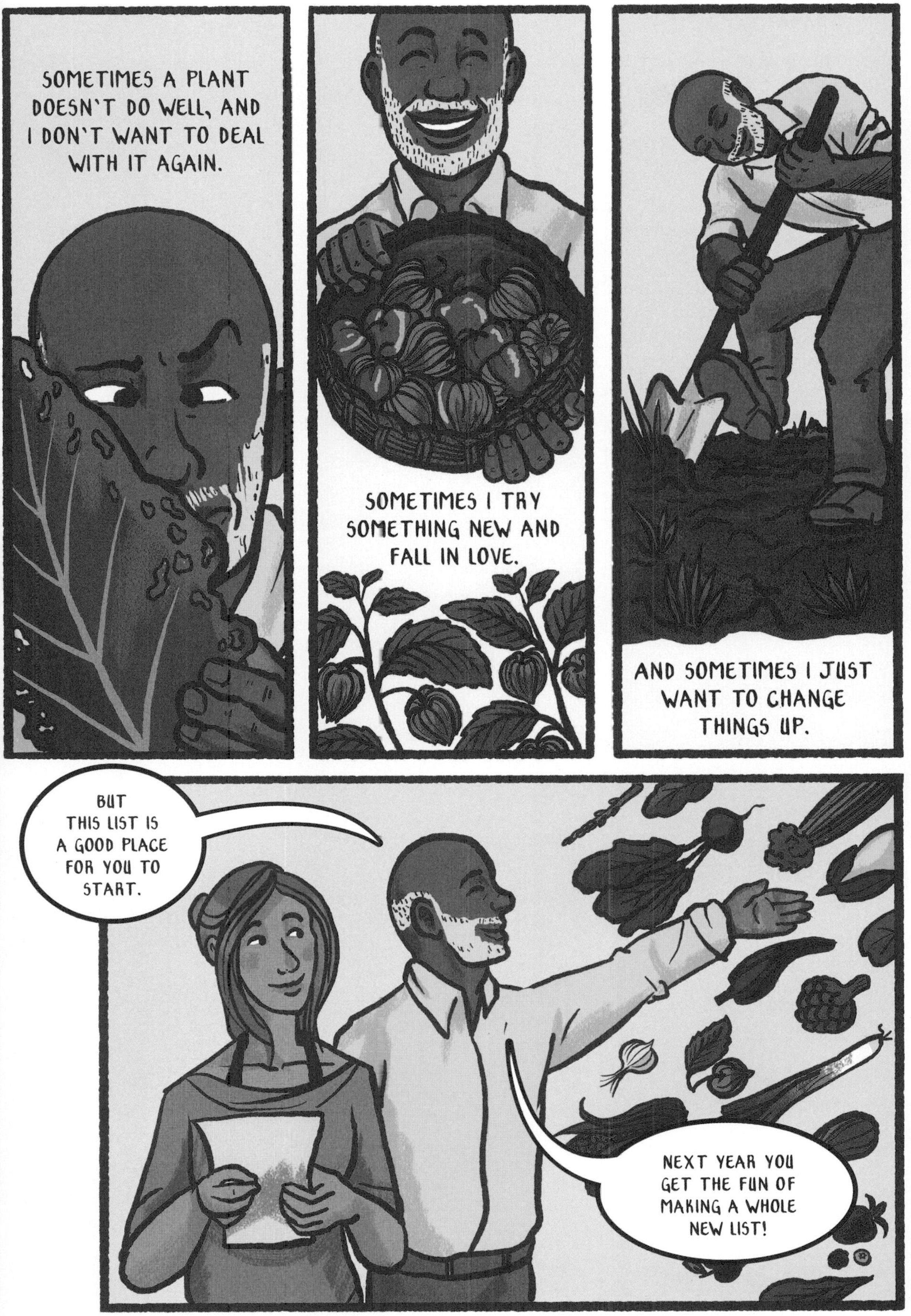
SOMETIMES A PLANT DOESN'T DO WELL, AND I DON'T WANT TO DEAL WITH IT AGAIN.
SOMETIMES I TRY SOMETHING NEW AND FALL IN LOVE.
AND SOMETIMES I JUST WANT TO CHANGE THINGS UP.
BUT THIS LIST IS A GOOD PLACE FOR YOU TO START.
NEXT YEAR YOU GET THE FUN OF MAKING A WHOLE NEW LIST!

THREE:
WHEN TO DO WHAT

MAKING A PLAN FOR PROPER TIMING.

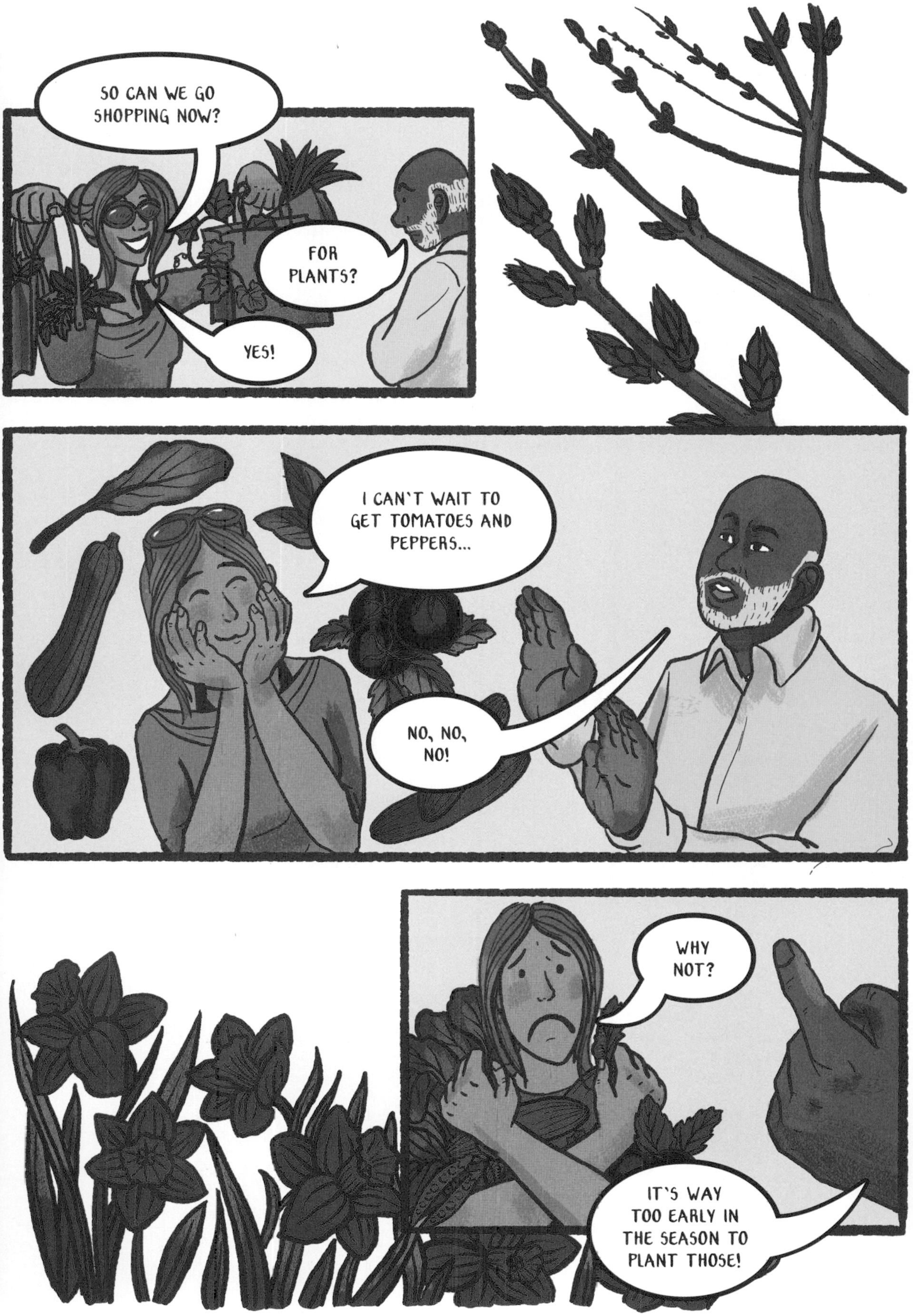
SO CAN WE GO SHOPPING NOW?
FOR PLANTS?
YES!
I CAN'T WAIT TO GET TOMATOES AND PEPPERS...
NO, NO, NO!
WHY NOT?
IT'S WAY TOO EARLY IN THE SEASON TO PLANT THOSE!

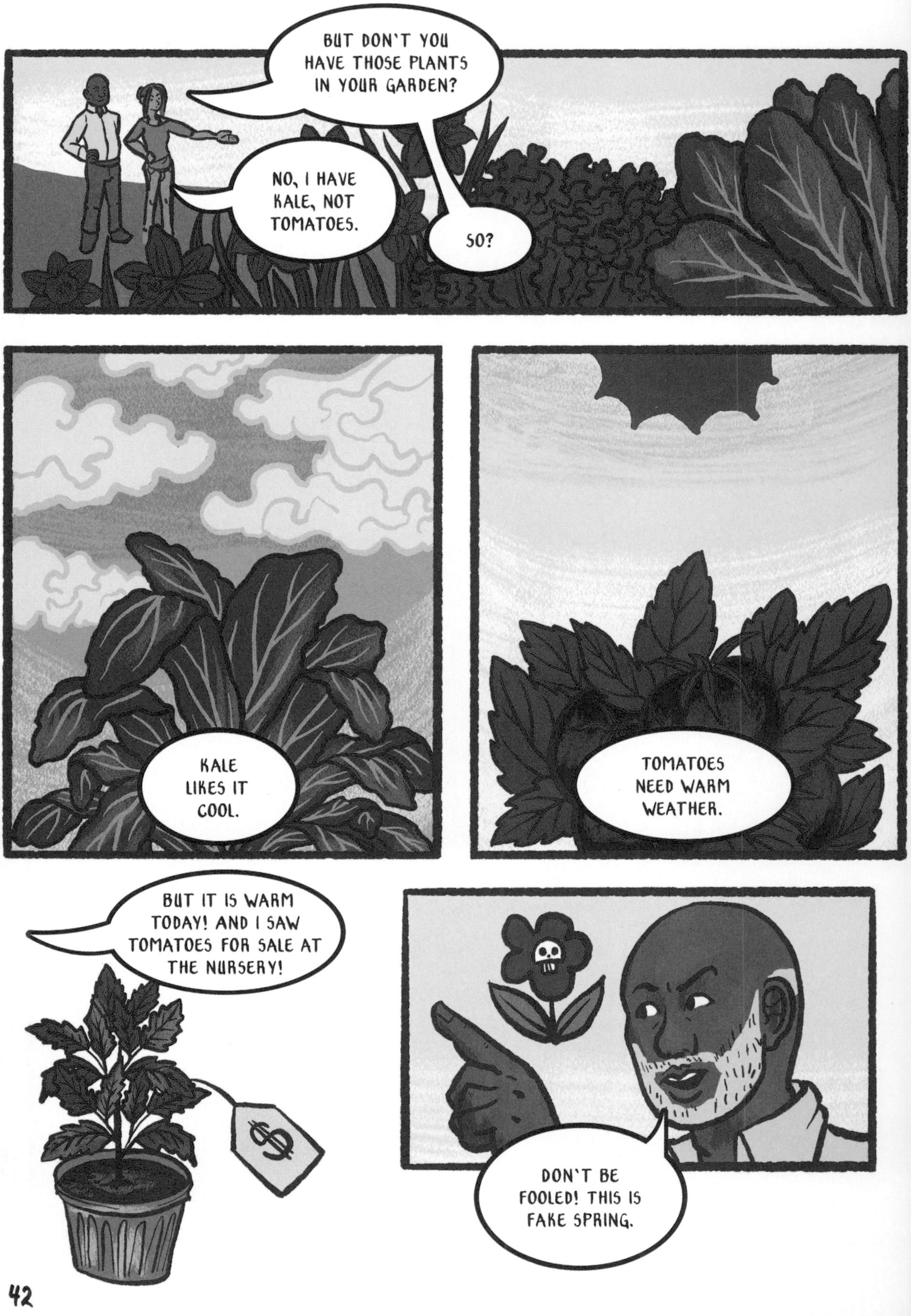
BUT DON'T YOU HAVE THOSE PLANTS IN YOUR GARDEN?
NO, I HAVE KALE, NOT TOMATOES.
SO?
KALE LIKES IT COOL.
TOMATOES NEED WARM WEATHER.
BUT IT IS WARM TODAY! AND I SAW TOMATOES FOR SALE AT THE NURSERY!
DON'T BE FOOLED! THIS IS FAKE SPRING.

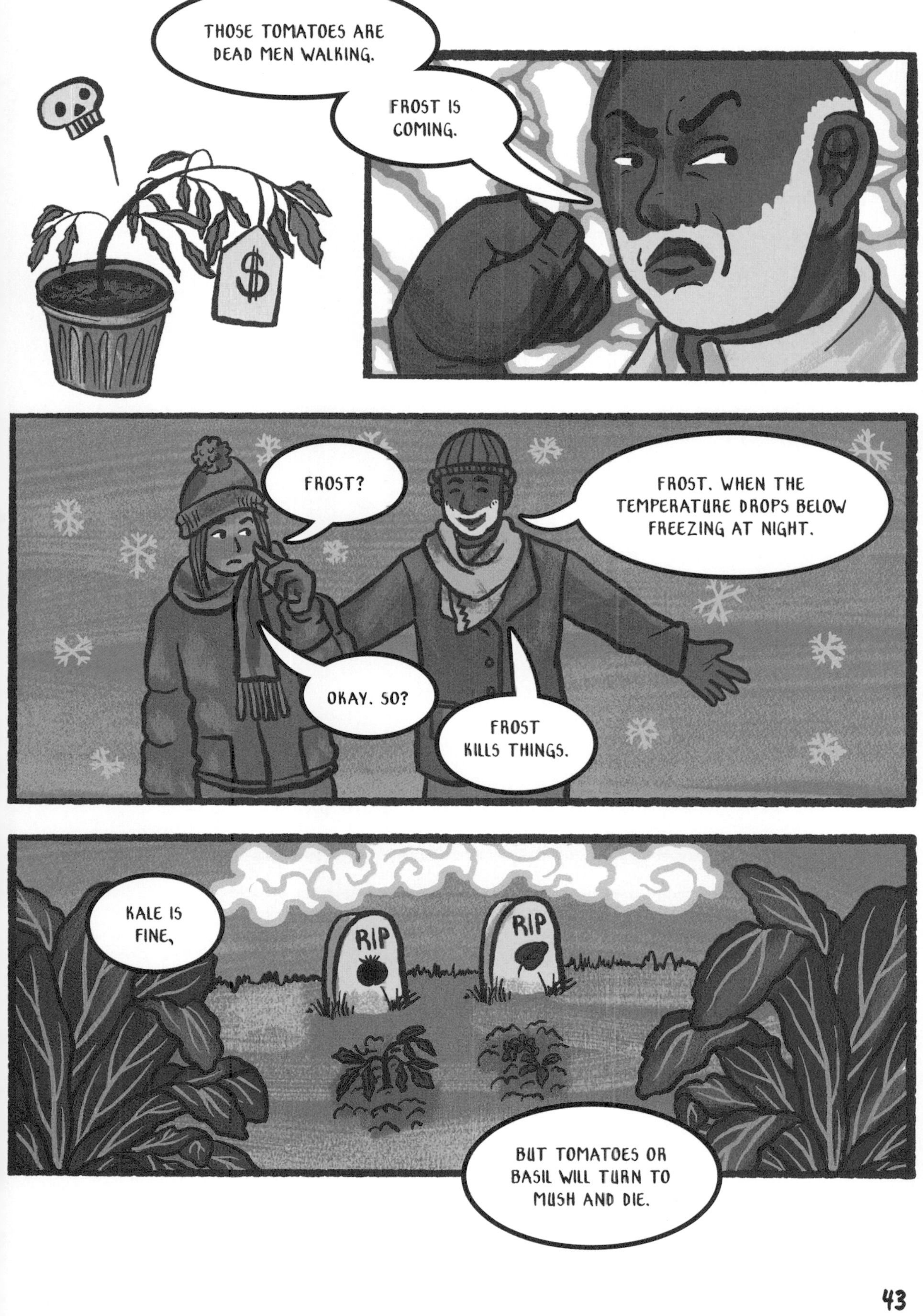
THOSE TOMATOES ARE DEAD MEN WALKING.
FROST IS COMING.
$
FROST?
FROST. WHEN THE TEMPERATURE DROPS BELOW FREEZING AT NIGHT.
OKAY. SO?
FROST KILLS THINGS.
KALE IS FINE,
RIP
RIP
BUT TOMATOES OR BASIL WILL TURN TO MUSH AND DIE.

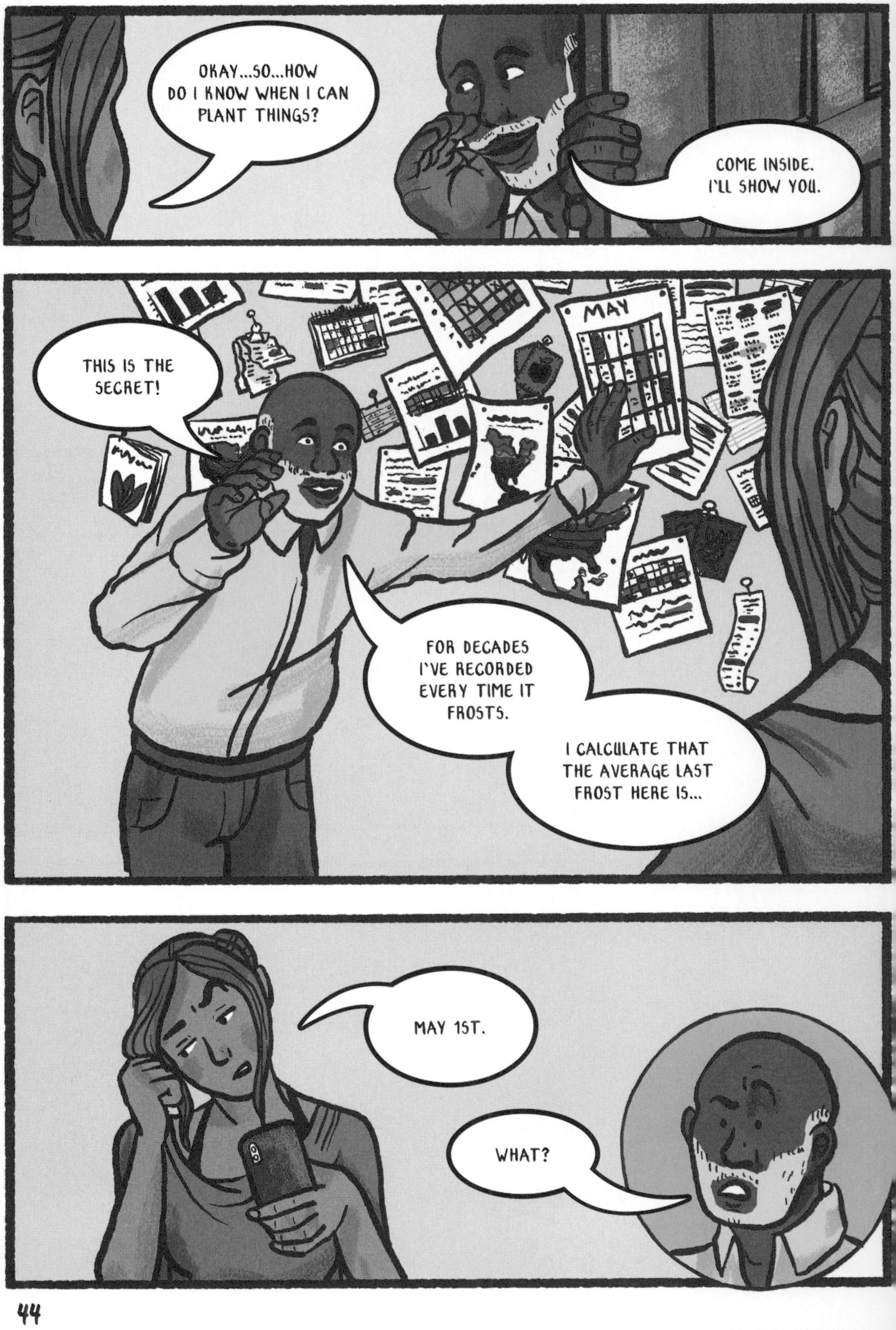

OKAY...SO...HOW DO I KNOW WHEN I CAN PLANT THINGS?
COME INSIDE. I'LL SHOW YOU.
THIS IS THE SECRET!
MAY
FOR DECADES I'VE RECORDED EVERY TIME IT FROSTS.
I CALCULATE THAT THE AVERAGE LAST FROST HERE IS...
MAY 1ST.
WHAT?

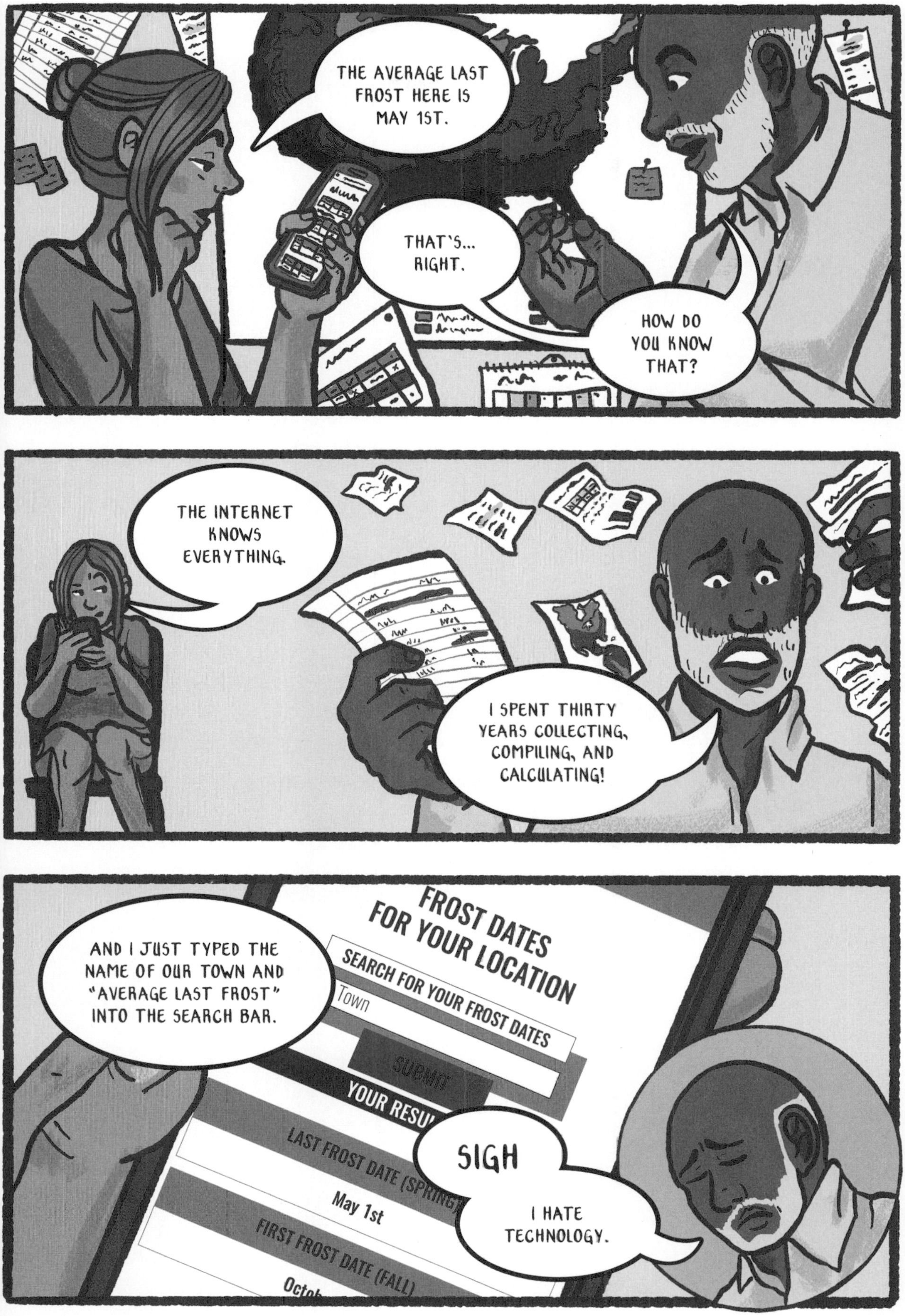
THE AVERAGE LAST FROST HERE IS MAY 1ST.
THAT'S... RIGHT.
HOW DO YOU KNOW THAT?
THE INTERNET KNOWS EVERYTHING.
I SPENT THIRTY YEARS COLLECTING, COMPILING, AND CALCULATING!
AND I JUST TYPED THE NAME OF OUR TOWN AND "AVERAGE LAST FROST" INTO THE SEARCH BAR.
FROST DATES FOR YOUR LOCATION
SEARCH FOR YOUR FROST DATES
Town
SUBMIT
LAST FROST DATE (SPRING)
May 1st
FIRST FROST DATE (FALL)
SIGH
I HATE TECHNOLOGY.

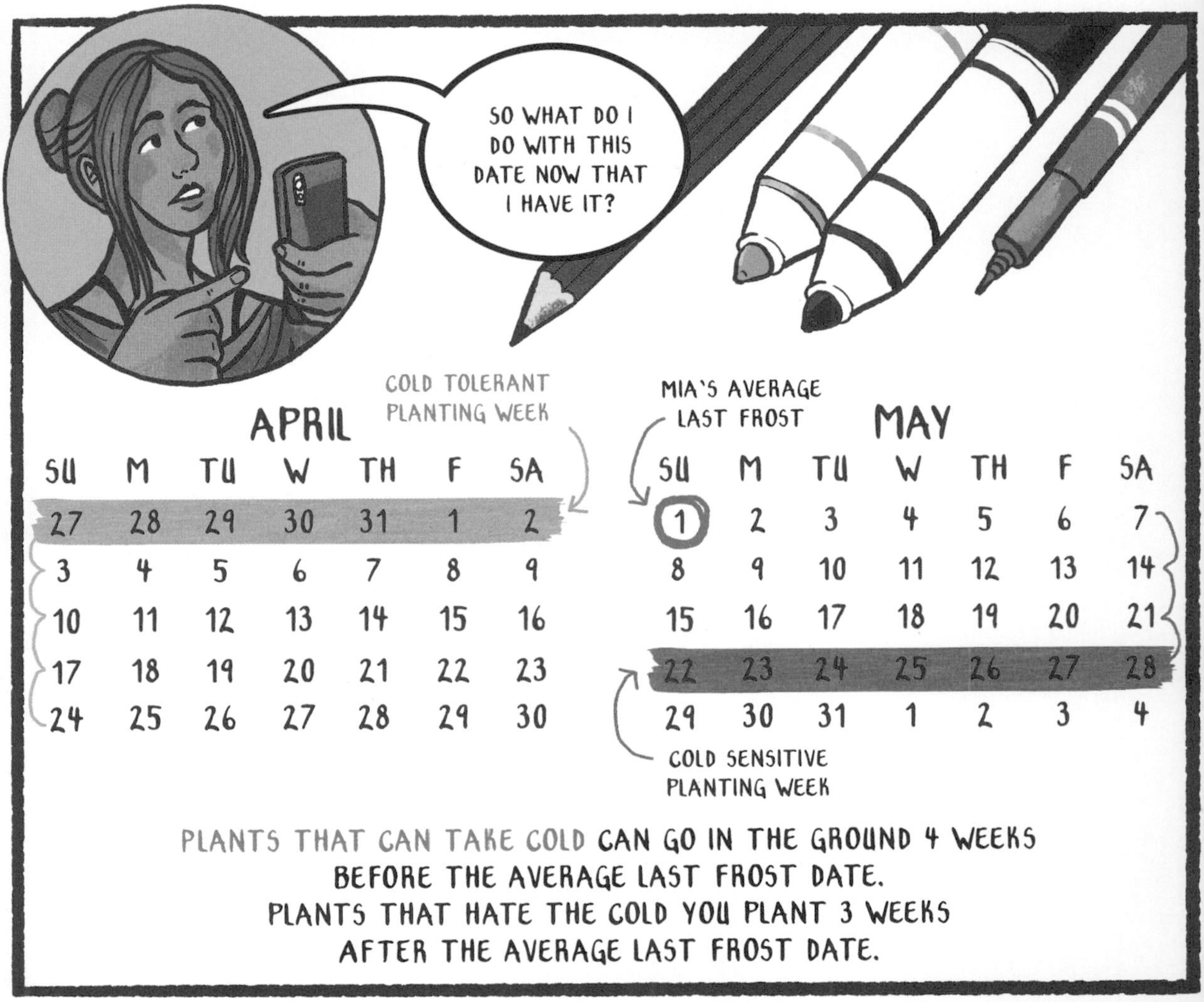
SO WHAT DO I DO WITH THIS DATE NOW THAT I HAVE IT?
COLD TOLERANT PLANTING WEEK
APRIL
SU M TU W TH F SA
27 28 29 30 31 1 2
3 4 5 6 7 8 9
10 11 12 13 14 15 16
17 18 19 20 21 22 23
24 25 26 27 28 29 30
MIA'S AVERAGE LAST FROST
MAY
SU M TU W TH F SA
1 2 3 4 5 6 7
8 9 10 11 12 13 14
15 16 17 18 19 20 21
22 23 24 25 26 27 28
29 30 31 1 2 3 4
COLD SENSITIVE PLANTING WEEK
PLANTS THAT CAN TAKE COLD CAN GO IN THE GROUND 4 WEEKS BEFORE THE AVERAGE LAST FROST DATE.
PLANTS THAT HATE THE COLD YOU PLANT 3 WEEKS AFTER THE AVERAGE LAST FROST DATE.

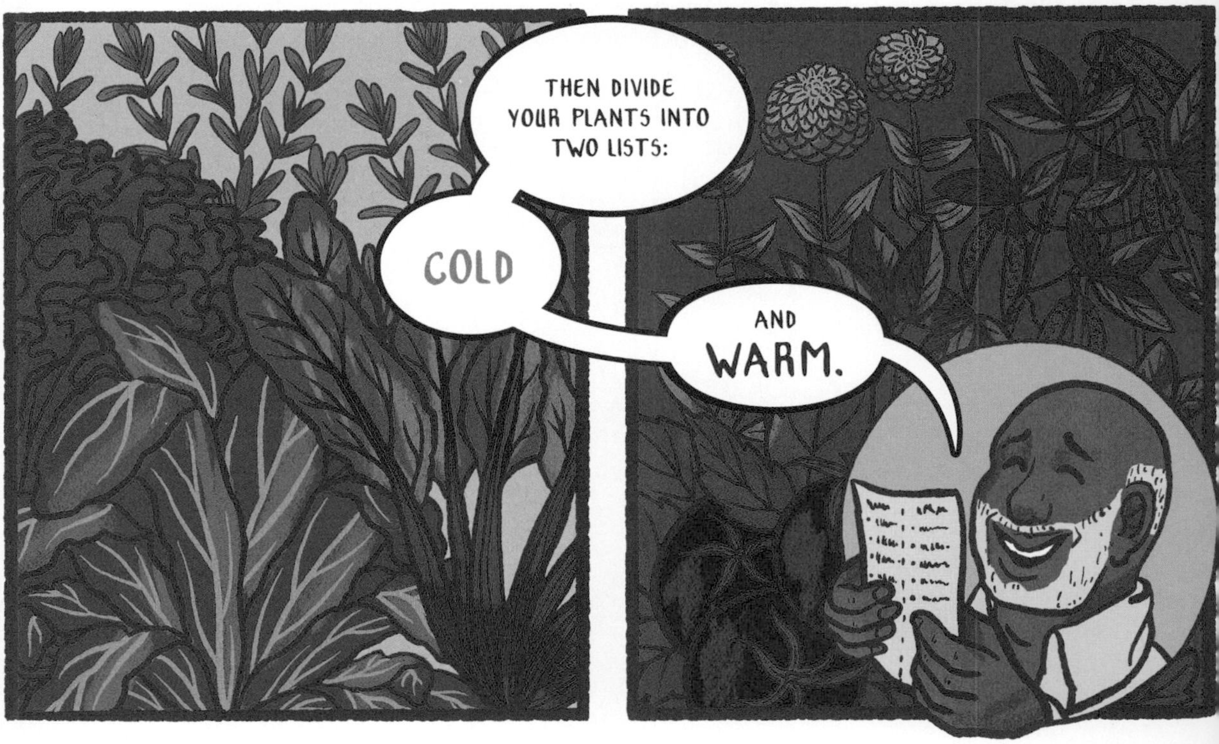
THEN DIVIDE YOUR PLANTS INTO TWO LISTS:
COLD
AND WARM.

GEORGE APPROVED CHEAT SHEET GARDEN TIPS

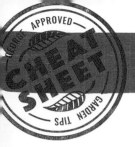

WHEN TO PLANT WHAT

YOUR AVERAGE LAST FROST:

____

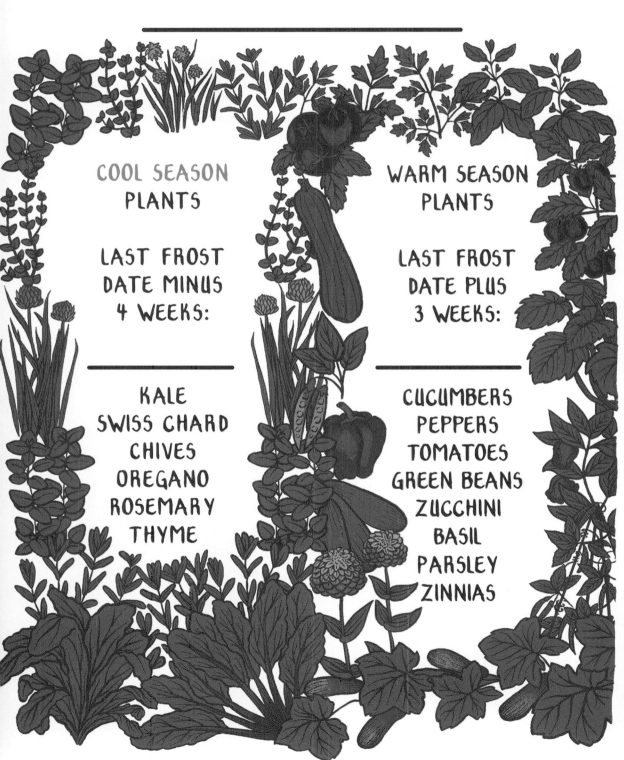

COOL SEASON PLANTS

LAST FROST DATE MINUS 4 WEEKS:

____

KALE
SWISS CHARD
CHIVES
OREGANO
ROSEMARY
THYME

WARM SEASON PLANTS

LAST FROST DATE PLUS 3 WEEKS:

____

CUCUMBERS
PEPPERS
TOMATOES
GREEN BEANS
ZUCCHINI
BASIL
PARSLEY
ZINNIAS

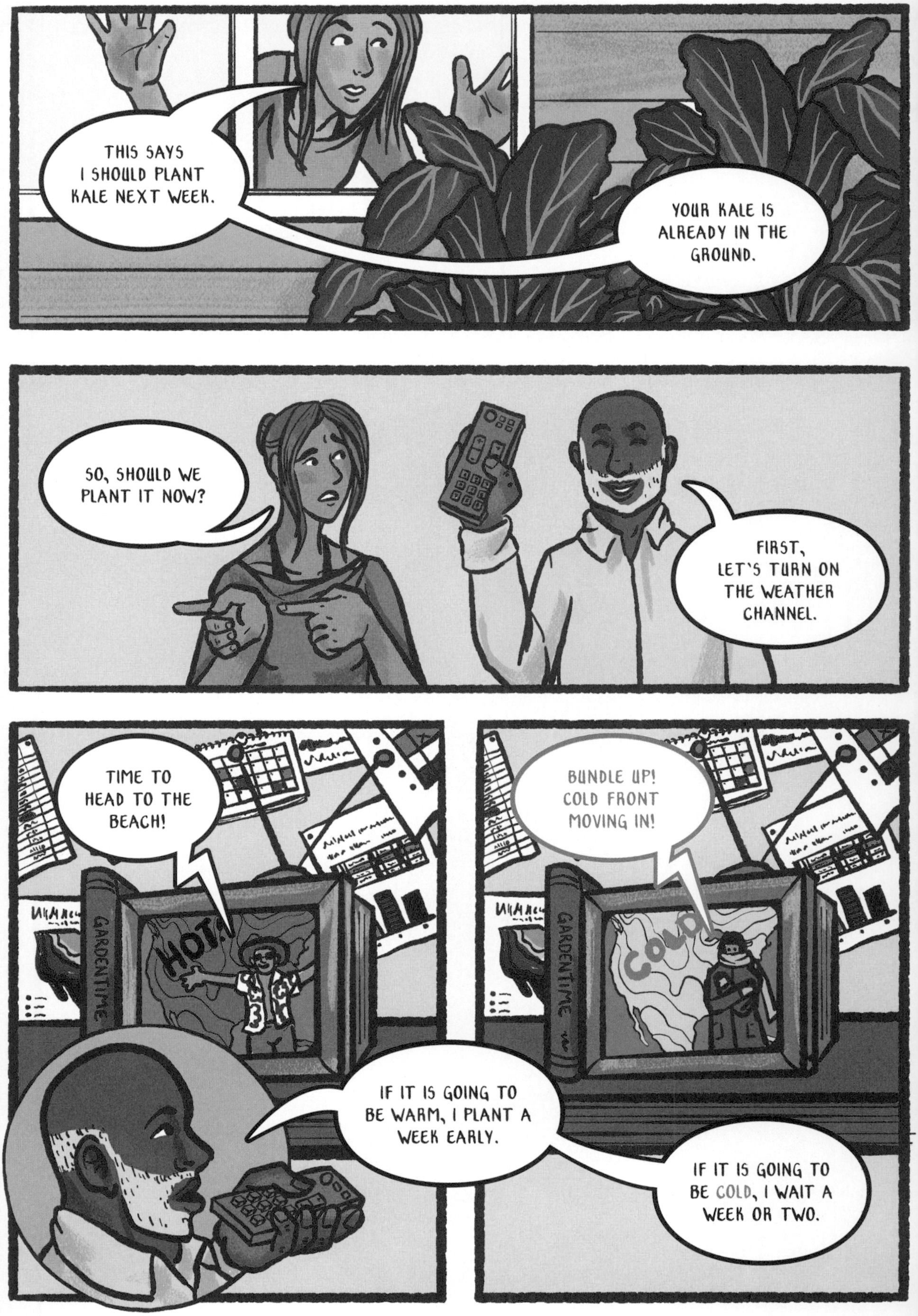
THIS SAYS I SHOULD PLANT KALE NEXT WEEK.
YOUR KALE IS ALREADY IN THE GROUND.
SO, SHOULD WE PLANT IT NOW?
FIRST, LET'S TURN ON THE WEATHER CHANNEL.
TIME TO HEAD TO THE BEACH!
HOT!
GARDENTIME
BUNDLE UP! COLD FRONT MOVING IN!
COLD
IF IT IS GOING TO BE WARM, I PLANT A WEEK EARLY.
IF IT IS GOING TO BE COLD, I WAIT A WEEK OR TWO.

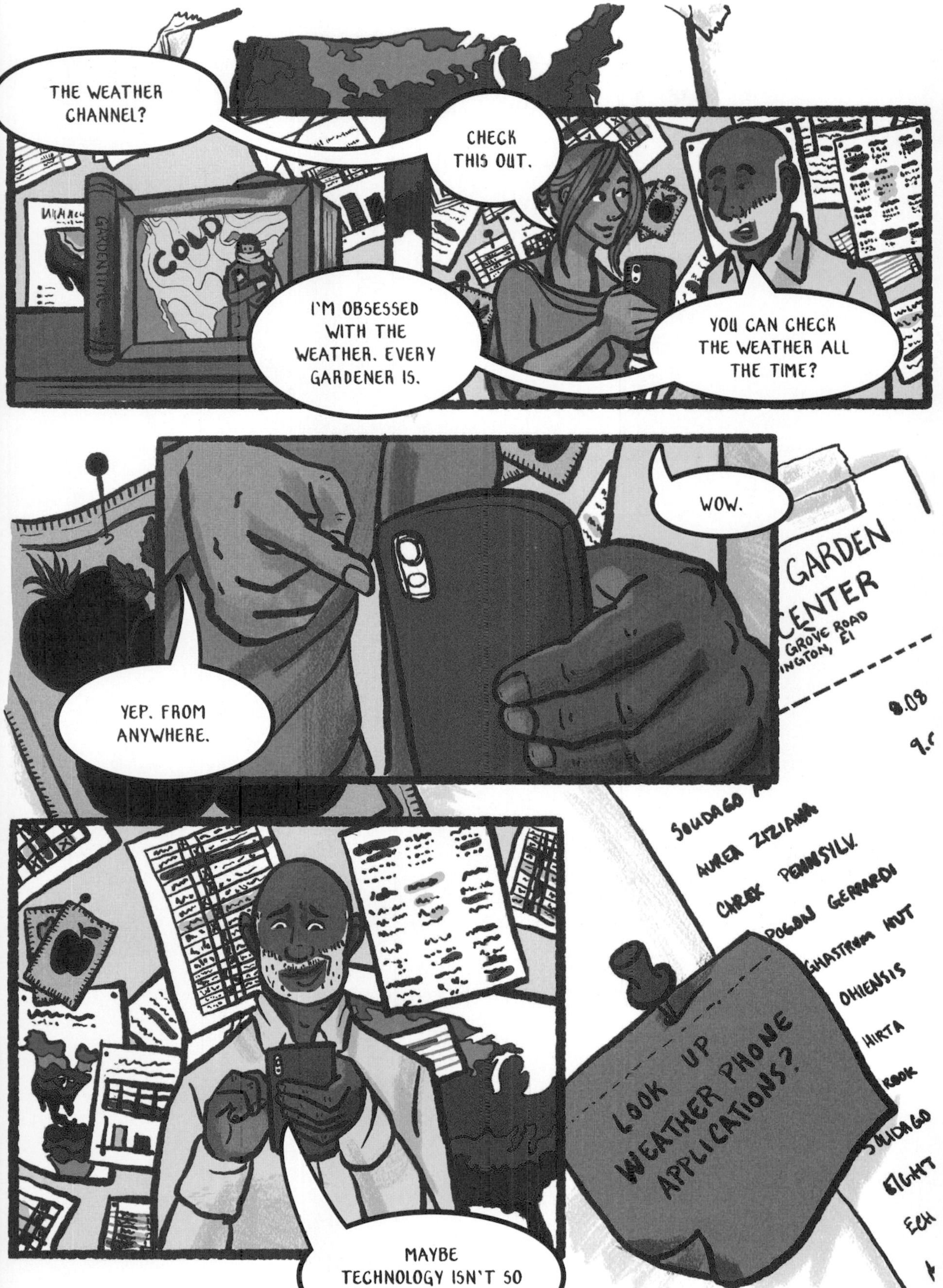
THE WEATHER CHANNEL?
CHECK THIS OUT.
COLD
I'M OBSESSED WITH THE WEATHER. EVERY GARDENER IS.
YOU CAN CHECK THE WEATHER ALL THE TIME?
WOW.
YEP. FROM ANYWHERE.
GARDEN CENTER
GROVE ROAD
MAYBE TECHNOLOGY ISN'T SO BAD AFTER ALL?
LOOK UP WEATHER PHONE APPLICATIONS?

GEORGE APPROVED CHEAT SHEET GARDEN TIPS

LEARN ABOUT YOUR LOCAL CLIMATE

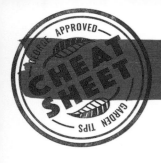

MARGARET ROACH'S PLANTING CALENDAR

AWAYTOGARDEN.COM/WHEN-TO-START-SEEDS-CALCULATOR

ENTER YOUR EXPECTED LAST FROST DATE AND GET TIMING ADVICE FOR A LONG LIST OF PLANTS.

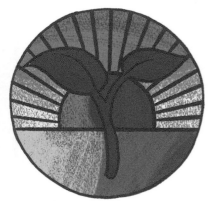

NATIONAL GARDENING ASSOCIATION

GARDEN.ORG/APPS/CALENDAR

ENTER YOUR ZIP CODE, AND YOU'LL GET SPECIFIC TIMING ADVICE FOR PLANTING ALL SORTS OF COMMON VEGETABLES.

USDA HARDINESS ZONE MAP

PLANTHARDINESS.ARS.USDA.GOV

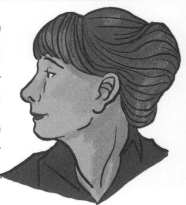

THE USDA DIVIDES THE UNITED STATES INTO HARDINESS ZONES BASED ON AVERAGE WINTER LOW TEMPERATURES. MANY PLANT CATALOGS AND BOOKS USE HARDINESS ZONES AS A BASIC MEASURE OF HOW WARM OR COLD YOUR LOCAL CLIMATE IS.

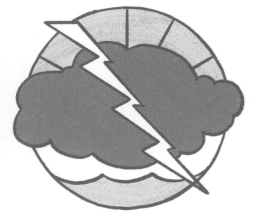

USDA

THE NATIONAL WEATHER SERVICE

WEATHER.GOV

THE NATIONAL WEATHER SERVICE IN THE UNITED STATES IS THE SOURCE FOR THE WEATHER FORECAST DATA USED BY OTHER FORECASTING SITES. GO STRAIGHT TO THE SOURCE TO GET THE MOST ACCURATE PREDICTIONS FOR UPCOMING WEATHER (THOUGH, OF COURSE, NO WEATHER PREDICTION IS PERFECT).

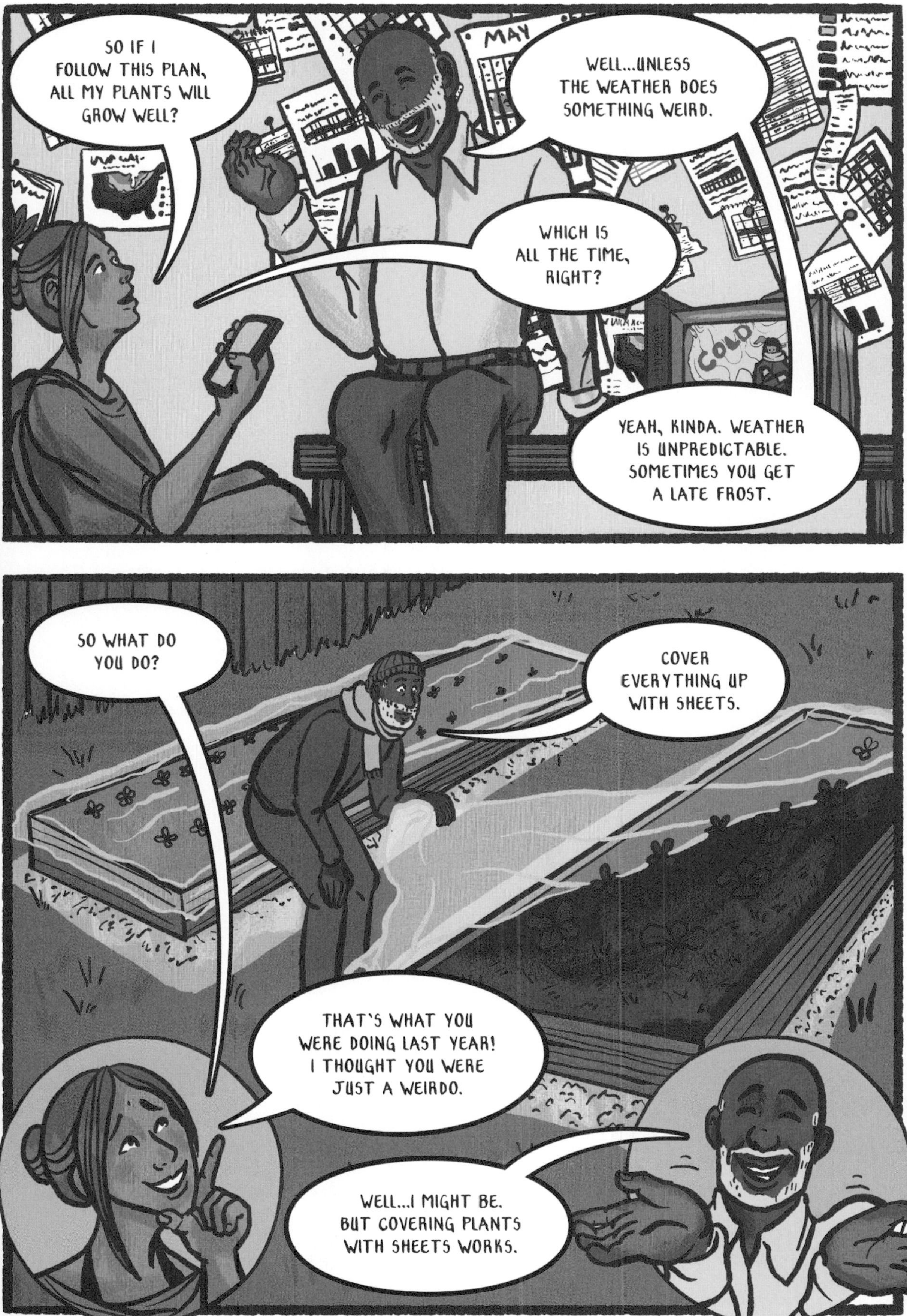
SO IF I FOLLOW THIS PLAN, ALL MY PLANTS WILL GROW WELL?
WELL...UNLESS THE WEATHER DOES SOMETHING WEIRD.
WHICH IS ALL THE TIME, RIGHT?
YEAH, KINDA. WEATHER IS UNPREDICTABLE. SOMETIMES YOU GET A LATE FROST.
MAY
COLD
SO WHAT DO YOU DO?
COVER EVERYTHING UP WITH SHEETS.
THAT'S WHAT YOU WERE DOING LAST YEAR! I THOUGHT YOU WERE JUST A WEIRDO.
WELL...I MIGHT BE. BUT COVERING PLANTS WITH SHEETS WORKS.

WHEN FROST THREATENS

WATCH FOR FROST

4:41
forecast.weather.gov
CURRENT CONDITIONS
HOME
43°F
FEELS LIKE 38°
Hi: 50° Lo:25°
RAIN
WIND
TONIGHT
Lo: 22°

KEEP AN EYE ON THE WEATHER.

IF LOW TEMPERATURES ARE PREDICTED TO BE WITHIN 5 DEGREES OF FREEZING, PROTECT YOUR WARM SEASON CROPS.

THE NATIONAL WEATHER SERVICE ISSUES FROST WARNINGS IF LATE FREEZES ARE POSSIBLE.

FROSTS ARE MOST LIKELY IF THE NIGHT IS CLOUDLESS AND WITHOUT WIND.

EXPOSED, OPEN, LOW-LYING AREAS FREEZE BEFORE THE TOPS OF SLOPES OR AREAS UNDER TREES OR BY HOUSE WALLS.

COVER PLANTS

WARMTH FROM THE SOIL CAN PROTECT PLANTS IF YOU GIVE THEM A LITTLE INSULATION.

COVER WITH AN OLD BEDSHEET, A ROW COVER SOLD AT YOUR NURSERY, OR EVEN CARDBOARD BOXES FROM YOUR ONLINE SHOPPING.

DO NOT USE PLASTIC. PLASTIC WILL CONDUCT COLD RATHER THAN INSULATE, AND WILL DAMAGE THE PLANT TISSUE TOUCHING IT.

USE ROCKS, BRICKS, OR ANYTHING ELSE AT HAND TO SECURE THE EDGES IF THE WIND PICKS UP.

IN THE MORNING, REMOVE THE COVERS ONCE IT HAS WARMED BACK UP OVER THE FREEZING MARK.

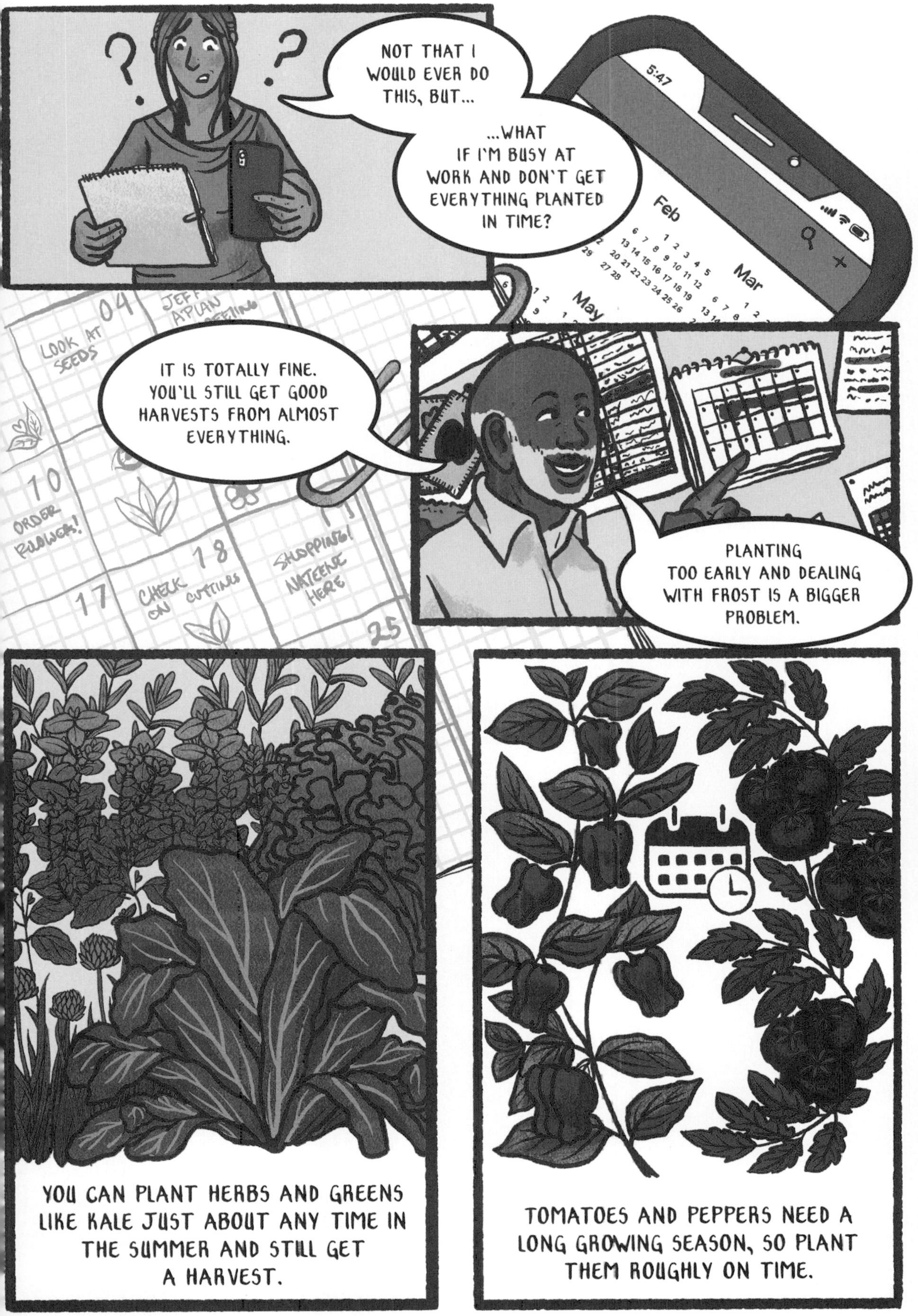
NOT THAT I WOULD EVER DO THIS, BUT...
...WHAT IF I'M BUSY AT WORK AND DON'T GET EVERYTHING PLANTED IN TIME?
IT IS TOTALLY FINE. YOU'LL STILL GET GOOD HARVESTS FROM ALMOST EVERYTHING.
PLANTING TOO EARLY AND DEALING WITH FROST IS A BIGGER PROBLEM.
YOU CAN PLANT HERBS AND GREENS LIKE KALE JUST ABOUT ANY TIME IN THE SUMMER AND STILL GET A HARVEST.
TOMATOES AND PEPPERS NEED A LONG GROWING SEASON, SO PLANT THEM ROUGHLY ON TIME.

FOUR:

SOIL TESTING AND FERTILIZING

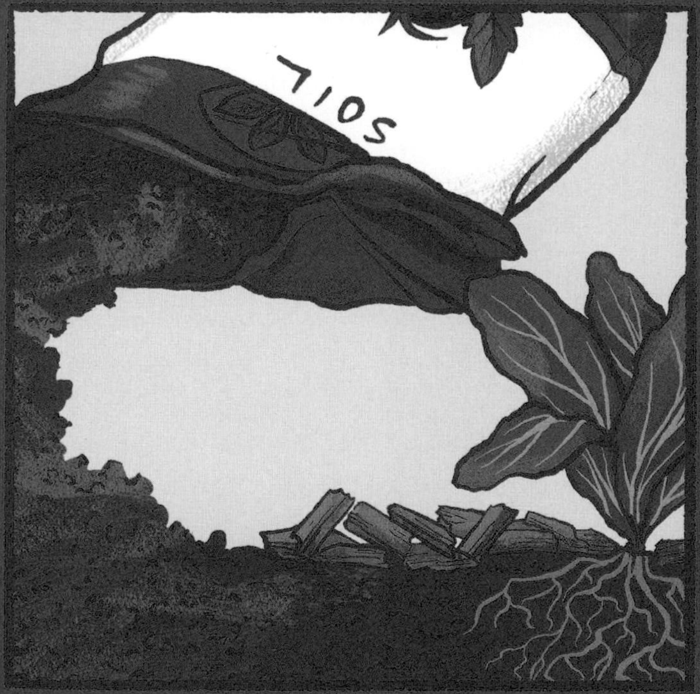
SOIL

MAKING SURE PLANTS GET THE NUTRIENTS THEY NEED.

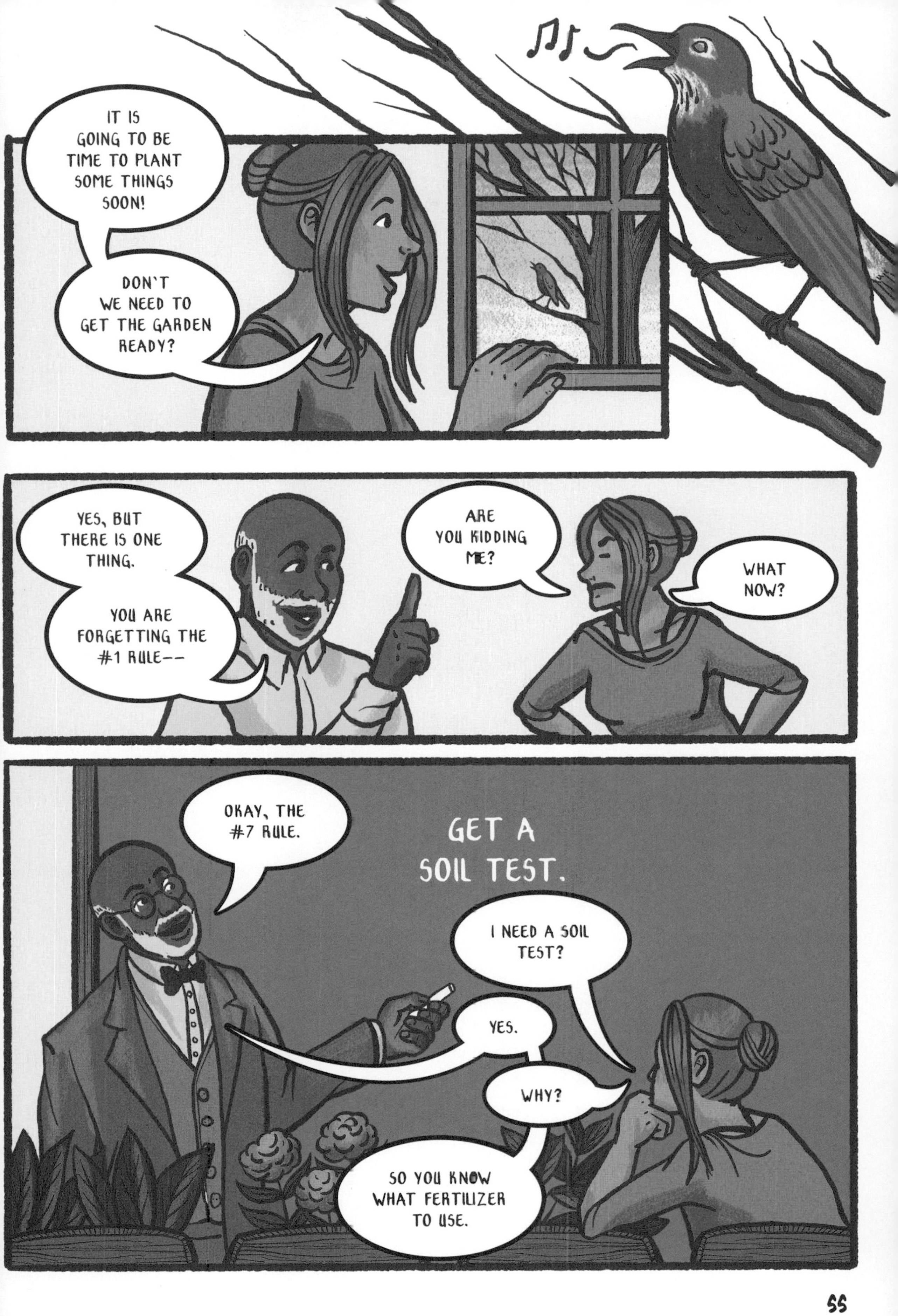

IT IS GOING TO BE TIME TO PLANT SOME THINGS SOON!
DON'T WE NEED TO GET THE GARDEN READY?
YES, BUT THERE IS ONE THING.
YOU ARE FORGETTING THE #1 RULE--
ARE YOU KIDDING ME?
WHAT NOW?
OKAY, THE #7 RULE.
GET A SOIL TEST.
I NEED A SOIL TEST?
YES.
WHY?
SO YOU KNOW WHAT FERTILIZER TO USE.

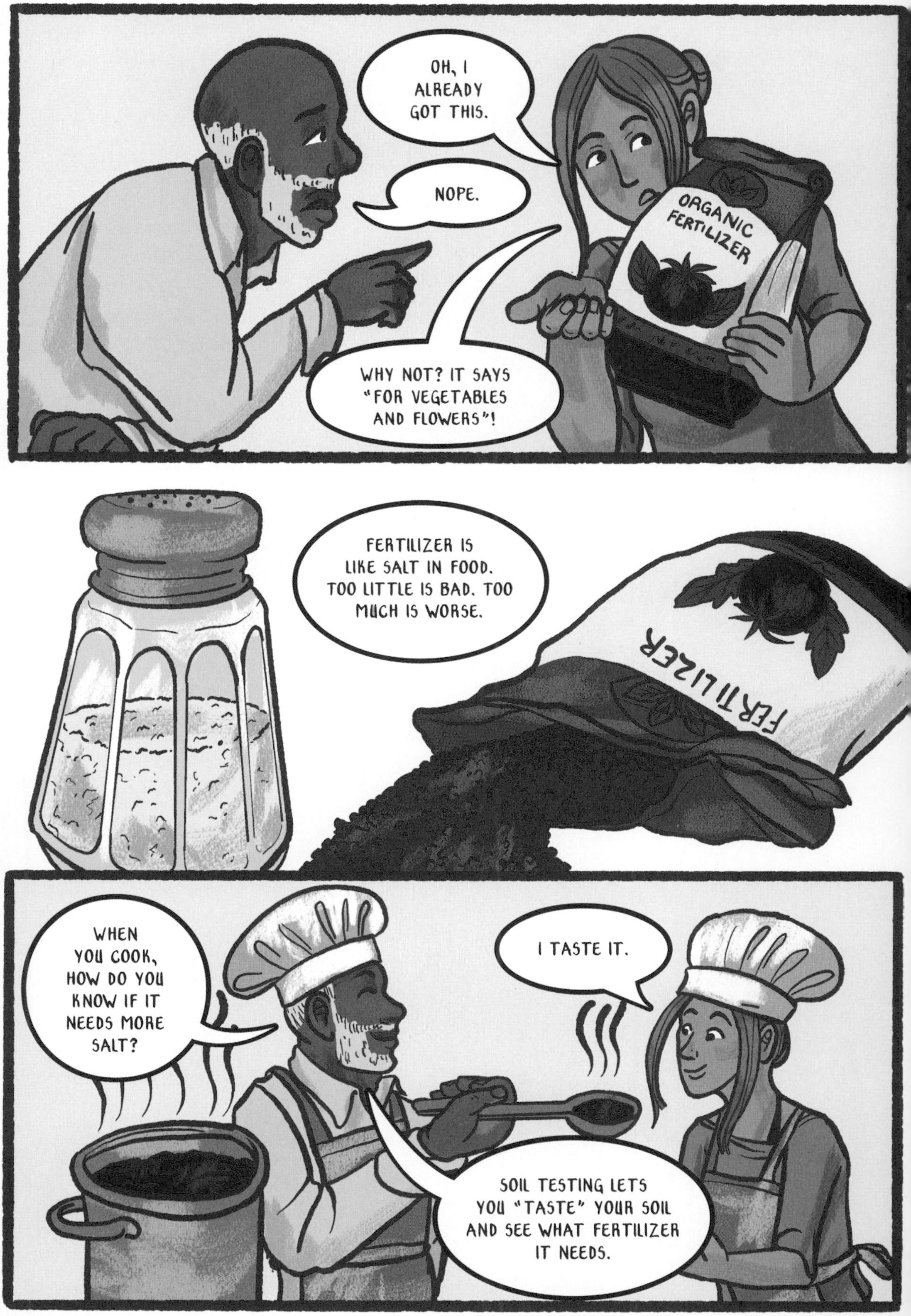
OH, I ALREADY GOT THIS.
NOPE.
ORGANIC FERTILIZER
WHY NOT? IT SAYS "FOR VEGETABLES AND FLOWERS"!
FERTILIZER IS LIKE SALT IN FOOD. TOO LITTLE IS BAD. TOO MUCH IS WORSE.
FERTILIZER
WHEN YOU COOK, HOW DO YOU KNOW IF IT NEEDS MORE SALT?
I TASTE IT.
SOIL TESTING LETS YOU "TASTE" YOUR SOIL AND SEE WHAT FERTILIZER IT NEEDS.

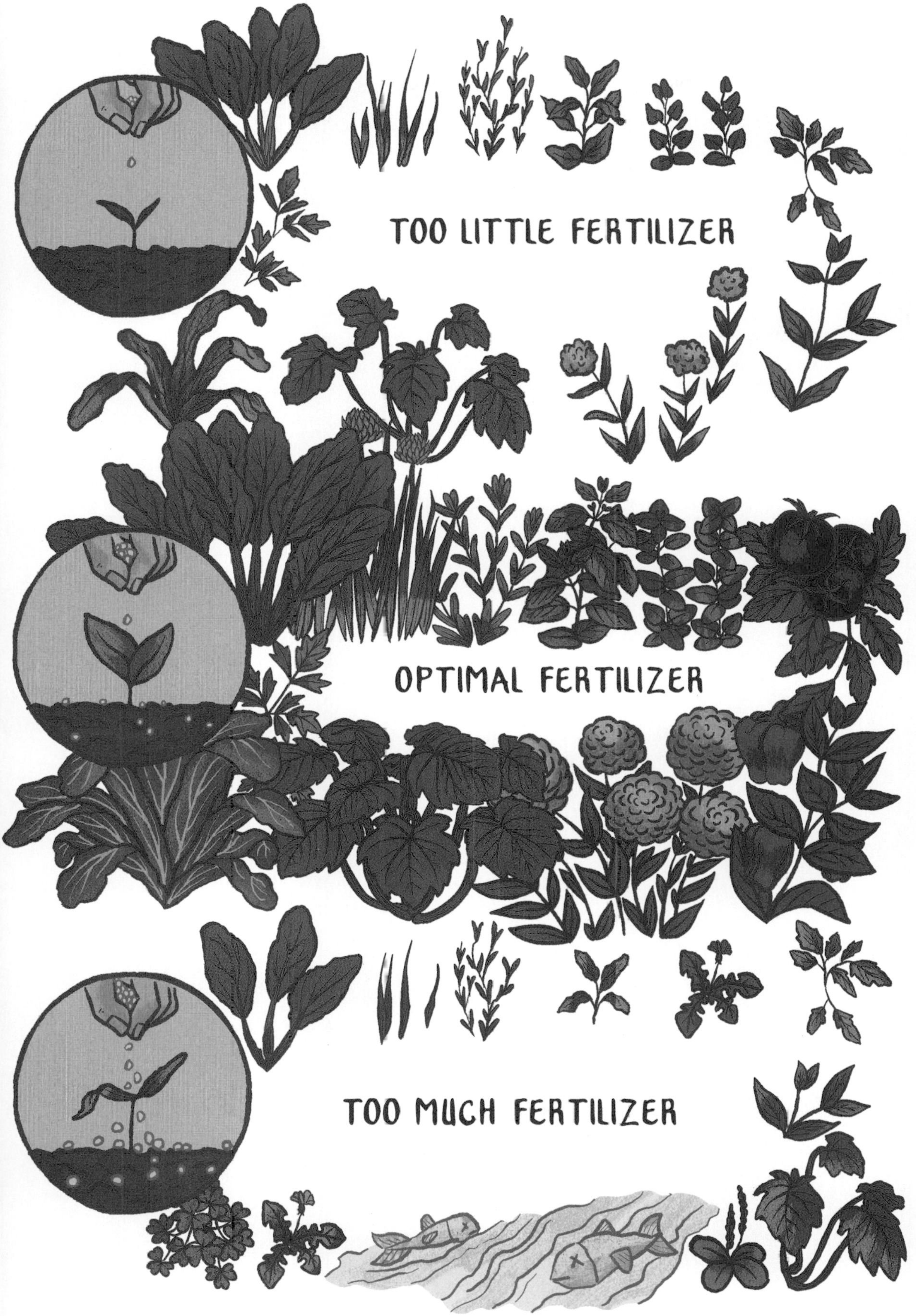
TOO LITTLE FERTILIZER
OPTIMAL FERTILIZER
TOO MUCH FERTILIZER

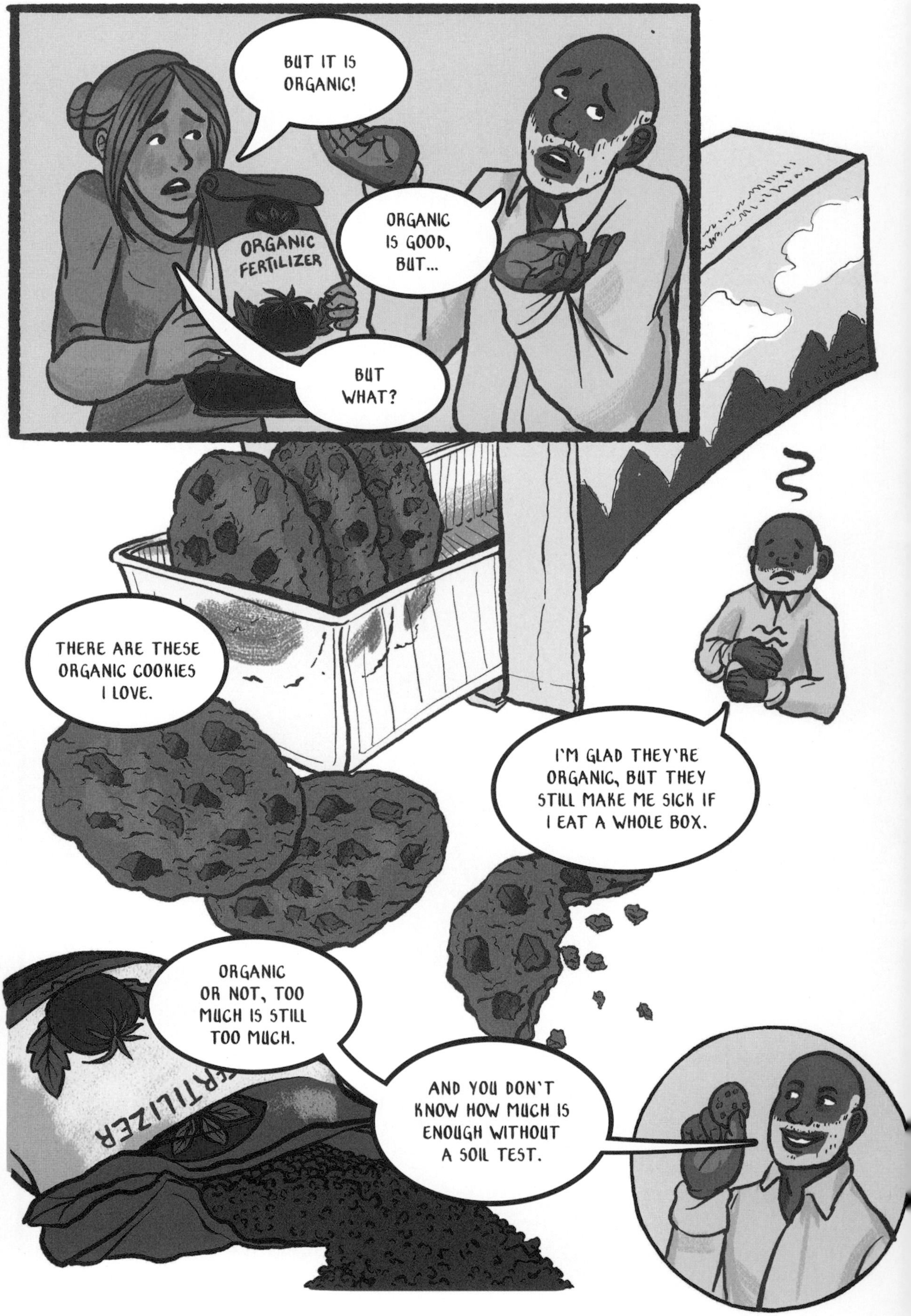

BUT IT IS ORGANIC!
ORGANIC FERTILIZER
ORGANIC IS GOOD, BUT...
BUT WHAT?
THERE ARE THESE ORGANIC COOKIES I LOVE.
I'M GLAD THEY'RE ORGANIC, BUT THEY STILL MAKE ME SICK IF I EAT A WHOLE BOX.
ORGANIC OR NOT, TOO MUCH IS STILL TOO MUCH.
AND YOU DON'T KNOW HOW MUCH IS ENOUGH WITHOUT A SOIL TEST.

HOW TO TEST YOUR SOIL

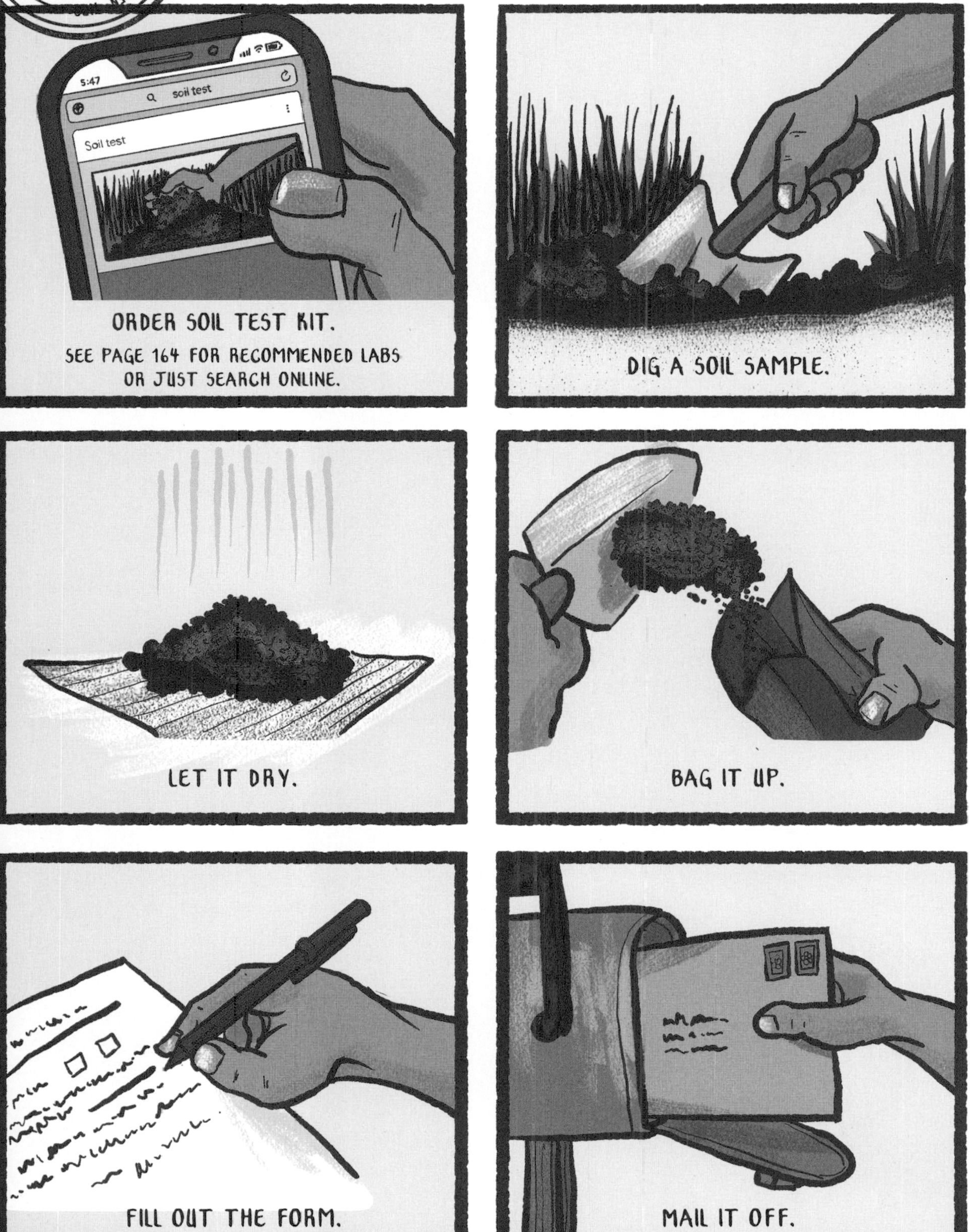

5:47
soil test
Soil test
ORDER SOIL TEST KIT.
SEE PAGE 164 FOR RECOMMENDED LABS OR JUST SEARCH ONLINE.
DIG A SOIL SAMPLE.
LET IT DRY.
BAG IT UP.
FILL OUT THE FORM.
MAIL IT OFF.

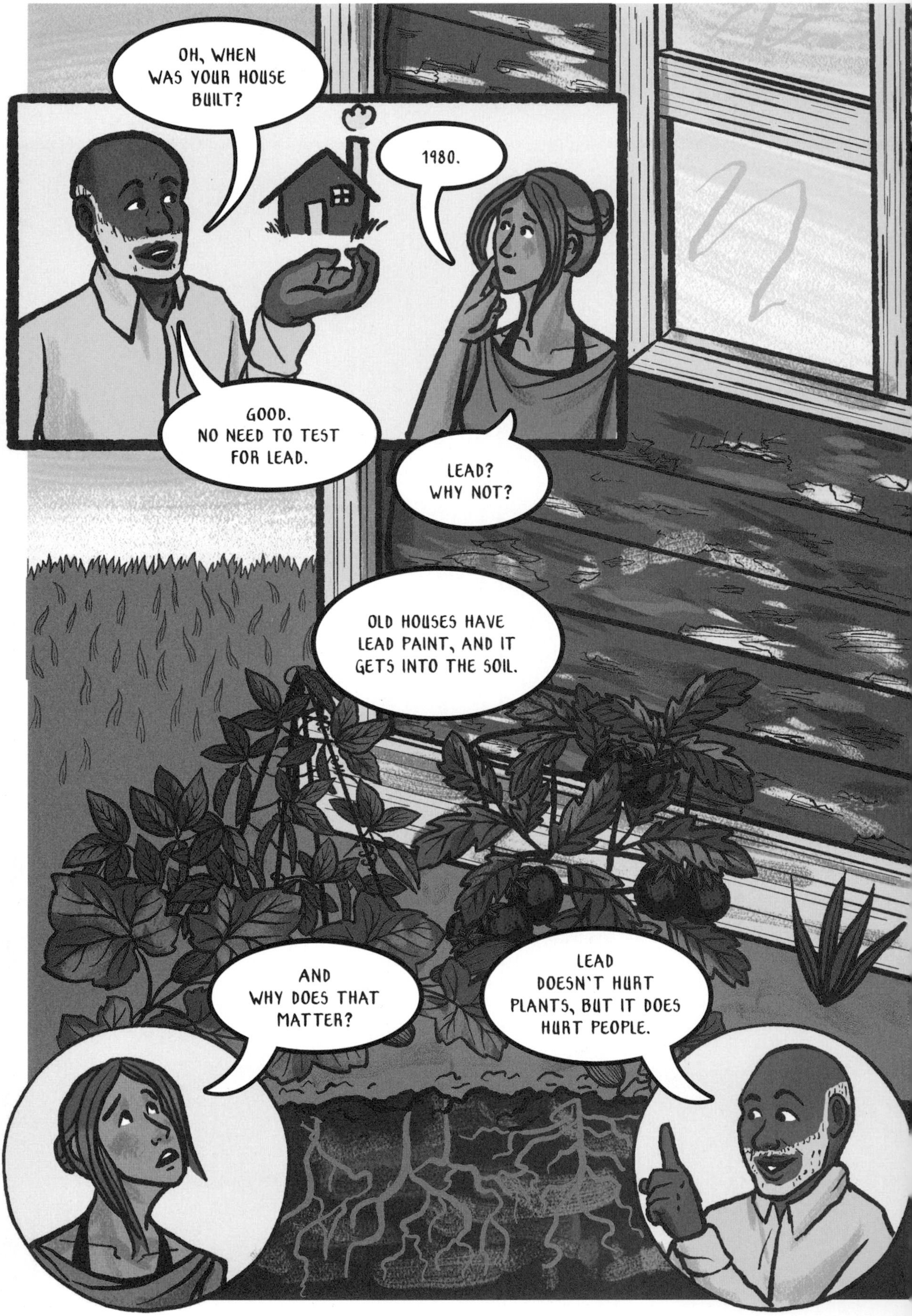
OH, WHEN WAS YOUR HOUSE BUILT?
1980.
GOOD. NO NEED TO TEST FOR LEAD.
LEAD? WHY NOT?
OLD HOUSES HAVE LEAD PAINT, AND IT GETS INTO THE SOIL.
AND WHY DOES THAT MATTER?
LEAD DOESN'T HURT PLANTS, BUT IT DOES HURT PEOPLE.

DEALING WITH LEAD

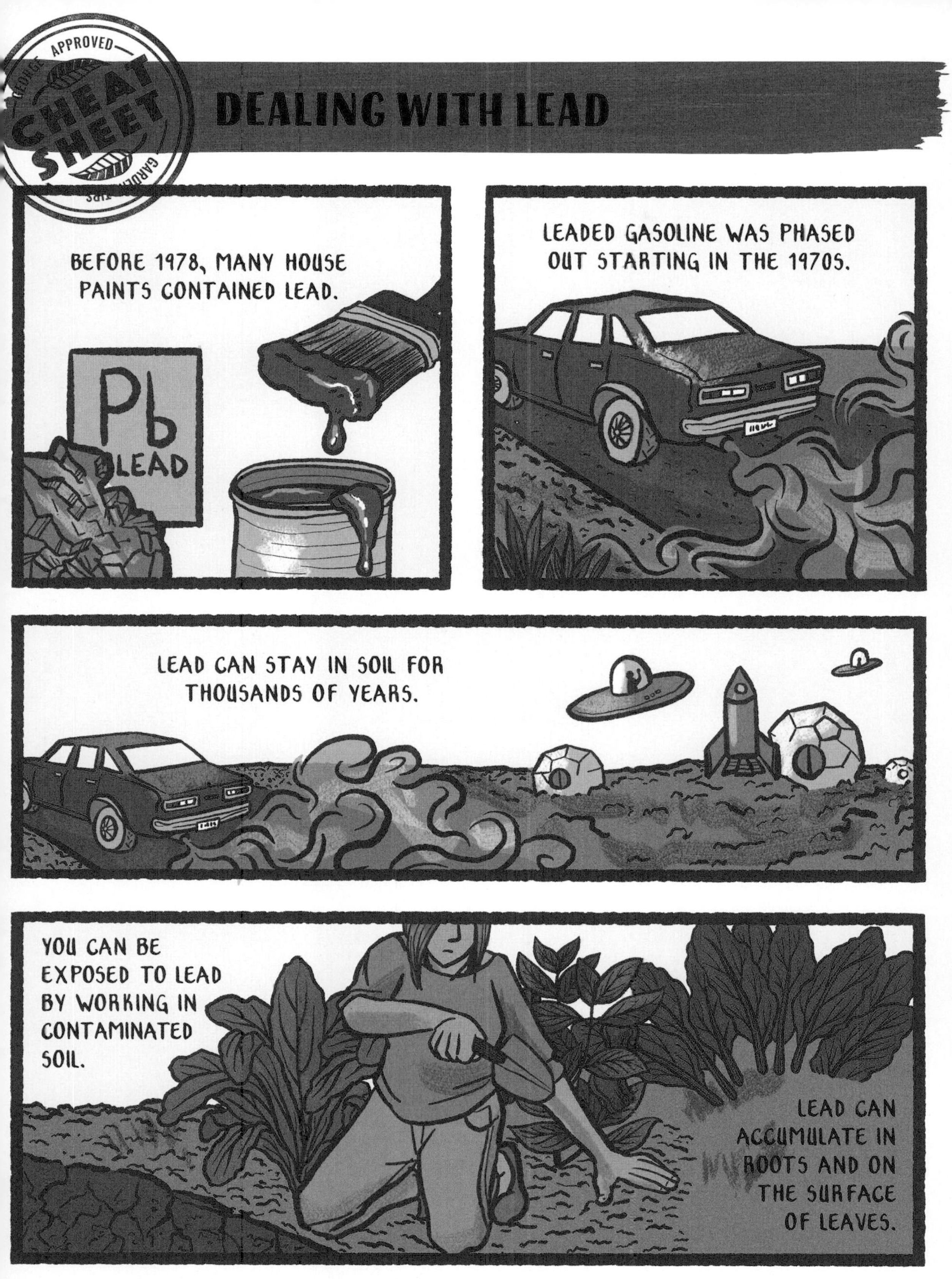
BEFORE 1978, MANY HOUSE PAINTS CONTAINED LEAD.
Pb
LEAD
LEADED GASOLINE WAS PHASED OUT STARTING IN THE 1970S.
LEAD CAN STAY IN SOIL FOR THOUSANDS OF YEARS.
YOU CAN BE EXPOSED TO LEAD BY WORKING IN CONTAMINATED SOIL.
LEAD CAN ACCUMULATE IN ROOTS AND ON THE SURFACE OF LEAVES.

TEST FOR LEAD IF GARDENING NEAR A HOUSE OLDER THAN 1978, OR NEAR A ROAD THAT WAS BUSY BEFORE AROUND 1980. YOU CAN REQUEST A LEAD TEST AS PART OF YOUR SOIL TEST.

GEORGE APPROVED CHEAT SHEET GARDEN

IF YOU FIND LEAD . . .

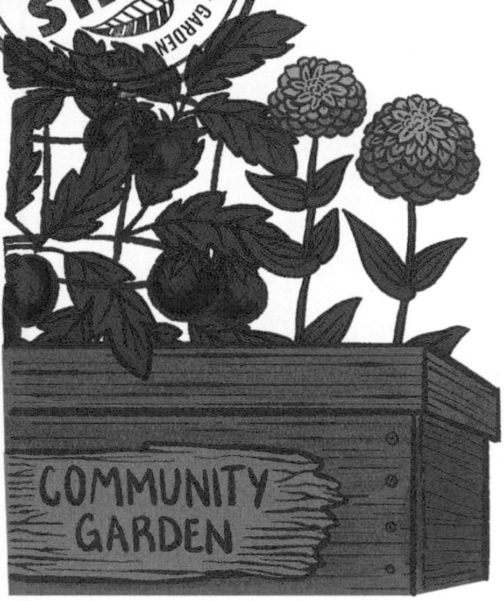
COMMUNITY GARDEN

GARDEN SOMEWHERE ELSE.

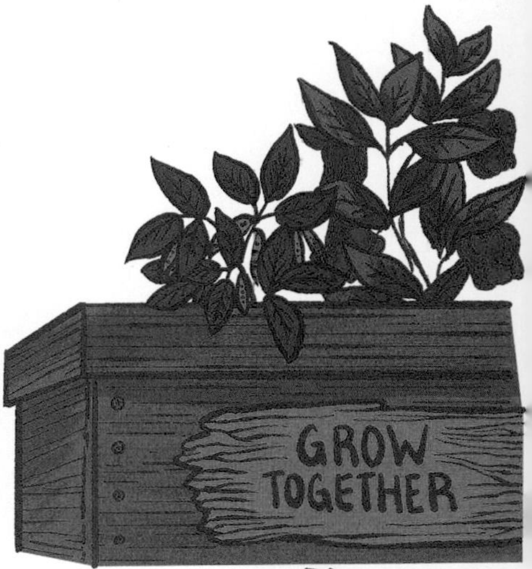
GROW TOGETHER

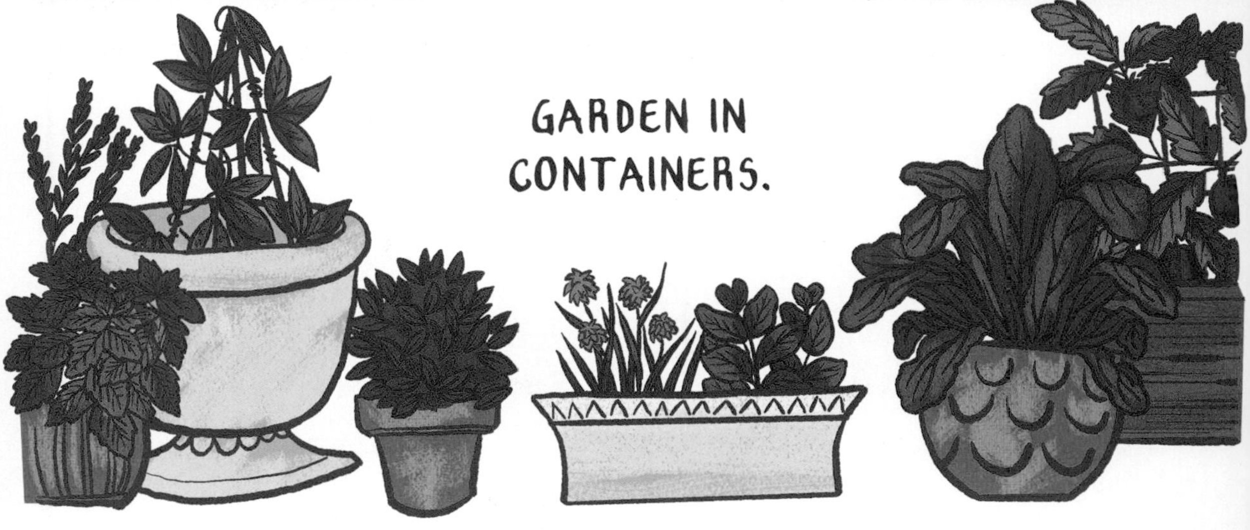

GARDEN IN CONTAINERS.

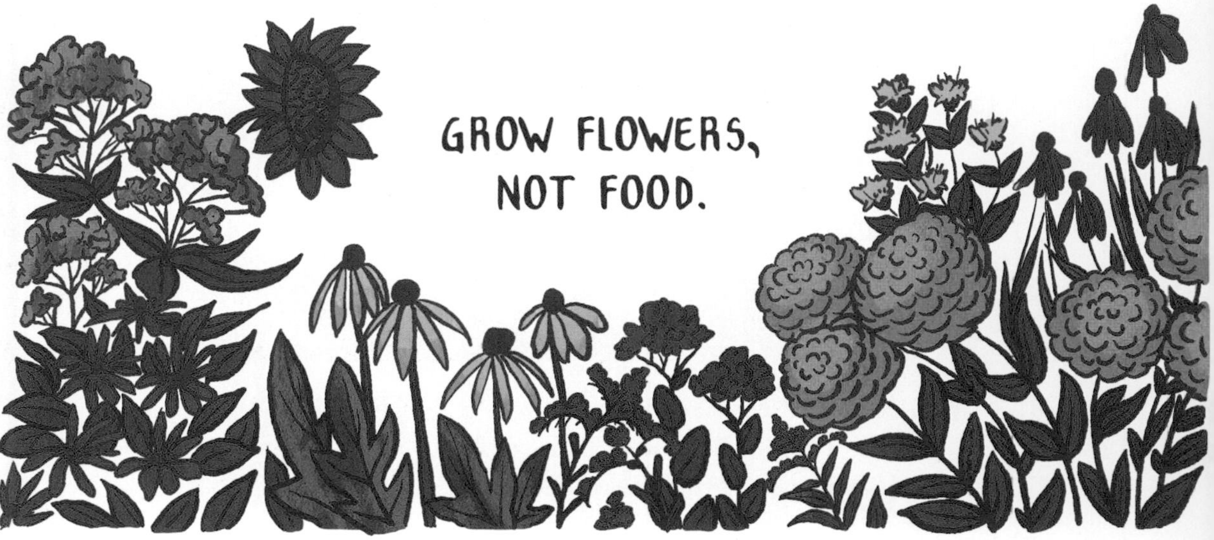

GROW FLOWERS, NOT FOOD.

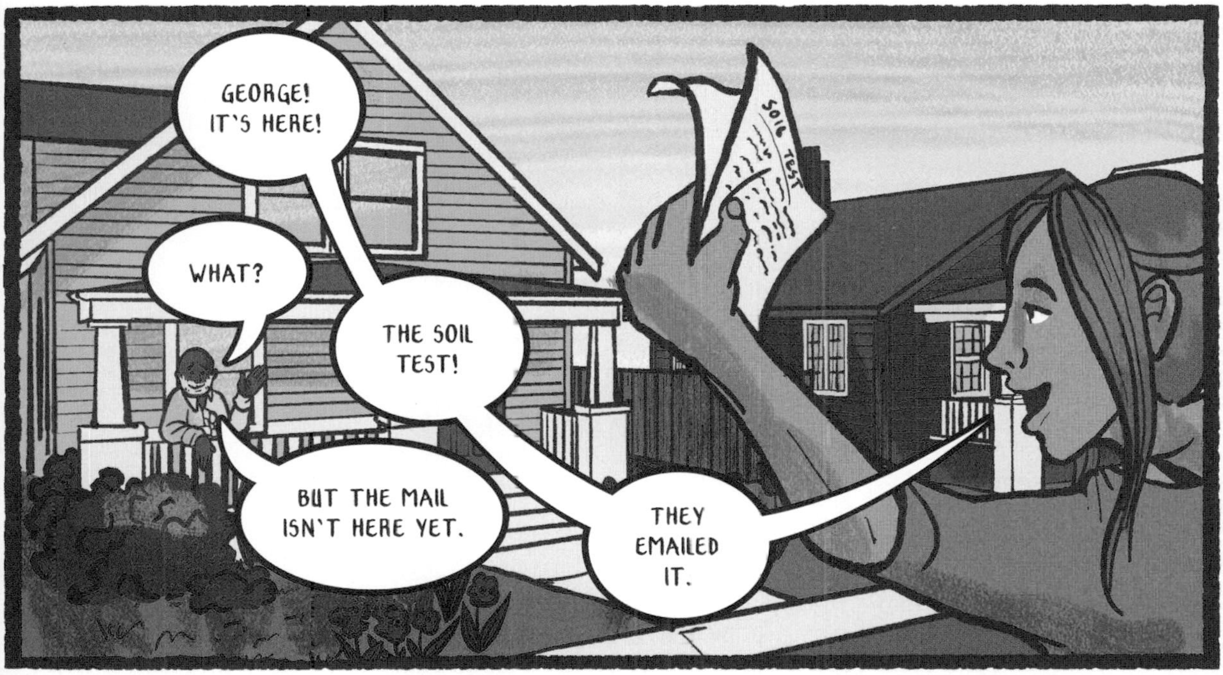
GEORGE!
IT'S HERE!
WHAT?
THE SOIL TEST!
BUT THE MAIL ISN'T HERE YET.
THEY EMAILED IT.
SOIL TEST

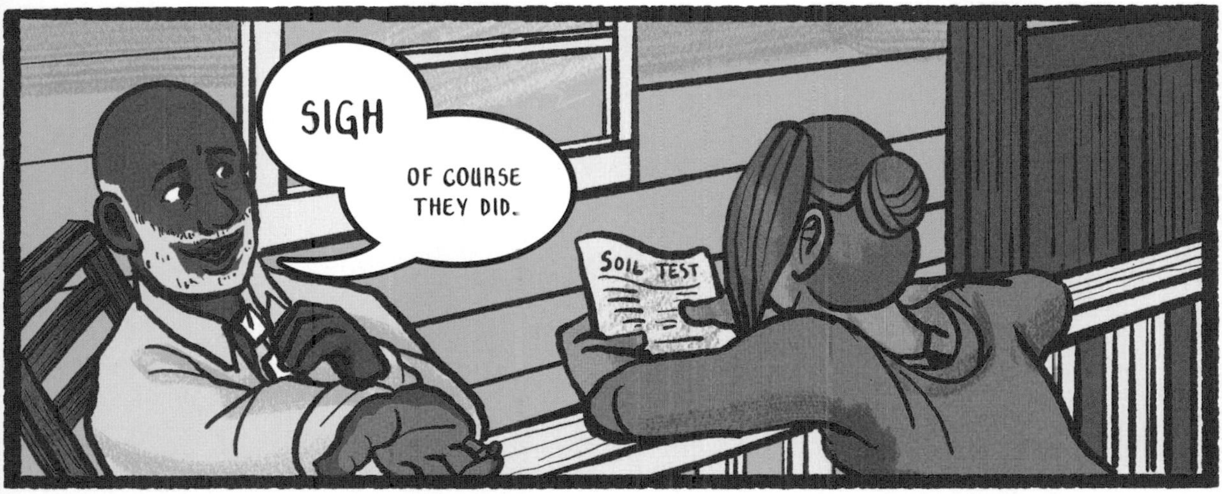
SIGH
OF COURSE THEY DID.
SOIL TEST

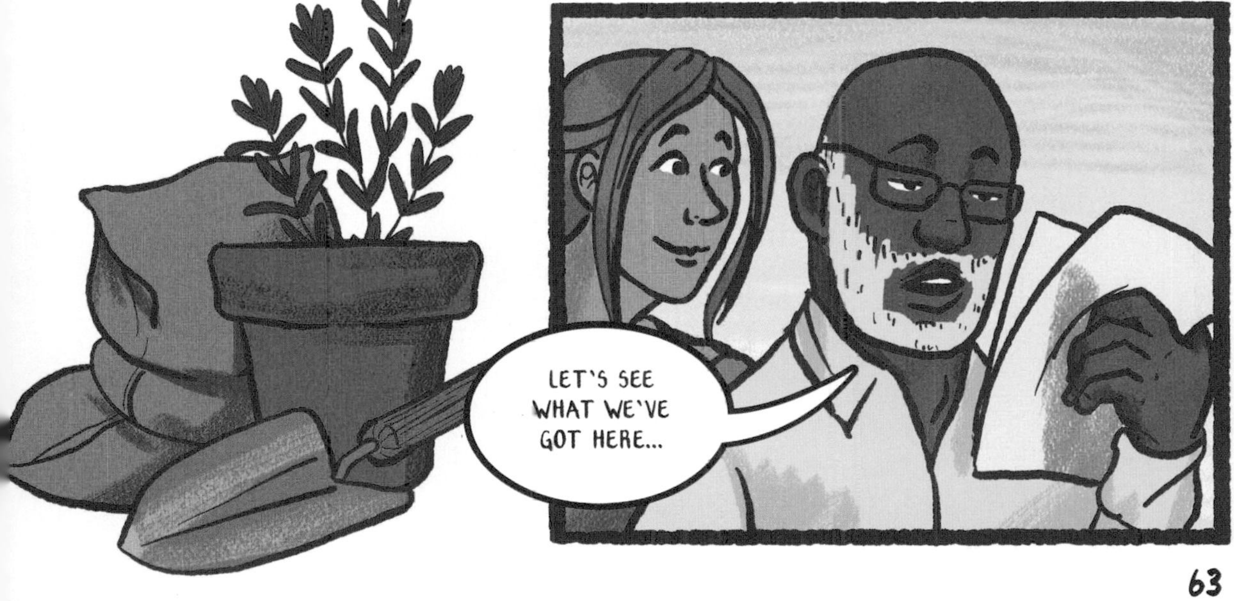
LET'S SEE WHAT WE'VE GOT HERE...

Soil Test

Soil test report for Mia Hernandez (Crop: Vegetables, Flowers)

		Below Optimum	Optimum	Above Optimum

Phosphorus (P)   91 ppm

Potassium (K)   127 ppm

Calcium (Ca)   1005 ppm

CEC   6.467 meq/100 g

Soil Type   Mineral, Sandy loam

Soil pH   7.6

Acidic   Basic

Lime Index   0

Organic Matter   2%

> LOOK FOR PERSONALIZED RECOMMENDATIONS FOR NITROGEN, PHOSPHORUS, AND POTASSIUM.

Your Personalized Recommendation:

Your soil test indicates you need to apply:

Nitrogen (N)   10 lbs / 100 sq. feet

Phosphorus (P_2O_5)   0 lbs / 100 sq. feet

Potassium (K_2O)   20 lbs / 100 sq. feet

> THESE ARE THE MOST COMMON NUTRIENTS THAT SOIL NEEDS, AND THE MAIN COMPONENTS OF MOST FERTILIZER.

WHICH FERTILIZER DO YOU NEED?

Your Personalized Recommendation:

Your soil test indicates you need to apply:

Nitrogen (N)	10 lbs	/ 100 sq. feet
Phosphrous (P_2O_5)	0 lbs	/ 100 sq. feet
Potassium (K_2O)	20 lbs	/ 100 sq. feet

CHECK YOUR TEST RESULTS

IN THIS EXAMPLE, THE RESULTS INDICATE A RATIO OF

1 : 0 : 2

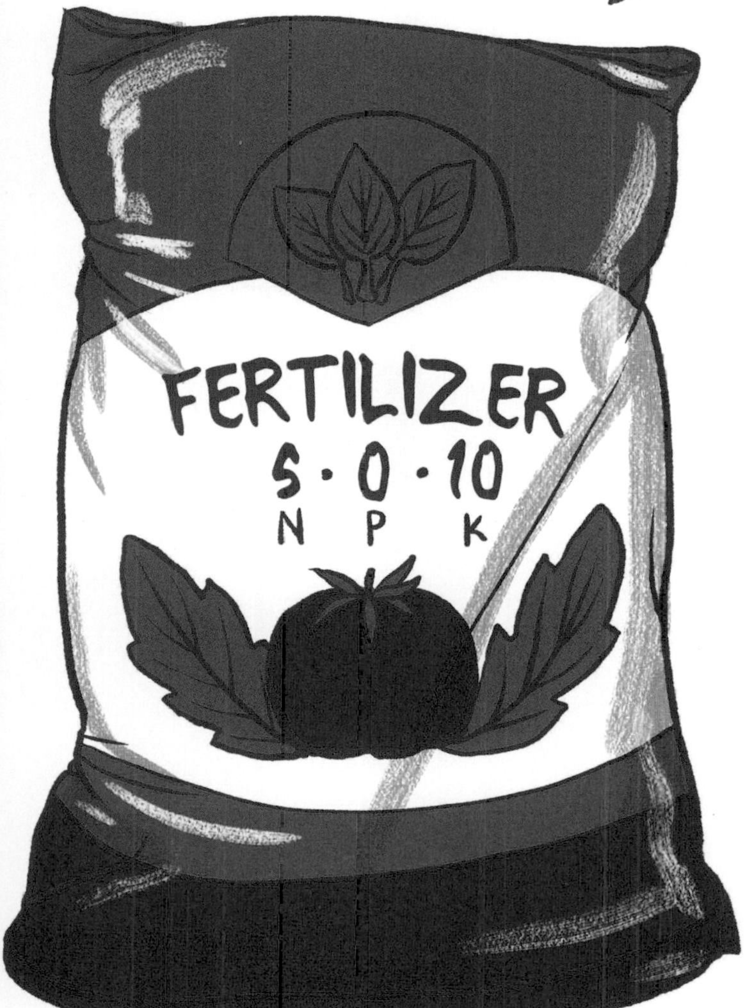

FERTILIZER
5 · 0 · 10
N P K

FIND A FERTILIZER WHOSE NUMBERS MOST CLOSELY MATCH THE RATIO OF FERTILIZER YOU NEED.

FERTILIZER BAGS ARE MARKED WITH THREE NUMBERS WHICH INDICATE PERCENTAGE OF

NITROGEN (N)
PHOSPHORUS (P)
AND
POTASSIUM (K)

HOW MUCH FERTILIZER DO YOU NEED?

GO TO:

SOILS.RS.UKY.EDU/CALCULATORS/MULT_FERT.ASP

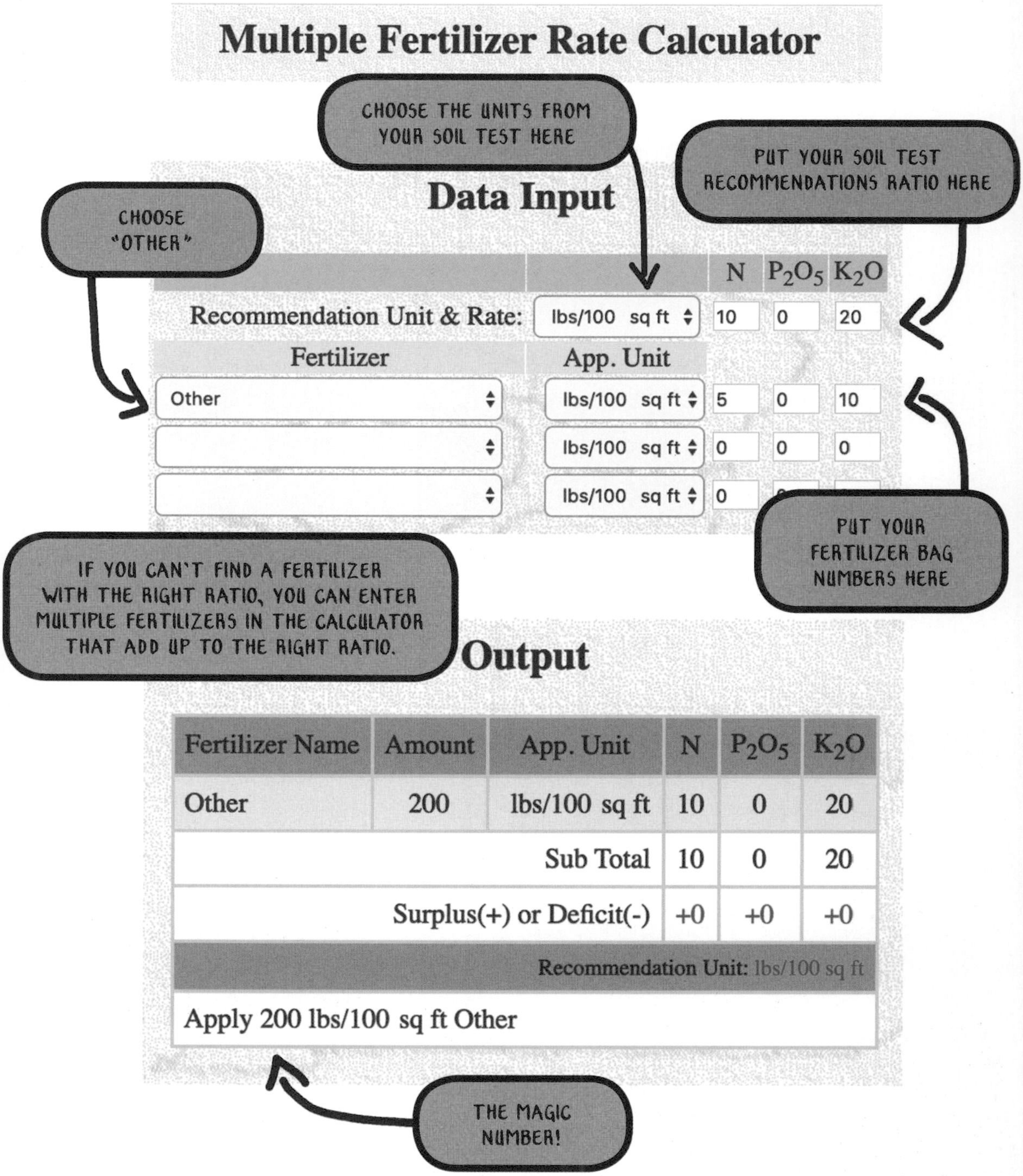

Multiple Fertilizer Rate Calculator
CHOOSE THE UNITS FROM YOUR SOIL TEST HERE
PUT YOUR SOIL TEST RECOMMENDATIONS RATIO HERE
CHOOSE "OTHER"
Data Input
N
P_2O_5
K_2O
Recommendation Unit & Rate:
lbs/100 sq ft
10
0
20
Fertilizer
App. Unit
Other
lbs/100 sq ft
5
0
10
lbs/100 sq ft
0
0
0
lbs/100 sq ft
0
PUT YOUR FERTILIZER BAG NUMBERS HERE
IF YOU CAN'T FIND A FERTILIZER WITH THE RIGHT RATIO, YOU CAN ENTER MULTIPLE FERTILIZERS IN THE CALCULATOR THAT ADD UP TO THE RIGHT RATIO.
Output
Fertilizer Name
Amount
App. Unit
N
P_2O_5
K_2O
Other
200
lbs/100 sq ft
10
0
20
Sub Total
10
0
20
Surplus(+) or Deficit(-)
+0
+0
+0
Recommendation Unit: lbs/100 sq ft
Apply 200 lbs/100 sq ft Other
THE MAGIC NUMBER!

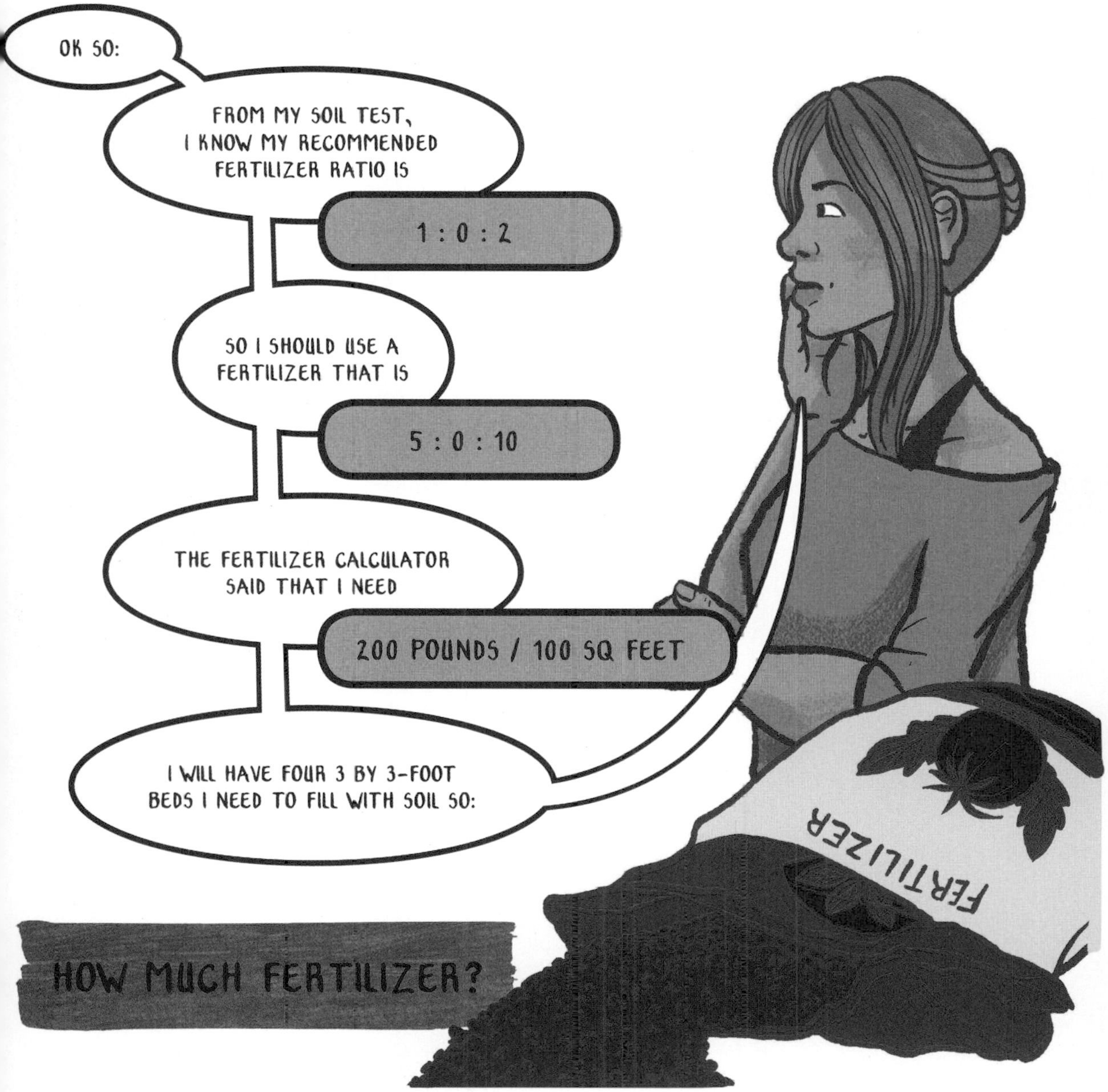
OK SO:
FROM MY SOIL TEST, I KNOW MY RECOMMENDED FERTILIZER RATIO IS
1 : 0 : 2
SO I SHOULD USE A FERTILIZER THAT IS
5 : 0 : 10
THE FERTILIZER CALCULATOR SAID THAT I NEED
200 POUNDS / 100 SQ FEET
I WILL HAVE FOUR 3 BY 3-FOOT BEDS I NEED TO FILL WITH SOIL SO:
FERTILIZER

HOW MUCH FERTILIZER?

IF OUTPUT IS OUNCES OR POUNDS PER 100 SQUARE FEET:

MULTIPLY BY 0.36 TO GET THE AMOUNT YOU NEED FOR ALL FOUR OF YOUR 3 BY 3–FOOT BEDS.

IF OUTPUT IS POUNDS PER 1,000 SQUARE FEET:

MULTIPLY BY 0.036 TO GET THE AMOUNT YOU NEED FOR ALL FOUR OF YOUR 3 BY 3–FOOT BEDS.

IF OUTPUT IS POUNDS PER ACRE:

MULTIPLY BY 0.008 TO GET THE AMOUNT YOU NEED FOR ALL FOUR OF YOUR 3 BY 3–FOOT BEDS.

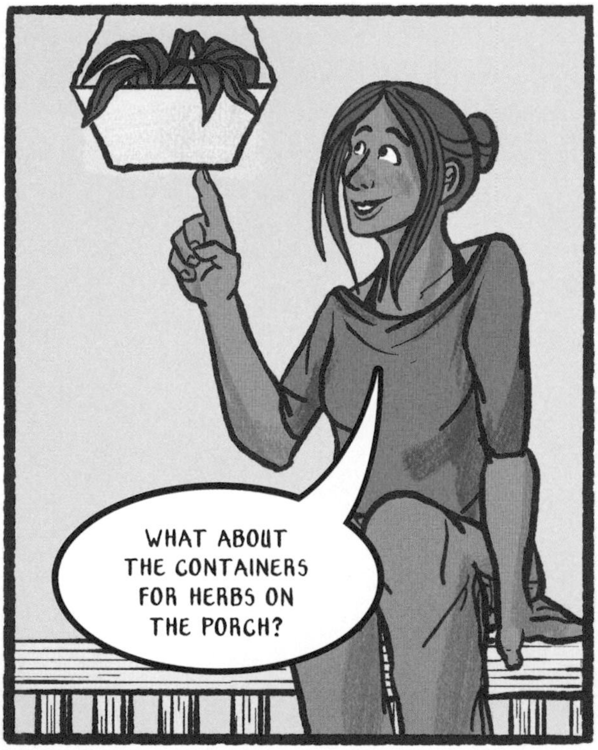
WHAT ABOUT THE CONTAINERS FOR HERBS ON THE PORCH?

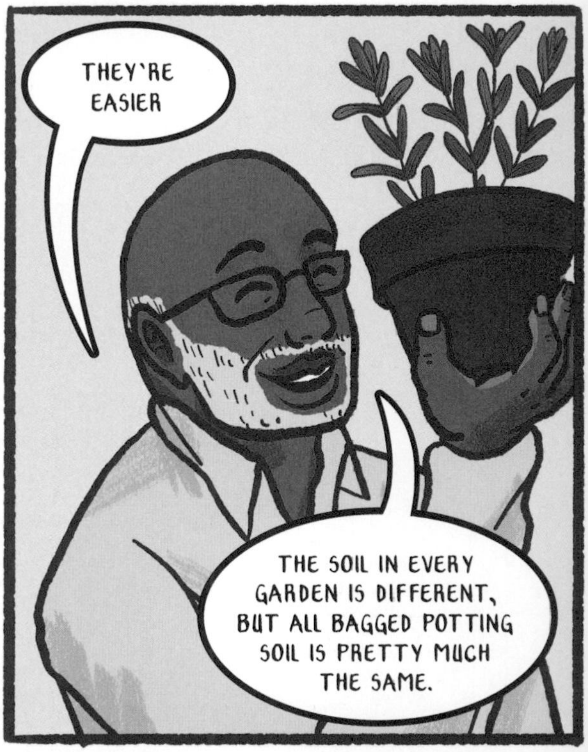
THEY'RE EASIER
THE SOIL IN EVERY GARDEN IS DIFFERENT, BUT ALL BAGGED POTTING SOIL IS PRETTY MUCH THE SAME.

POTTING SOIL: CHECK THE BAG.

IF IT DOESN'T CONTAIN FERTILIZER, ADD A GENERAL-PURPOSE FERTILIZER RIGHT AWAY, FOLLOWING THE BAG DIRECTIONS.

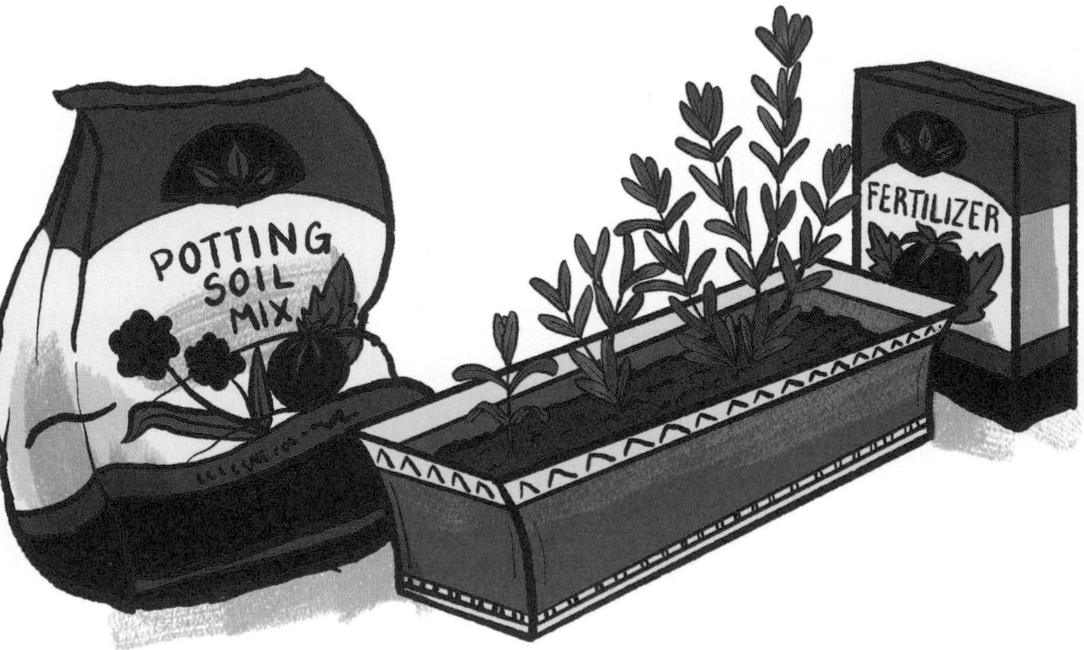
POTTING SOIL MIX
FERTILIZER

IF IT HAS FERTILIZER, WAIT UNTIL AFTER THE FIRST 3 MONTHS TO ADD MORE.

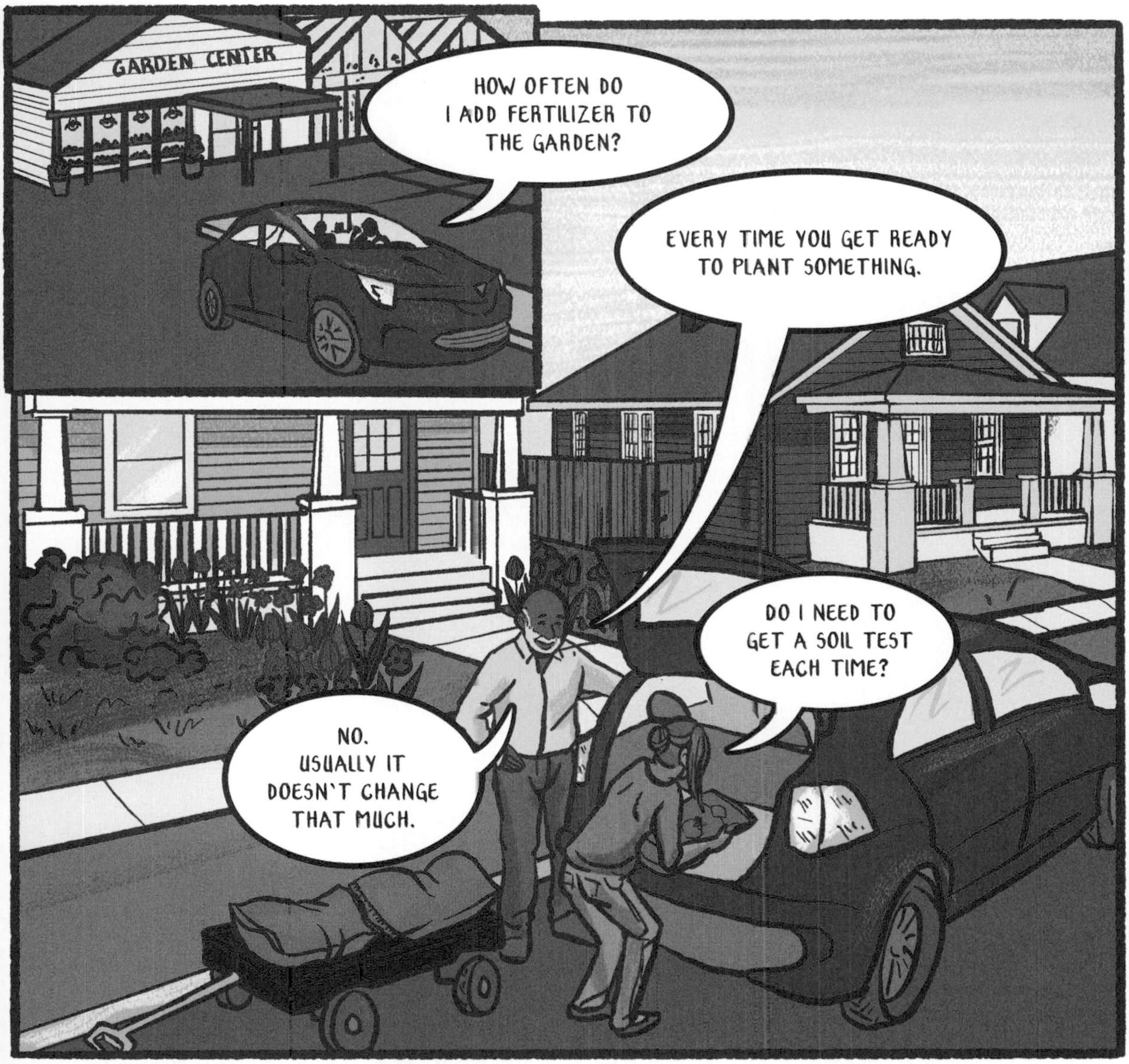
GARDEN CENTER
HOW OFTEN DO I ADD FERTILIZER TO THE GARDEN?
EVERY TIME YOU GET READY TO PLANT SOMETHING.
DO I NEED TO GET A SOIL TEST EACH TIME?
NO. USUALLY IT DOESN'T CHANGE THAT MUCH.

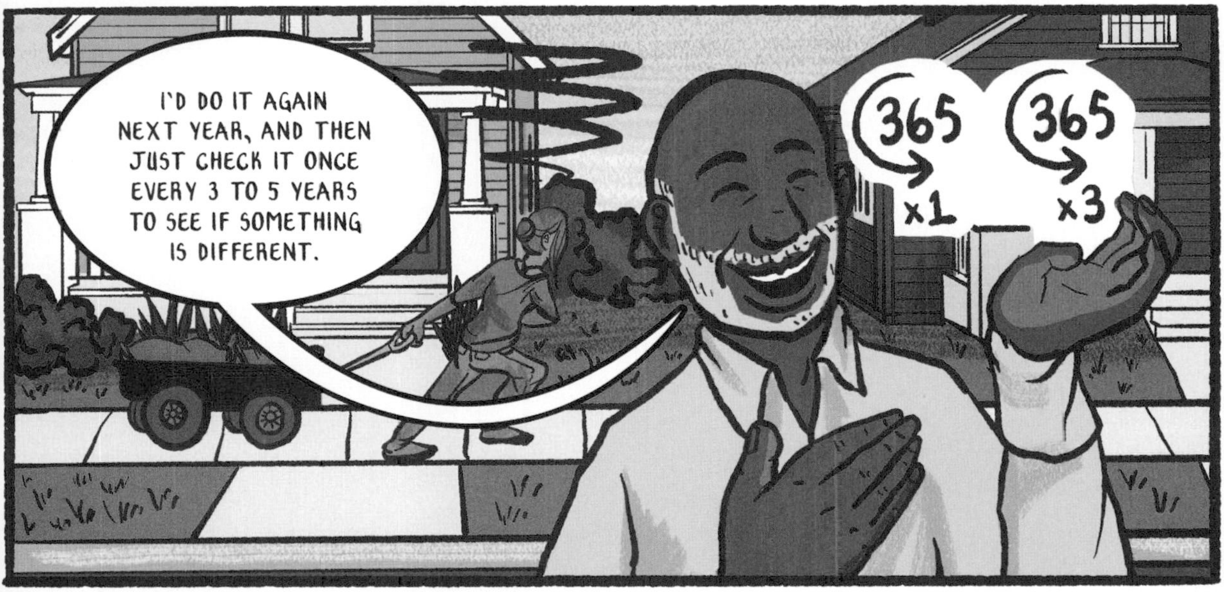
I'D DO IT AGAIN NEXT YEAR, AND THEN JUST CHECK IT ONCE EVERY 3 TO 5 YEARS TO SEE IF SOMETHING IS DIFFERENT.
365 x1
365 x3

FIVE:
PREPARING
THE SPACE

MAKING A NEW GARDEN BED.

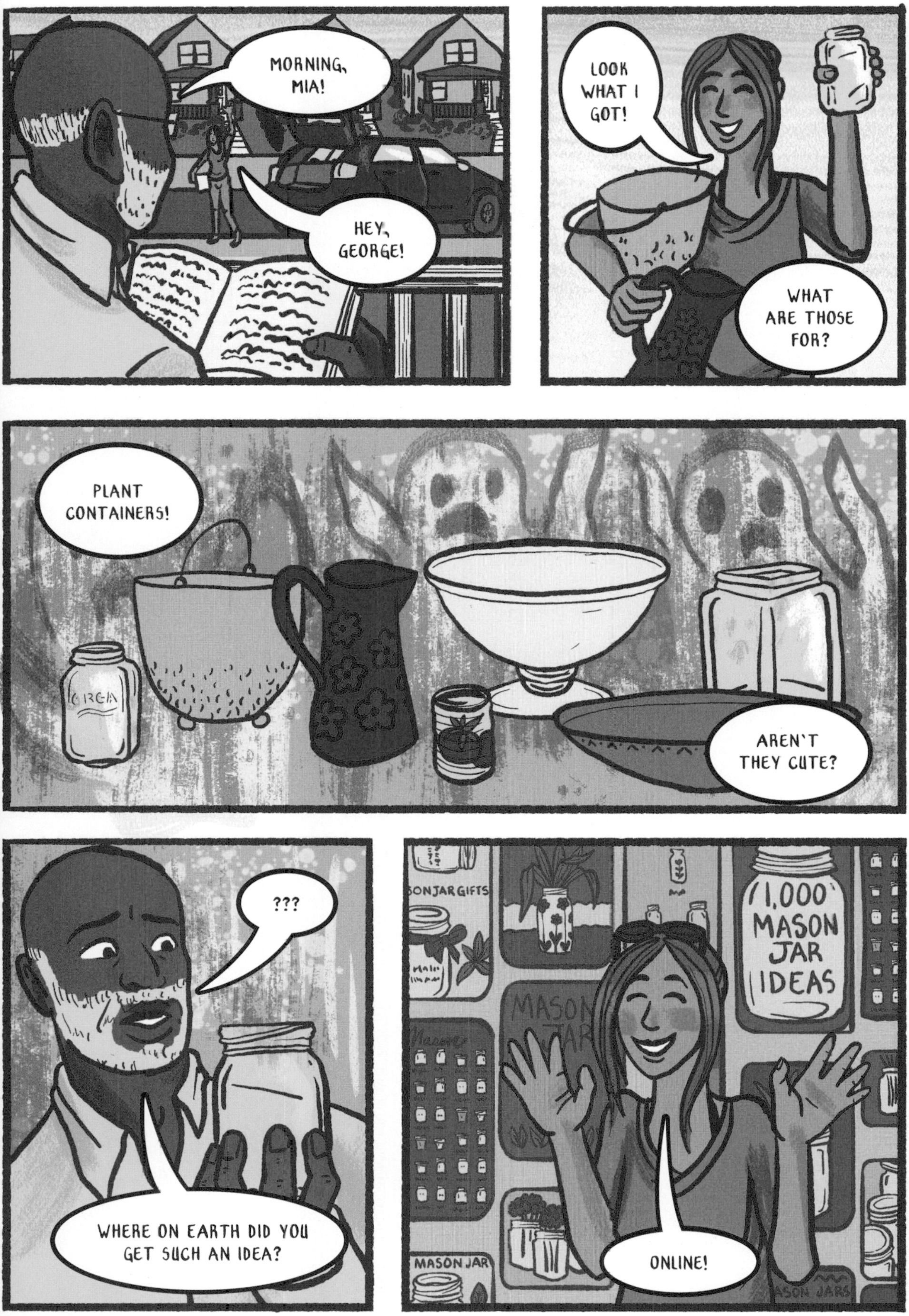
MORNING, MIA!
HEY, GEORGE!
LOOK WHAT I GOT!
WHAT ARE THOSE FOR?
PLANT CONTAINERS!
AREN'T THEY CUTE?
???
WHERE ON EARTH DID YOU GET SUCH AN IDEA?
1,000 MASON JAR IDEAS
MASON JAR
ONLINE!

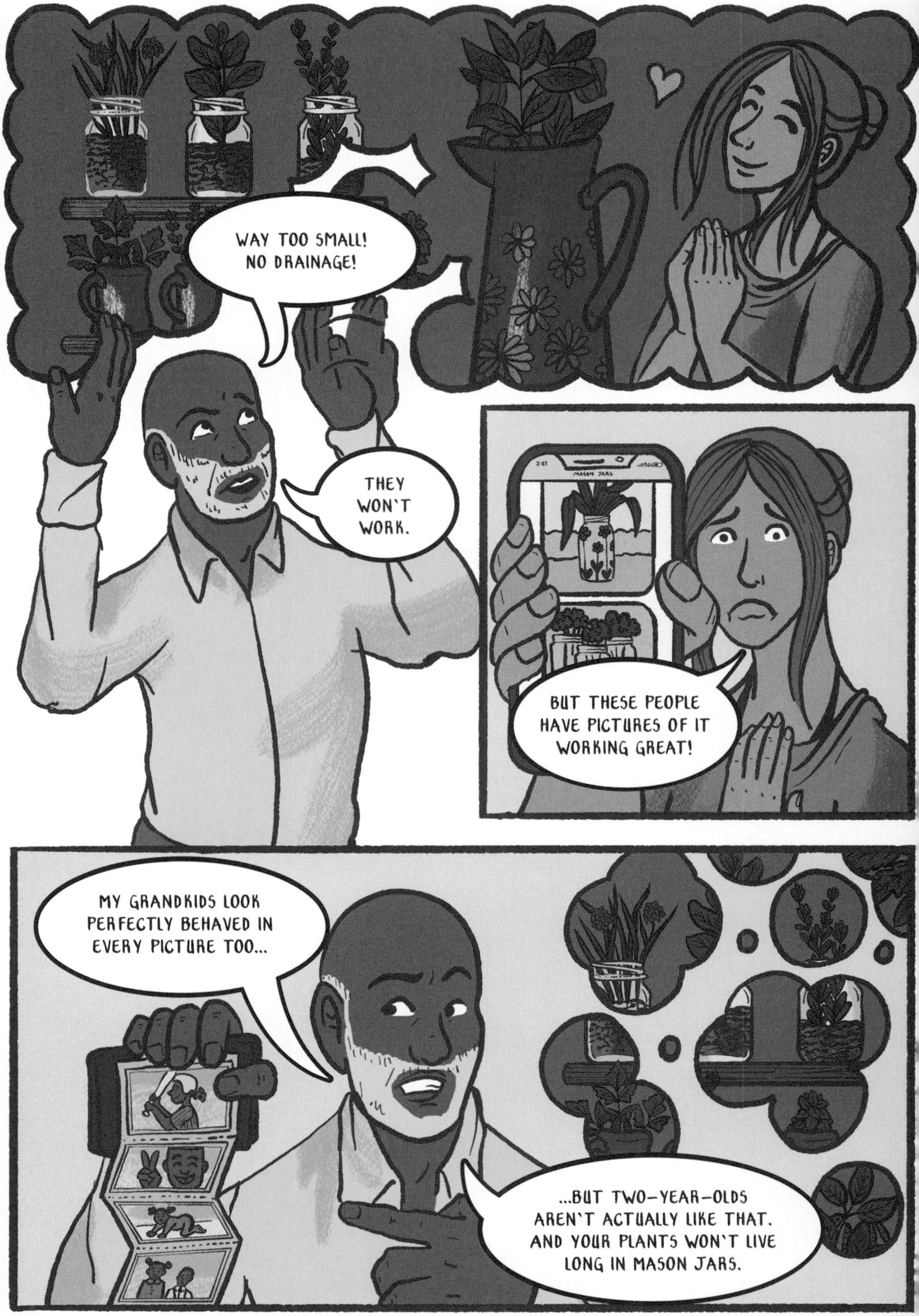
WAY TOO SMALL! NO DRAINAGE!
THEY WON'T WORK.
MASON JARS
BUT THESE PEOPLE HAVE PICTURES OF IT WORKING GREAT!
MY GRANDKIDS LOOK PERFECTLY BEHAVED IN EVERY PICTURE TOO...
...BUT TWO-YEAR-OLDS AREN'T ACTUALLY LIKE THAT. AND YOUR PLANTS WON'T LIVE LONG IN MASON JARS.

GEORGE APPROVED CHEAT SHEET GARDEN TIPS

GOOD CONTAINERS . . .

ARE LARGE. AT LEAST 8 INCHES WIDE AND DEEP.

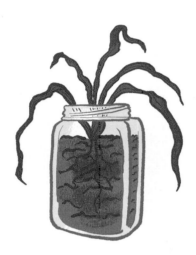

SMALL CONTAINERS STUNT PLANTS, NEED FREQUENT WATERING.

LARGE CONTAINERS GROW BIG HEALTHY PLANTS, NEED LESS WATERING.

AND HAVE GOOD DRAINAGE.

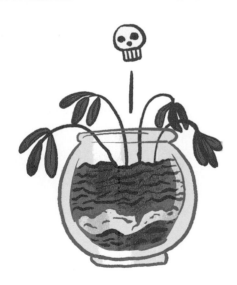

NO DRAINAGE HOLES: WATER ACCUMULATES, DROWNS AND KILLS PLANTS.

DRAINAGE HOLES: EXCESS WATER DRAINS OUT, PLANTS THRIVE.

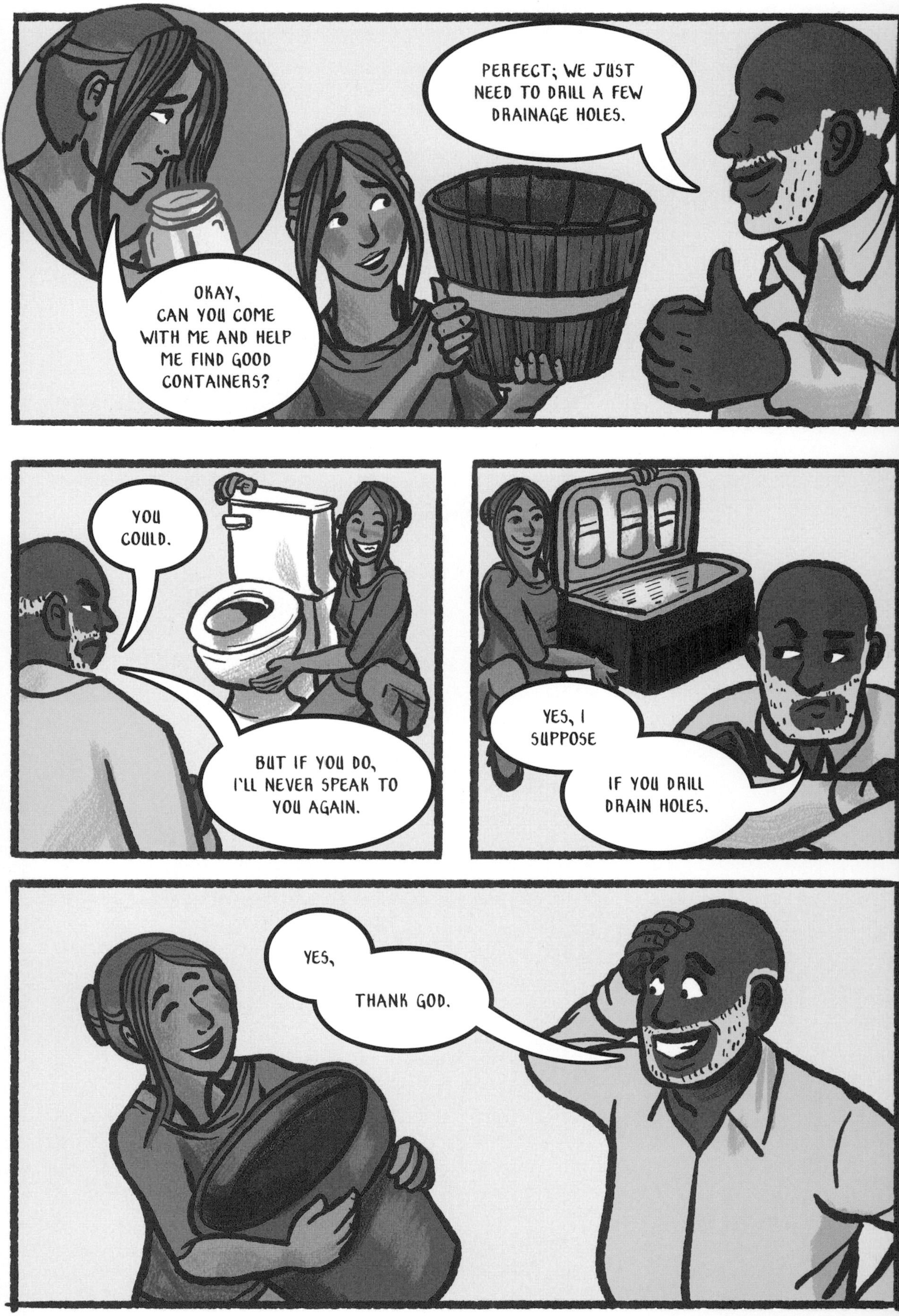
PERFECT; WE JUST NEED TO DRILL A FEW DRAINAGE HOLES.
OKAY, CAN YOU COME WITH ME AND HELP ME FIND GOOD CONTAINERS?
YOU COULD.
BUT IF YOU DO, I'LL NEVER SPEAK TO YOU AGAIN.
YES, I SUPPOSE
IF YOU DRILL DRAIN HOLES.
YES,
THANK GOD.

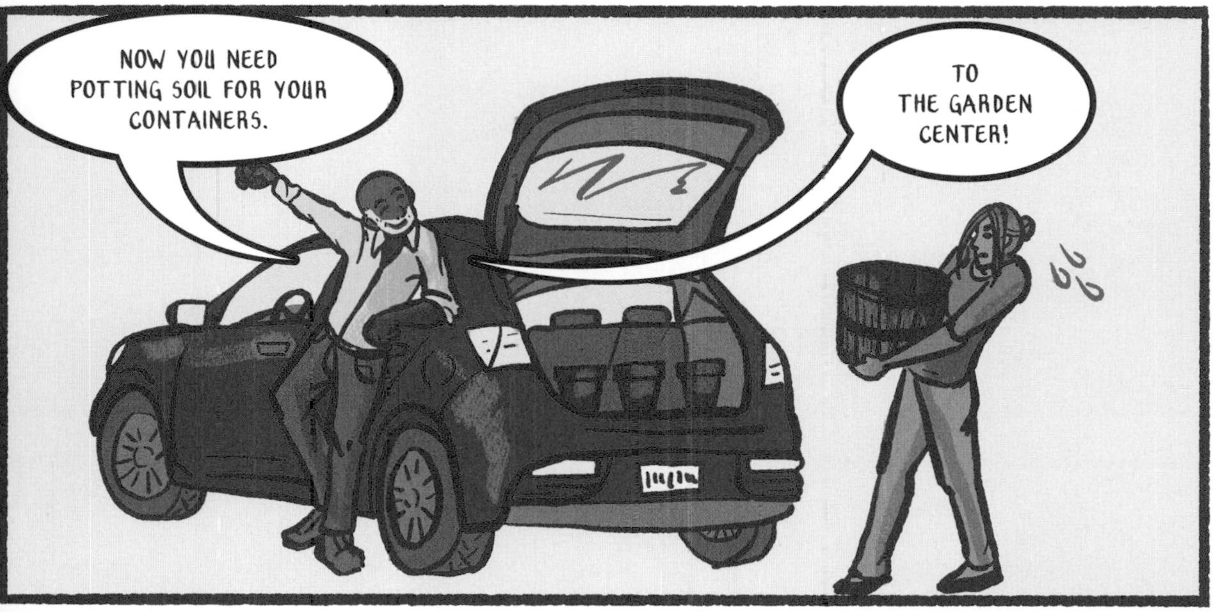
NOW YOU NEED POTTING SOIL FOR YOUR CONTAINERS.
TO THE GARDEN CENTER!

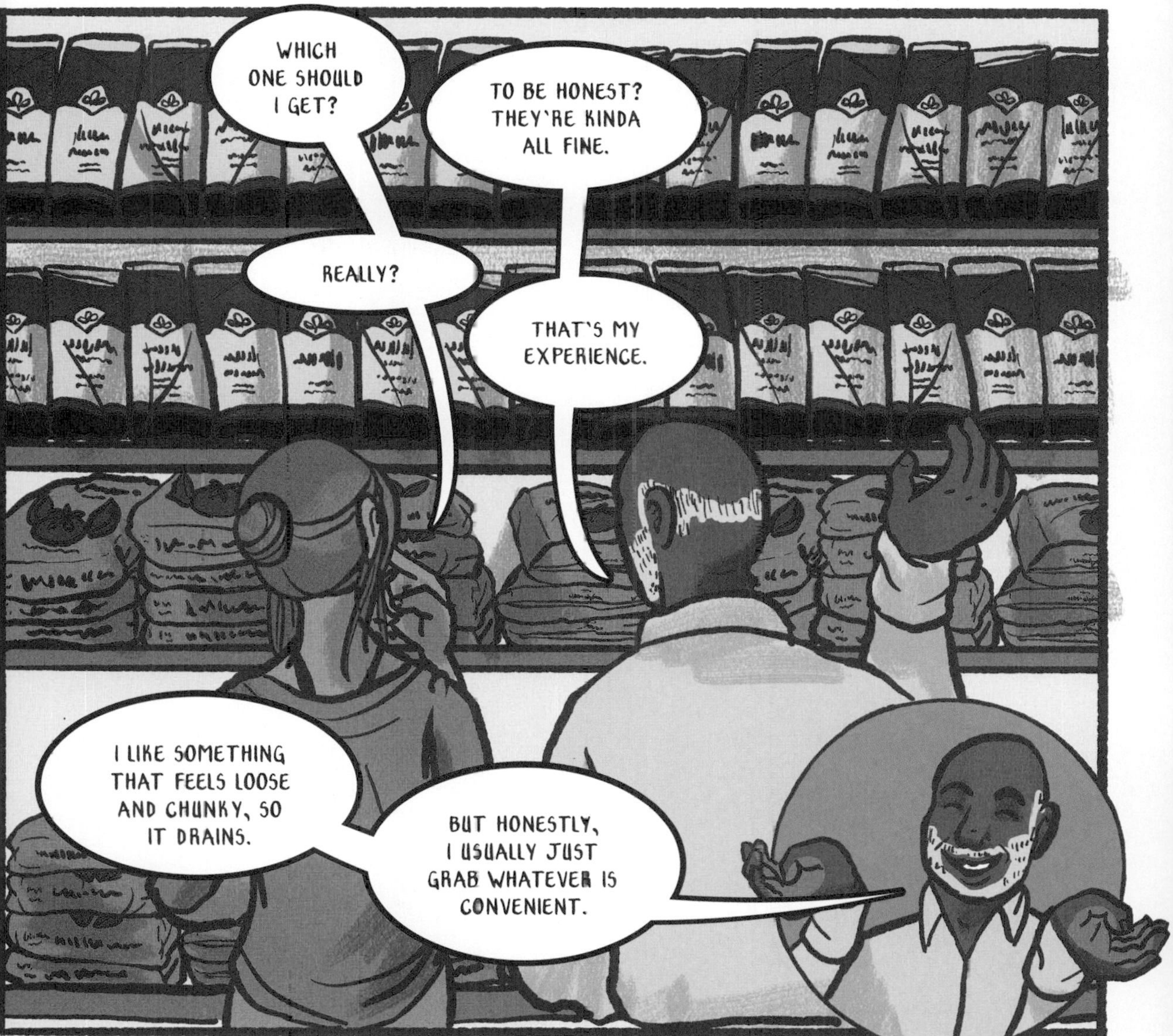
WHICH ONE SHOULD I GET?
TO BE HONEST? THEY'RE KINDA ALL FINE.
REALLY?
THAT'S MY EXPERIENCE.
I LIKE SOMETHING THAT FEELS LOOSE AND CHUNKY, SO IT DRAINS.
BUT HONESTLY, I USUALLY JUST GRAB WHATEVER IS CONVENIENT.

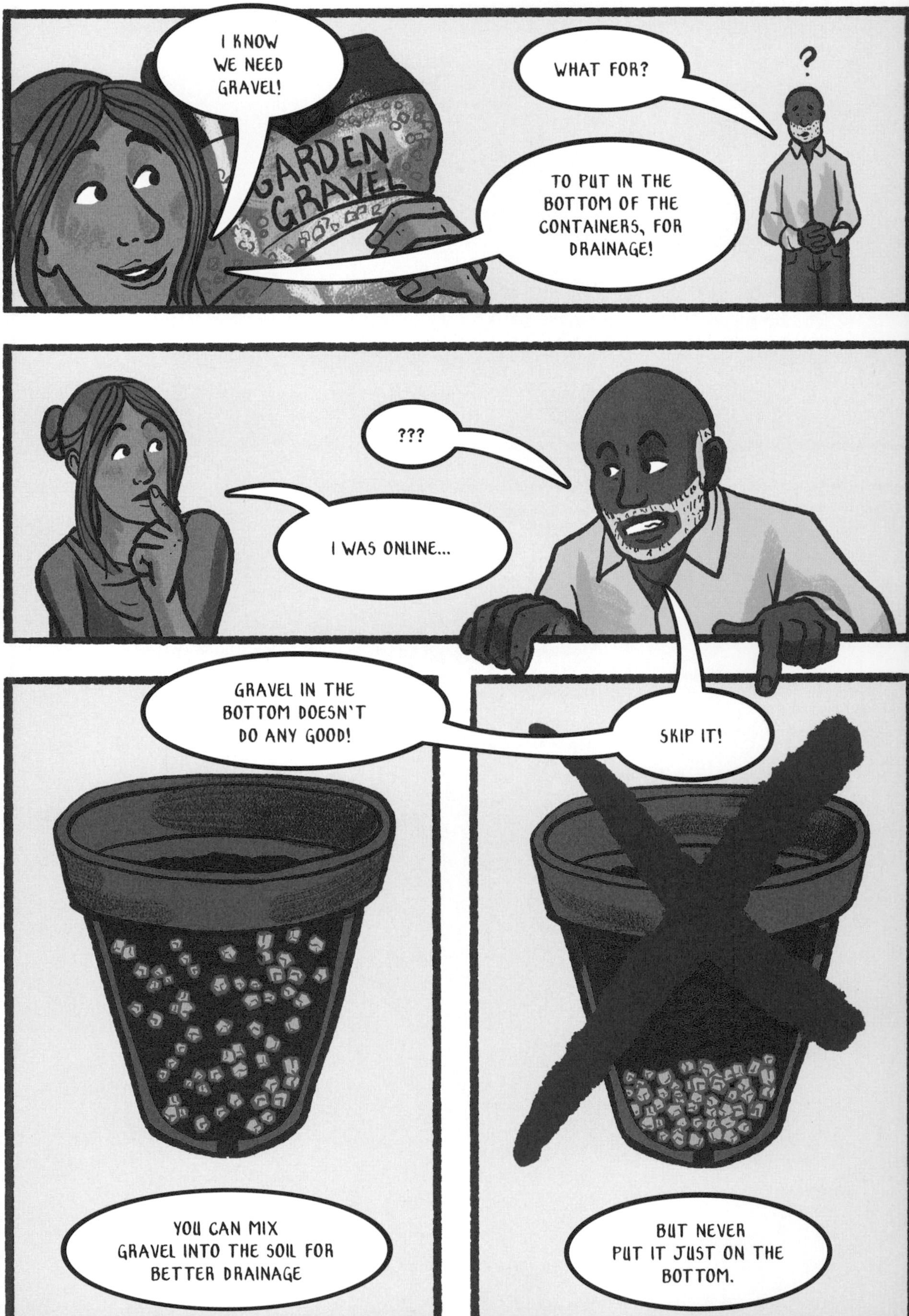
I KNOW WE NEED GRAVEL!
GARDEN GRAVEL
WHAT FOR?
?
TO PUT IN THE BOTTOM OF THE CONTAINERS, FOR DRAINAGE!
???
I WAS ONLINE...
GRAVEL IN THE BOTTOM DOESN'T DO ANY GOOD!
SKIP IT!
YOU CAN MIX GRAVEL INTO THE SOIL FOR BETTER DRAINAGE
BUT NEVER PUT IT JUST ON THE BOTTOM.

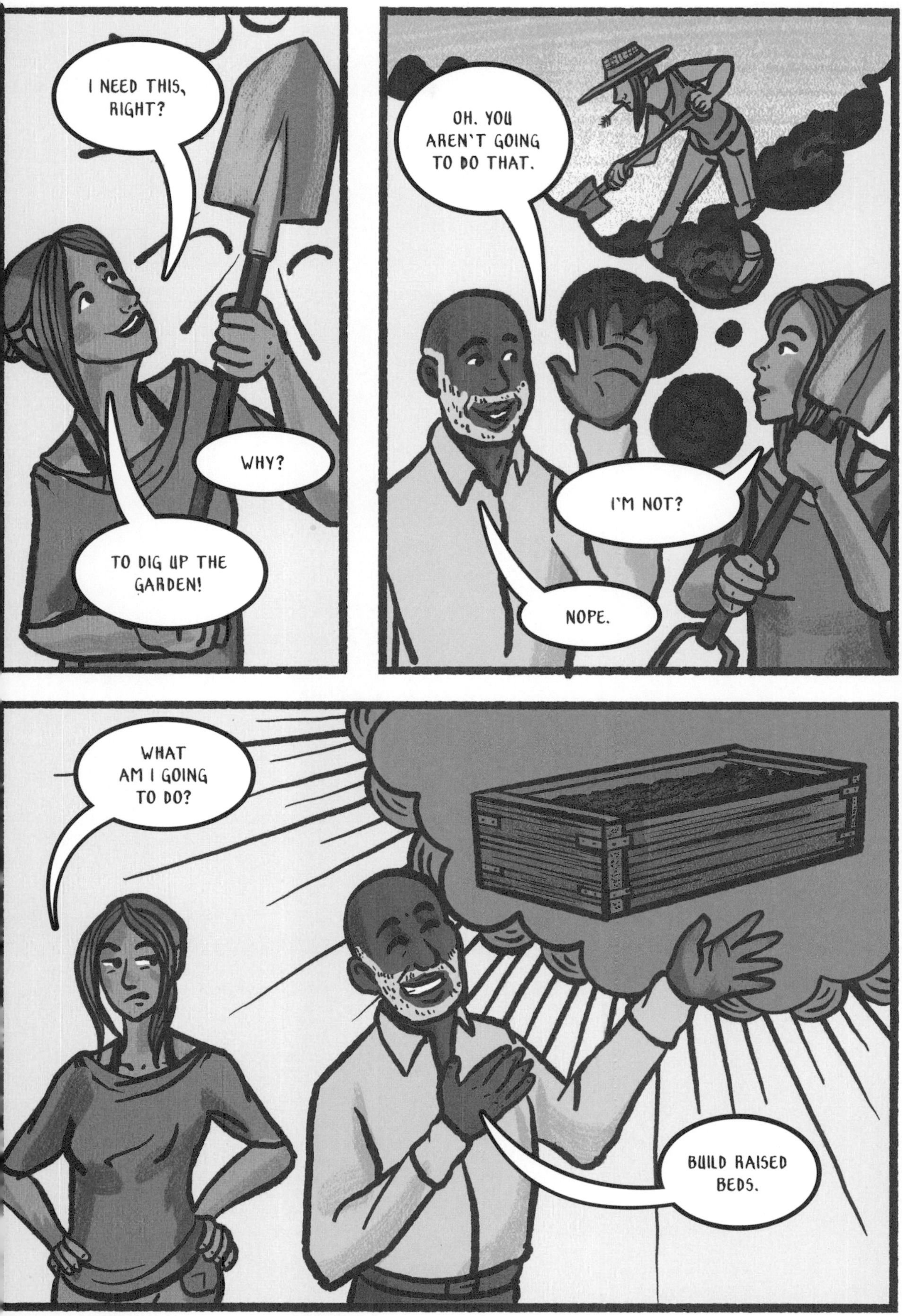
I NEED THIS, RIGHT?
WHY?
TO DIG UP THE GARDEN!
OH. YOU AREN'T GOING TO DO THAT.
I'M NOT?
NOPE.
WHAT AM I GOING TO DO?
BUILD RAISED BEDS.

GEORGE APPROVED CHEAT SHEET GARDEN TIPS

RAISED BEDS VERSUS DIGGING

DIGGING	RAISED BED

LOTS OF WORK.
DUMP TOPSOIL AND DONE.
SOIL WILL BE FULL OF WEED SEEDS.
NO WEED SEEDS.
CAN HAVE POOR DRAINAGE.
GOOD DRAINAGE.

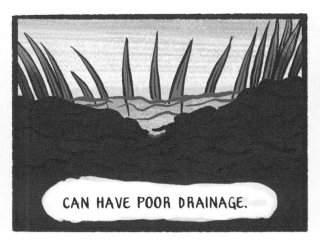

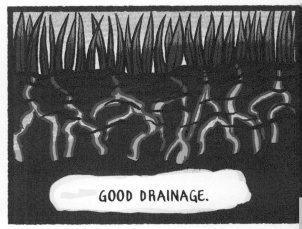

BUILDING RAISED BEDS

WHAT YOU NEED

WOOD PLANKS

8 (1-INCH BY 6-INCH BY 6-FOOT) PLANKS LUMBER, CUT INTO 3-FOOT PIECES (MOST LUMBERYARDS AND HOME IMPROVEMENT STORES WILL CUT YOUR WOOD FOR YOU IF YOU DON'T HAVE A SAW.)

ALTERNATIVES: PLAIN PINE LUMBER IS THE CHEAPEST OPTION, BUT WILL NEED TO BE REPLACED EVERY FEW YEARS. ROT-RESISTANT WOODS LIKE CEDAR, PLASTIC LUMBER (SOLD FOR DECKING), BRICKS, STONES, OR CONCRETE BLOCKS ARE LONGER-LASTING, BUT MORE EXPENSIVE, OPTIONS.

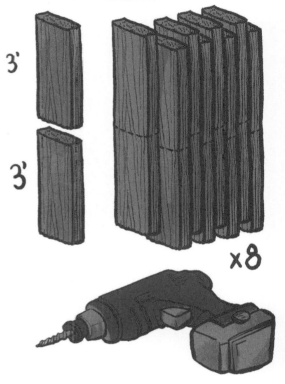

3'

3'

x8

x32

CORNER BRACES

32 (2-INCH) CORNER BRACES (GENERALLY COME IN PACKS OF 4 WITH SCREWS INCLUDED)

ELECTRIC DRILL

IF YOU DON'T HAVE ONE, ASK AROUND AND BORROW FROM A FRIEND.

TOPSOIL

15 CUBIC FEET (ROUGHLY ½ CUBIC YARD) MAY BE LABELED AS GARDEN SOIL, VEGETABLE GARDEN SOIL, OR RAISED BED SOIL.

MULCH

3 CUBIC FEET (ENOUGH TO COVER THE BEDS ROUGHLY 1 INCH DEEP)

PEA GRAVEL

4 CUBIC FEET (OPTIONAL)

CARDBOARD

ENOUGH TO COVER 64 SQUARE FEET

HOW TO BUILD A BED

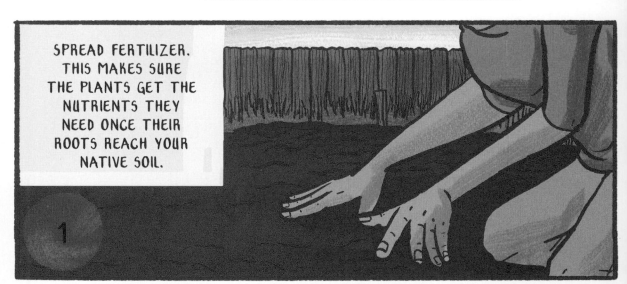

SPREAD FERTILIZER. THIS MAKES SURE THE PLANTS GET THE NUTRIENTS THEY NEED ONCE THEIR ROOTS REACH YOUR NATIVE SOIL.

1

COVER AN 8 BY 8-FOOT AREA WITH LAYER OF CARDBOARD.

2

CARDBOARD SMOTHERS WEEDS, THEN DECOMPOSES TO LET PLANT ROOTS GROW THROUGH.

SCREW TOGETHER THE BOARDS USING TWO CORNER BRACES PER CORNER TO MAKE FOUR 3 BY 3-FOOT SQUARE FRAMES.

3

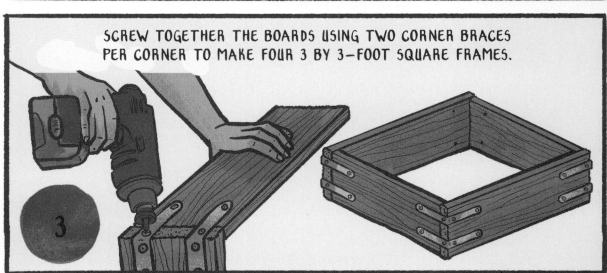

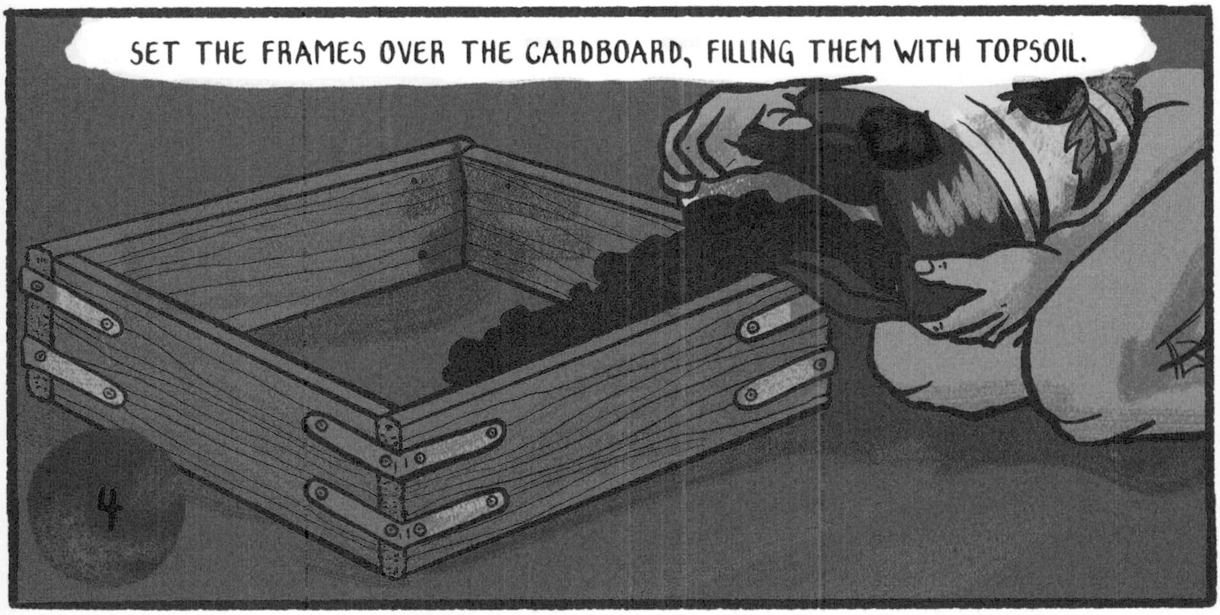
SET THE FRAMES OVER THE CARDBOARD, FILLING THEM WITH TOPSOIL.
4

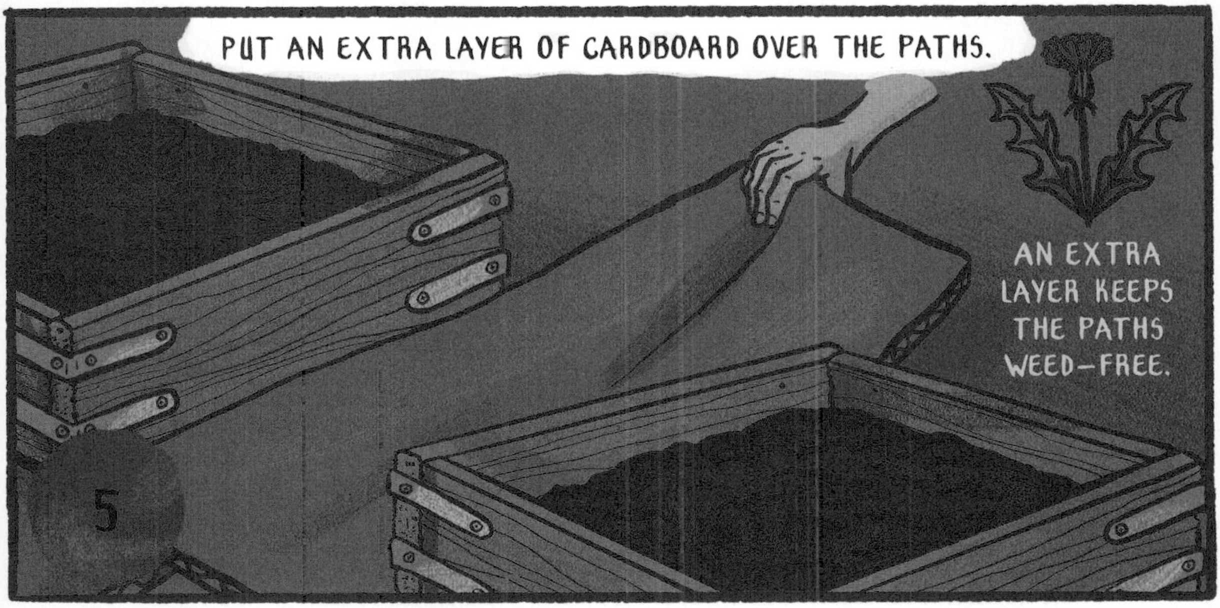
PUT AN EXTRA LAYER OF CARDBOARD OVER THE PATHS.
AN EXTRA LAYER KEEPS THE PATHS WEED-FREE.
5

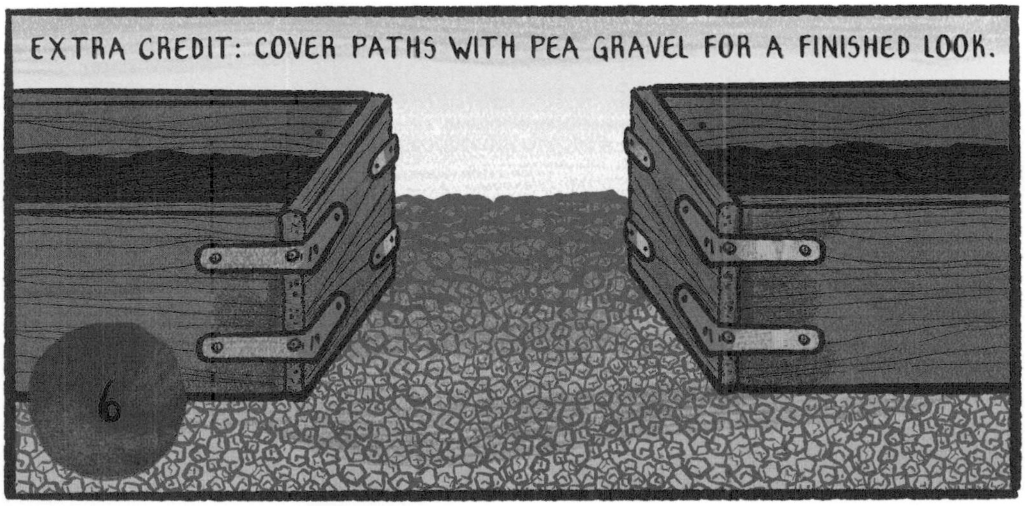
EXTRA CREDIT: COVER PATHS WITH PEA GRAVEL FOR A FINISHED LOOK.
6

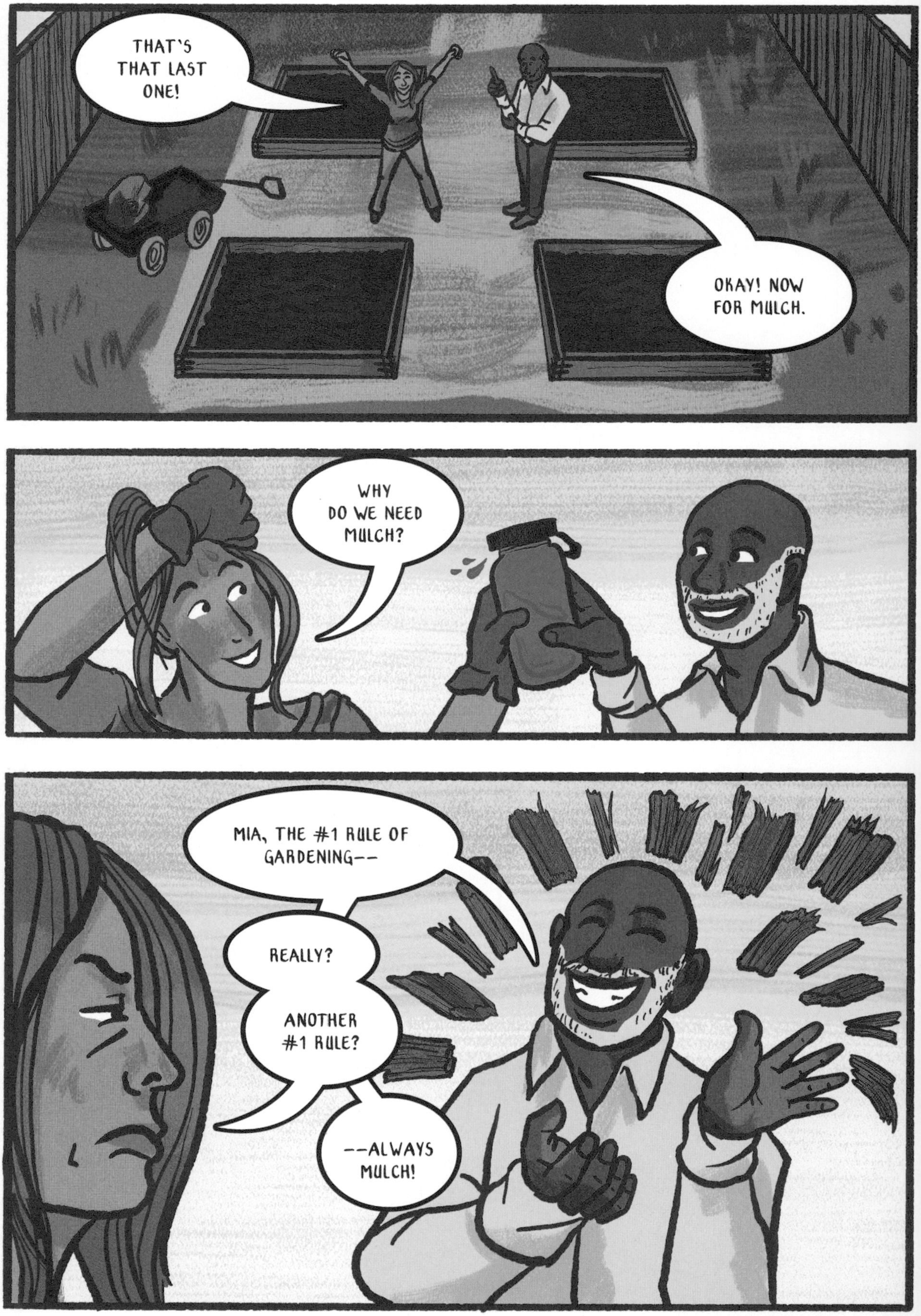
THAT'S THAT LAST ONE!
OKAY! NOW FOR MULCH.
WHY DO WE NEED MULCH?
MIA, THE #1 RULE OF GARDENING--
REALLY?
ANOTHER #1 RULE?
--ALWAYS MULCH!

GEORGE APPROVED CHEAT SHEET GARDEN TIPS

THE MAGIC OF MULCH

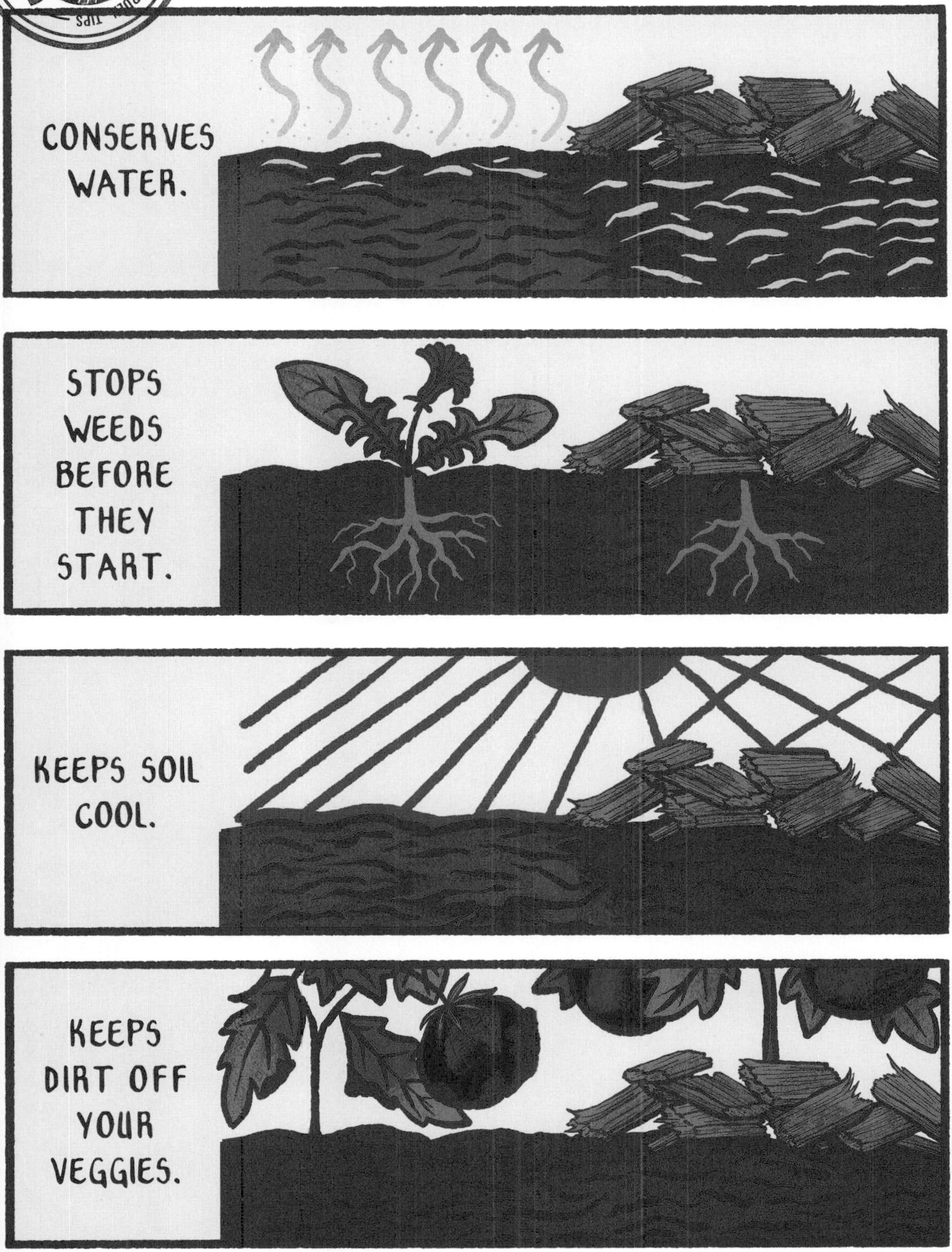
CONSERVES WATER.
STOPS WEEDS BEFORE THEY START.
KEEPS SOIL COOL.
KEEPS DIRT OFF YOUR VEGGIES.

APPROVED CHEAT SHEET GARDEN TIPS

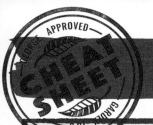

TYPES OF MULCH

STRAW:
USE CLEAN WHEAT, BARLEY, OAT, OR RICE STRAW, NOT HAY WHICH CAN BE FULL OF WEED SEEDS.

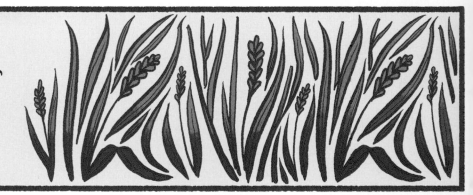

SHREDDED FALL LEAVES:
FREE, EASY. SHRED WITH LAWN MOWER.

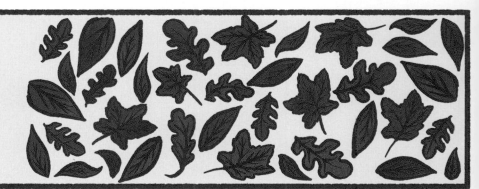

BULK OR BAGGED BARK/ WOOD CHIP MULCH:
CONVENIENT. GET THE CHEAPEST YOU CAN FIND.

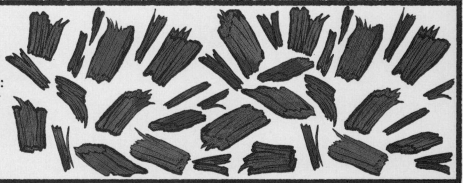

LAWN CLIPPINGS:
DON'T USE ALONE. MIX 50/50 WITH LEAVES OR BAGGED MULCH.

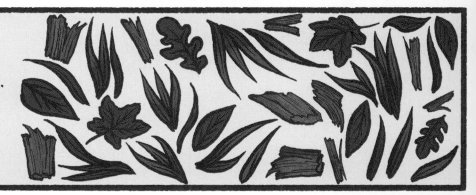

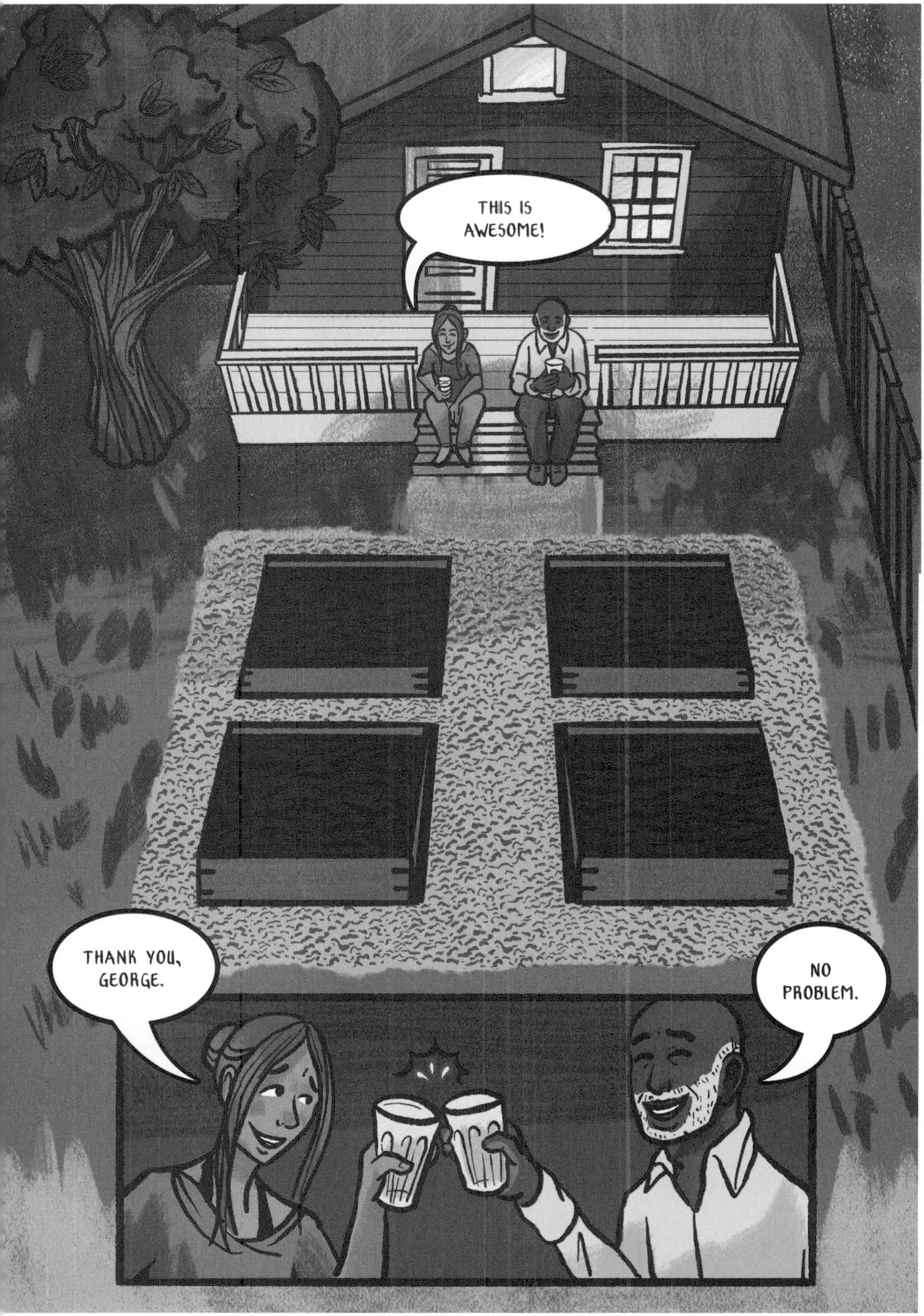
THIS IS AWESOME!
THANK YOU, GEORGE.
NO PROBLEM.

SIX:
GETTING PLANTS

BUYING HEALTHY PLANTS FOR THE GARDEN.

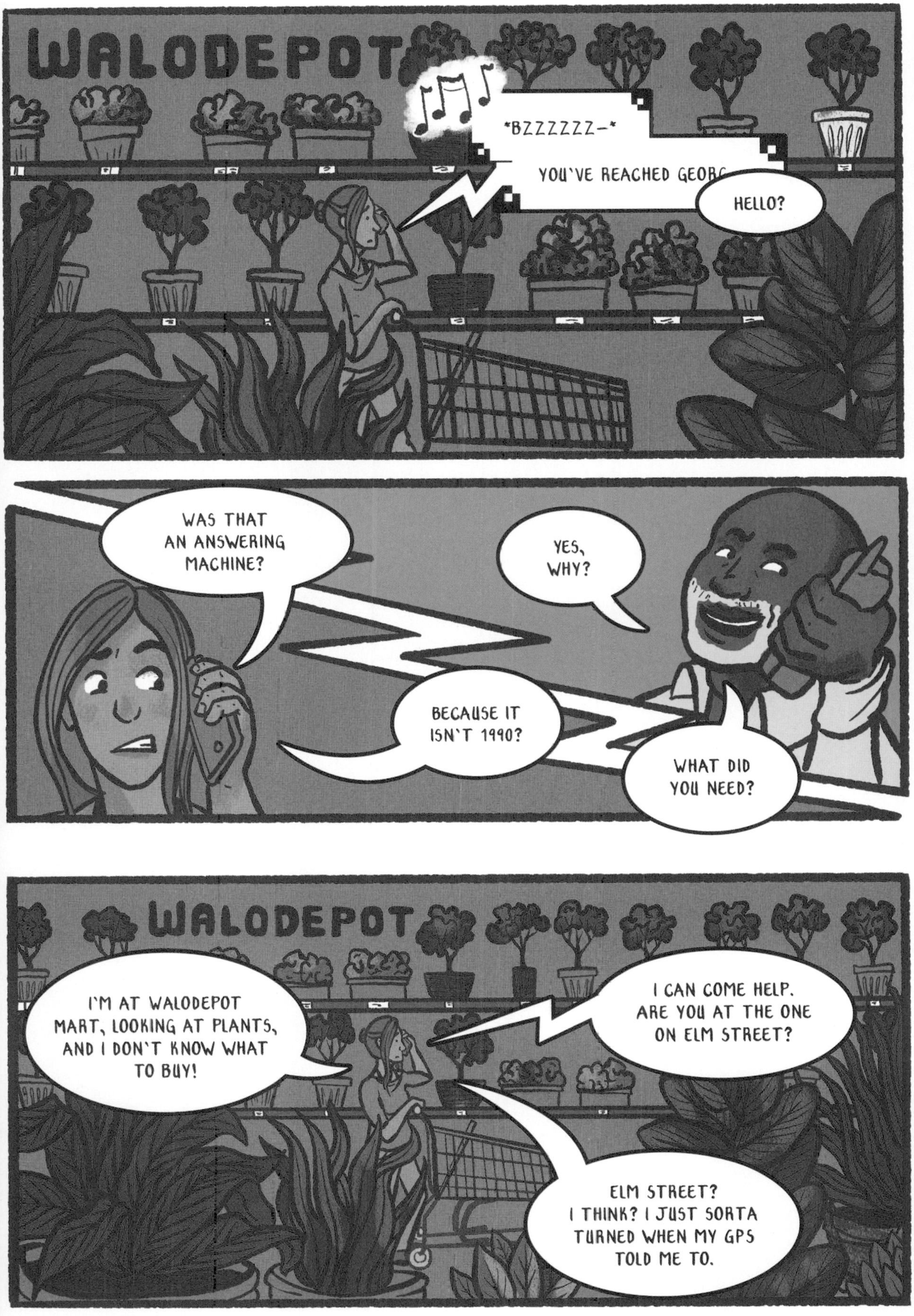
WALODEPOT
BZZZZZZ-
YOU'VE REACHED GEORG
HELLO?
WAS THAT AN ANSWERING MACHINE?
YES, WHY?
BECAUSE IT ISN'T 1990?
WHAT DID YOU NEED?
WALODEPOT
I'M AT WALODEPOT MART, LOOKING AT PLANTS, AND I DON'T KNOW WHAT TO BUY!
I CAN COME HELP. ARE YOU AT THE ONE ON ELM STREET?
ELM STREET? I THINK? I JUST SORTA TURNED WHEN MY GPS TOLD ME TO.

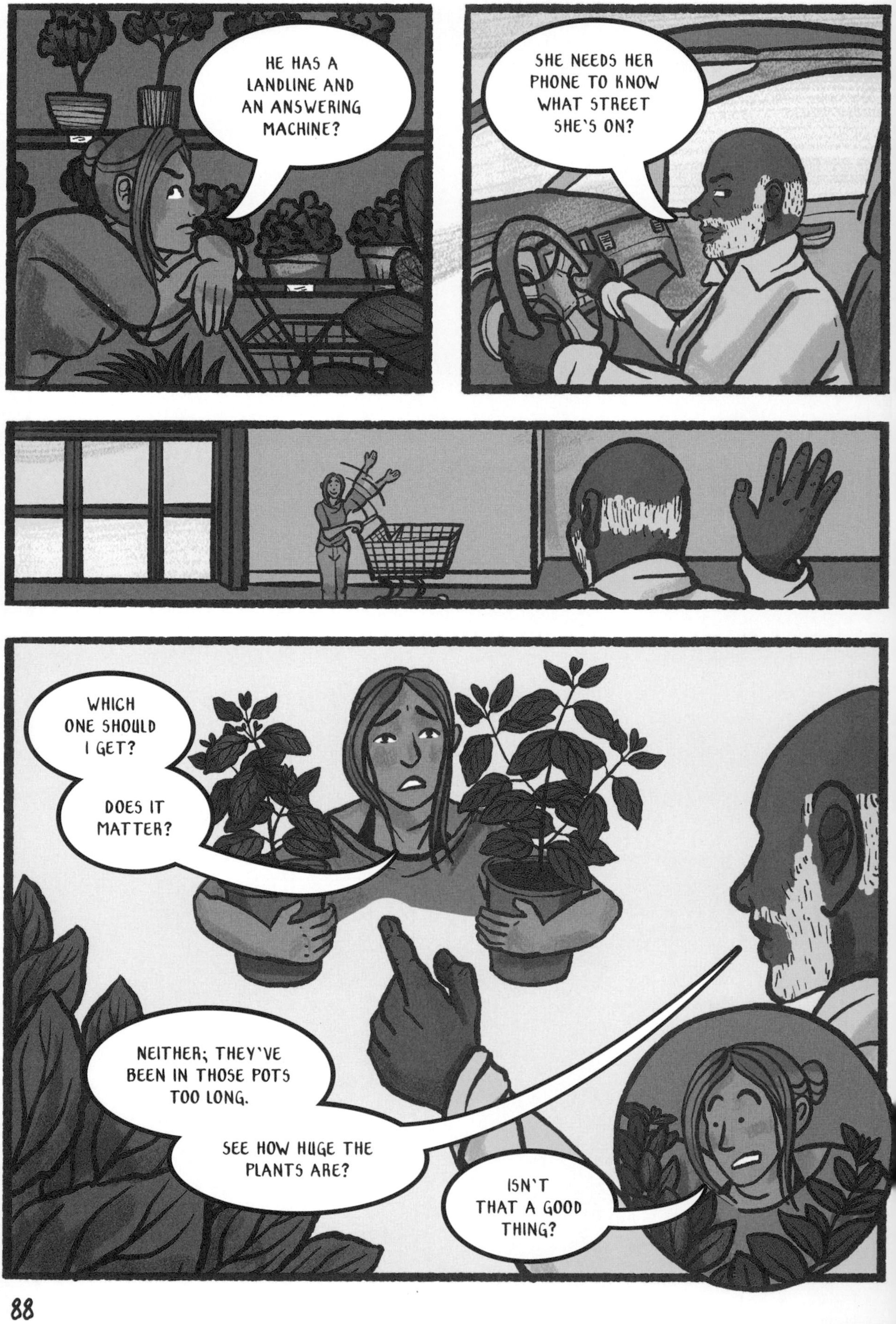
HE HAS A LANDLINE AND AN ANSWERING MACHINE?
SHE NEEDS HER PHONE TO KNOW WHAT STREET SHE'S ON?
WHICH ONE SHOULD I GET?
DOES IT MATTER?
NEITHER; THEY'VE BEEN IN THOSE POTS TOO LONG.
SEE HOW HUGE THE PLANTS ARE?
ISN'T THAT A GOOD THING?

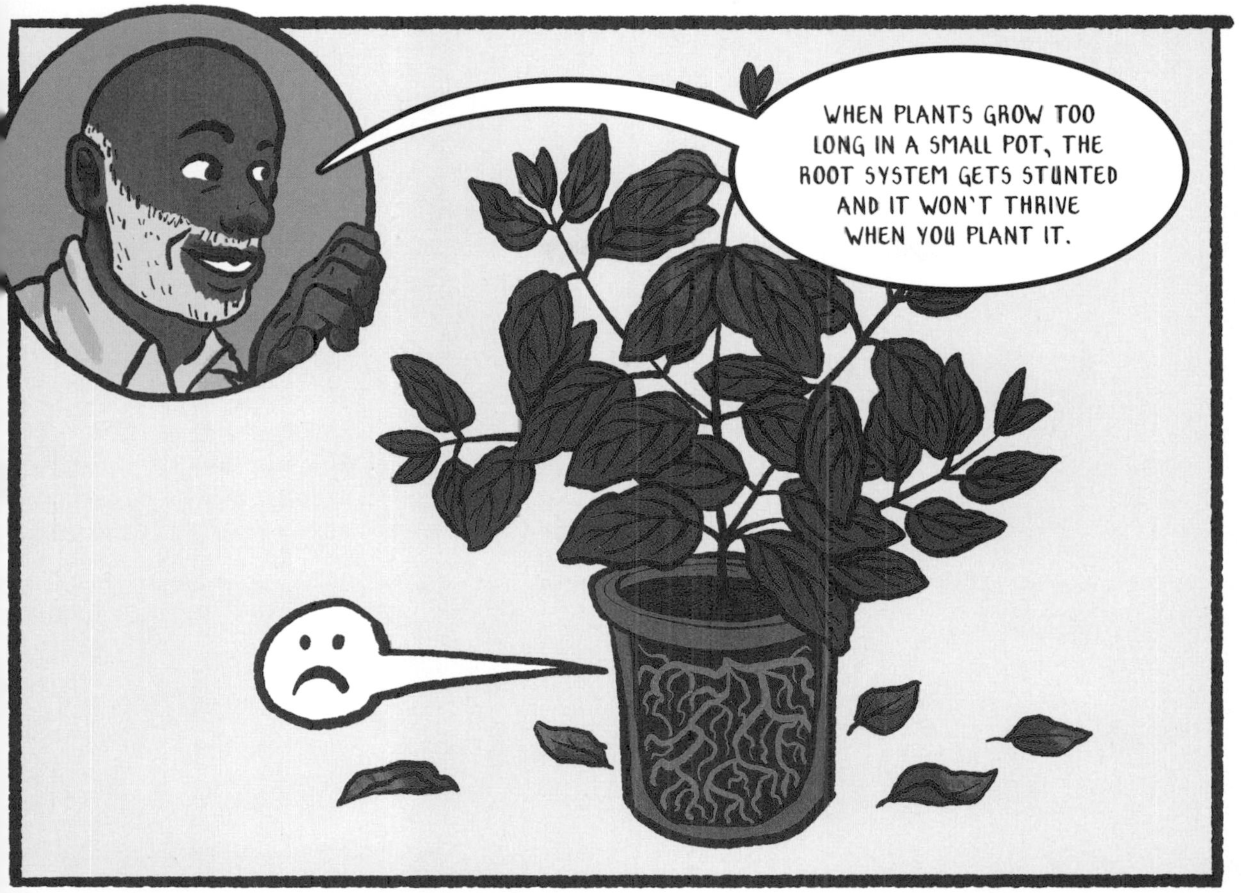
WHEN PLANTS GROW TOO LONG IN A SMALL POT, THE ROOT SYSTEM GETS STUNTED AND IT WON'T THRIVE WHEN YOU PLANT IT.

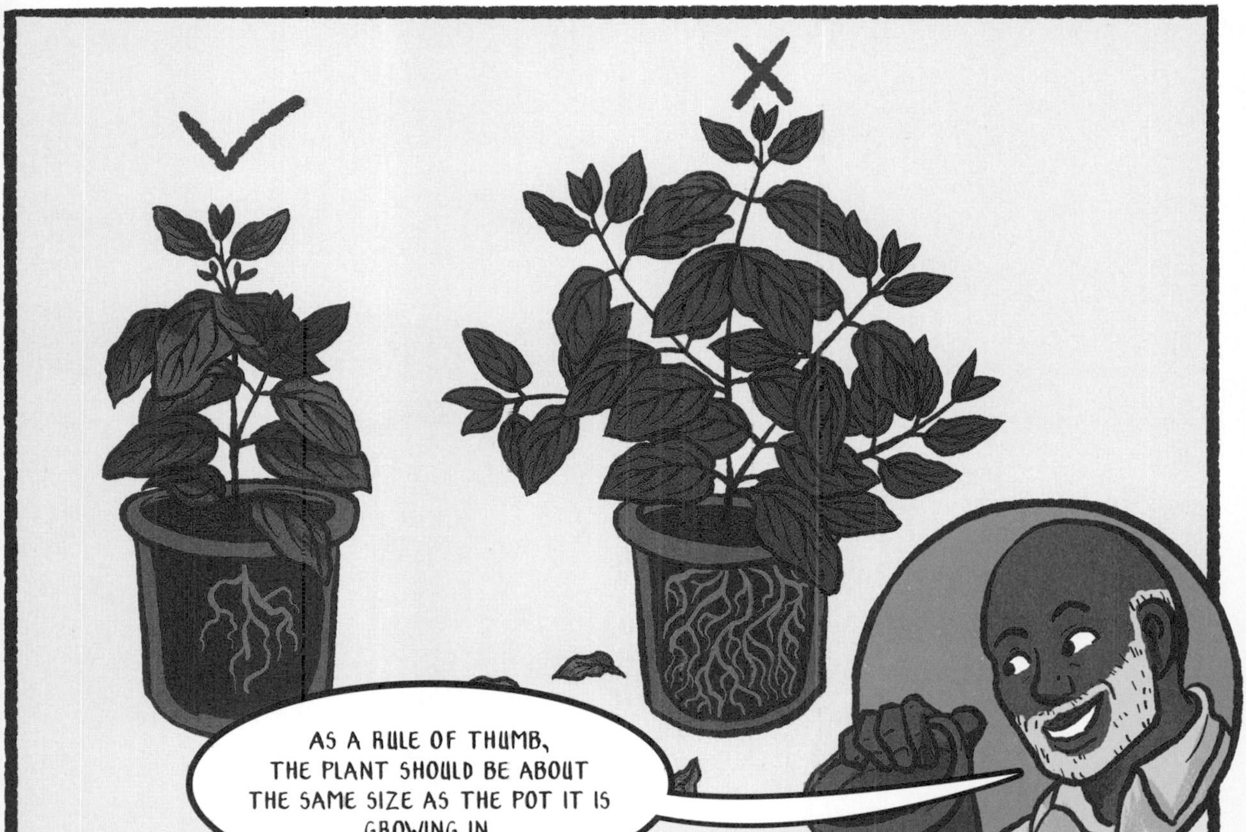
AS A RULE OF THUMB, THE PLANT SHOULD BE ABOUT THE SAME SIZE AS THE POT IT IS GROWING IN.

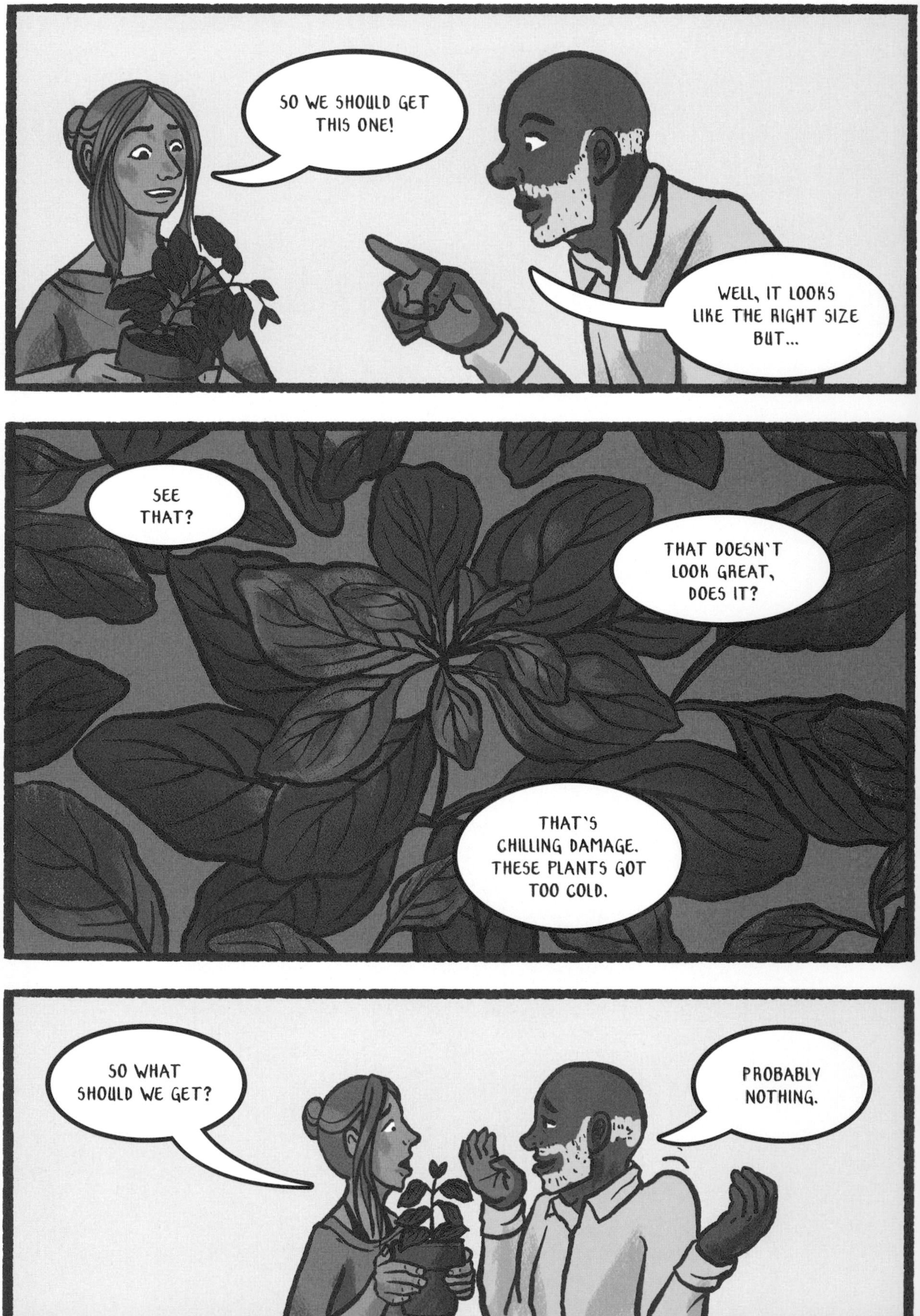
SO WE SHOULD GET THIS ONE!
WELL, IT LOOKS LIKE THE RIGHT SIZE BUT...
SEE THAT?
THAT DOESN'T LOOK GREAT, DOES IT?
THAT'S CHILLING DAMAGE. THESE PLANTS GOT TOO COLD.
SO WHAT SHOULD WE GET?
PROBABLY NOTHING.

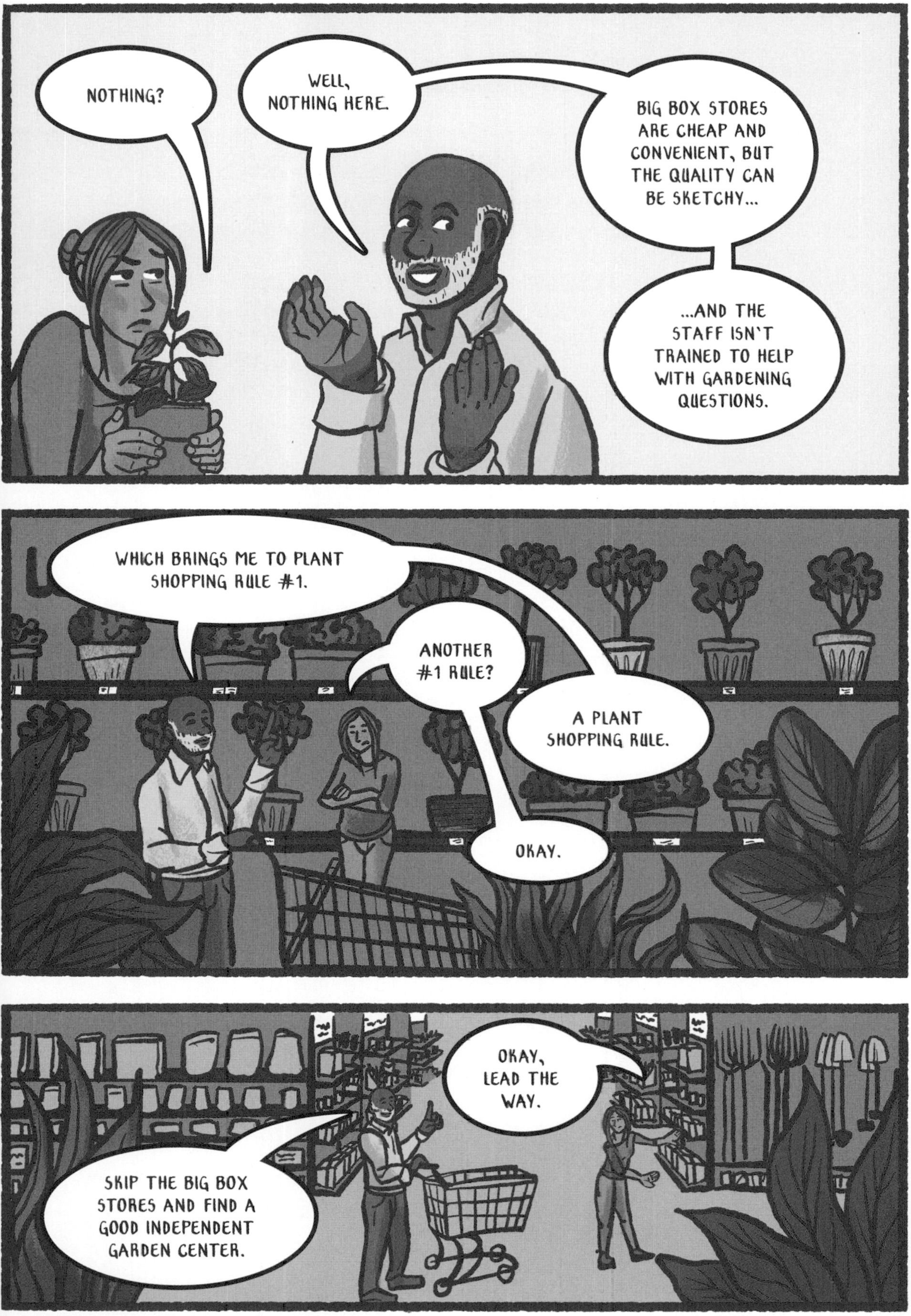
NOTHING?
WELL, NOTHING HERE.
BIG BOX STORES ARE CHEAP AND CONVENIENT, BUT THE QUALITY CAN BE SKETCHY...
...AND THE STAFF ISN'T TRAINED TO HELP WITH GARDENING QUESTIONS.
WHICH BRINGS ME TO PLANT SHOPPING RULE #1.
ANOTHER #1 RULE?
A PLANT SHOPPING RULE.
OKAY.
SKIP THE BIG BOX STORES AND FIND A GOOD INDEPENDENT GARDEN CENTER.
OKAY, LEAD THE WAY.

CHEAT SHEET

THE BEST PLACES TO GET PLANTS

INDEPENDENT GARDEN CENTERS

PROS: WIDE SELECTION, STAFF ON HAND TO ANSWER QUESTIONS, CARRIES VARIETIES WELL SUITED TO YOUR LOCAL CONDITIONS.

CONS: CAN BE MORE EXPENSIVE. EACH ONE IS DIFFERENT. IF THE PLANTS ARE LOW QUALITY OR STAFF CAN'T HELP YOU, TRY SOMEWHERE ELSE.

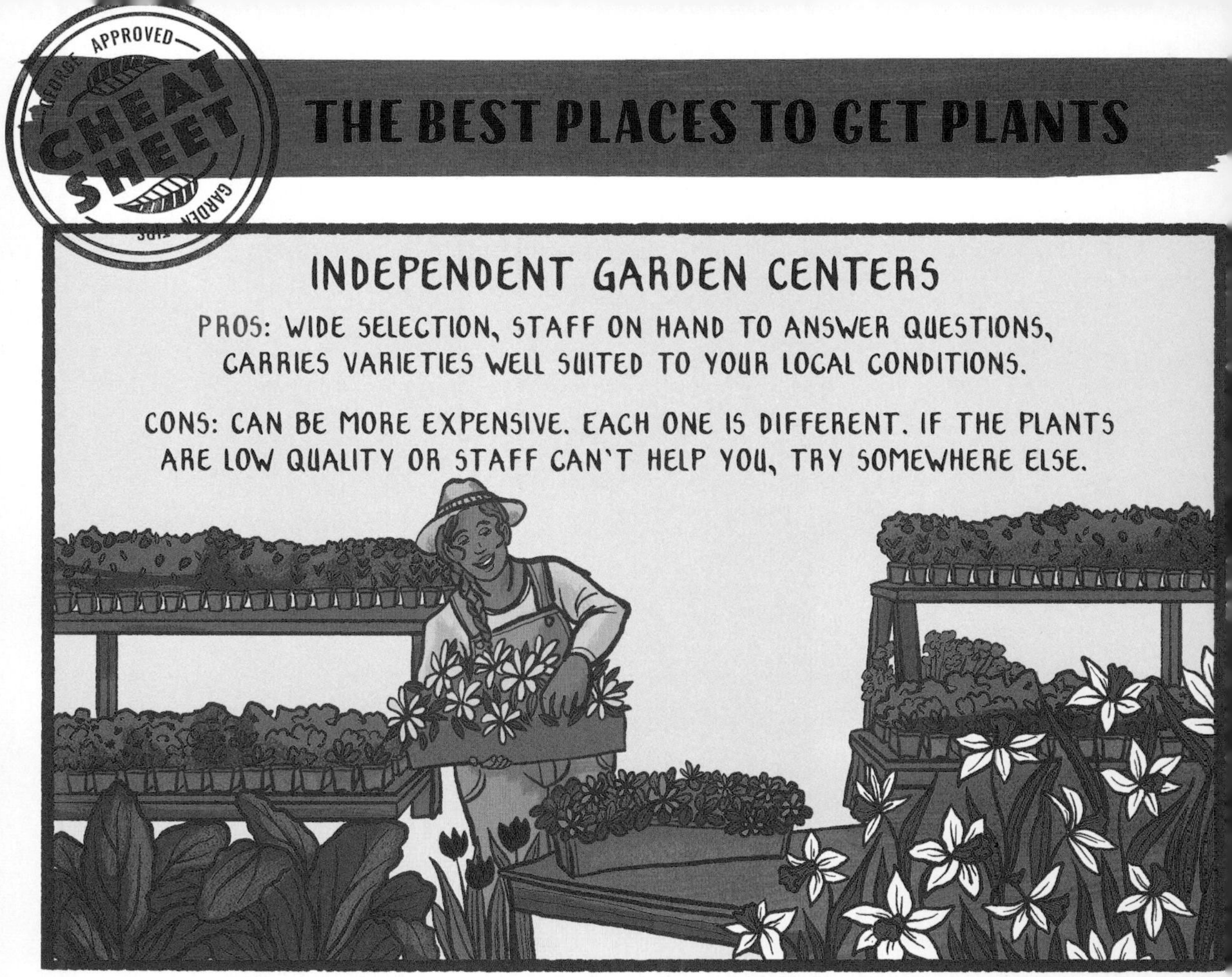

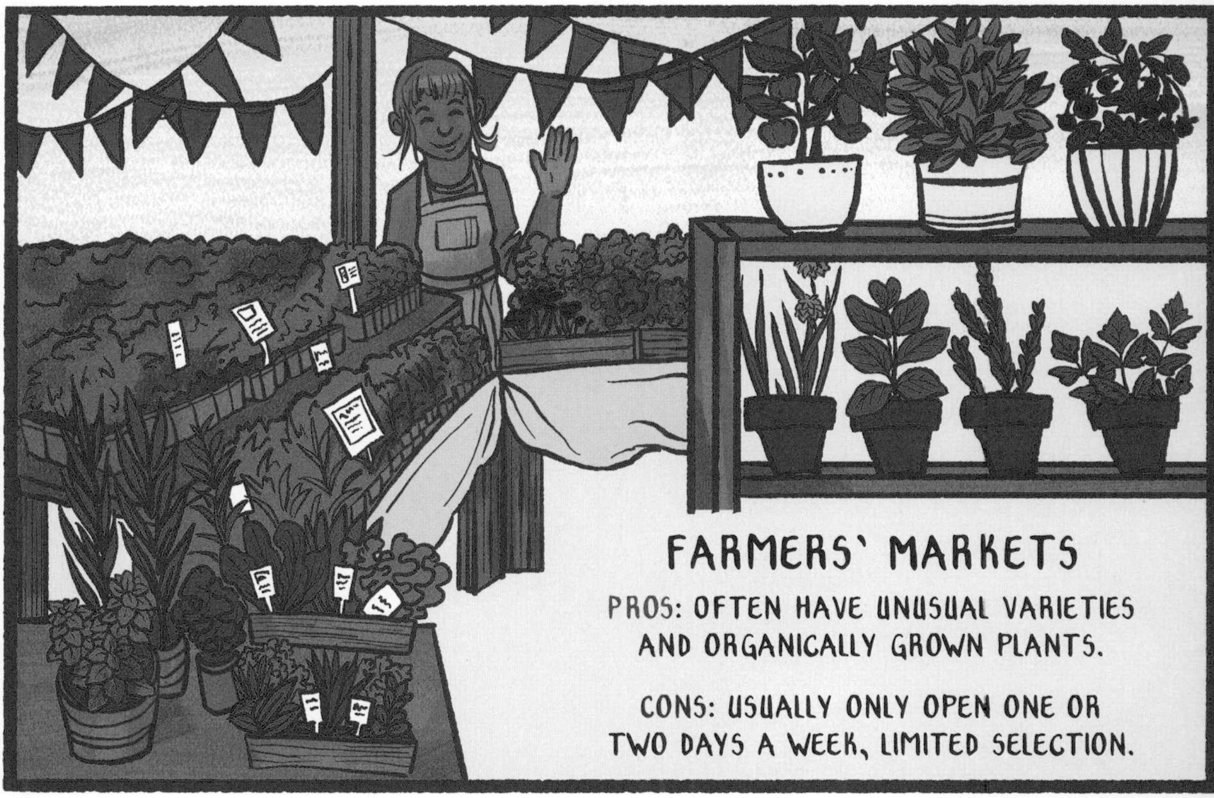

FARMERS' MARKETS

PROS: OFTEN HAVE UNUSUAL VARIETIES AND ORGANICALLY GROWN PLANTS.

CONS: USUALLY ONLY OPEN ONE OR TWO DAYS A WEEK, LIMITED SELECTION.

THE BEST PLACES TO GET PLANTS

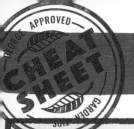

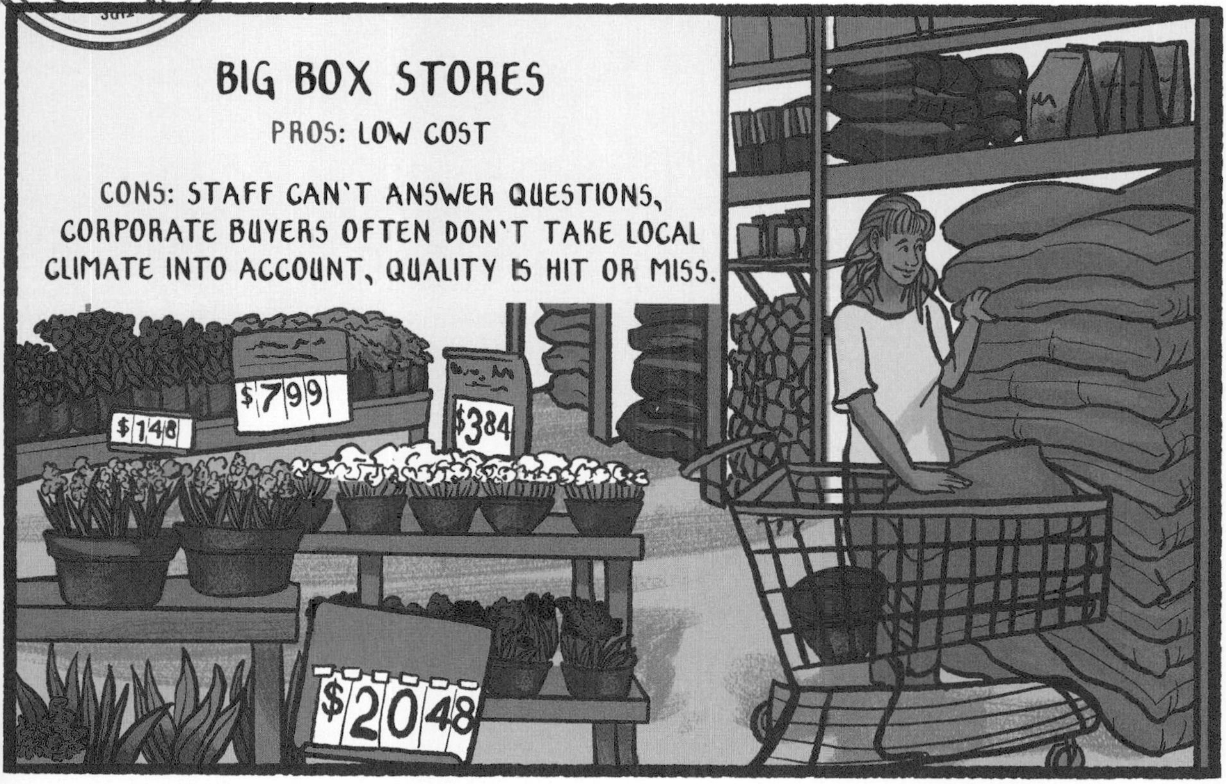
BIG BOX STORES
PROS: LOW COST
CONS: STAFF CAN'T ANSWER QUESTIONS, CORPORATE BUYERS OFTEN DON'T TAKE LOCAL CLIMATE INTO ACCOUNT, QUALITY IS HIT OR MISS.
$799
$148
$384
$2048

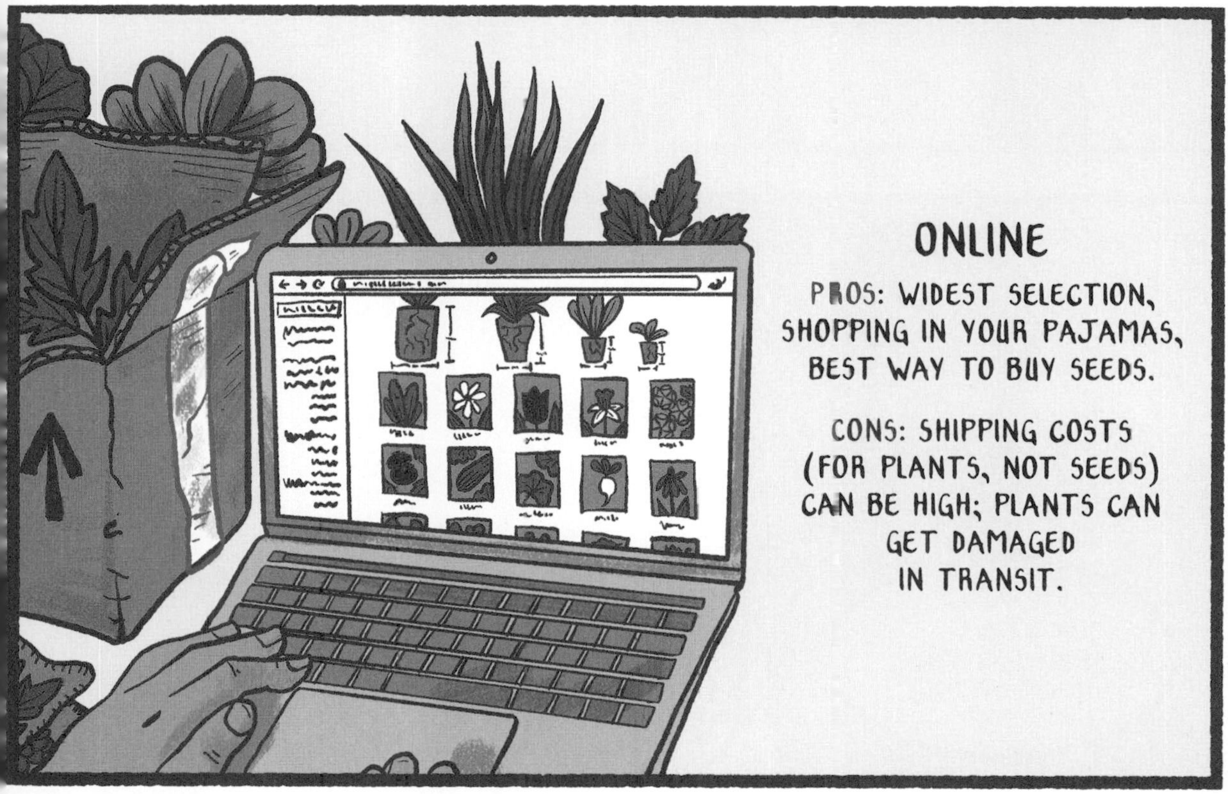
ONLINE
PROS: WIDEST SELECTION, SHOPPING IN YOUR PAJAMAS, BEST WAY TO BUY SEEDS.
CONS: SHIPPING COSTS (FOR PLANTS, NOT SEEDS) CAN BE HIGH; PLANTS CAN GET DAMAGED IN TRANSIT.

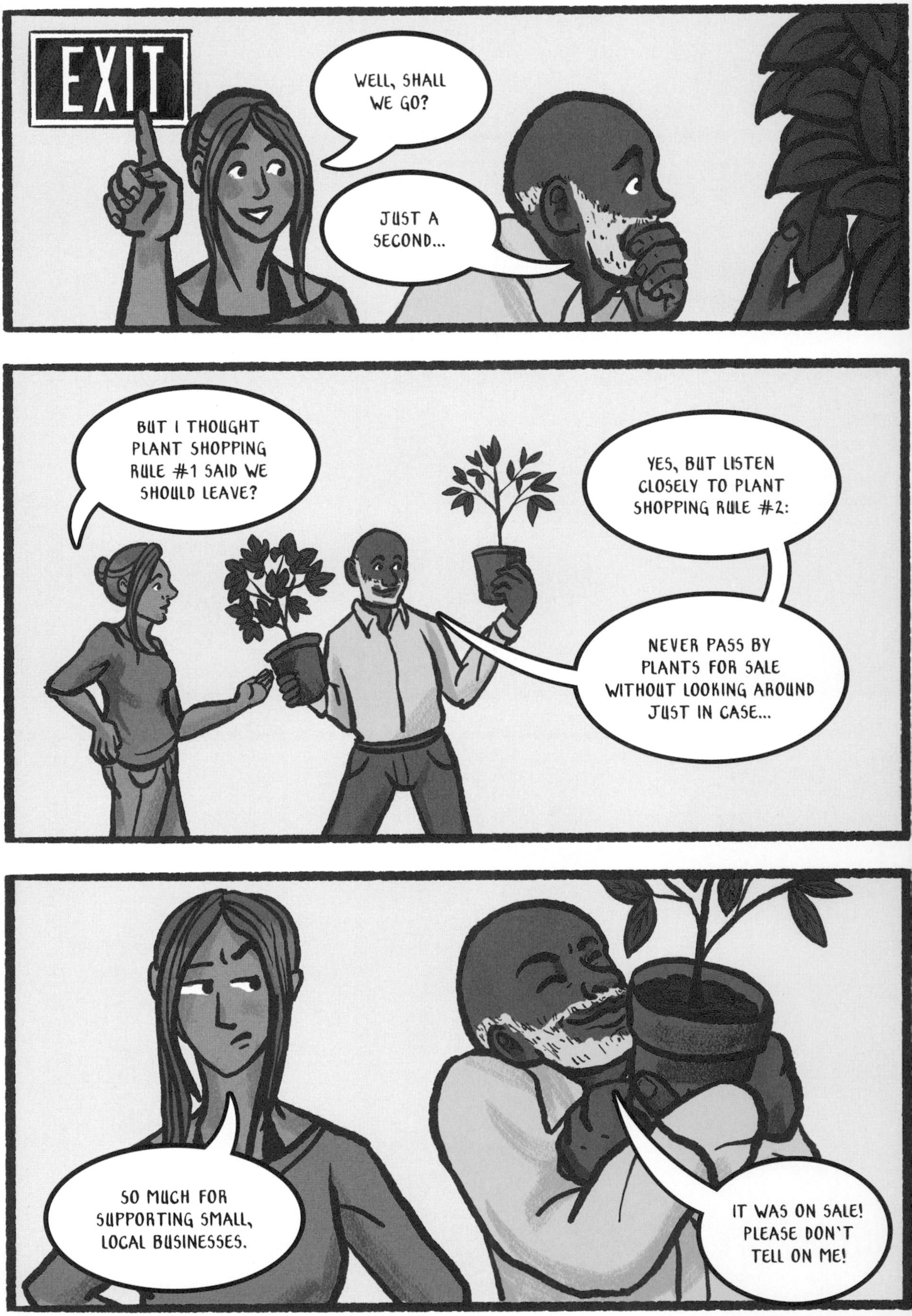
EXIT
WELL, SHALL WE GO?
JUST A SECOND...
BUT I THOUGHT PLANT SHOPPING RULE #1 SAID WE SHOULD LEAVE?
YES, BUT LISTEN CLOSELY TO PLANT SHOPPING RULE #2:
NEVER PASS BY PLANTS FOR SALE WITHOUT LOOKING AROUND JUST IN CASE...
SO MUCH FOR SUPPORTING SMALL, LOCAL BUSINESSES.
IT WAS ON SALE! PLEASE DON'T TELL ON ME!

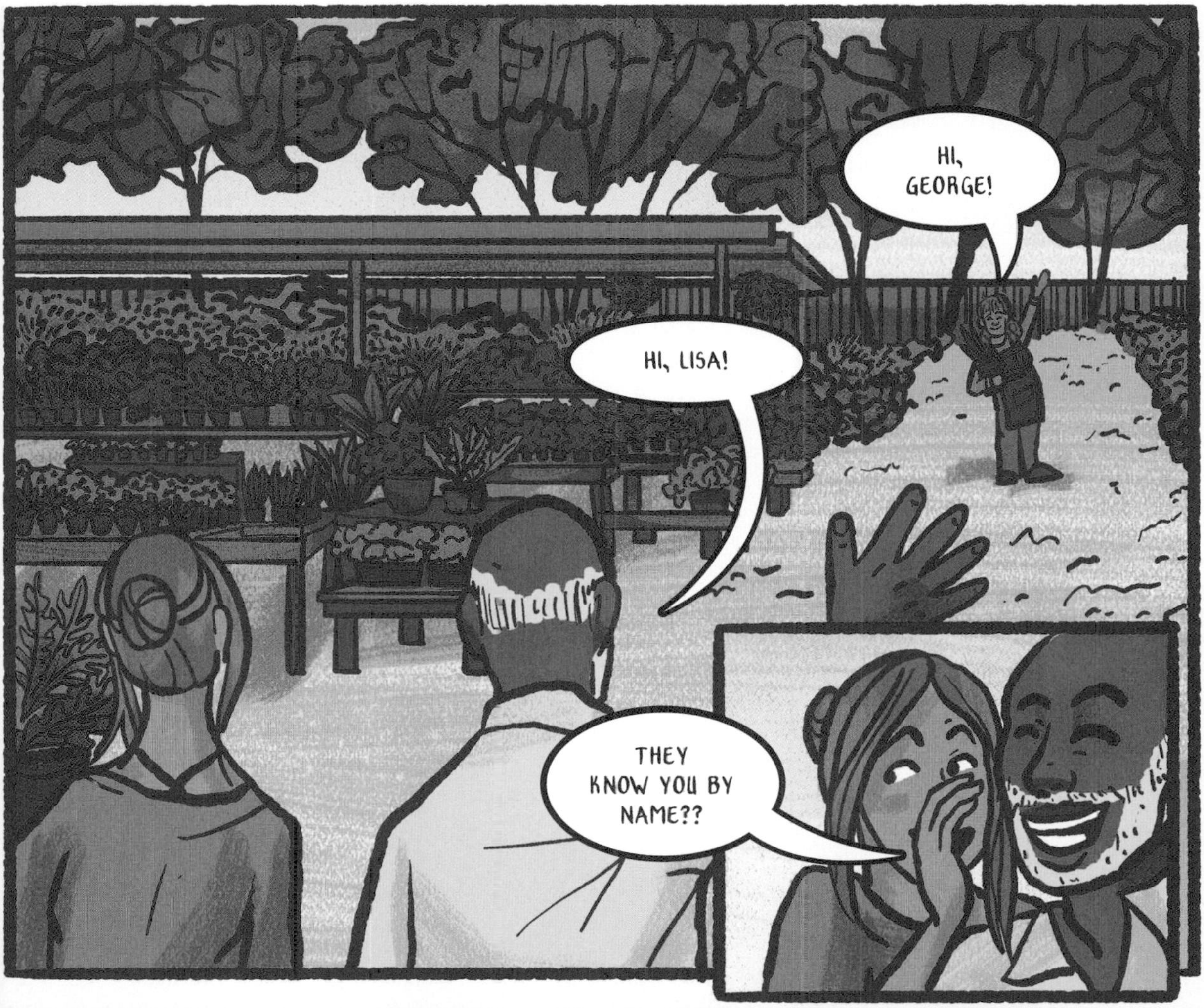
HI, GEORGE!
HI, LISA!
THEY KNOW YOU BY NAME??

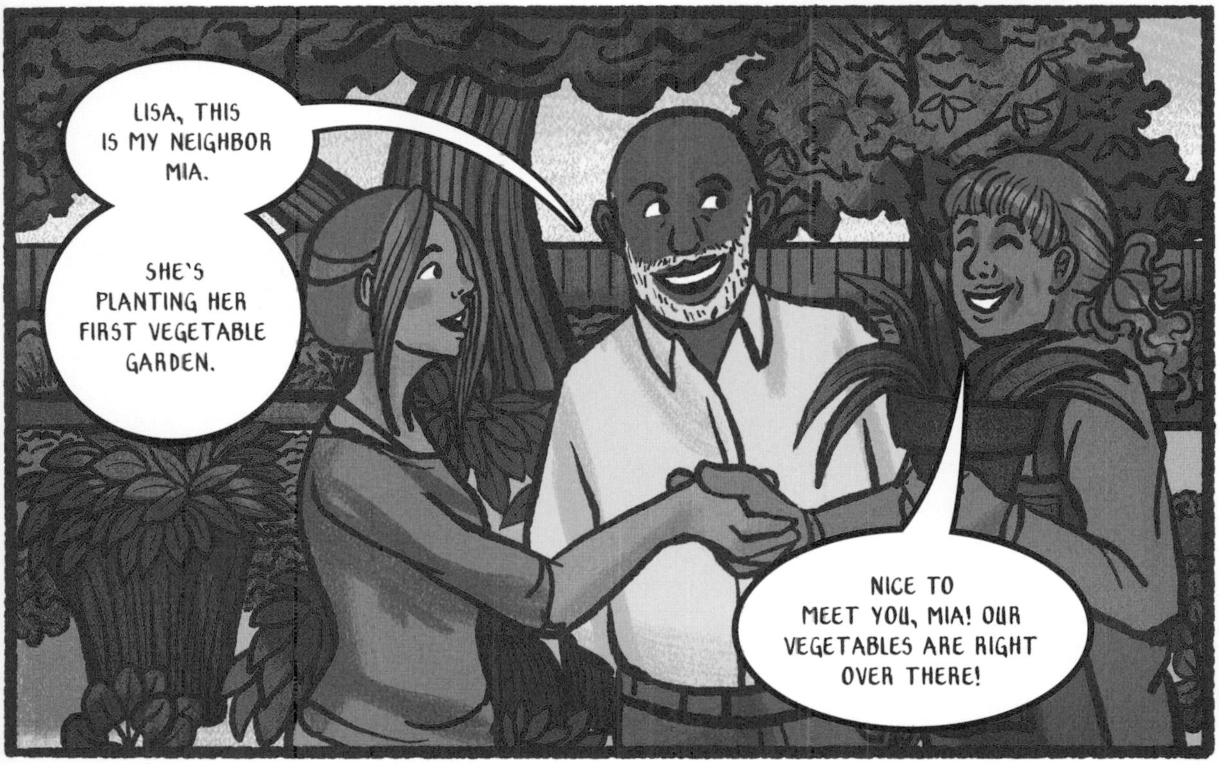
LISA, THIS IS MY NEIGHBOR MIA.
SHE'S PLANTING HER FIRST VEGETABLE GARDEN.
NICE TO MEET YOU, MIA! OUR VEGETABLES ARE RIGHT OVER THERE!

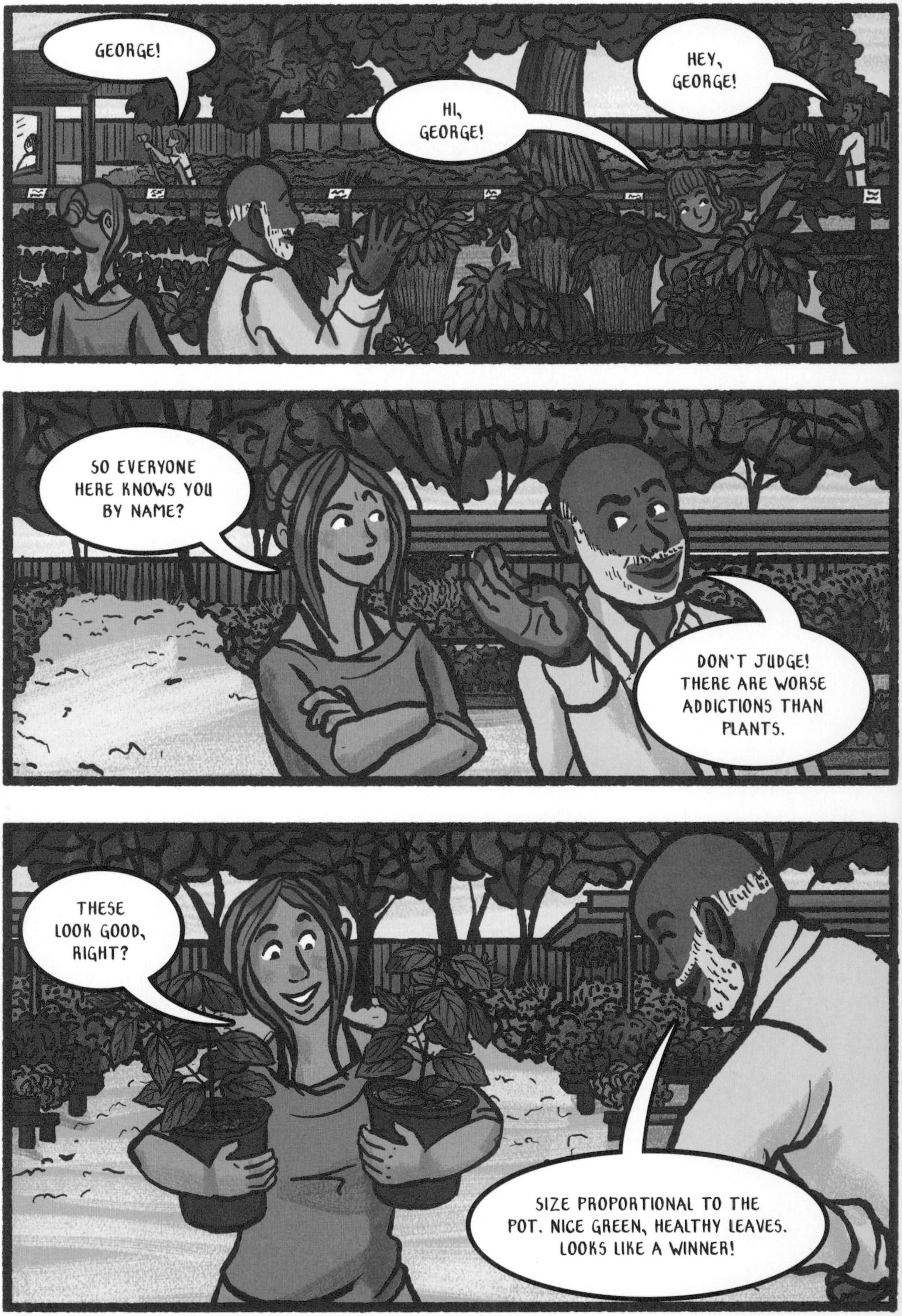
GEORGE!
HI, GEORGE!
HEY, GEORGE!
SO EVERYONE HERE KNOWS YOU BY NAME?
DON'T JUDGE! THERE ARE WORSE ADDICTIONS THAN PLANTS.
THESE LOOK GOOD, RIGHT?
SIZE PROPORTIONAL TO THE POT. NICE GREEN, HEALTHY LEAVES. LOOKS LIKE A WINNER!

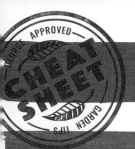

BUYING PLANTS

GOOD

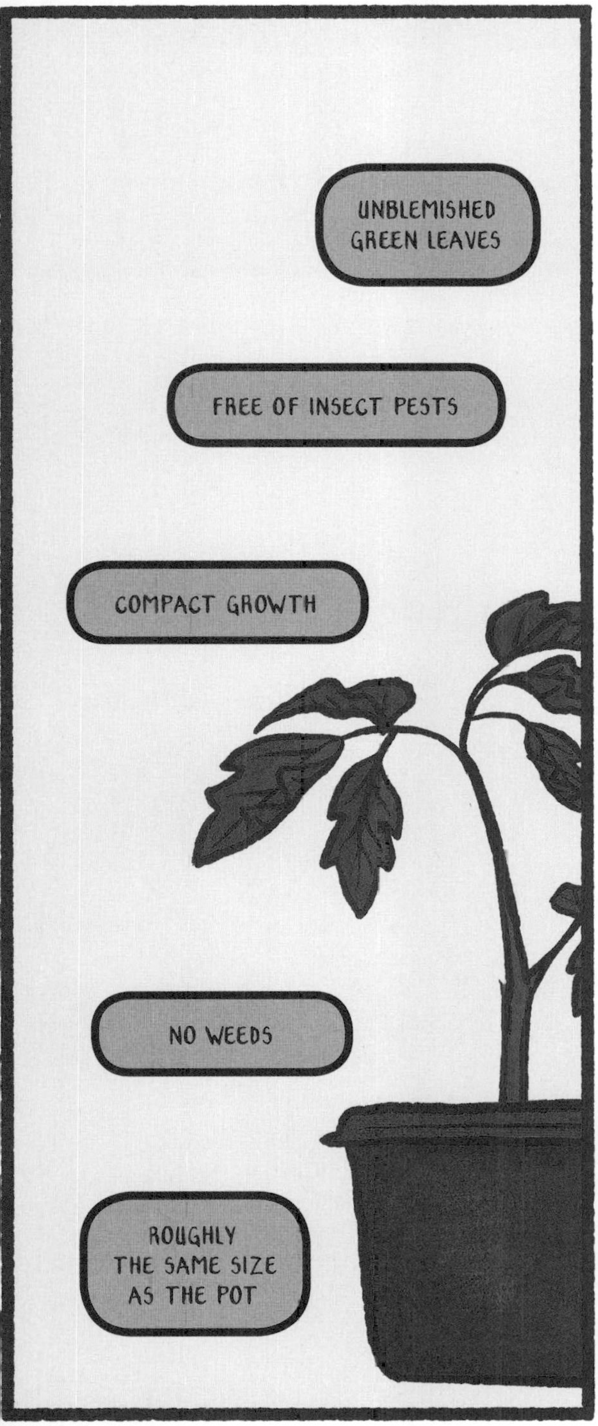
UNBLEMISHED GREEN LEAVES
FREE OF INSECT PESTS
COMPACT GROWTH
NO WEEDS
ROUGHLY THE SAME SIZE AS THE POT

BAD

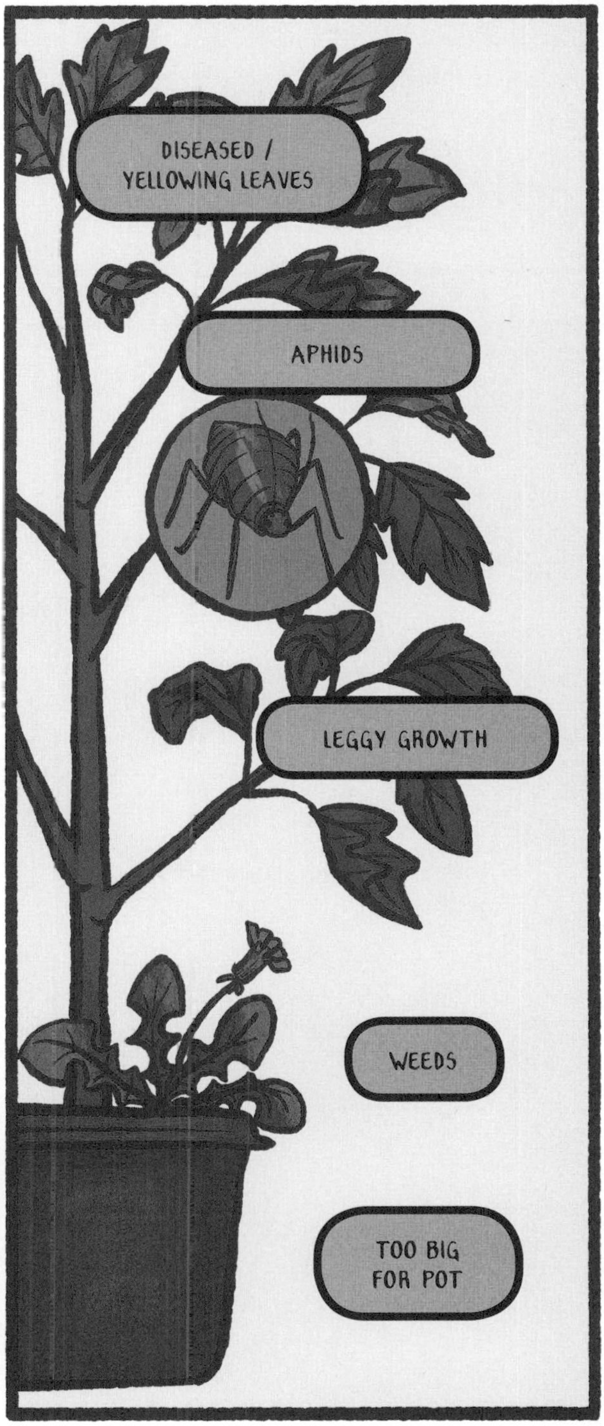
DISEASED / YELLOWING LEAVES
APHIDS
LEGGY GROWTH
WEEDS
TOO BIG FOR POT

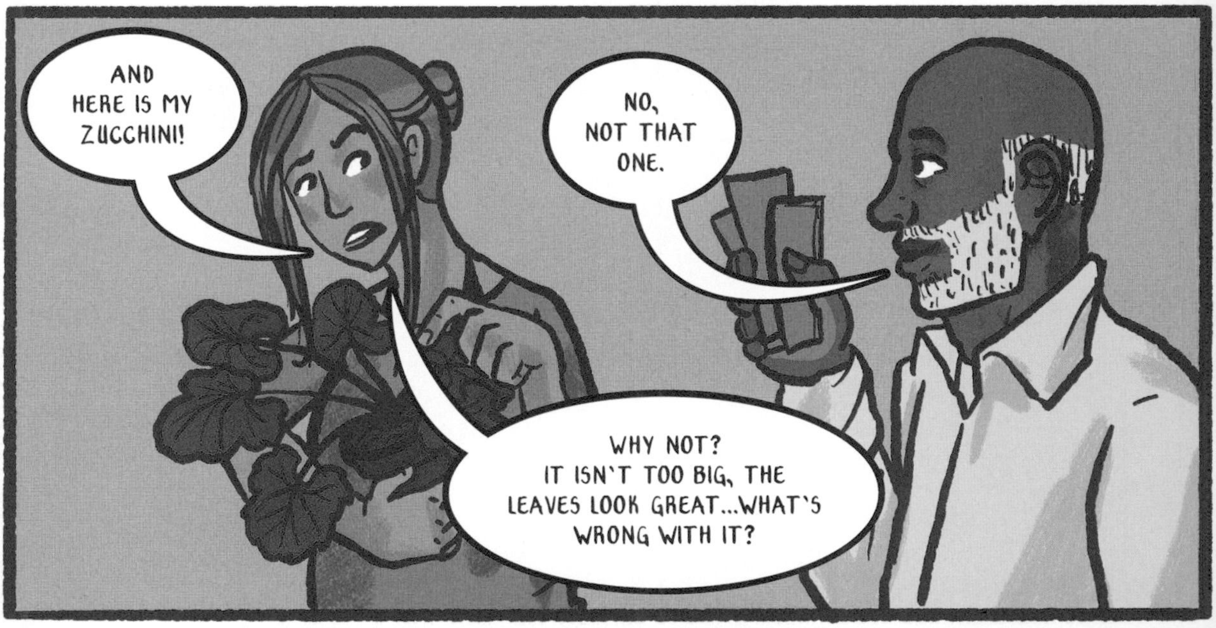
AND HERE IS MY ZUCCHINI!
NO, NOT THAT ONE.
WHY NOT? IT ISN'T TOO BIG, THE LEAVES LOOK GREAT...WHAT'S WRONG WITH IT?

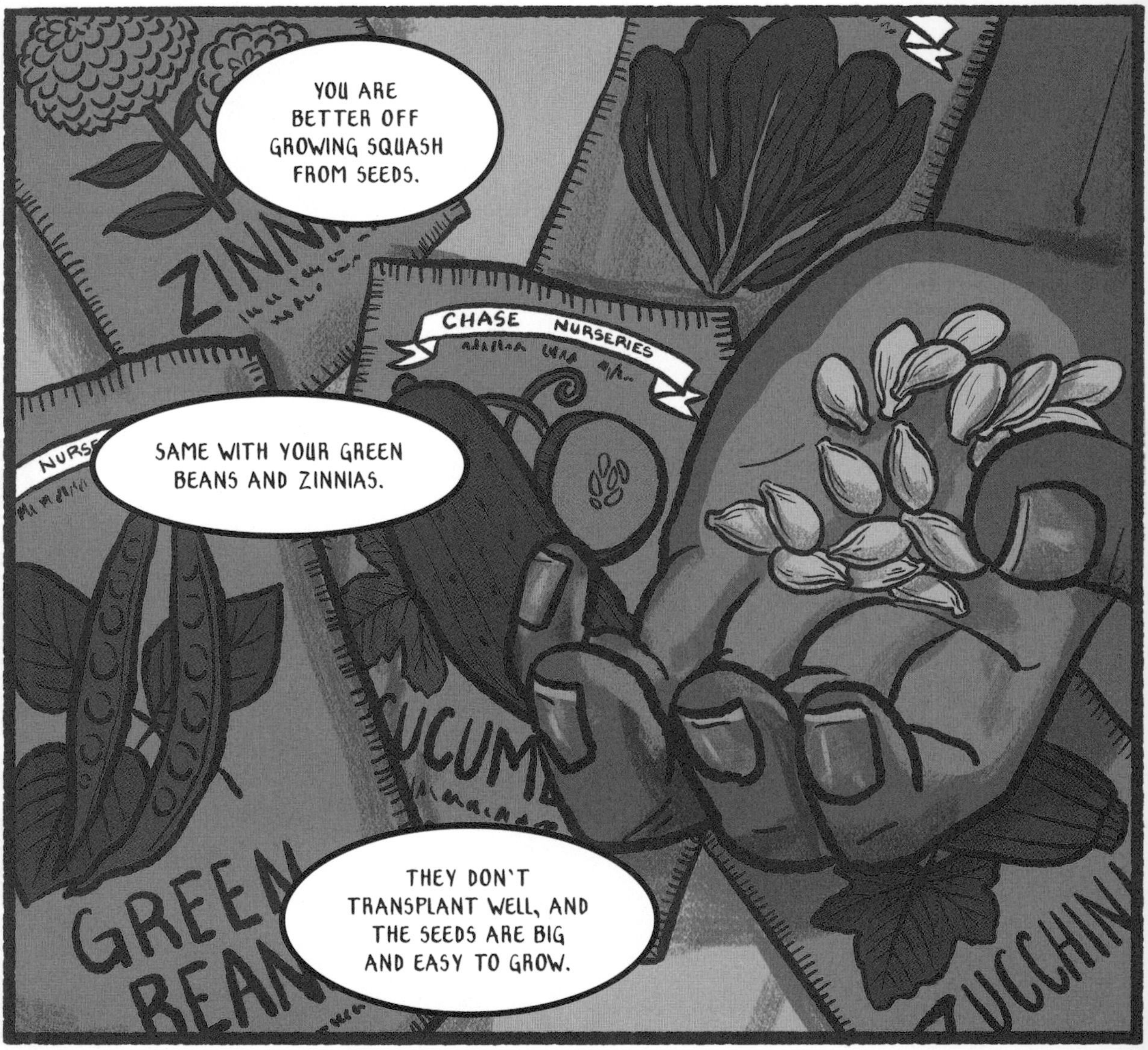
YOU ARE BETTER OFF GROWING SQUASH FROM SEEDS.
ZINNI
CHASE NURSERIES
NURSE
SAME WITH YOUR GREEN BEANS AND ZINNIAS.
CUCUM
THEY DON'T TRANSPLANT WELL, AND THE SEEDS ARE BIG AND EASY TO GROW.
GREEN BEAN
ZUCCHINI

GEORGE APPROVED CHEAT SHEET GARDEN TIPS

BUY AS SEEDS OR PLANTS?

SEEDS*

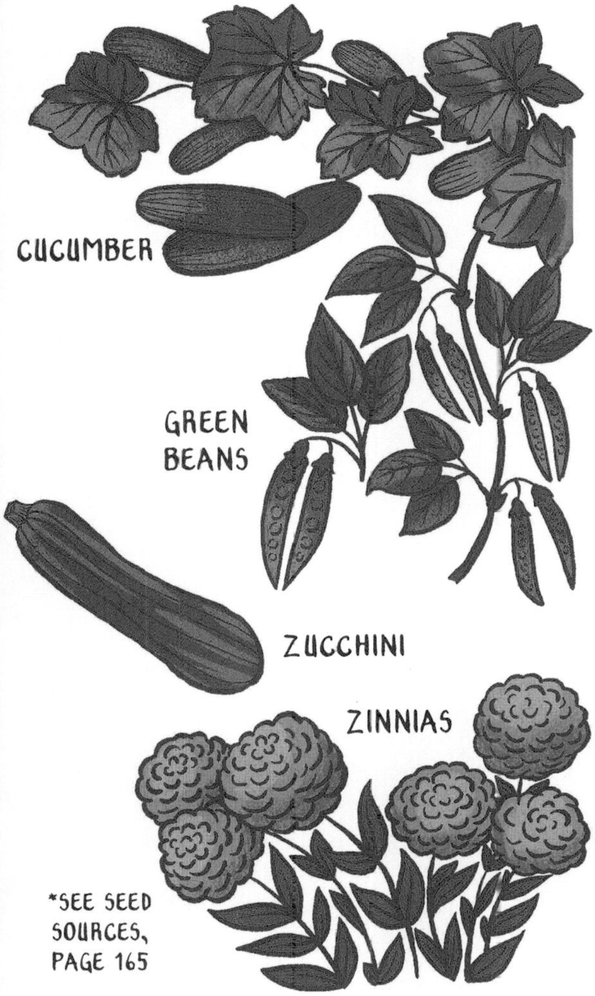
CUCUMBER
GREEN BEANS
ZUCCHINI
ZINNIAS

*SEE SEED SOURCES, PAGE 165

PLANTS

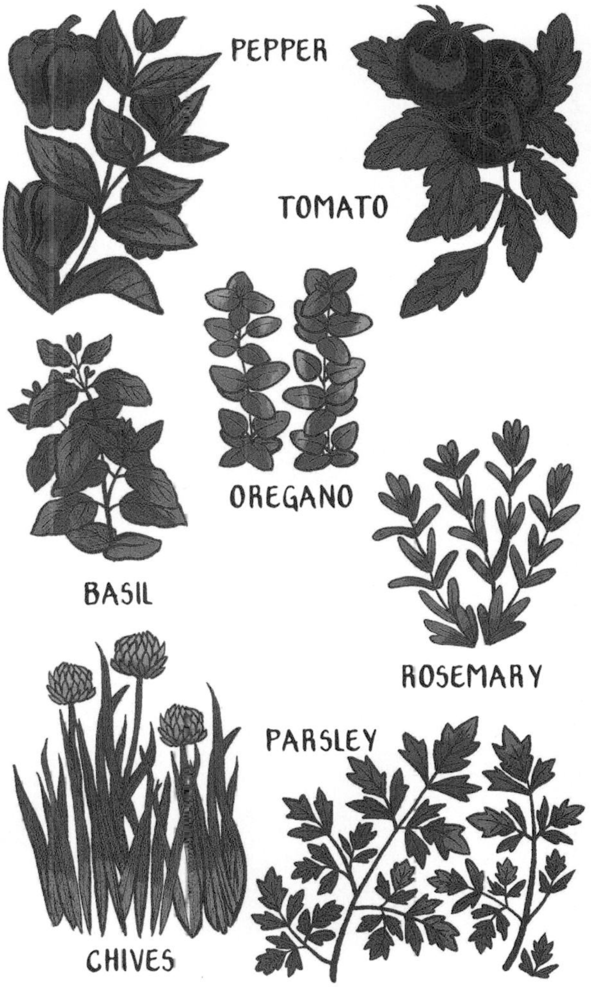
PEPPER
TOMATO
OREGANO
BASIL
ROSEMARY
PARSLEY
CHIVES

EITHER IS FINE

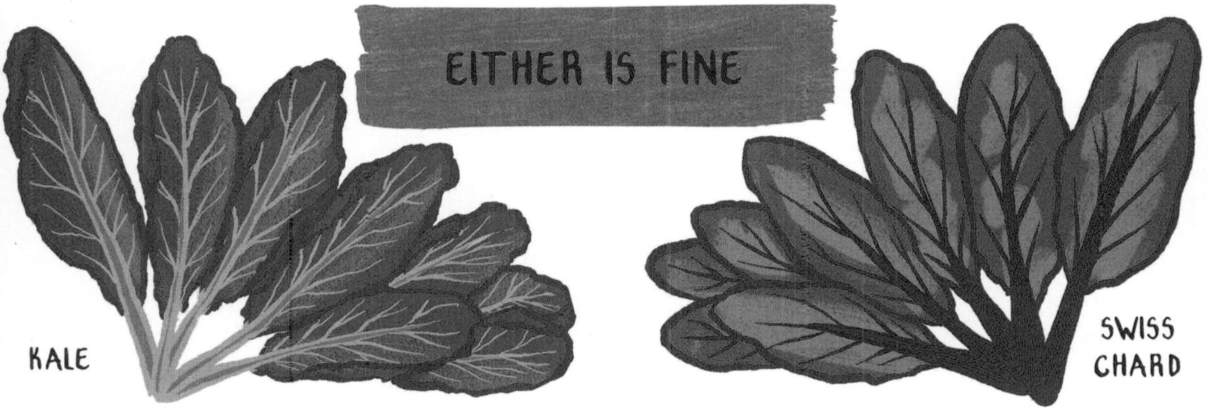
KALE
SWISS CHARD

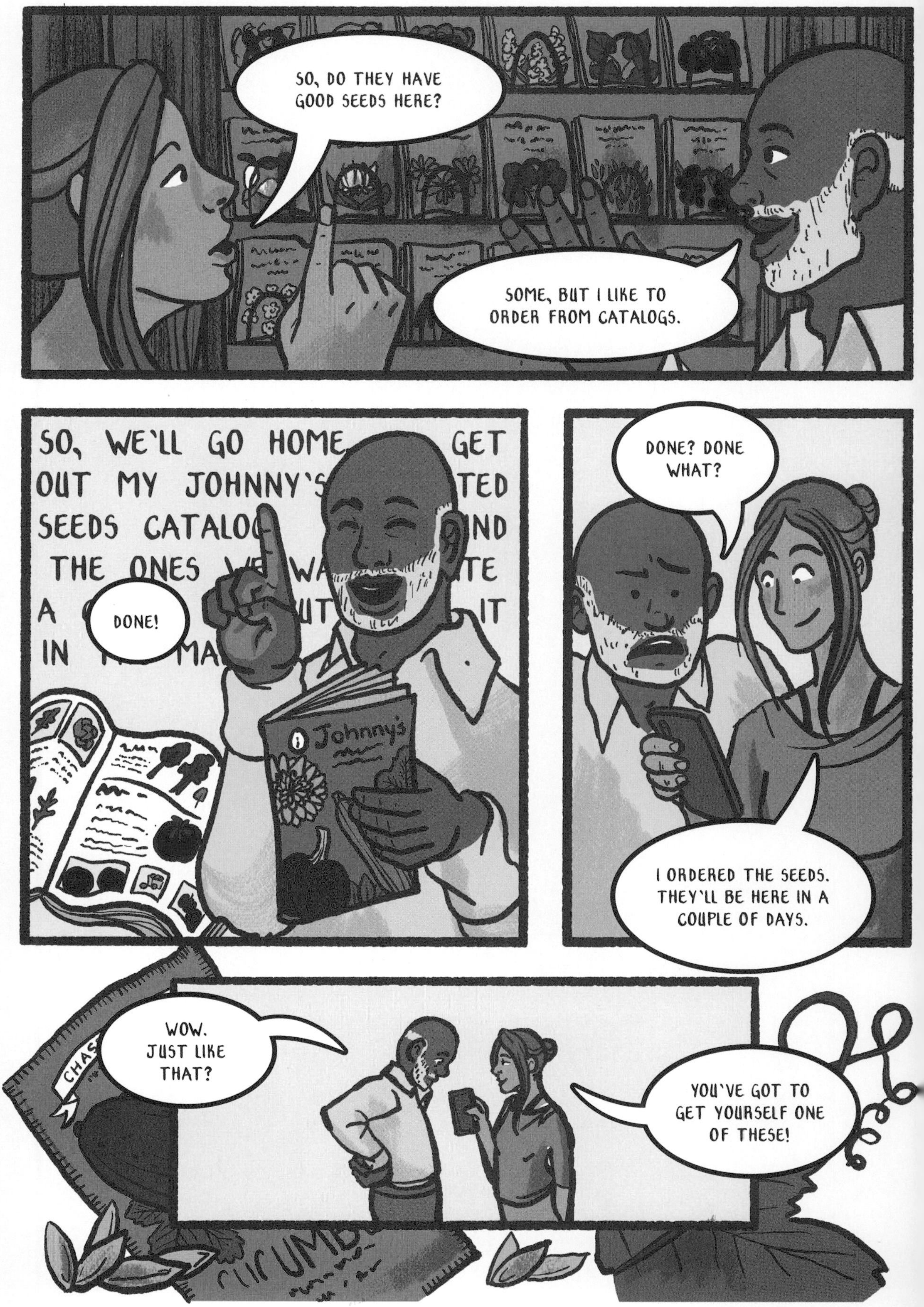
SO, DO THEY HAVE GOOD SEEDS HERE?
SOME, BUT I LIKE TO ORDER FROM CATALOGS.
SO, WE'LL GO HOME GET
OUT MY JOHNNY'S TED
SEEDS CATALOG ND
THE ONES WE WA TE
A UT IT
IN MA
DONE!
Johnny's
DONE? DONE WHAT?
I ORDERED THE SEEDS. THEY'LL BE HERE IN A COUPLE OF DAYS.
WOW. JUST LIKE THAT?
YOU'VE GOT TO GET YOURSELF ONE OF THESE!

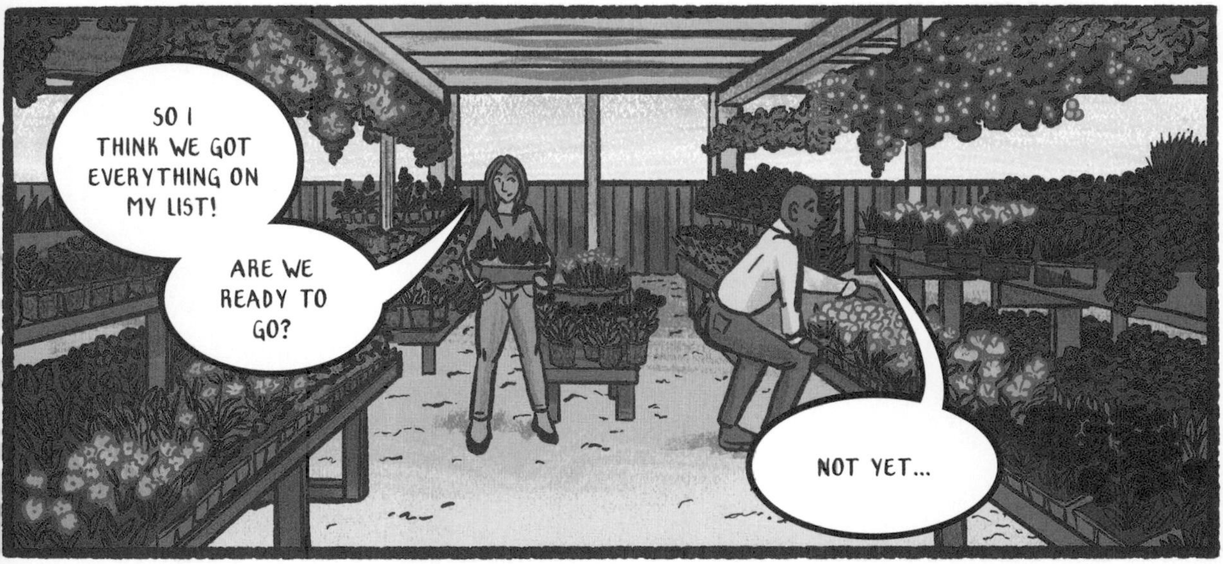
SO I THINK WE GOT EVERYTHING ON MY LIST!
ARE WE READY TO GO?
NOT YET...

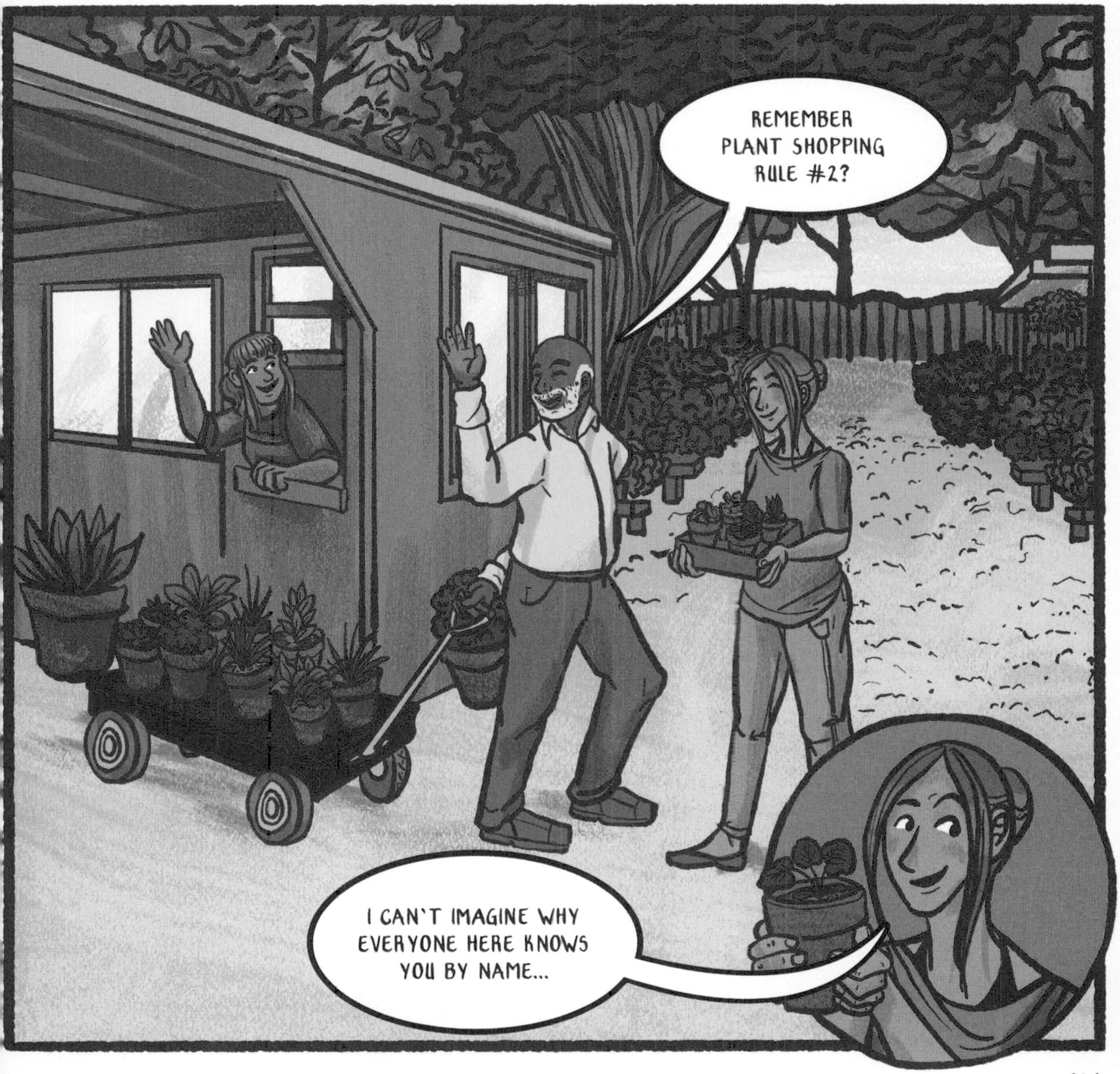
REMEMBER PLANT SHOPPING RULE #2?
I CAN'T IMAGINE WHY EVERYONE HERE KNOWS YOU BY NAME...

SEVEN:
PLANTING

THE RIGHT WAY TO PUT PLANTS IN THE GROUND.

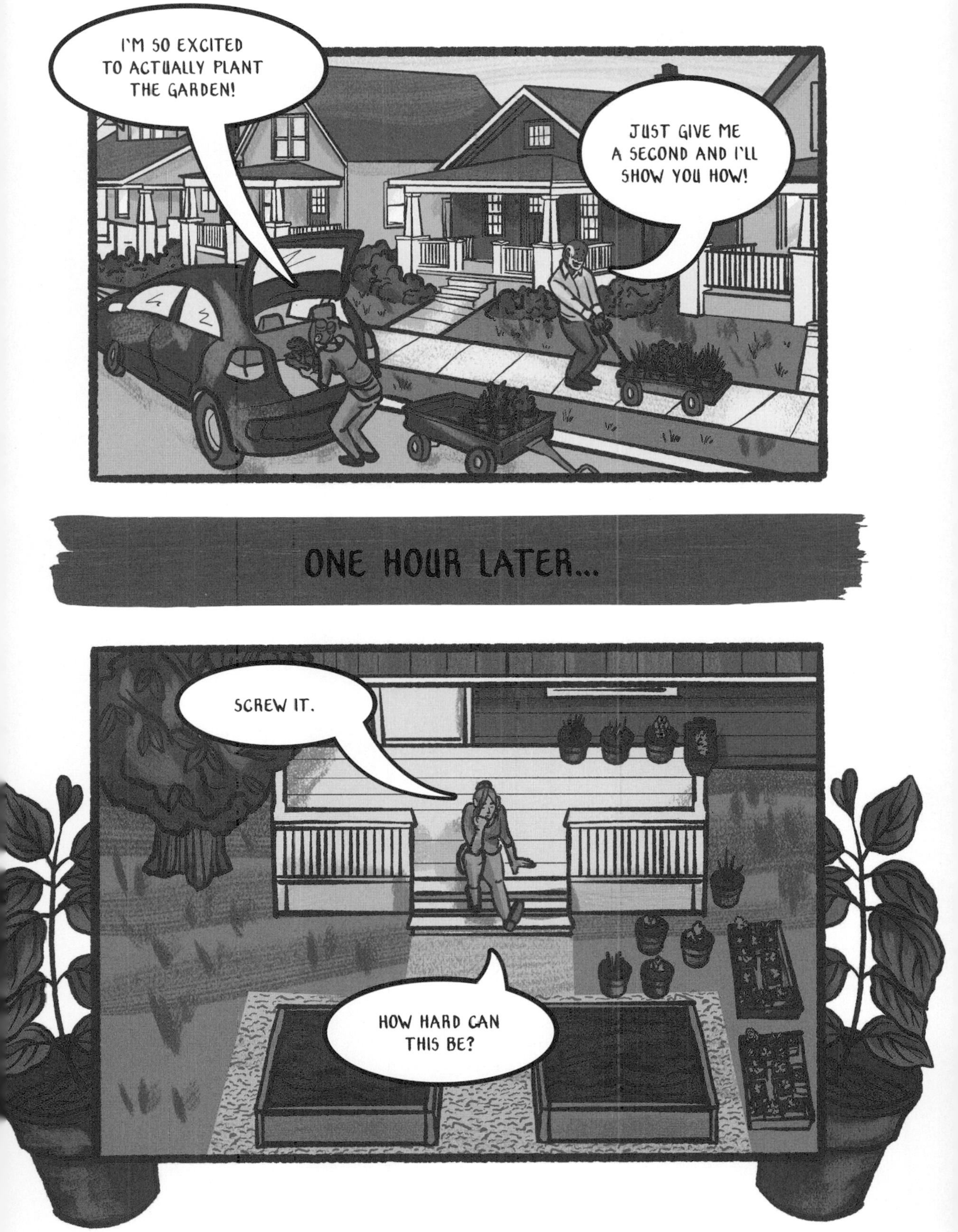
I'M SO EXCITED TO ACTUALLY PLANT THE GARDEN!
JUST GIVE ME A SECOND AND I'LL SHOW YOU HOW!
ONE HOUR LATER...
SCREW IT.
HOW HARD CAN THIS BE?

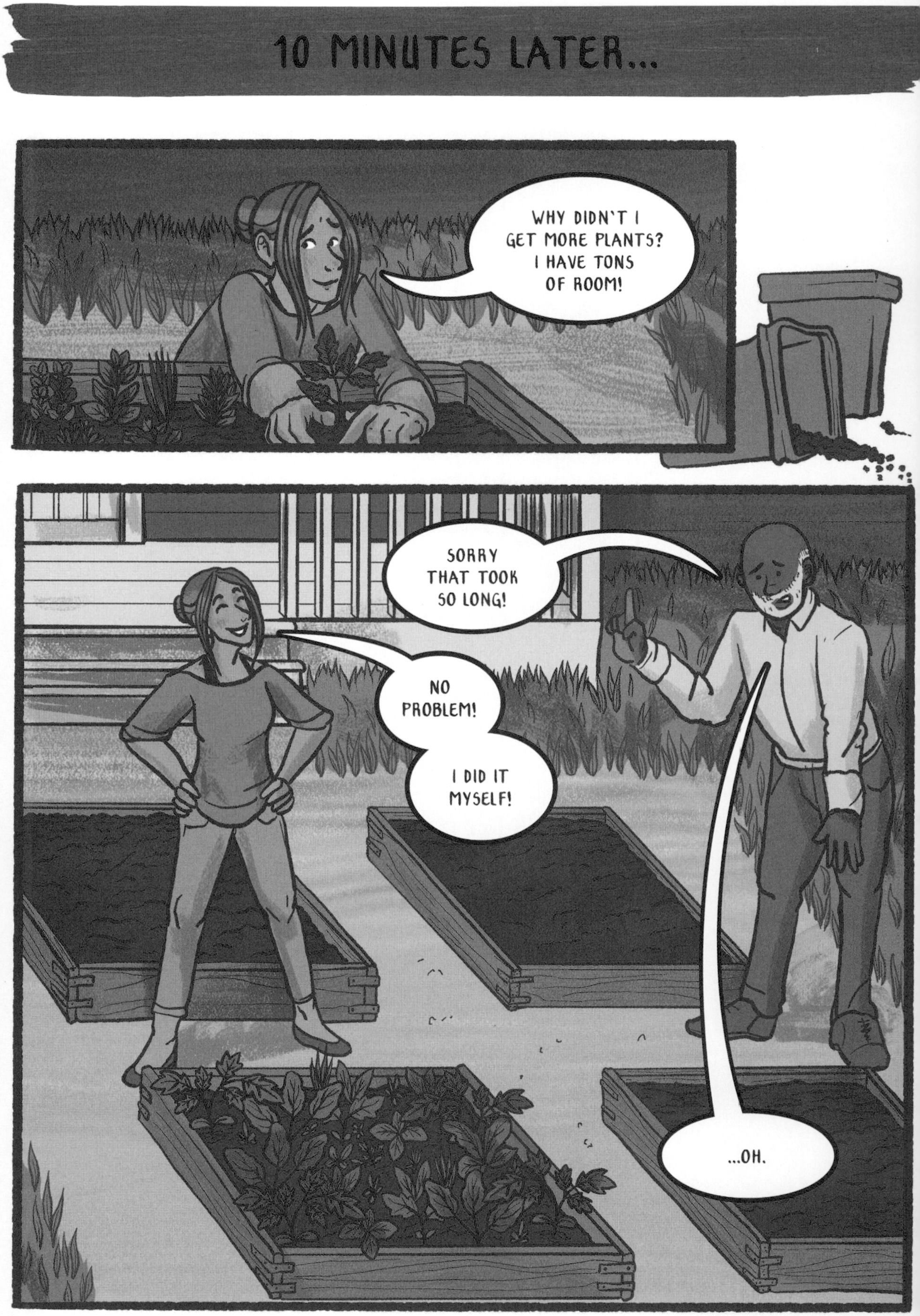
10 MINUTES LATER...
WHY DIDN'T I GET MORE PLANTS? I HAVE TONS OF ROOM!
SORRY THAT TOOK SO LONG!
NO PROBLEM!
I DID IT MYSELF!
...OH.

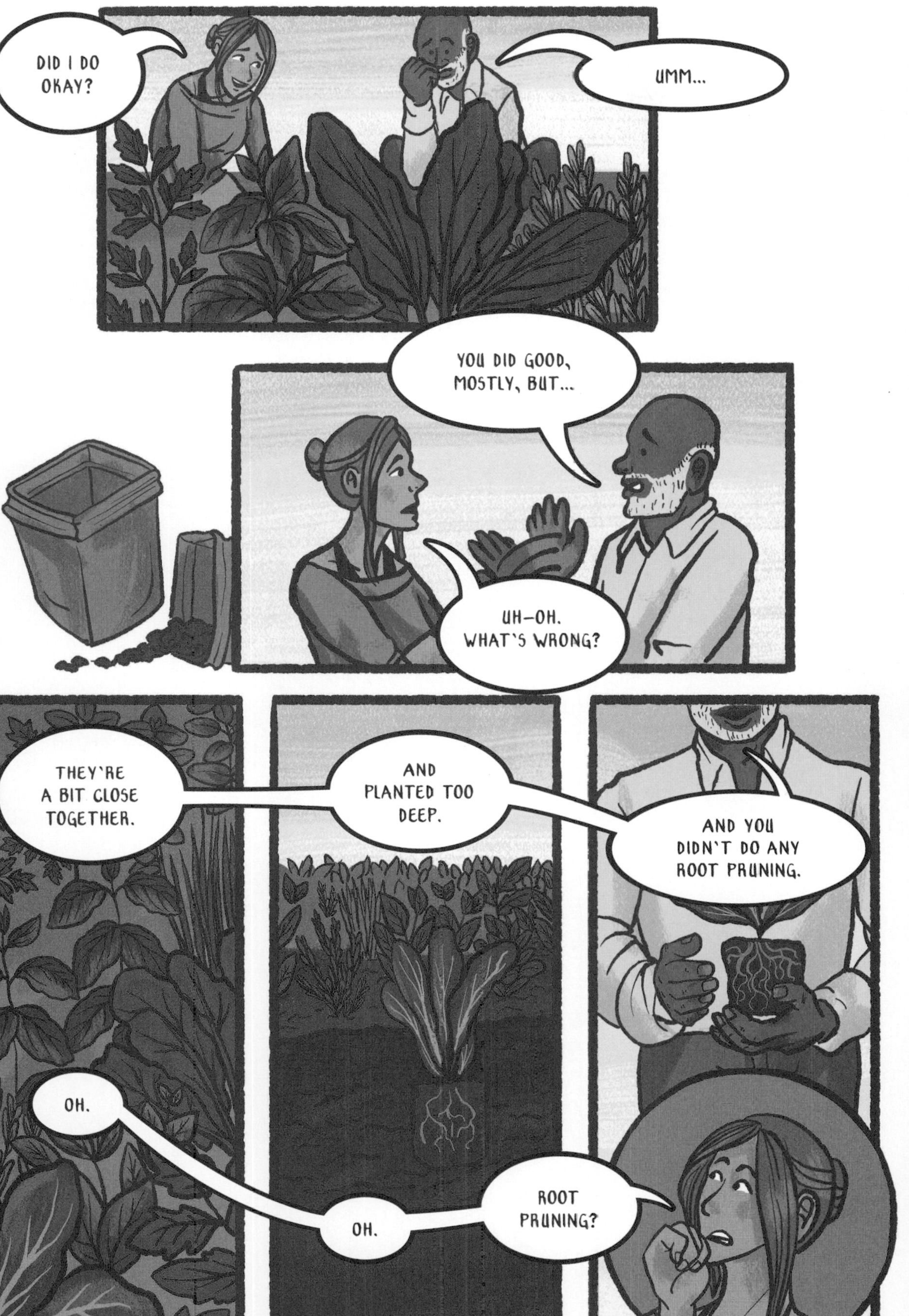
DID I DO OKAY?
UMM...
YOU DID GOOD, MOSTLY, BUT...
UH-OH. WHAT'S WRONG?
THEY'RE A BIT CLOSE TOGETHER.
AND PLANTED TOO DEEP.
AND YOU DIDN'T DO ANY ROOT PRUNING.
OH.
OH.
ROOT PRUNING?

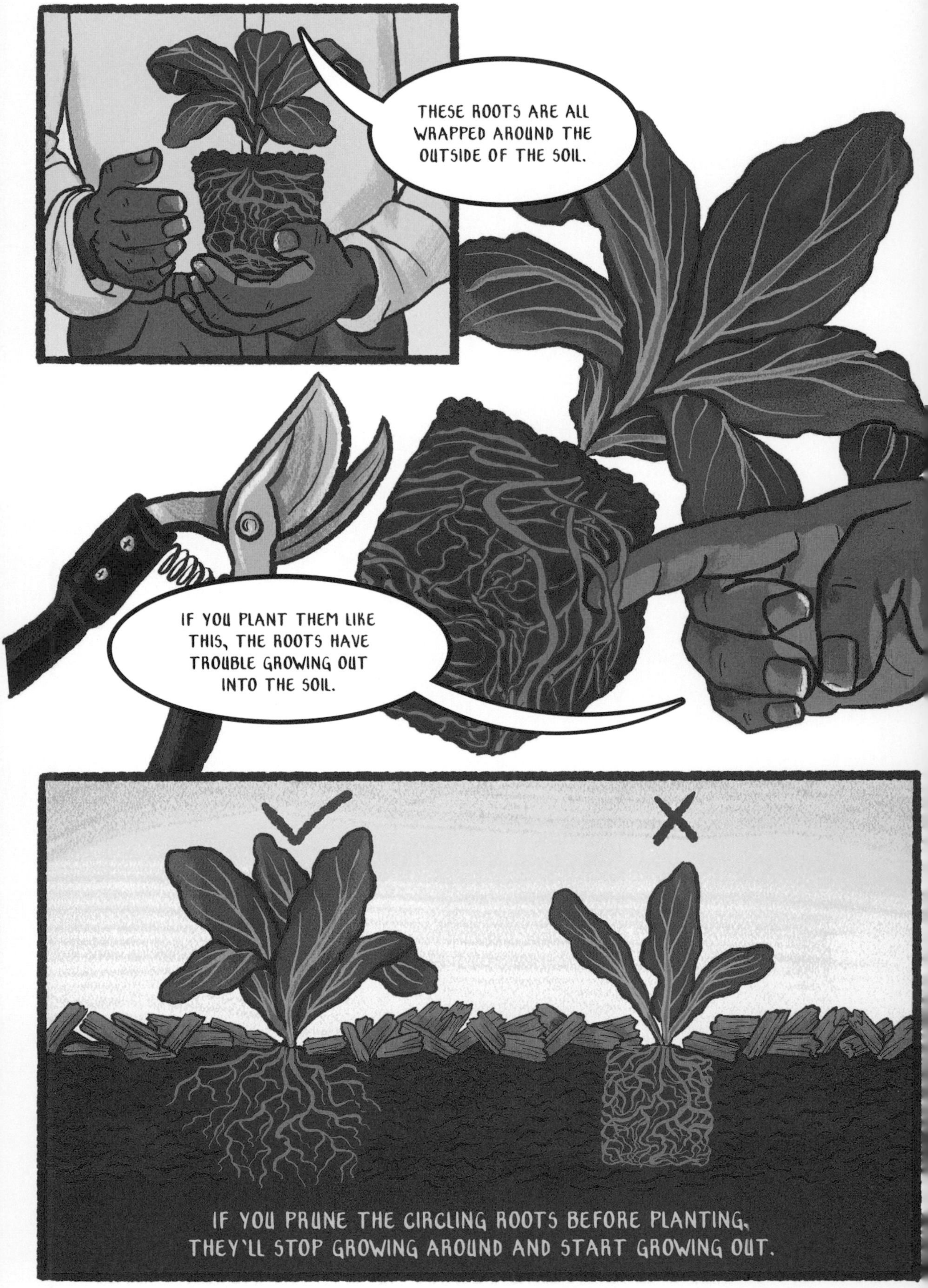
THESE ROOTS ARE ALL WRAPPED AROUND THE OUTSIDE OF THE SOIL.
IF YOU PLANT THEM LIKE THIS, THE ROOTS HAVE TROUBLE GROWING OUT INTO THE SOIL.
IF YOU PRUNE THE CIRCLING ROOTS BEFORE PLANTING, THEY'LL STOP GROWING AROUND AND START GROWING OUT.

HOW TO ROOT PRUNE

IF JUST A FEW ROOTS ARE VISIBLE, NO NEED TO ROOT PRUNE.

IF YOU SEE LOTS OF VISIBLE ROOTS, YOU NEED TO PRUNE THEM OFF.

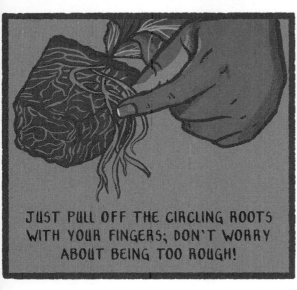

JUST PULL OFF THE CIRCLING ROOTS WITH YOUR FINGERS; DON'T WORRY ABOUT BEING TOO ROUGH!

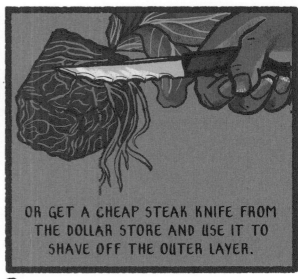

OR GET A CHEAP STEAK KNIFE FROM THE DOLLAR STORE AND USE IT TO SHAVE OFF THE OUTER LAYER.

ALL READY TO PLANT!

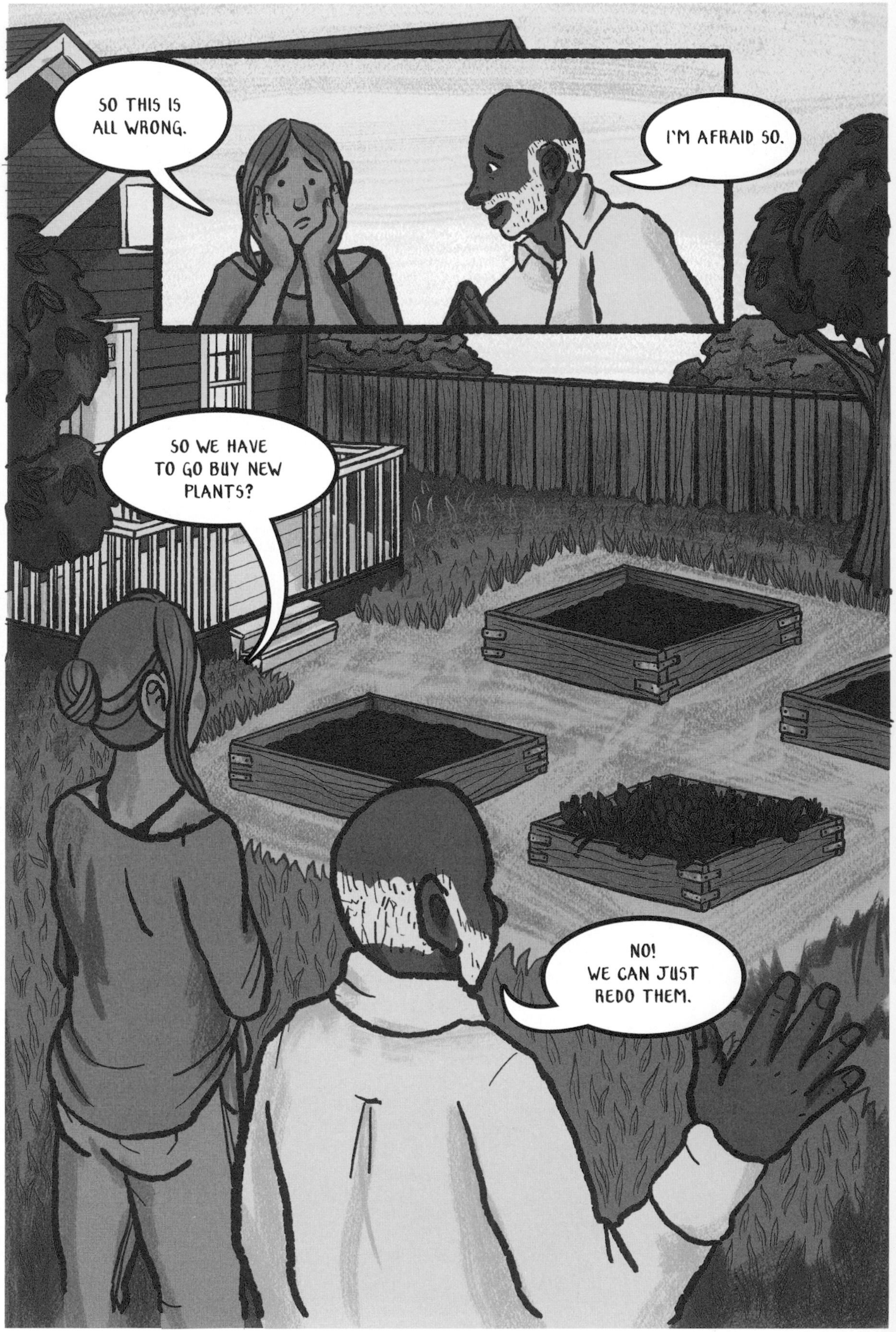
SO THIS IS ALL WRONG.
I'M AFRAID SO.
SO WE HAVE TO GO BUY NEW PLANTS?
NO! WE CAN JUST REDO THEM.

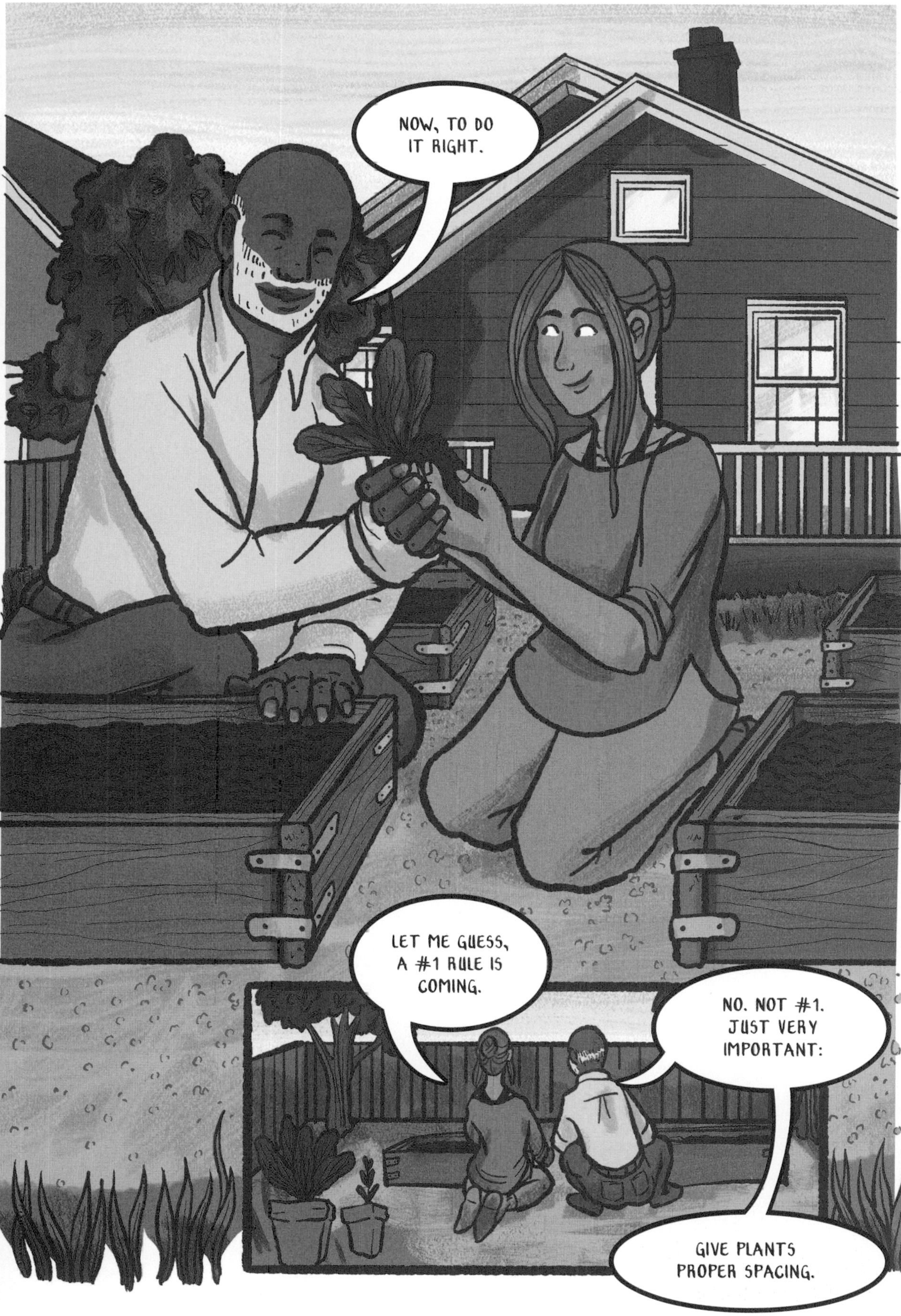
NOW, TO DO IT RIGHT.
LET ME GUESS, A #1 RULE IS COMING.
NO. NOT #1. JUST VERY IMPORTANT:
GIVE PLANTS PROPER SPACING.

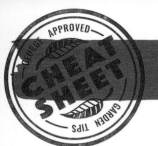

GIVE PLANTS PROPER SPACING

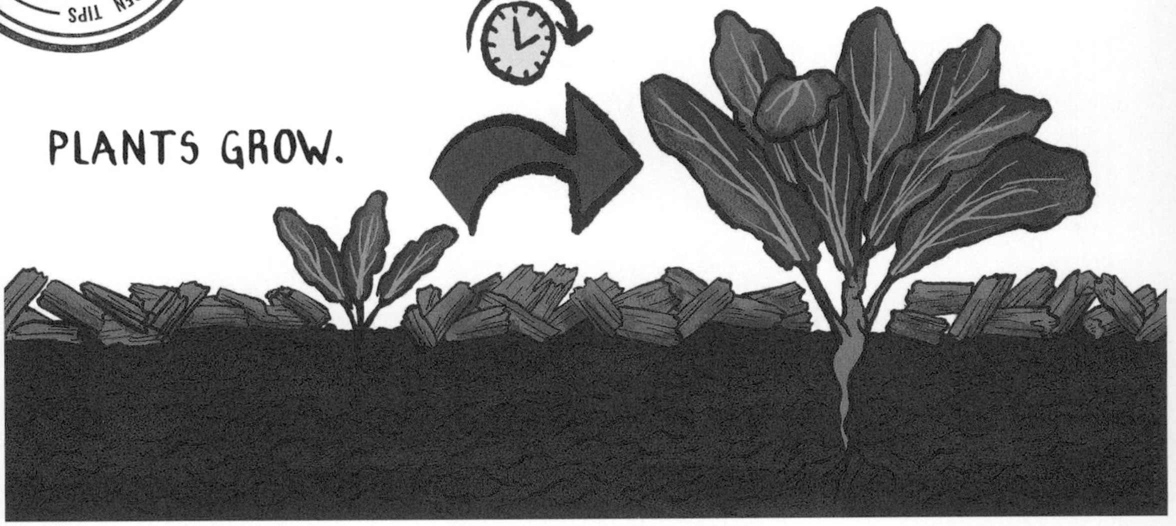
PLANTS GROW.

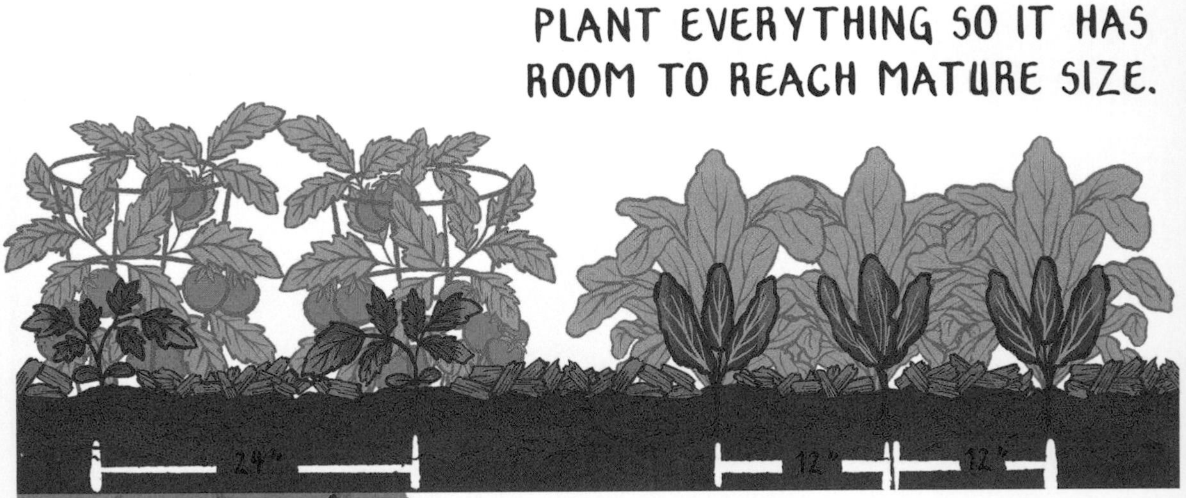
PLANT EVERYTHING SO IT HAS ROOM TO REACH MATURE SIZE.
24"
12"
12"

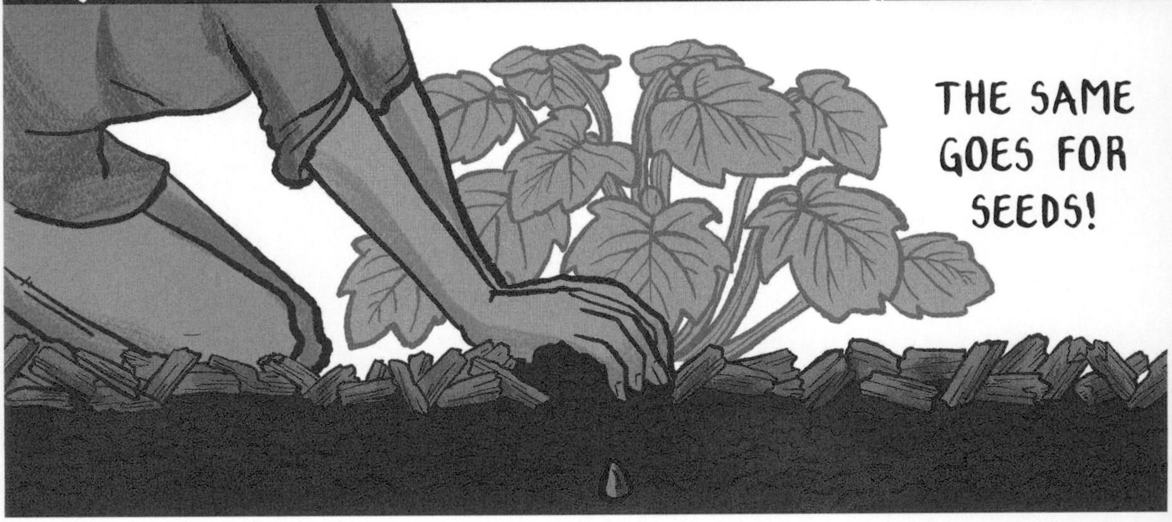
THE SAME GOES FOR SEEDS!

CHEAT SHEET

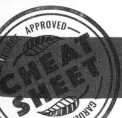

RECOMMENDED PLANT SPACINGS

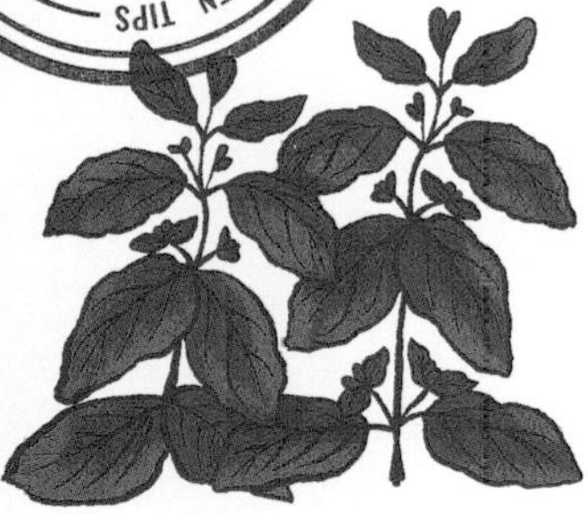
BASIL 18"

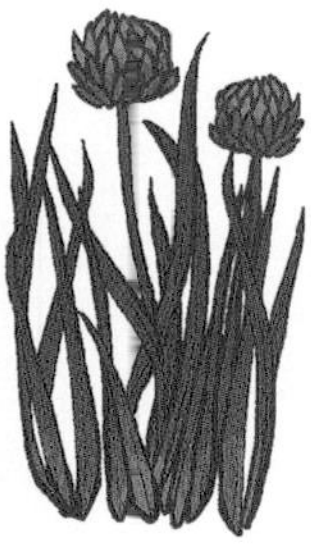
CHIVES 8"

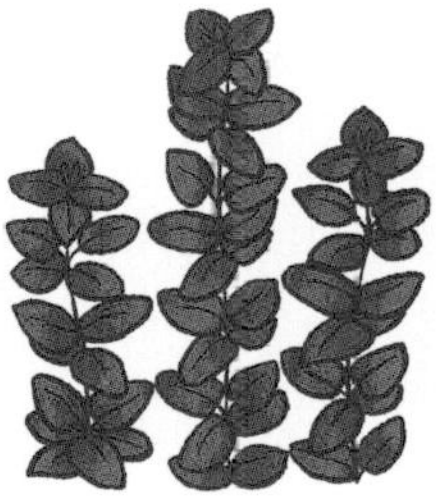
OREGANO 12"

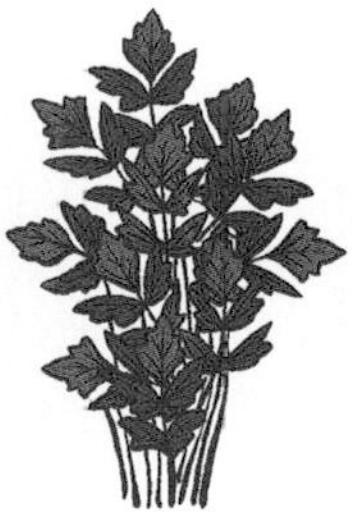
PARSLEY 8"

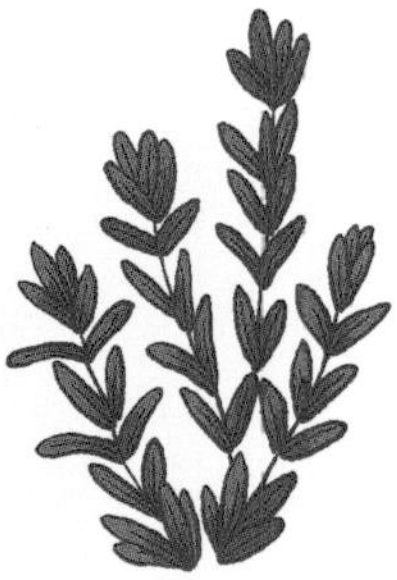
ROSEMARY 12"

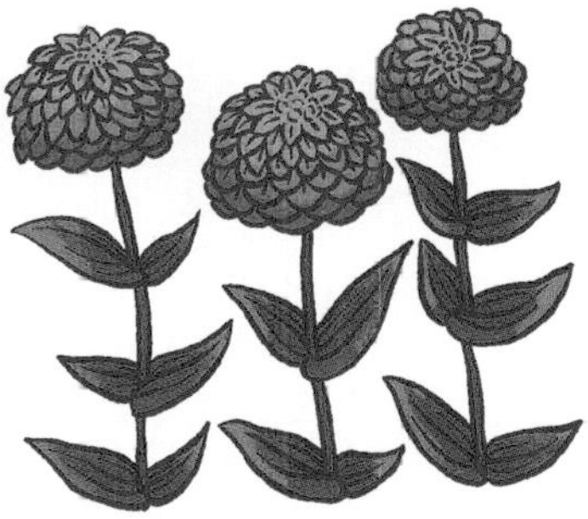
ZINNIAS 12"

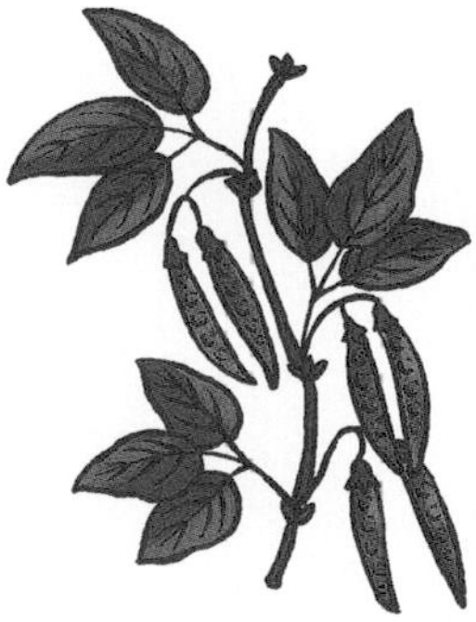
GREEN BEANS 12"

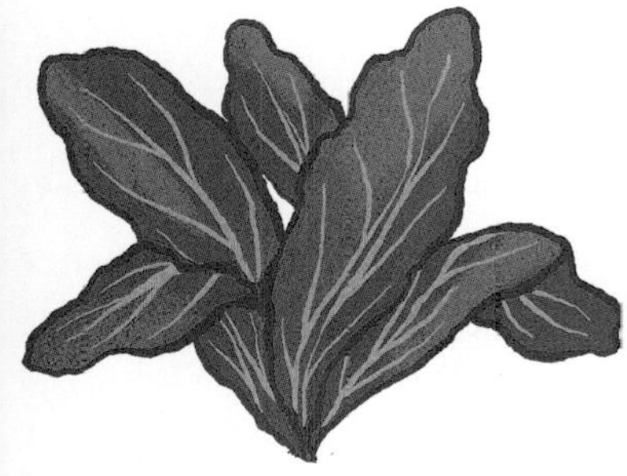
KALE 12"

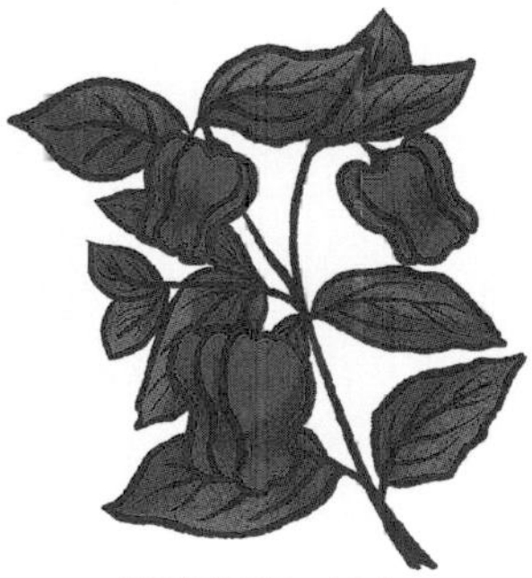
PEPPER 18"

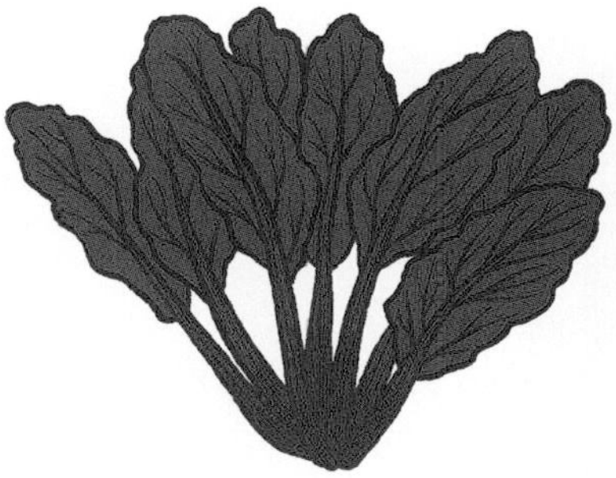
SWISS CHARD 12"

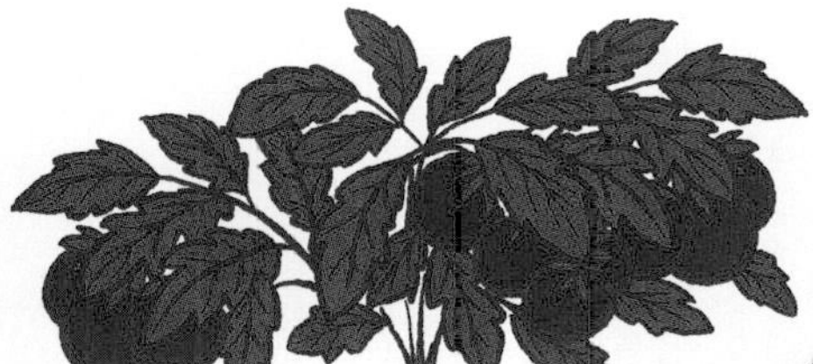
TOMATO 24"

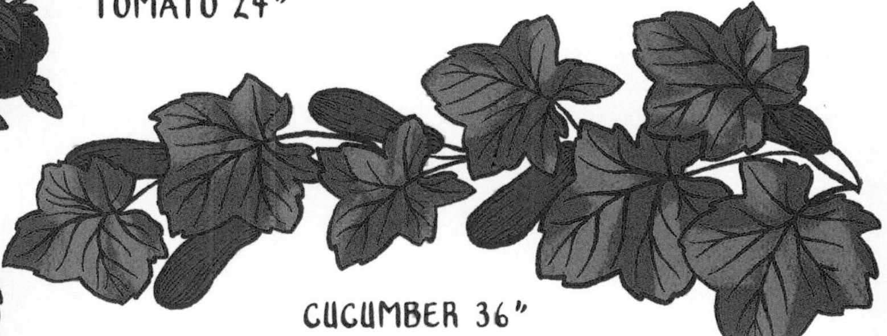
CUCUMBER 36"

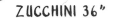

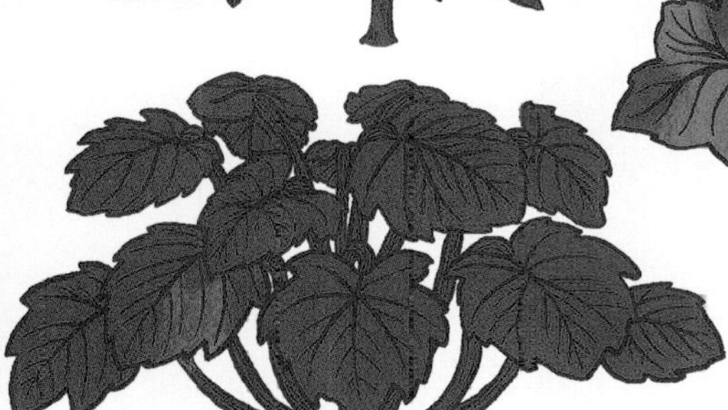
ZUCCHINI 36"

HOW TO PLANT

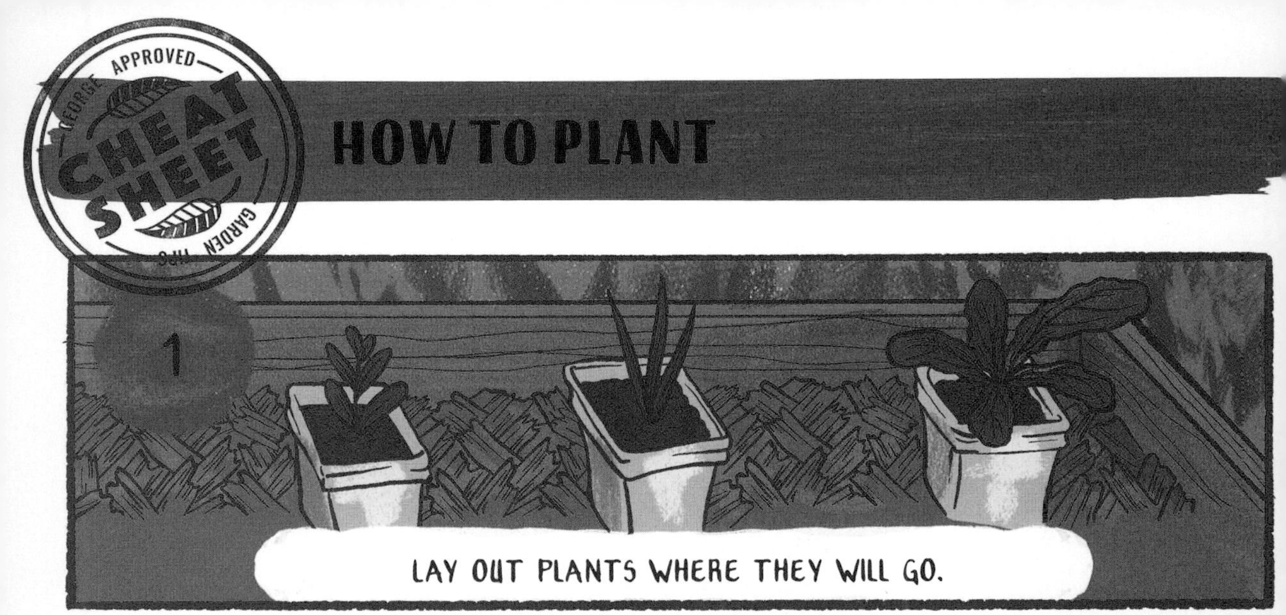
1
LAY OUT PLANTS WHERE THEY WILL GO.

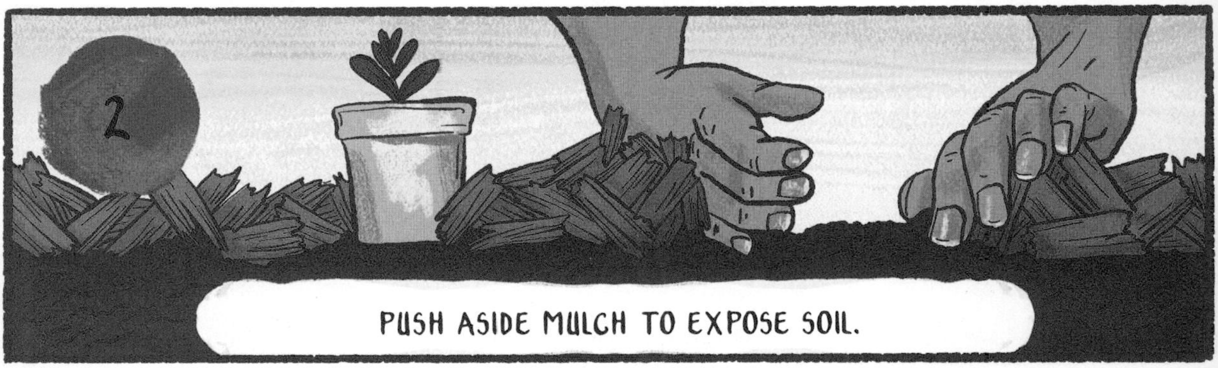
2
PUSH ASIDE MULCH TO EXPOSE SOIL.

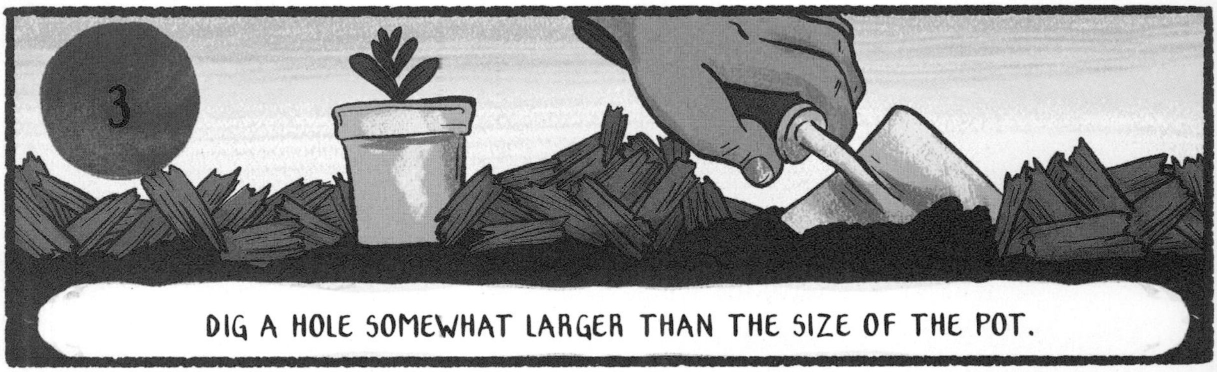
3
DIG A HOLE SOMEWHAT LARGER THAN THE SIZE OF THE POT.

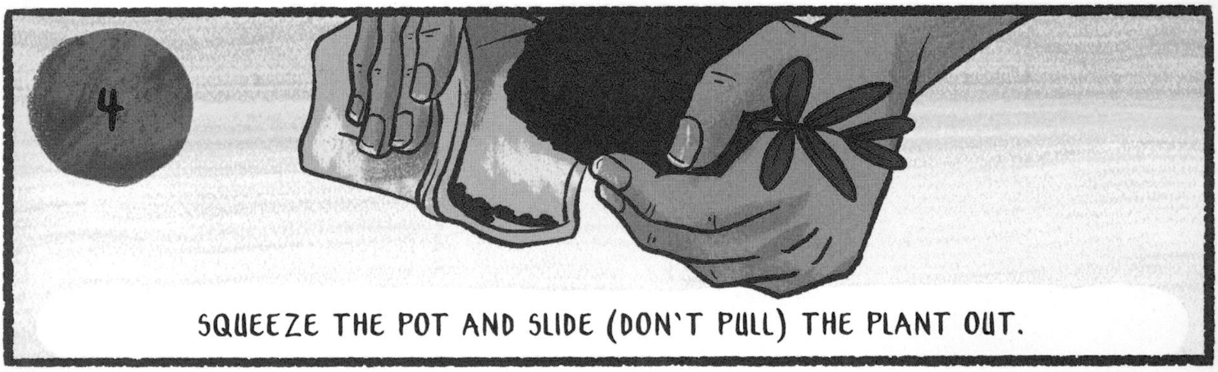
4
SQUEEZE THE POT AND SLIDE (DON'T PULL) THE PLANT OUT.

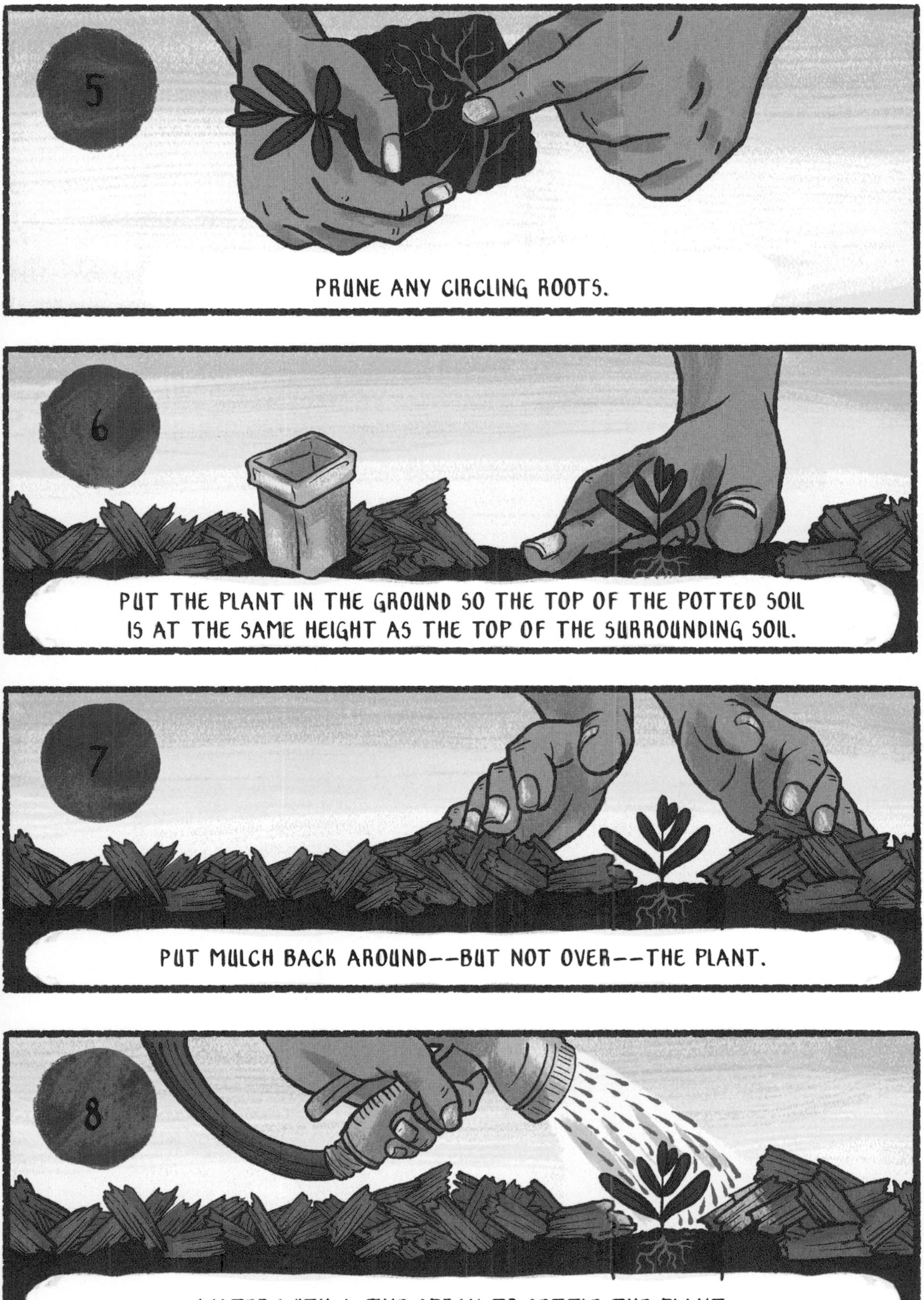
5
PRUNE ANY CIRCLING ROOTS.
6
PUT THE PLANT IN THE GROUND SO THE TOP OF THE POTTED SOIL IS AT THE SAME HEIGHT AS THE TOP OF THE SURROUNDING SOIL.
7
PUT MULCH BACK AROUND--BUT NOT OVER--THE PLANT.
8
WATER WITH A FINE SPRAY TO SETTLE THE PLANT.

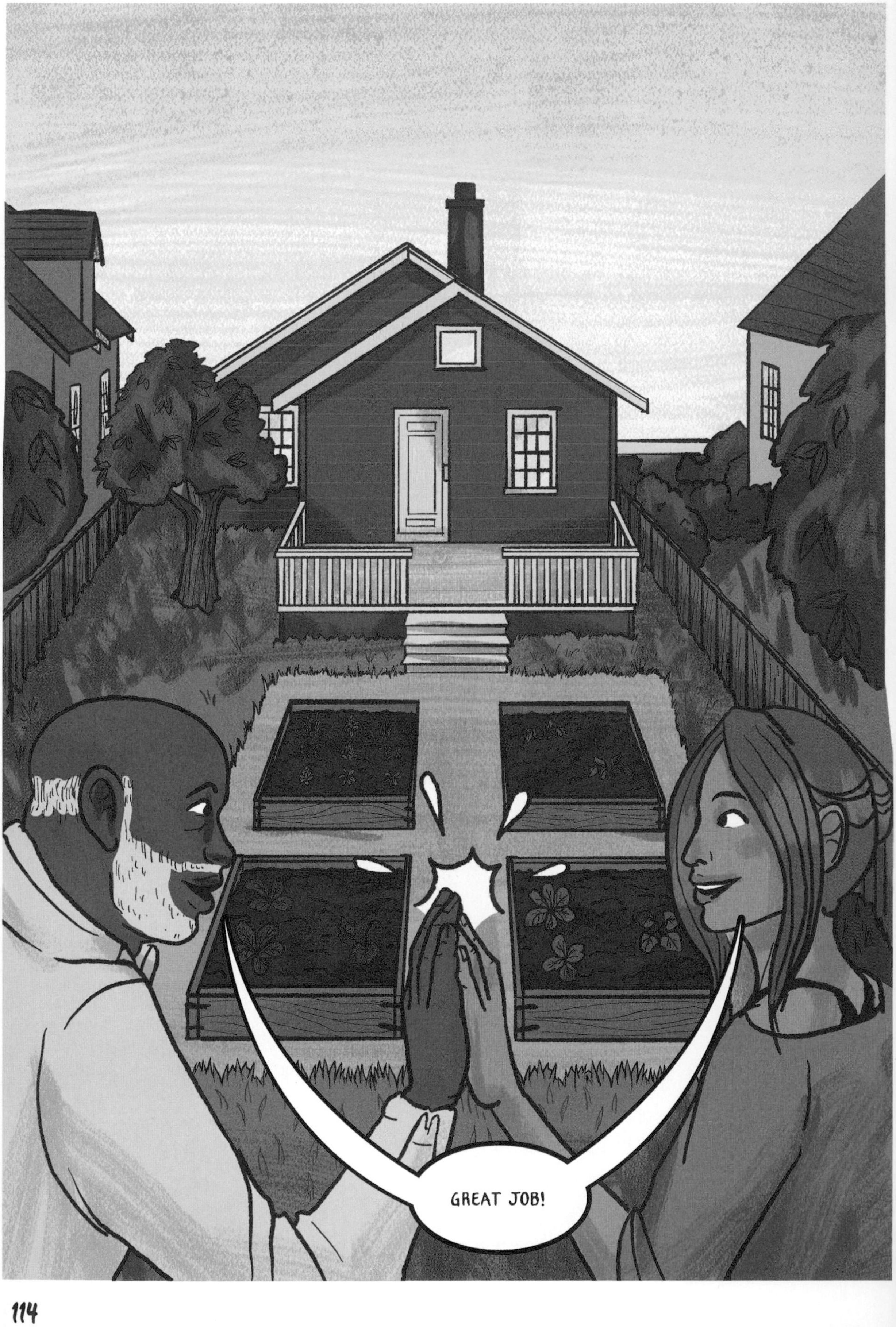
GREAT JOB!

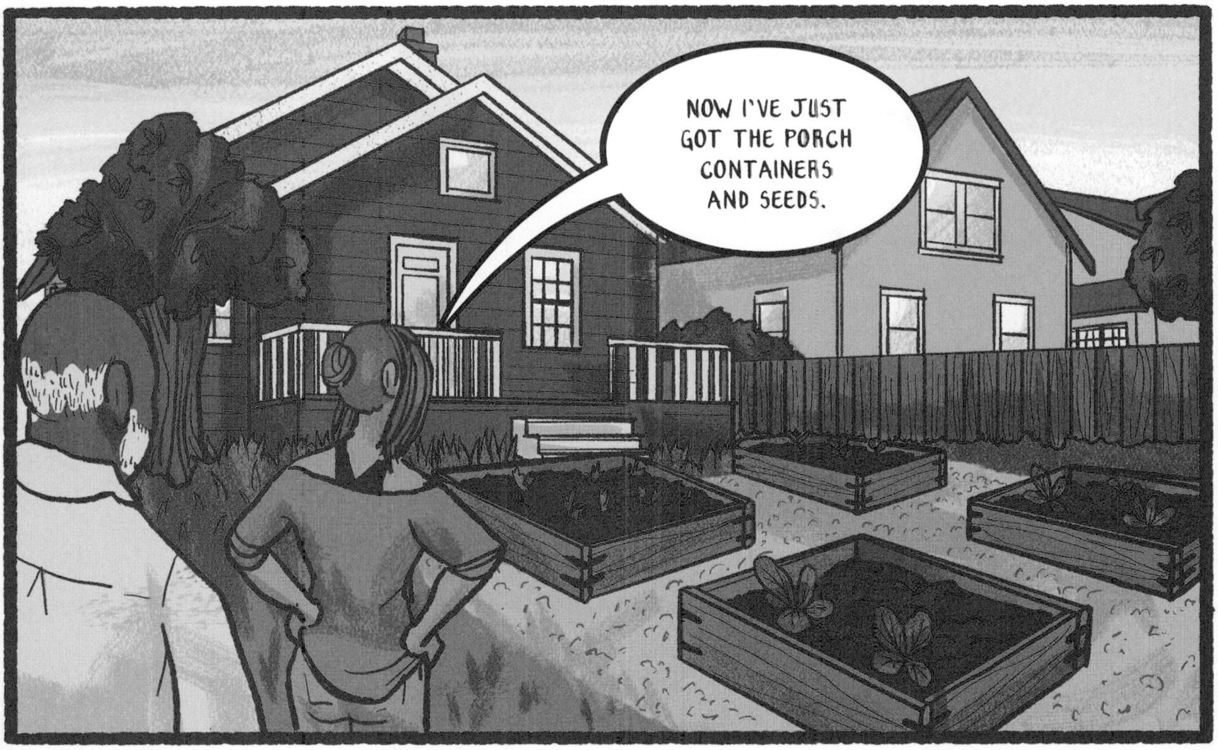
NOW I'VE JUST GOT THE PORCH CONTAINERS AND SEEDS.

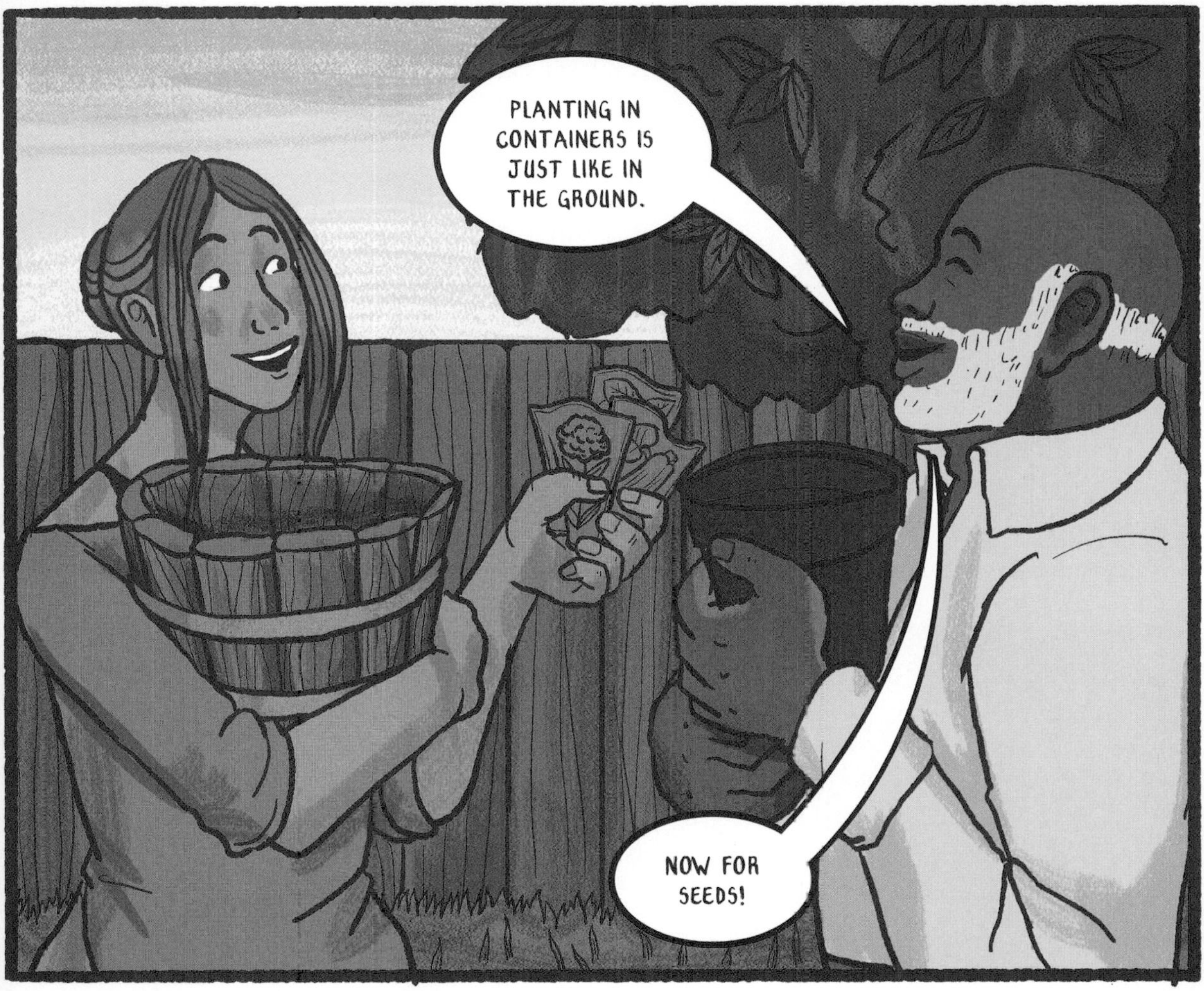
PLANTING IN CONTAINERS IS JUST LIKE IN THE GROUND.
NOW FOR SEEDS!

GEORGE APPROVED CHEAT SHEET GARDEN TIPS

HOW TO SOW SEEDS

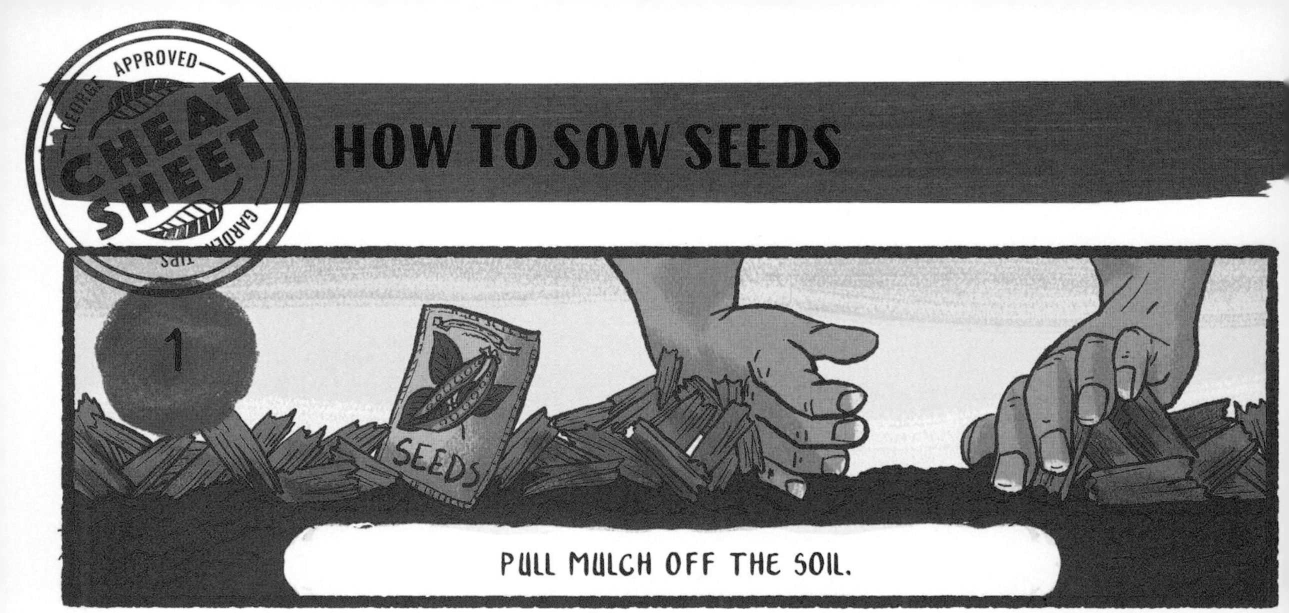
1
SEEDS
PULL MULCH OFF THE SOIL.

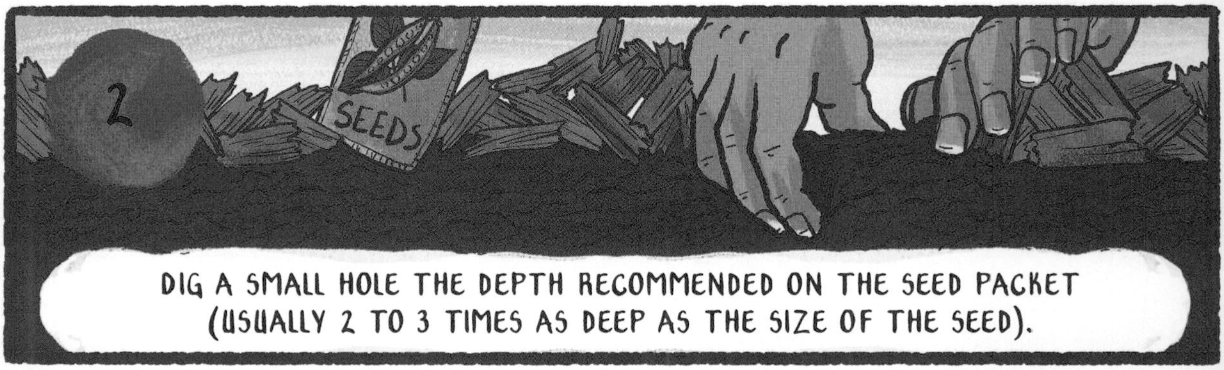
2
SEEDS
DIG A SMALL HOLE THE DEPTH RECOMMENDED ON THE SEED PACKET (USUALLY 2 TO 3 TIMES AS DEEP AS THE SIZE OF THE SEED).

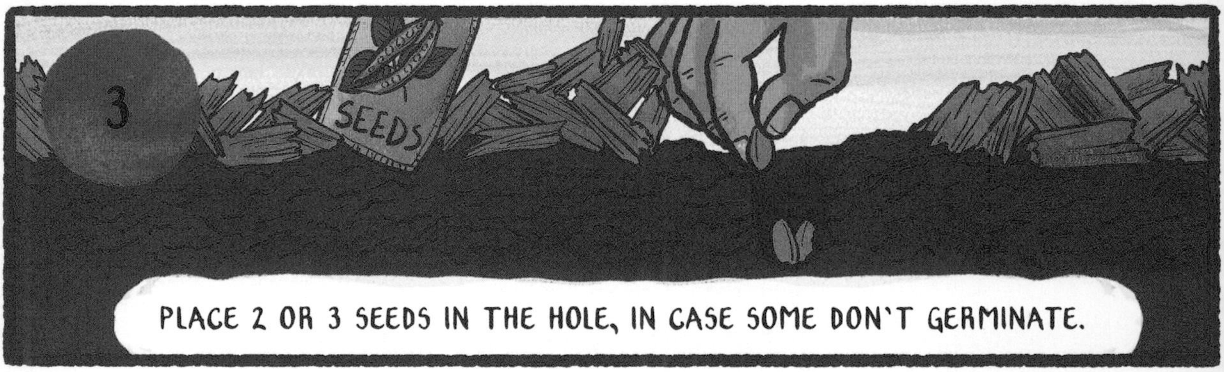
3
SEEDS
PLACE 2 OR 3 SEEDS IN THE HOLE, IN CASE SOME DON'T GERMINATE.

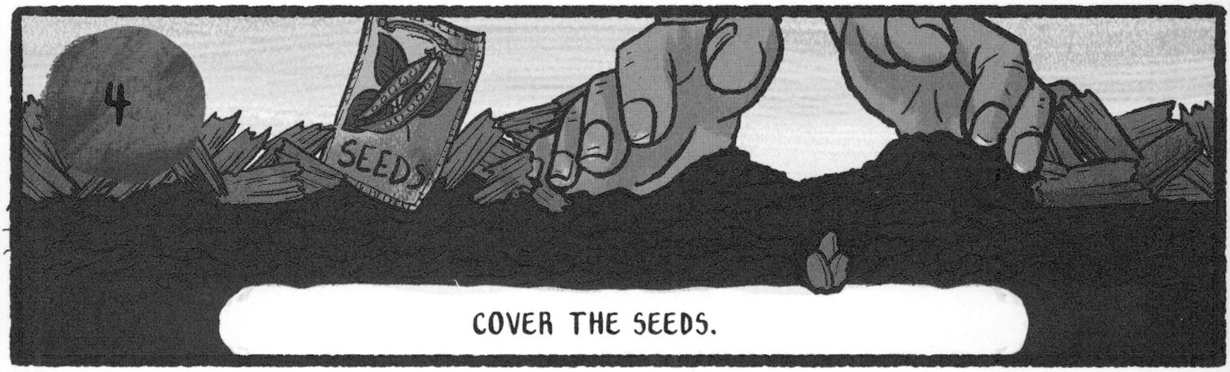
4
SEEDS
COVER THE SEEDS.

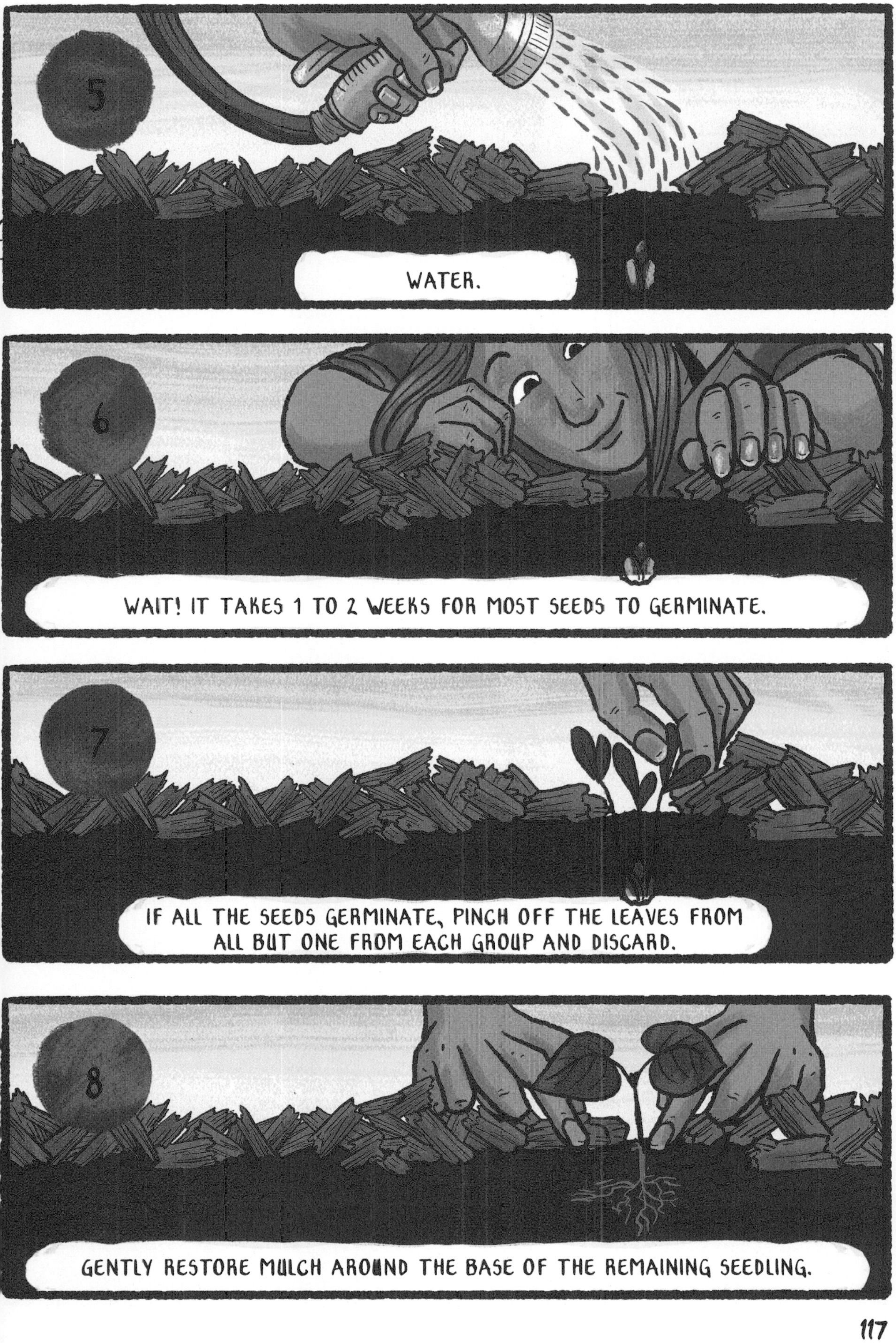
5
WATER.
6
WAIT! IT TAKES 1 TO 2 WEEKS FOR MOST SEEDS TO GERMINATE.
7
IF ALL THE SEEDS GERMINATE, PINCH OFF THE LEAVES FROM ALL BUT ONE FROM EACH GROUP AND DISCARD.
8
GENTLY RESTORE MULCH AROUND THE BASE OF THE REMAINING SEEDLING.

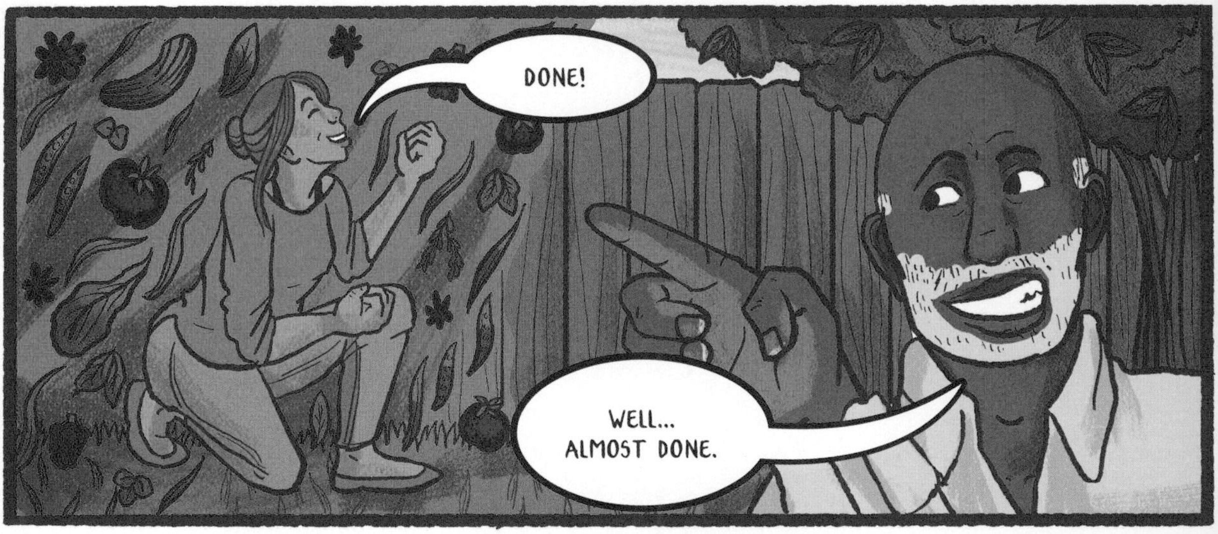
DONE!
WELL... ALMOST DONE.

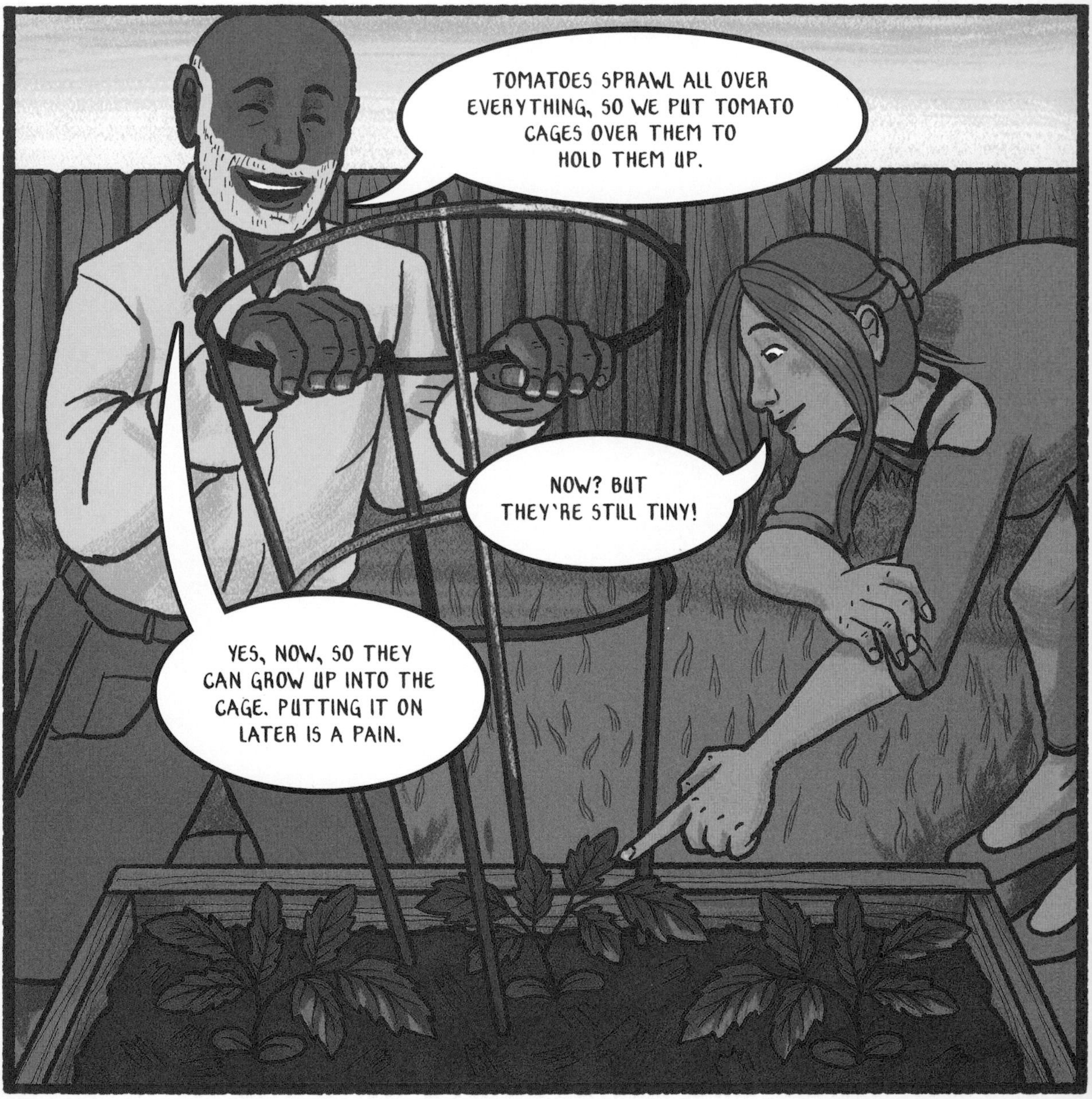
TOMATOES SPRAWL ALL OVER EVERYTHING, SO WE PUT TOMATO CAGES OVER THEM TO HOLD THEM UP.
NOW? BUT THEY'RE STILL TINY!
YES, NOW, SO THEY CAN GROW UP INTO THE CAGE. PUTTING IT ON LATER IS A PAIN.

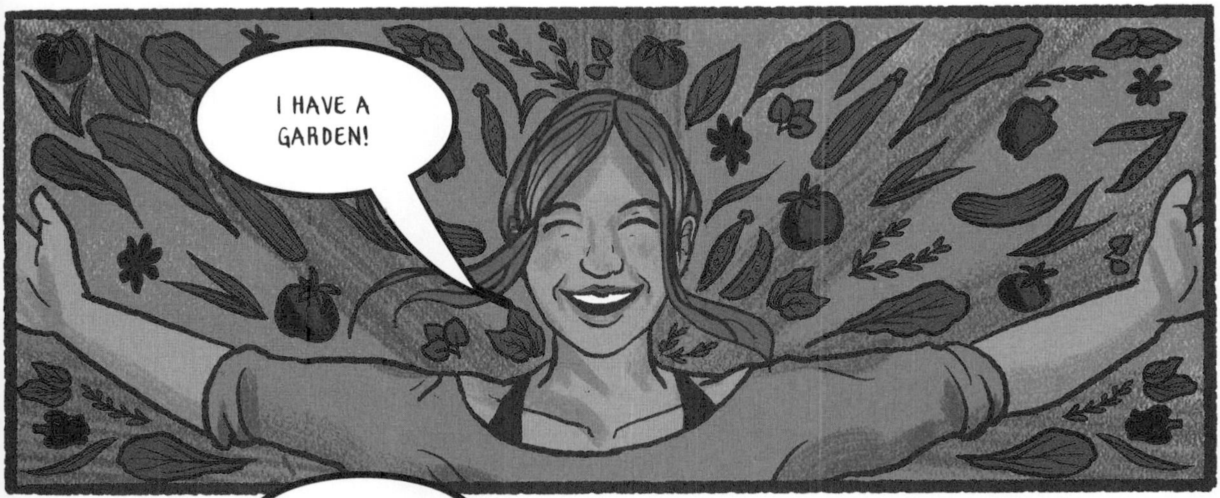
I HAVE A GARDEN!

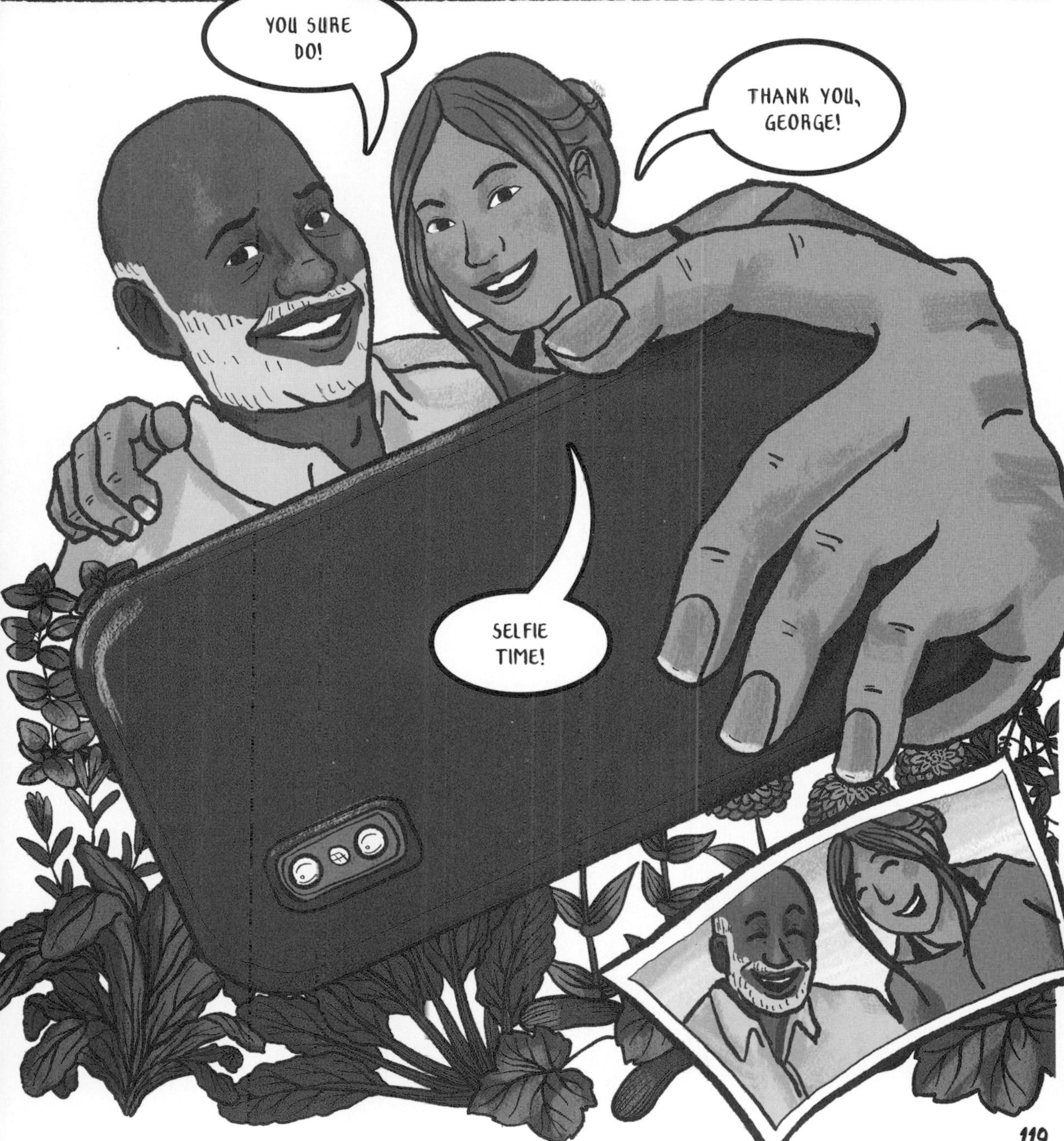
YOU SURE DO!
THANK YOU, GEORGE!
SELFIE TIME!

EIGHT:
MAINTAINING AND TROUBLESHOOTING

WEEKLY CHORES AND WHAT TO DO WHEN THINGS GO WRONG.

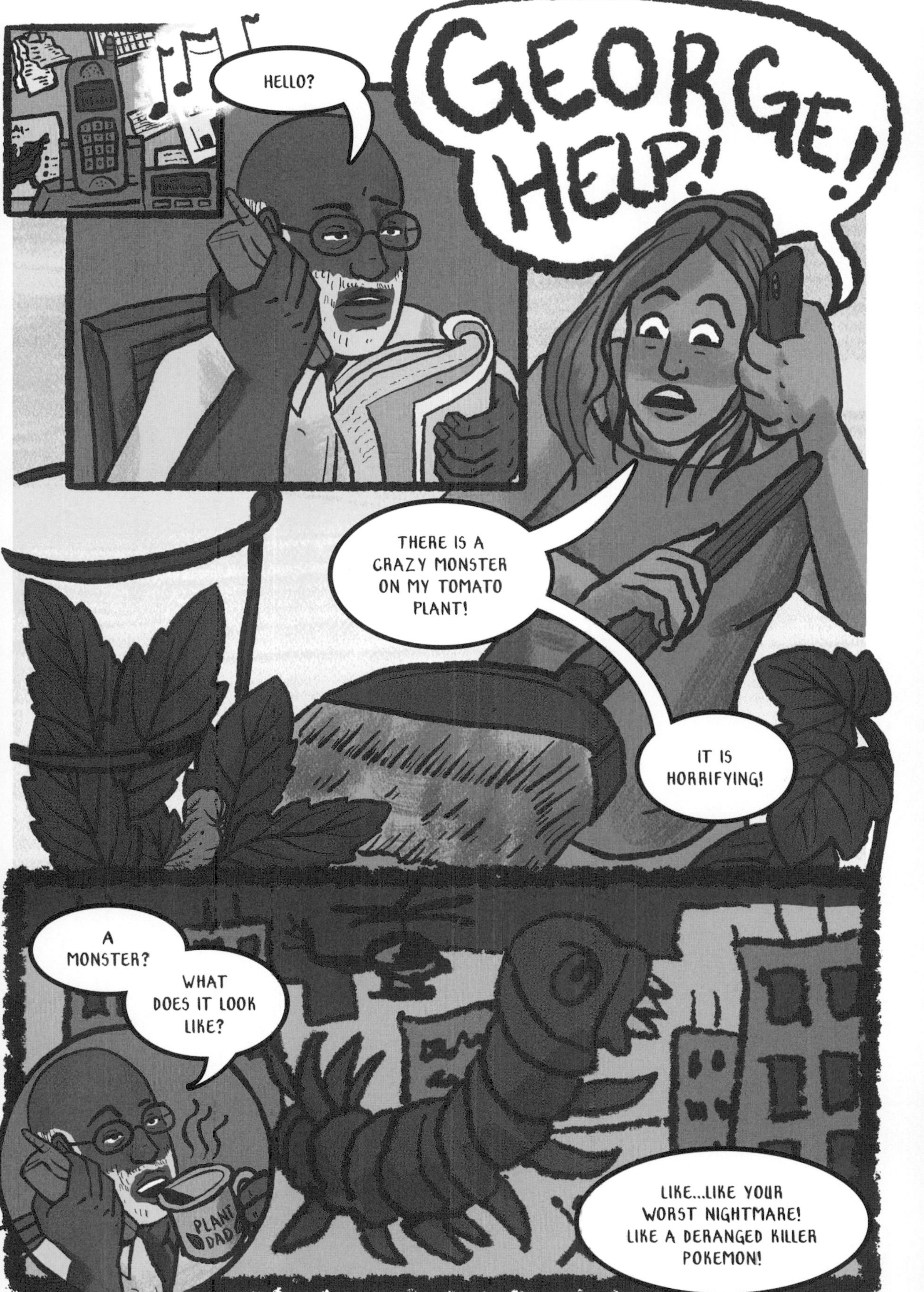
HELLO?
GEORGE HELP!
THERE IS A CRAZY MONSTER ON MY TOMATO PLANT!
IT IS HORRIFYING!
A MONSTER?
WHAT DOES IT LOOK LIKE?
PLANT DAD
LIKE...LIKE YOUR WORST NIGHTMARE! LIKE A DERANGED KILLER POKEMON!

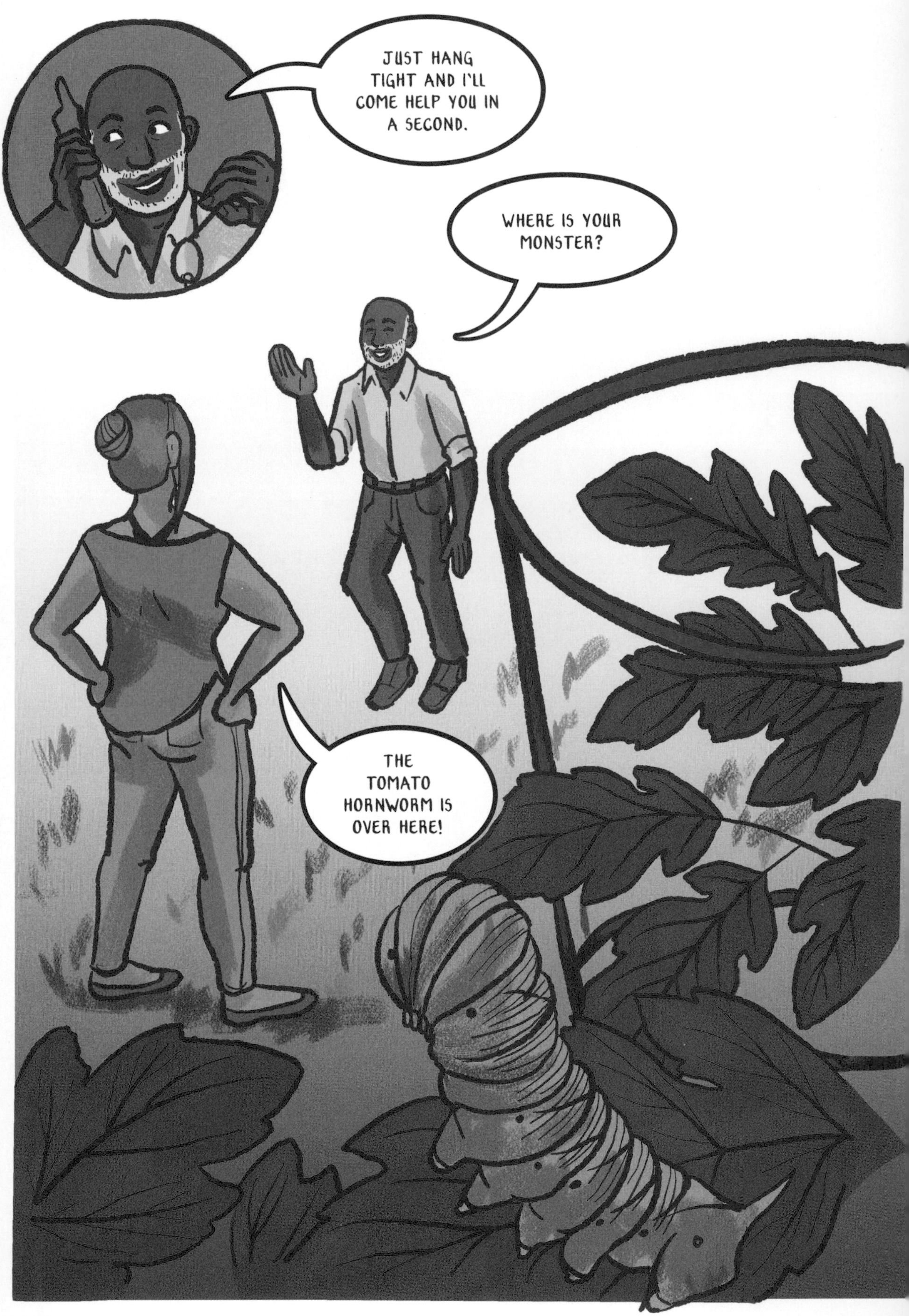
JUST HANG TIGHT AND I'LL COME HELP YOU IN A SECOND.
WHERE IS YOUR MONSTER?
THE TOMATO HORNWORM IS OVER HERE!

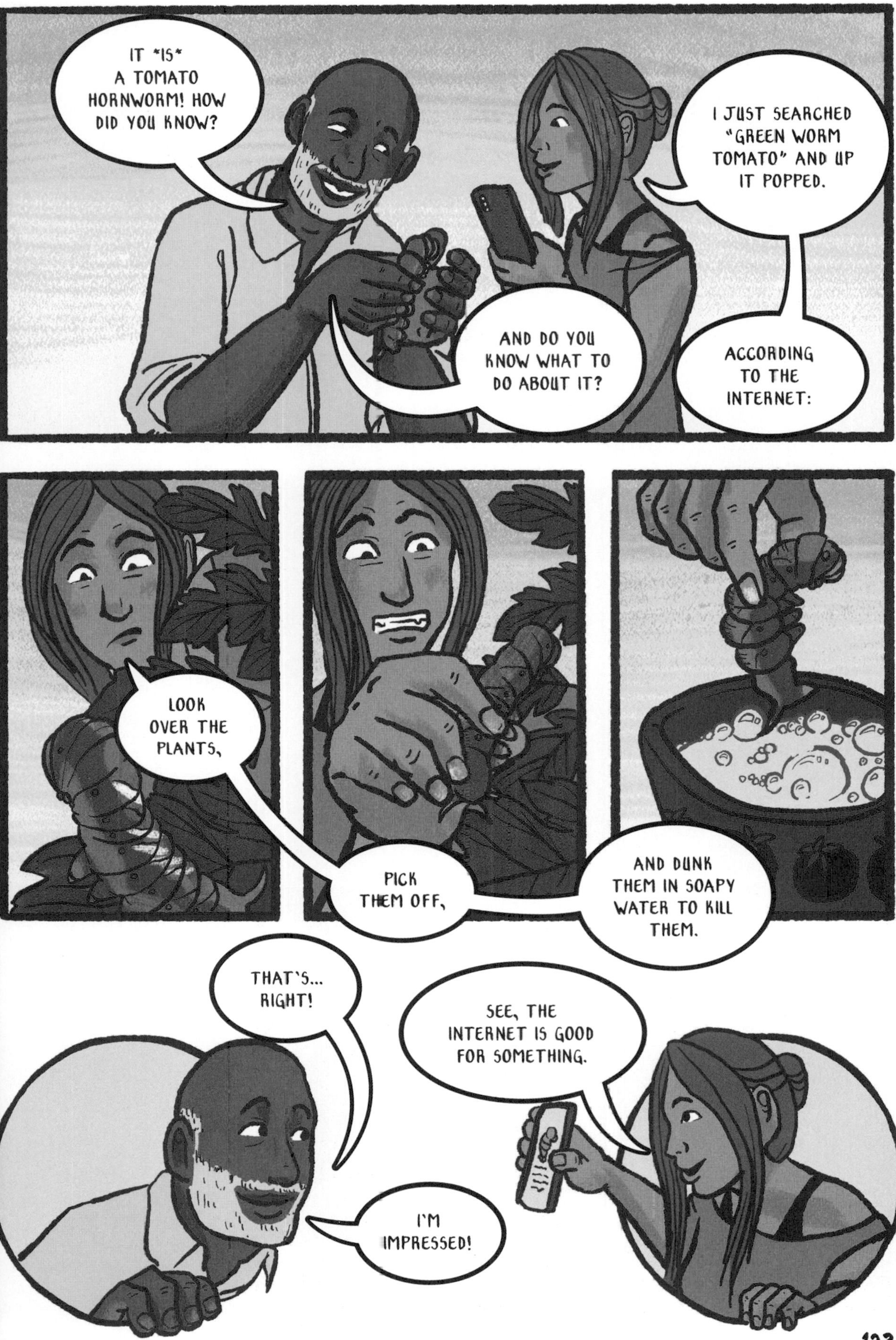
IT *IS* A TOMATO HORNWORM! HOW DID YOU KNOW?
I JUST SEARCHED "GREEN WORM TOMATO" AND UP IT POPPED.
AND DO YOU KNOW WHAT TO DO ABOUT IT?
ACCORDING TO THE INTERNET:
LOOK OVER THE PLANTS,
PICK THEM OFF,
AND DUNK THEM IN SOAPY WATER TO KILL THEM.
THAT'S... RIGHT!
I'M IMPRESSED!
SEE, THE INTERNET IS GOOD FOR SOMETHING.

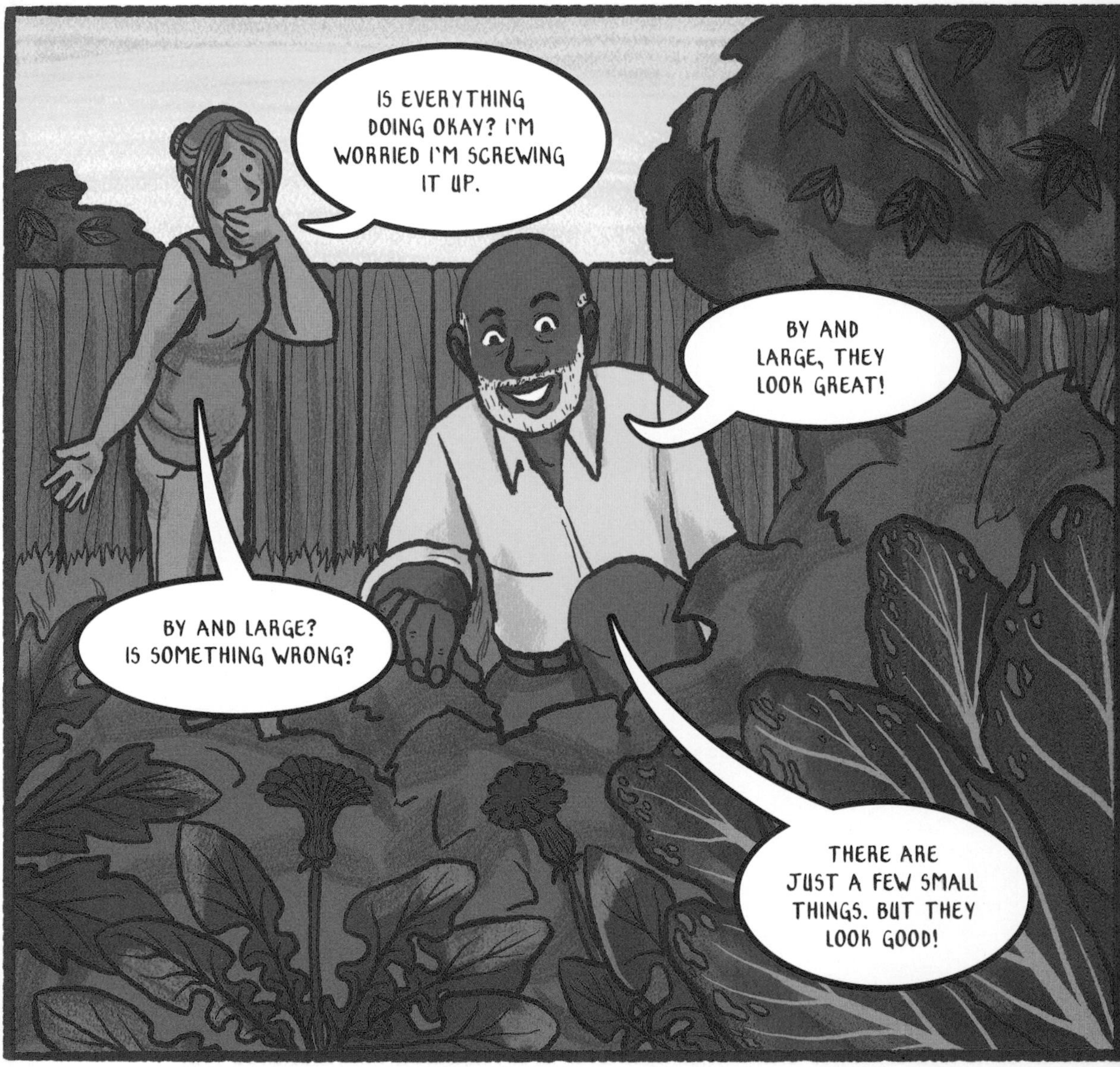
IS EVERYTHING DOING OKAY? I'M WORRIED I'M SCREWING IT UP.
BY AND LARGE, THEY LOOK GREAT!
BY AND LARGE? IS SOMETHING WRONG?
THERE ARE JUST A FEW SMALL THINGS. BUT THEY LOOK GOOD!

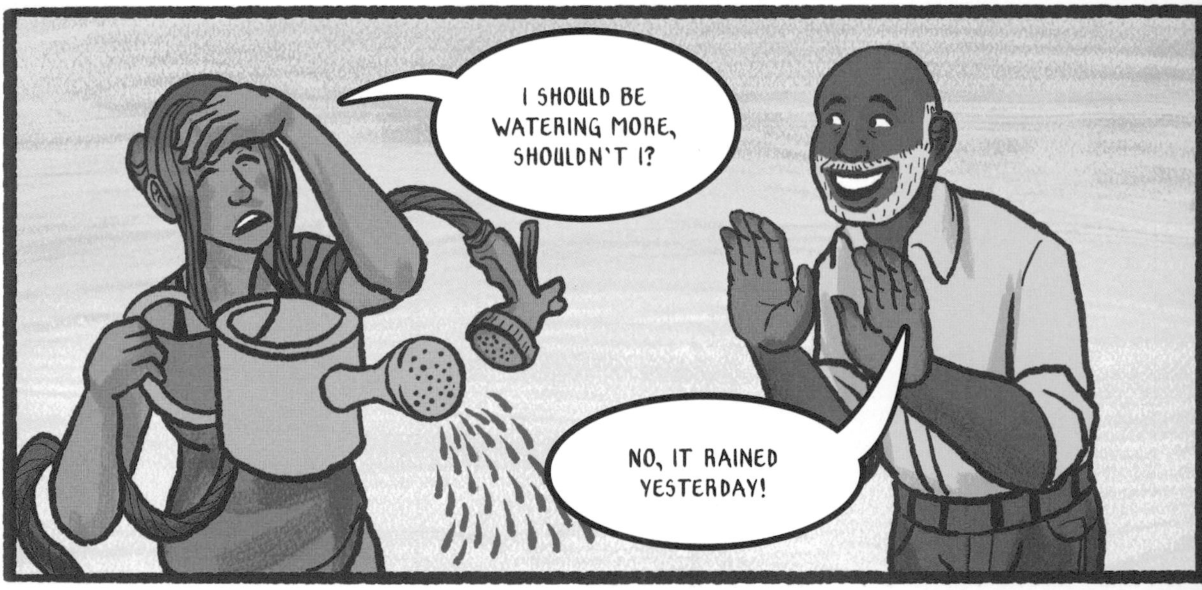
I SHOULD BE WATERING MORE, SHOULDN'T I?
NO, IT RAINED YESTERDAY!

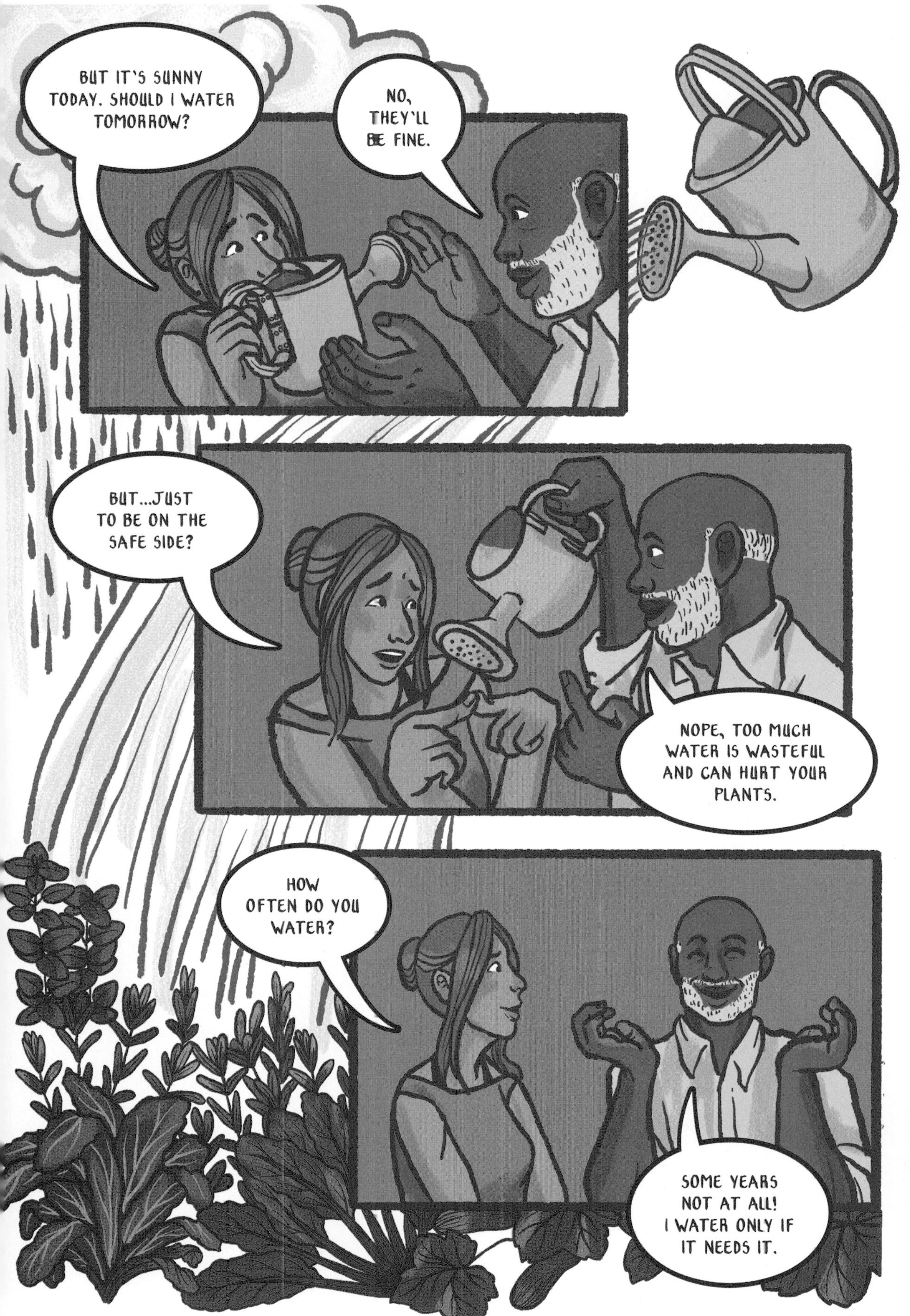
BUT IT'S SUNNY TODAY. SHOULD I WATER TOMORROW?
NO, THEY'LL BE FINE.
BUT...JUST TO BE ON THE SAFE SIDE?
NOPE, TOO MUCH WATER IS WASTEFUL AND CAN HURT YOUR PLANTS.
HOW OFTEN DO YOU WATER?
SOME YEARS NOT AT ALL! I WATER ONLY IF IT NEEDS IT.

GEORGE APPROVED CHEAT SHEET GARDEN TIPS

DO YOU NEED TO WATER?

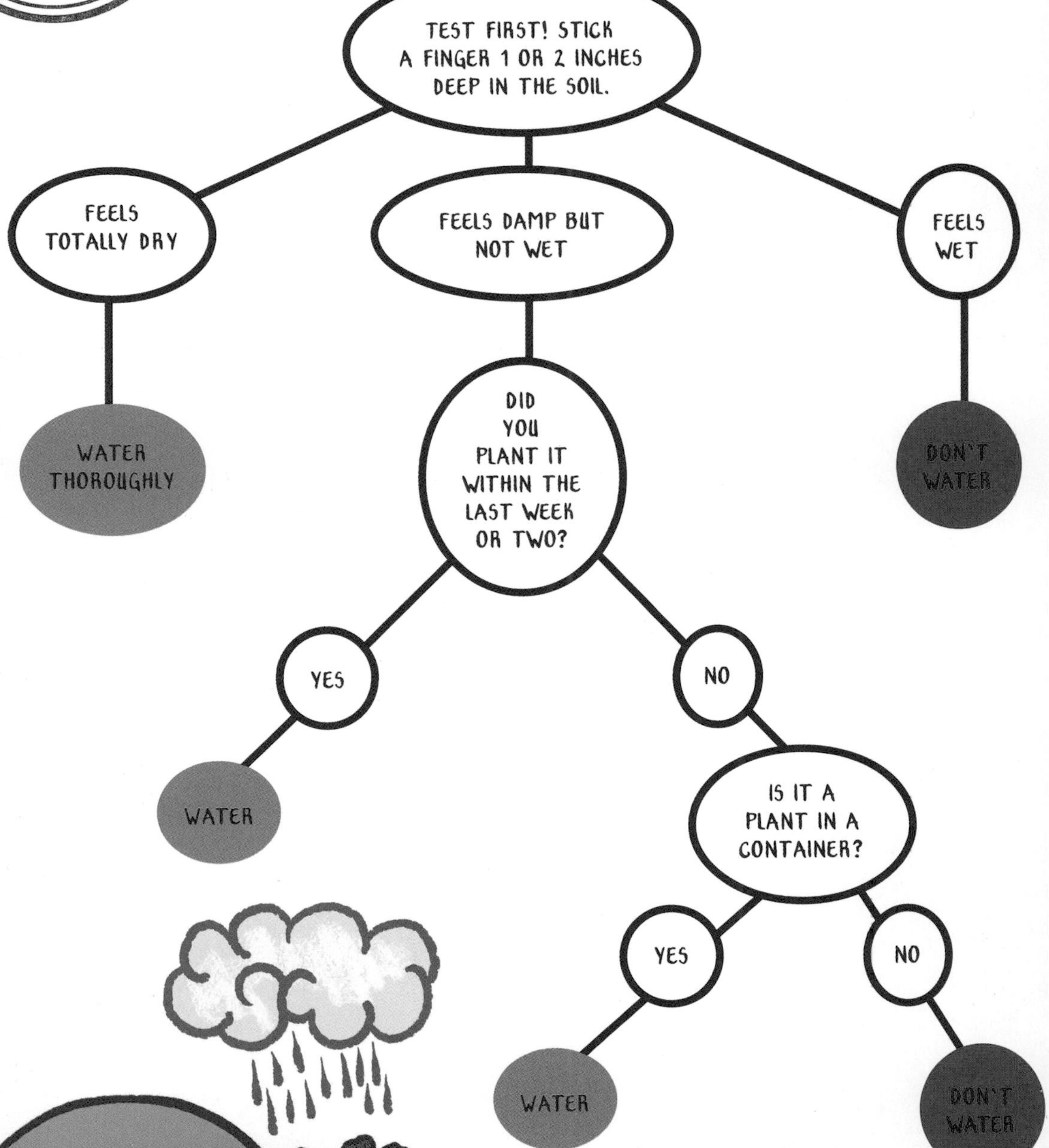
TEST FIRST! STICK A FINGER 1 OR 2 INCHES DEEP IN THE SOIL.
FEELS TOTALLY DRY
WATER THOROUGHLY
FEELS DAMP BUT NOT WET
DID YOU PLANT IT WITHIN THE LAST WEEK OR TWO?
YES
WATER
NO
IS IT A PLANT IN A CONTAINER?
YES
WATER
NO
DON'T WATER
FEELS WET
DON'T WATER

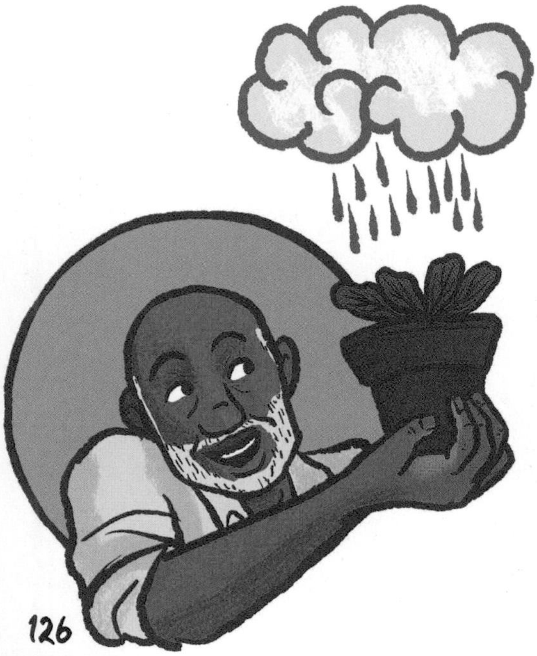

BRAND NEW PLANTS NEED A LITTLE EXTRA WATER AND CONTAINER SOIL DRIES OUT MUCH FASTER THAN THE GROUND.

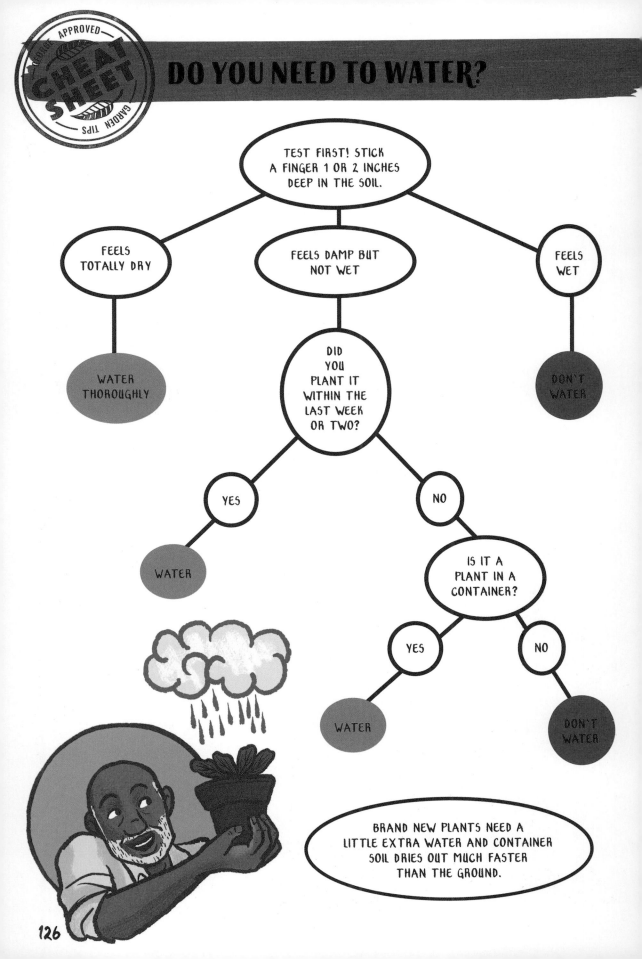

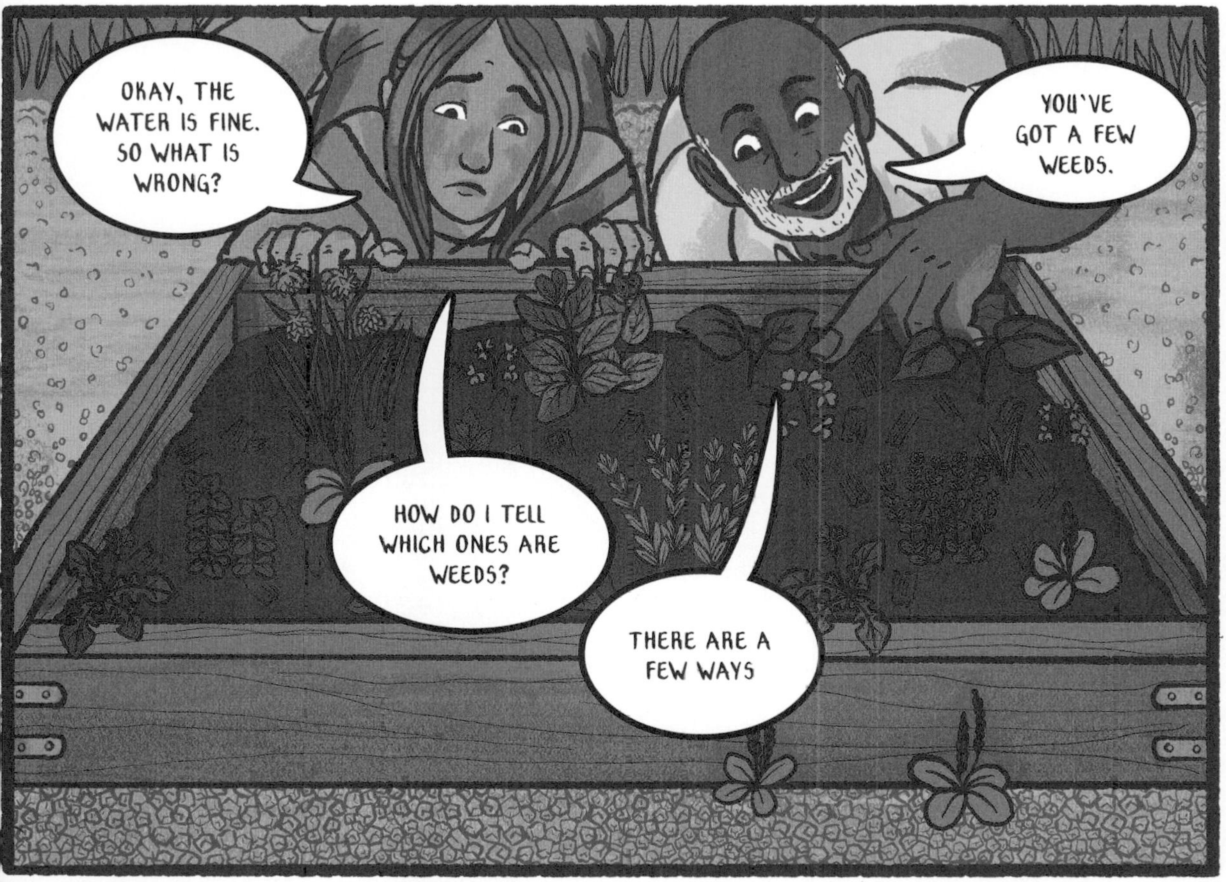
OKAY, THE WATER IS FINE. SO WHAT IS WRONG?
YOU'VE GOT A FEW WEEDS.
HOW DO I TELL WHICH ONES ARE WEEDS?
THERE ARE A FEW WAYS

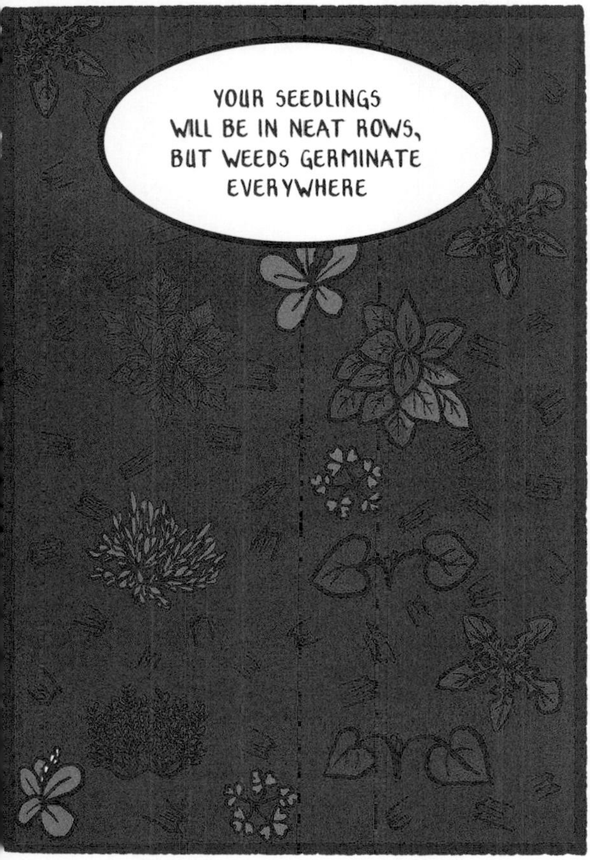
YOUR SEEDLINGS WILL BE IN NEAT ROWS, BUT WEEDS GERMINATE EVERYWHERE

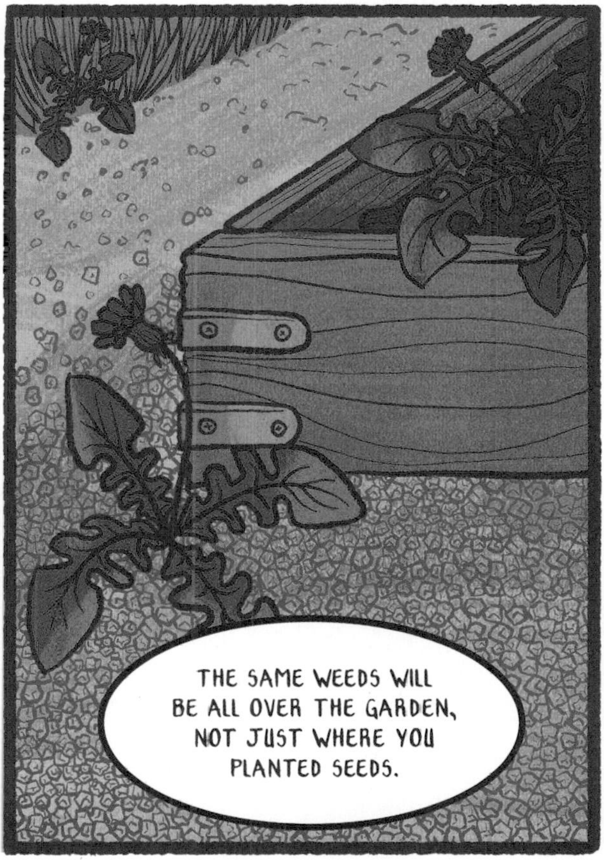
THE SAME WEEDS WILL BE ALL OVER THE GARDEN, NOT JUST WHERE YOU PLANTED SEEDS.

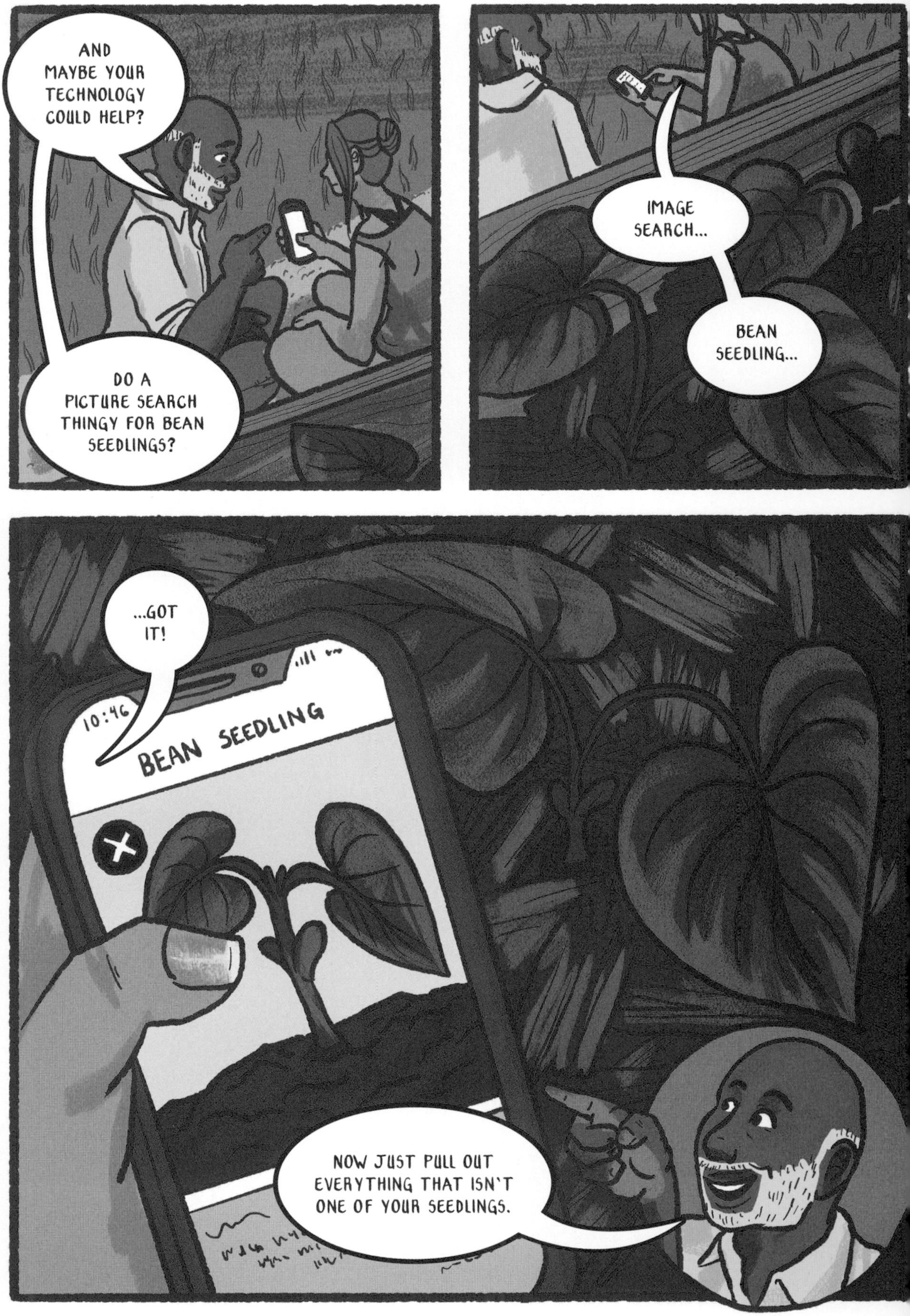
AND MAYBE YOUR TECHNOLOGY COULD HELP?
DO A PICTURE SEARCH THINGY FOR BEAN SEEDLINGS?
IMAGE SEARCH...
BEAN SEEDLING...
...GOT IT!
10:46
BEAN SEEDLING
NOW JUST PULL OUT EVERYTHING THAT ISN'T ONE OF YOUR SEEDLINGS.

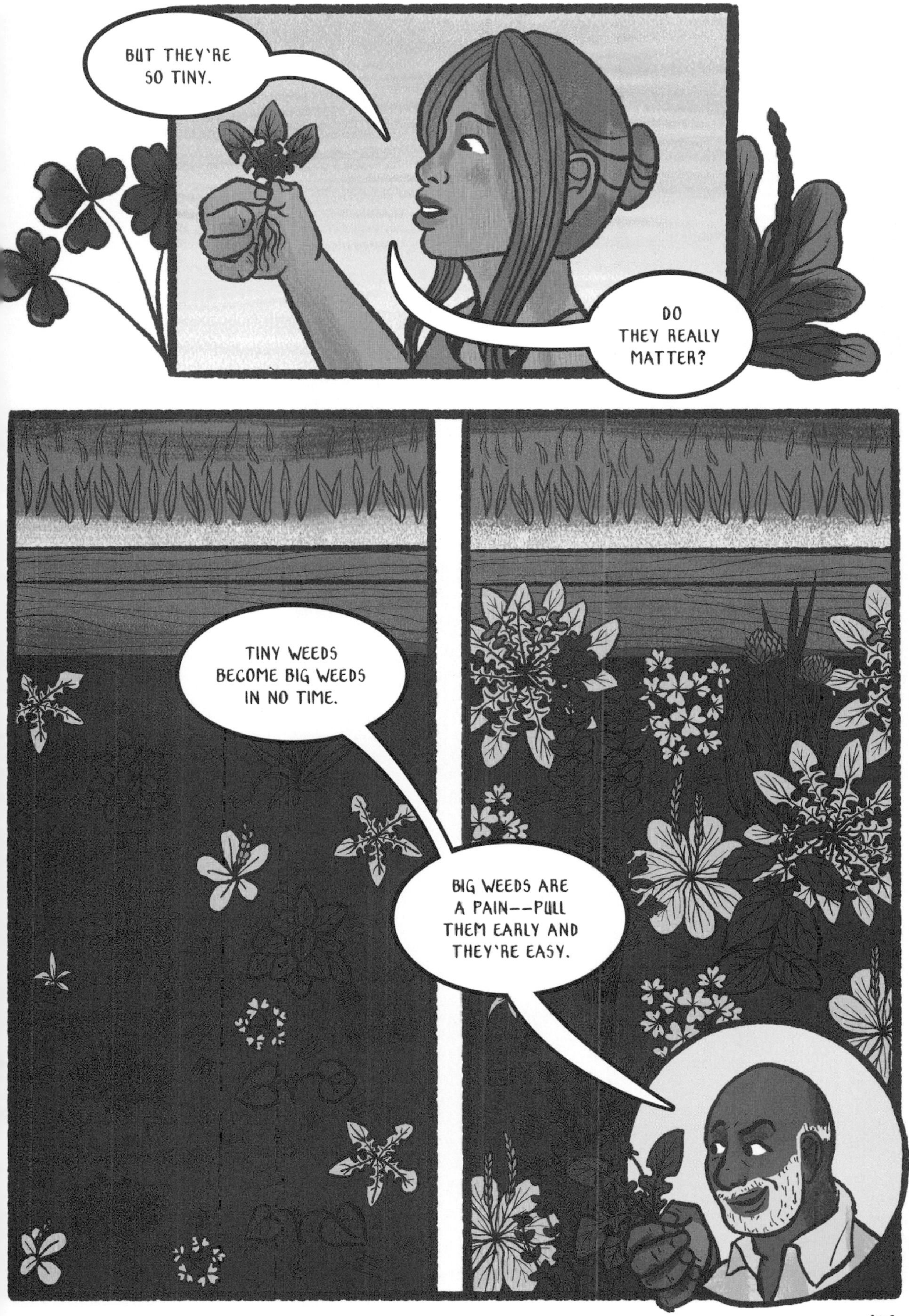
BUT THEY'RE SO TINY.
DO THEY REALLY MATTER?
TINY WEEDS BECOME BIG WEEDS IN NO TIME.
BIG WEEDS ARE A PAIN--PULL THEM EARLY AND THEY'RE EASY.

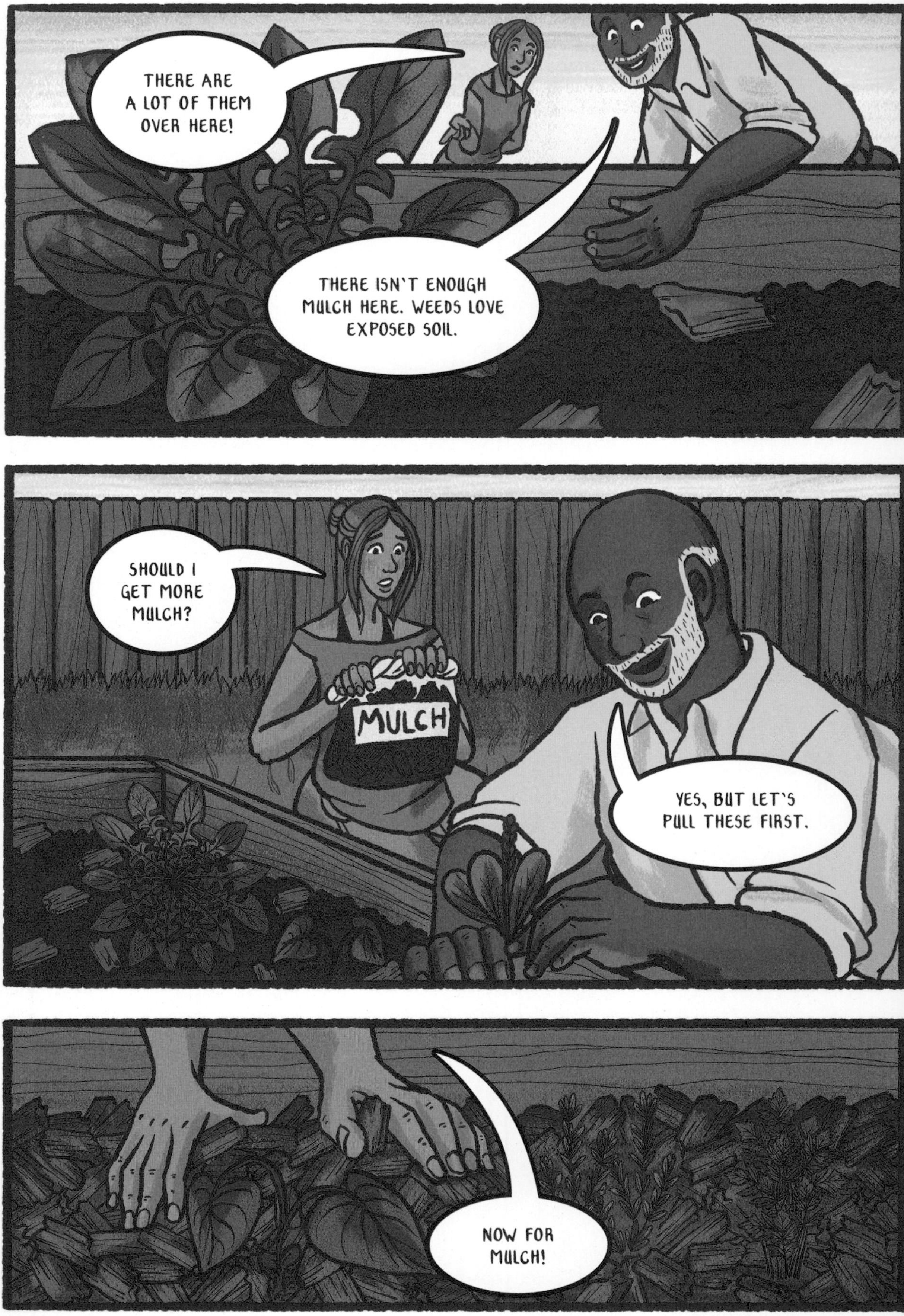
THERE ARE A LOT OF THEM OVER HERE!
THERE ISN'T ENOUGH MULCH HERE. WEEDS LOVE EXPOSED SOIL.
SHOULD I GET MORE MULCH?
MULCH
YES, BUT LET'S PULL THESE FIRST.
NOW FOR MULCH!

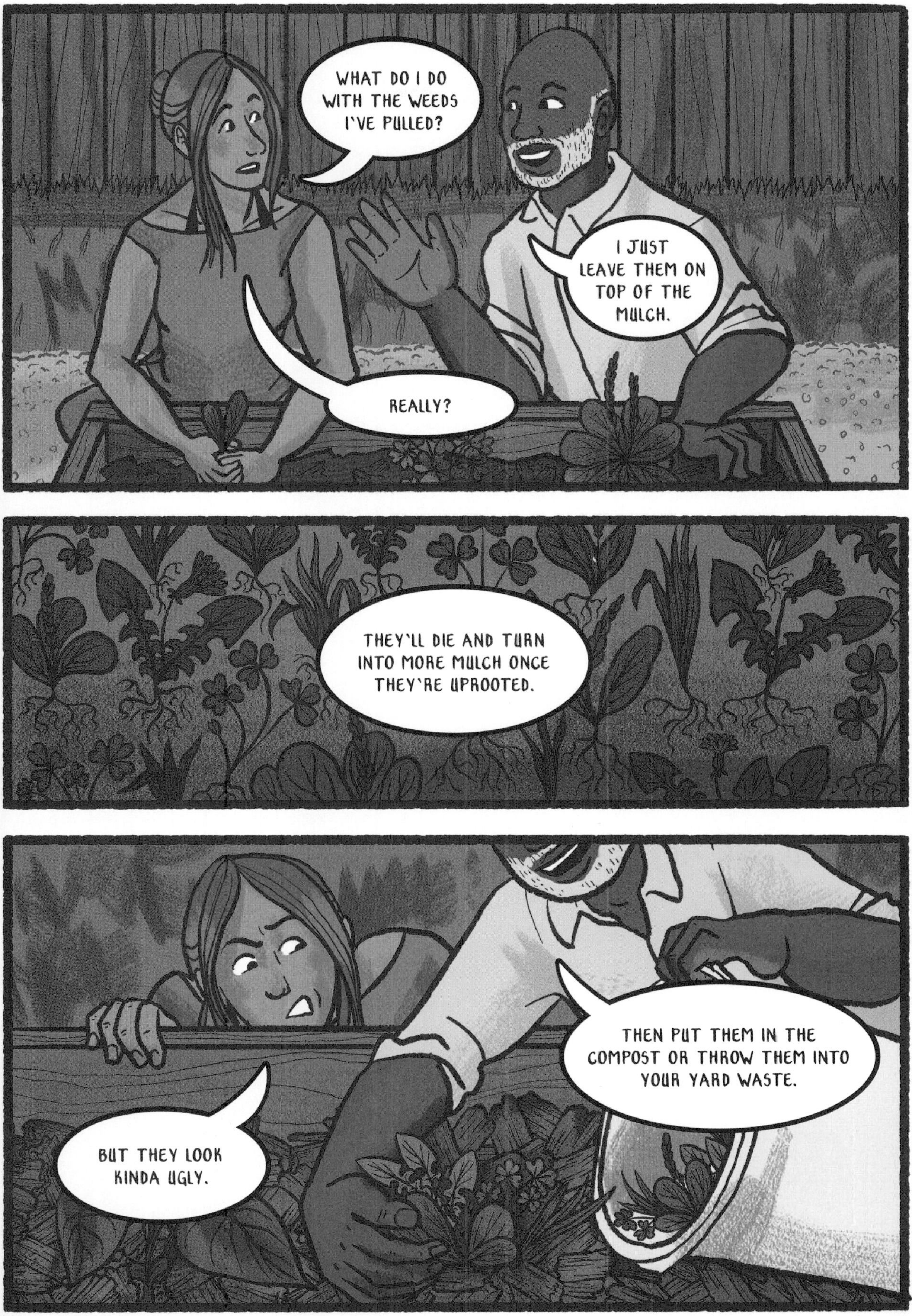
WHAT DO I DO WITH THE WEEDS I'VE PULLED?
I JUST LEAVE THEM ON TOP OF THE MULCH.
REALLY?
THEY'LL DIE AND TURN INTO MORE MULCH ONCE THEY'RE UPROOTED.
BUT THEY LOOK KINDA UGLY.
THEN PUT THEM IN THE COMPOST OR THROW THEM INTO YOUR YARD WASTE.

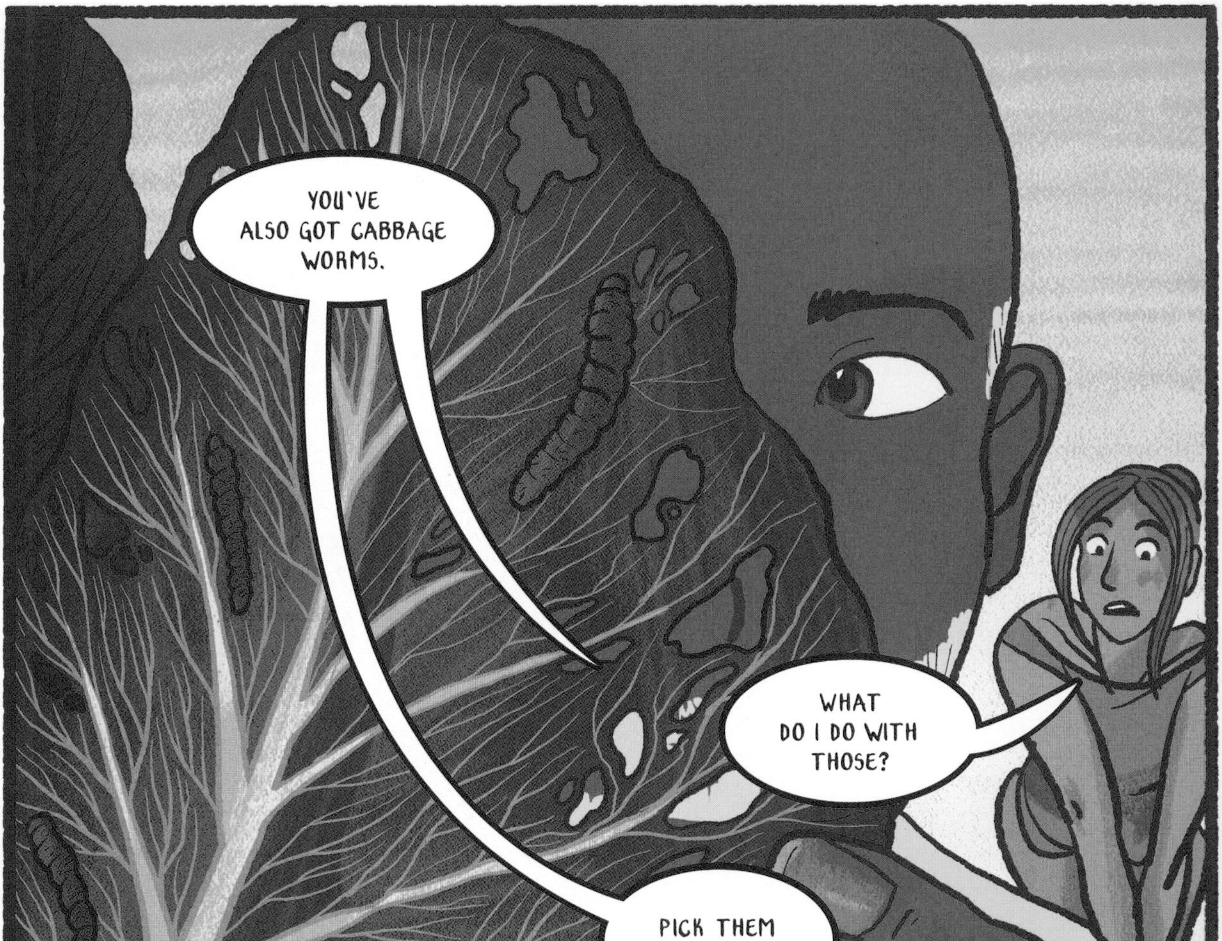
YOU'VE ALSO GOT CABBAGE WORMS.
WHAT DO I DO WITH THOSE?
PICK THEM OFF.

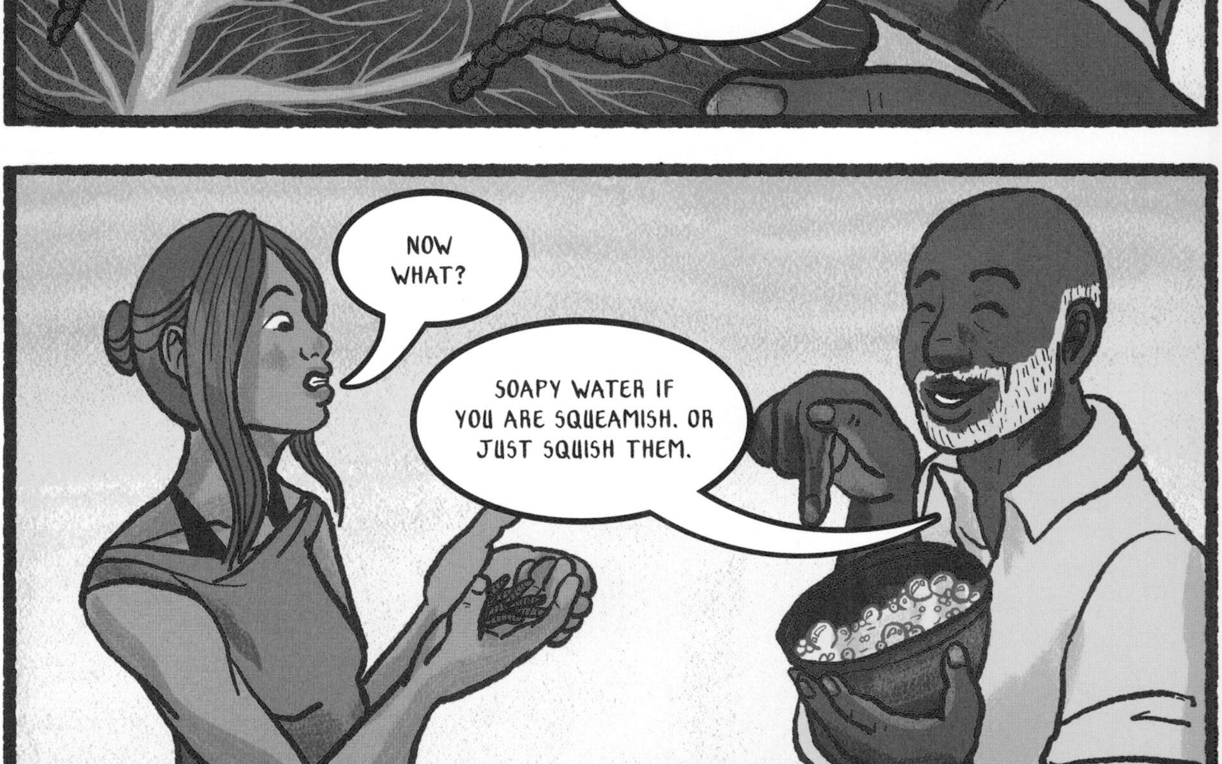
NOW WHAT?
SOAPY WATER IF YOU ARE SQUEAMISH. OR JUST SQUISH THEM.

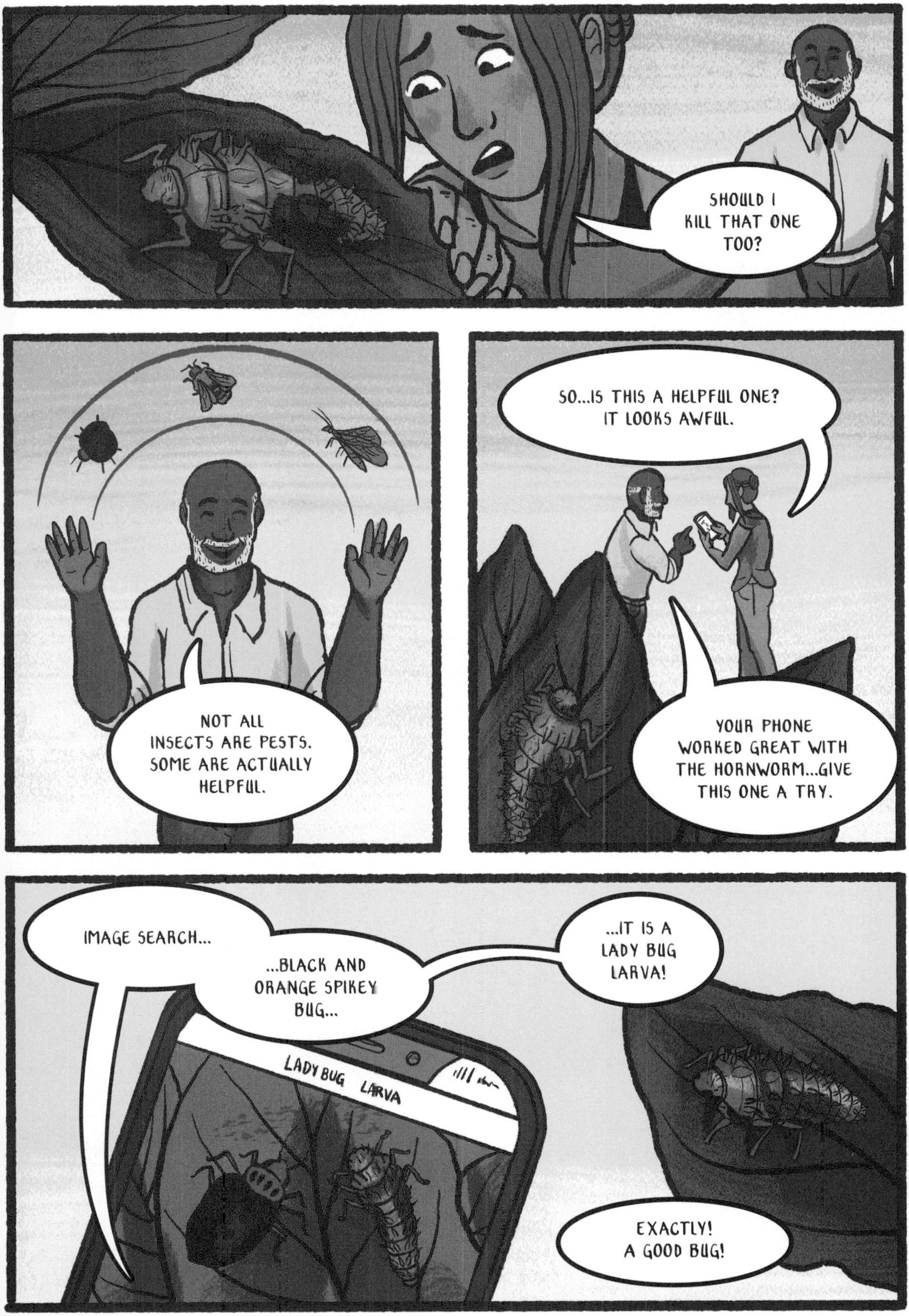
SHOULD I KILL THAT ONE TOO?
NOT ALL INSECTS ARE PESTS. SOME ARE ACTUALLY HELPFUL.
SO...IS THIS A HELPFUL ONE? IT LOOKS AWFUL.
YOUR PHONE WORKED GREAT WITH THE HORNWORM...GIVE THIS ONE A TRY.
IMAGE SEARCH...
...BLACK AND ORANGE SPIKEY BUG...
...IT IS A LADY BUG LARVA!
LADY BUG LARVA
EXACTLY! A GOOD BUG!

WHAT TO CHECK EACH WEEK

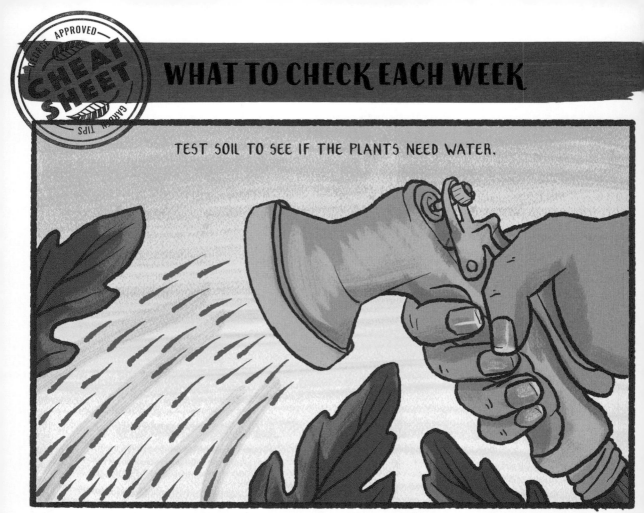

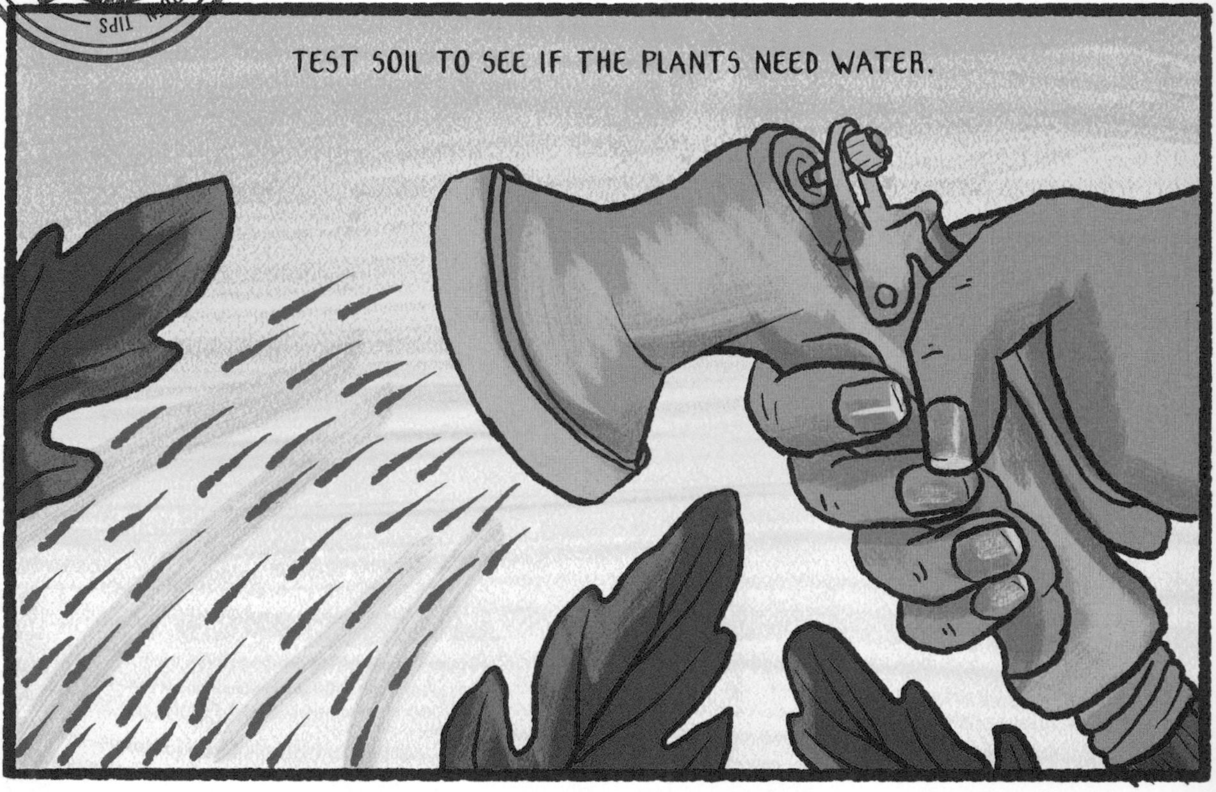
TEST SOIL TO SEE IF THE PLANTS NEED WATER.

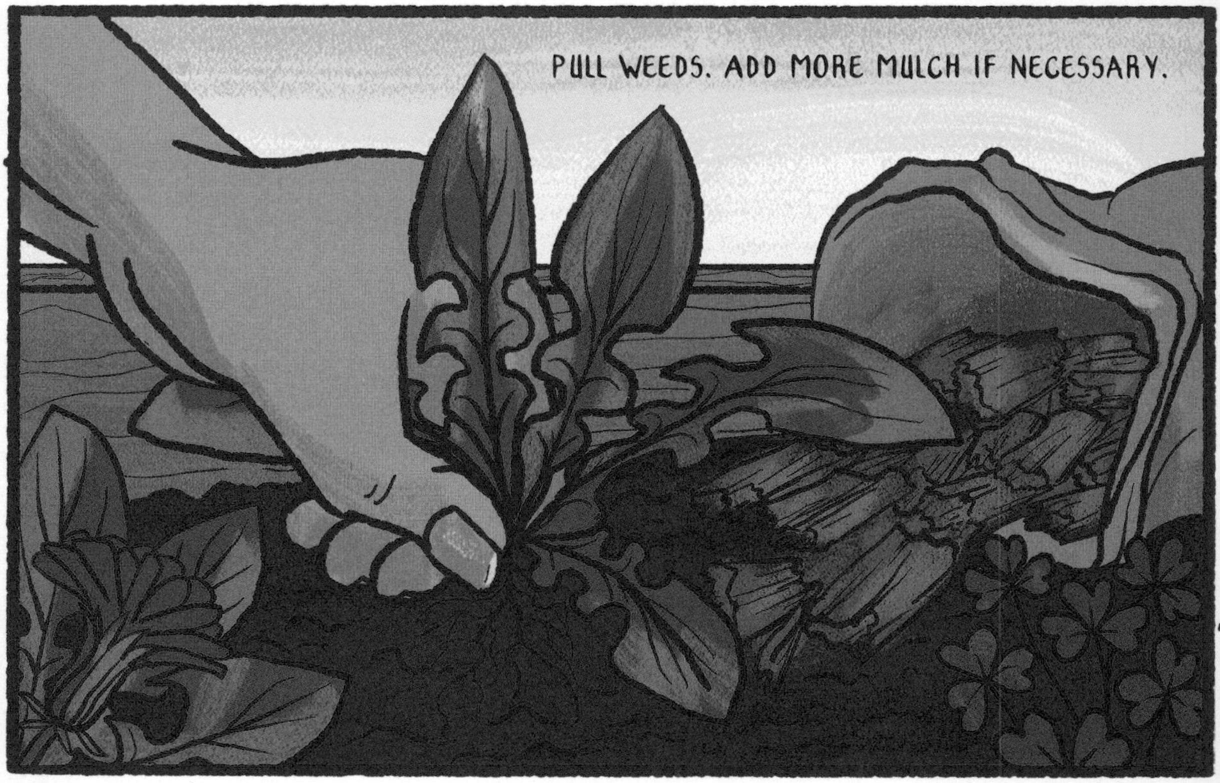
PULL WEEDS. ADD MORE MULCH IF NECESSARY.

GEORGE APPROVED CHEAT SHEET GARDEN TIPS

WHAT TO CHECK EACH WEEK

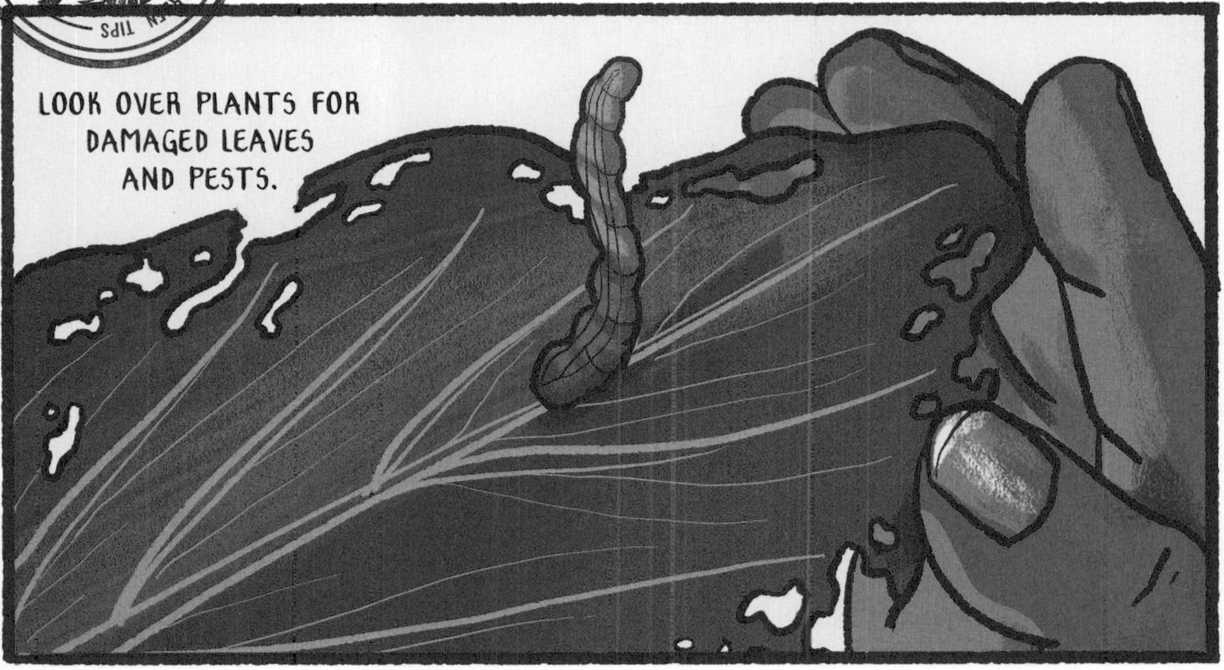
LOOK OVER PLANTS FOR DAMAGED LEAVES AND PESTS.

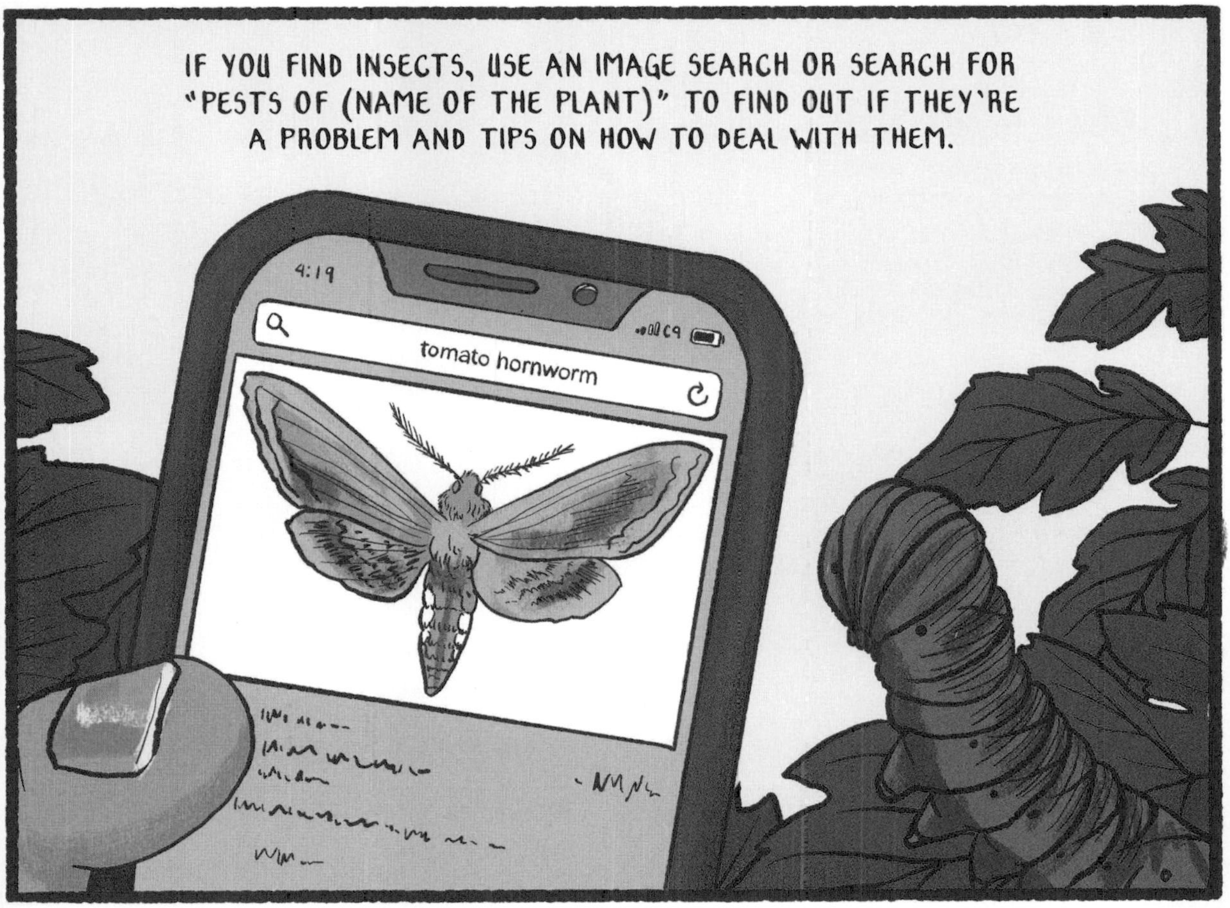
IF YOU FIND INSECTS, USE AN IMAGE SEARCH OR SEARCH FOR "PESTS OF (NAME OF THE PLANT)" TO FIND OUT IF THEY'RE A PROBLEM AND TIPS ON HOW TO DEAL WITH THEM.
4:19
tomato hornworm

SOME BUGS YOU SHOULD KNOW

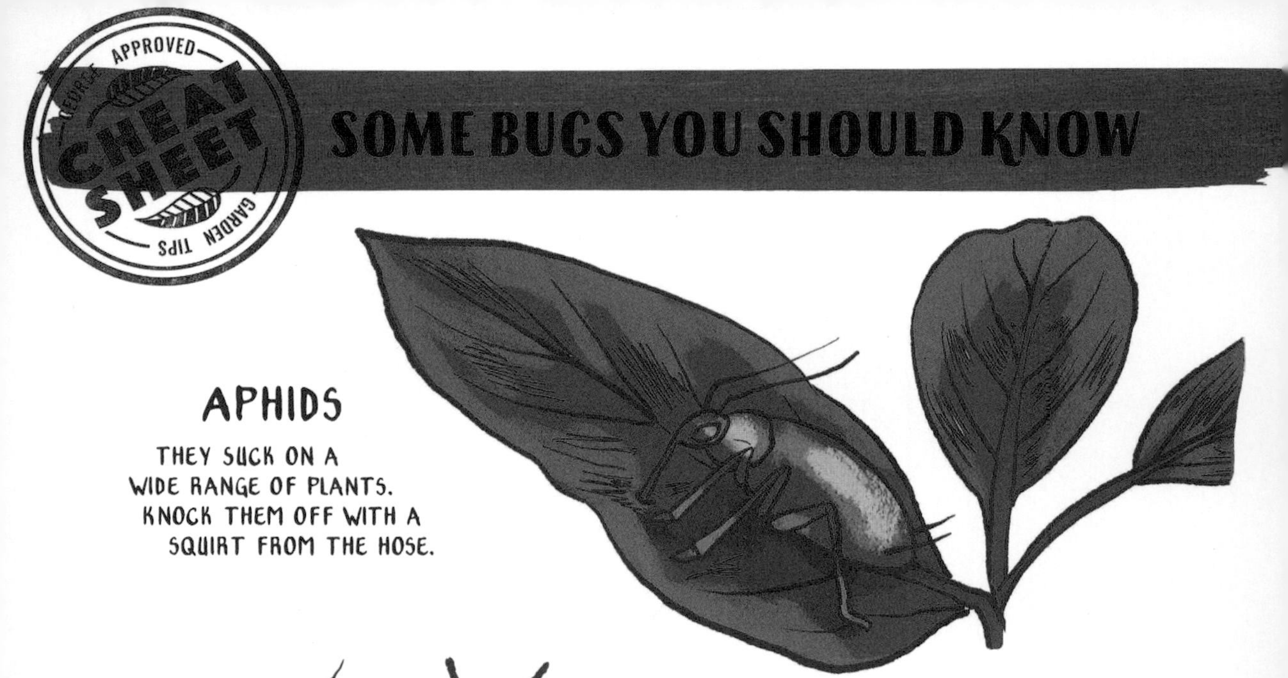

APHIDS

THEY SUCK ON A WIDE RANGE OF PLANTS. KNOCK THEM OFF WITH A SQUIRT FROM THE HOSE.

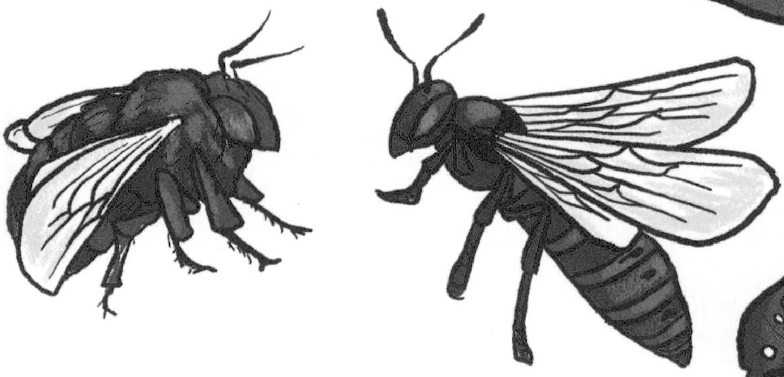

BEES + WASPS

BEES POLLINATE VEGETABLES AND FLOWERS, AND WASPS ARE VORACIOUS PREDATORS OF A WIDE RANGE OF GARDEN PESTS. DON'T HARASS THEM AND YOU WON'T GET STUNG.

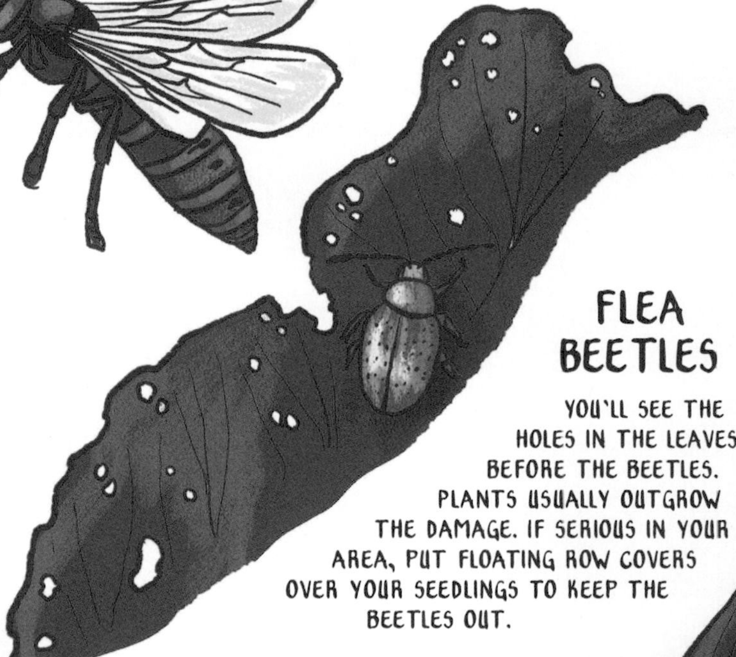

FLEA BEETLES

YOU'LL SEE THE HOLES IN THE LEAVES BEFORE THE BEETLES. PLANTS USUALLY OUTGROW THE DAMAGE. IF SERIOUS IN YOUR AREA, PUT FLOATING ROW COVERS OVER YOUR SEEDLINGS TO KEEP THE BEETLES OUT.

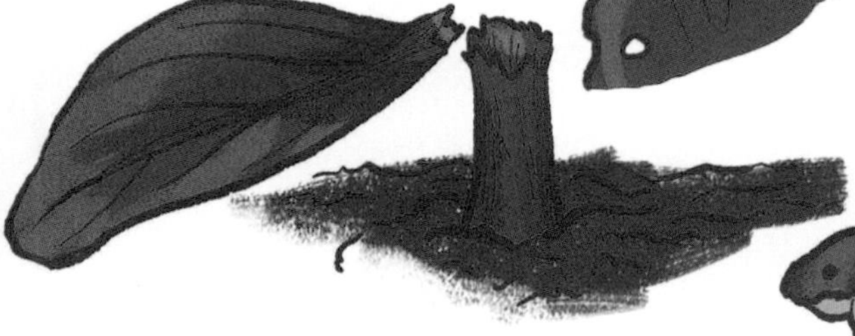

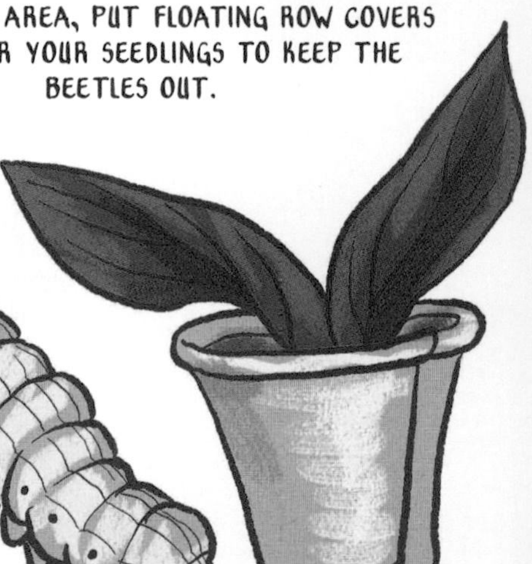

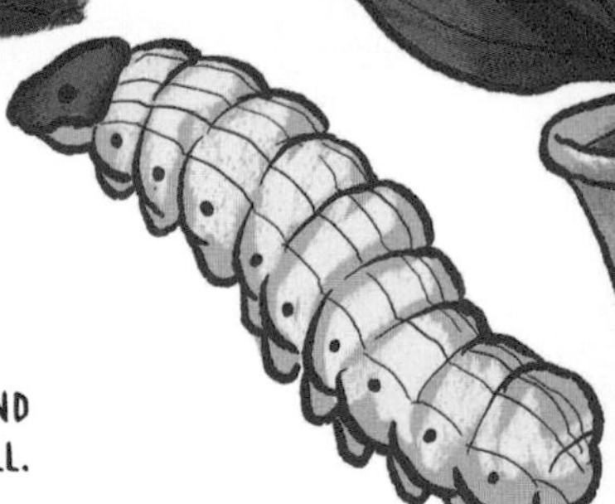

CUTWORMS

FEED AT THE SOIL SURFACE AND CAN CUT THROUGH THE STEMS OF SEEDLINGS. CUT THE BOTTOM OUT OF A PAPER CUP, AND PUT IT AROUND YOUR SEEDLINGS AS A 2- TO 3-INCH TALL WALL.

APPROVED CHEAT SHEET GARDEN TIPS

SOME BUGS YOU SHOULD KNOW

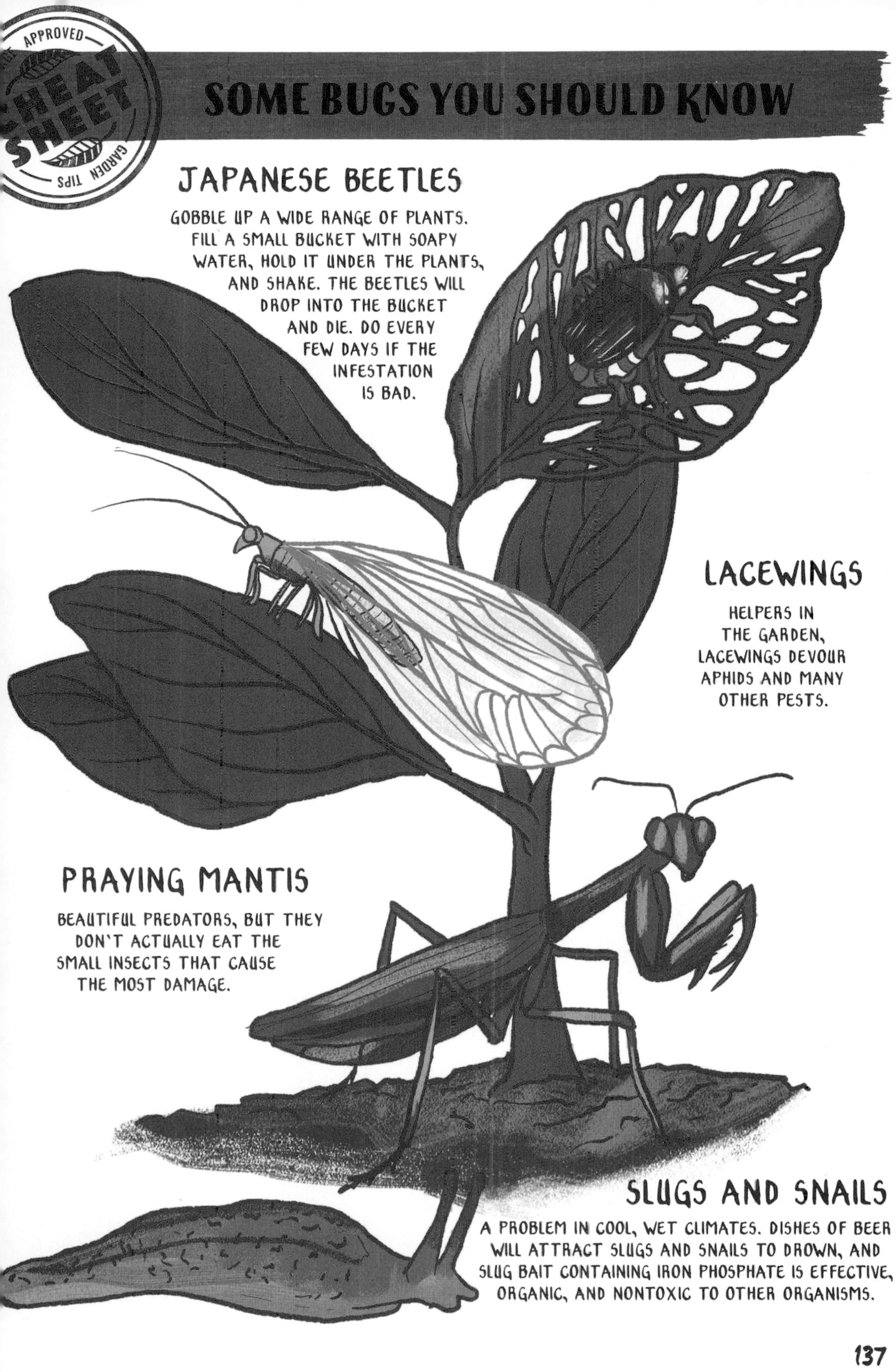

JAPANESE BEETLES

GOBBLE UP A WIDE RANGE OF PLANTS. FILL A SMALL BUCKET WITH SOAPY WATER, HOLD IT UNDER THE PLANTS, AND SHAKE. THE BEETLES WILL DROP INTO THE BUCKET AND DIE. DO EVERY FEW DAYS IF THE INFESTATION IS BAD.

LACEWINGS

HELPERS IN THE GARDEN, LACEWINGS DEVOUR APHIDS AND MANY OTHER PESTS.

PRAYING MANTIS

BEAUTIFUL PREDATORS, BUT THEY DON'T ACTUALLY EAT THE SMALL INSECTS THAT CAUSE THE MOST DAMAGE.

SLUGS AND SNAILS

A PROBLEM IN COOL, WET CLIMATES. DISHES OF BEER WILL ATTRACT SLUGS AND SNAILS TO DROWN, AND SLUG BAIT CONTAINING IRON PHOSPHATE IS EFFECTIVE, ORGANIC, AND NONTOXIC TO OTHER ORGANISMS.

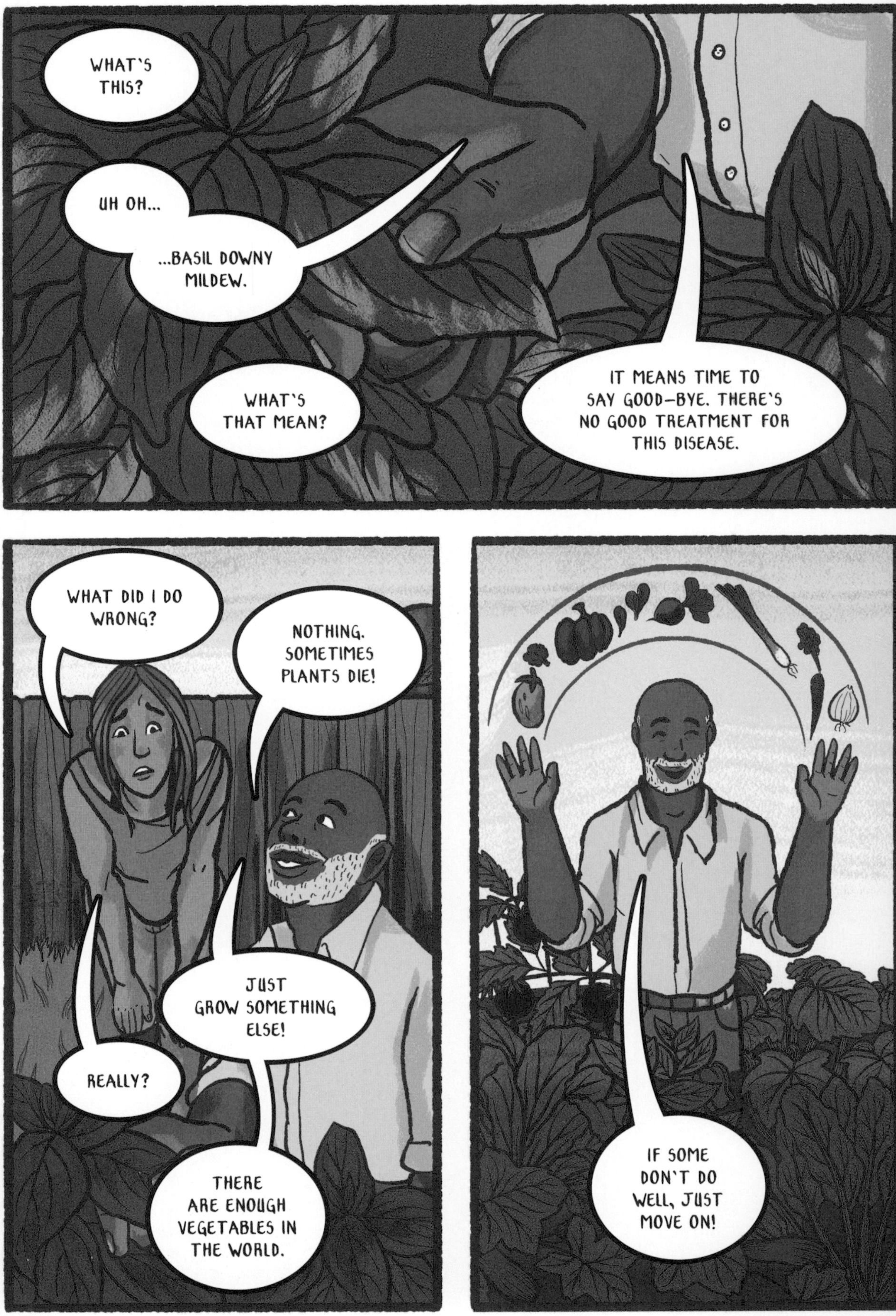
WHAT'S THIS?
UH OH...
...BASIL DOWNY MILDEW.
WHAT'S THAT MEAN?
IT MEANS TIME TO SAY GOOD-BYE. THERE'S NO GOOD TREATMENT FOR THIS DISEASE.
WHAT DID I DO WRONG?
NOTHING. SOMETIMES PLANTS DIE!
JUST GROW SOMETHING ELSE!
REALLY?
THERE ARE ENOUGH VEGETABLES IN THE WORLD.
IF SOME DON'T DO WELL, JUST MOVE ON!

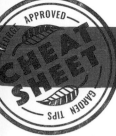

PLANTS THAT ARE USUALLY CAREFREE

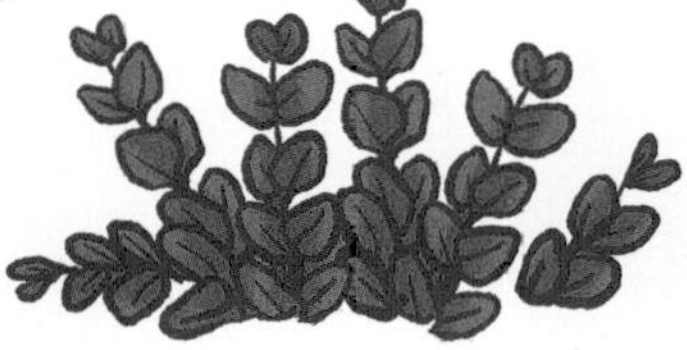

OREGANO

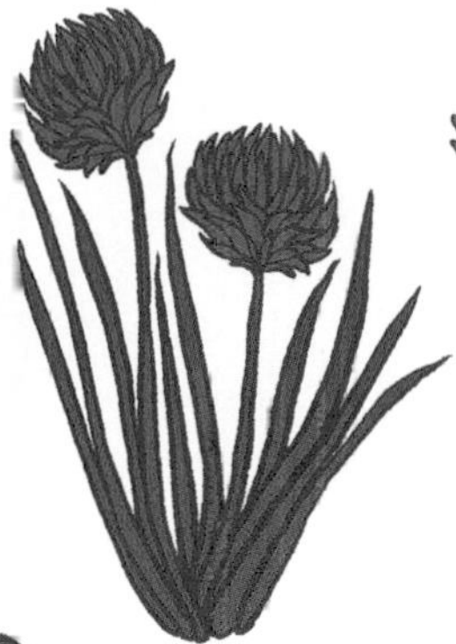

CHIVES

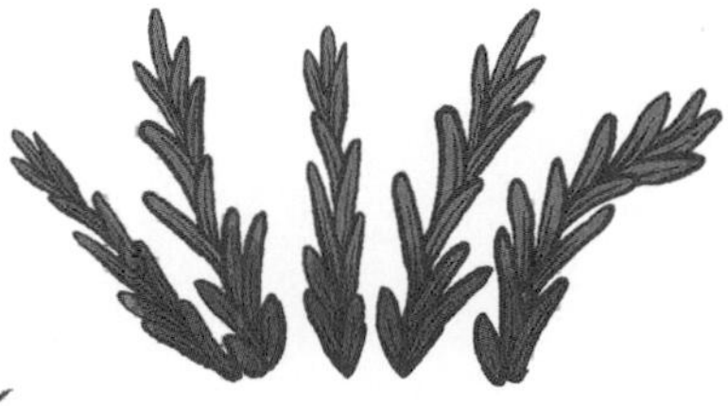

ROSEMARY

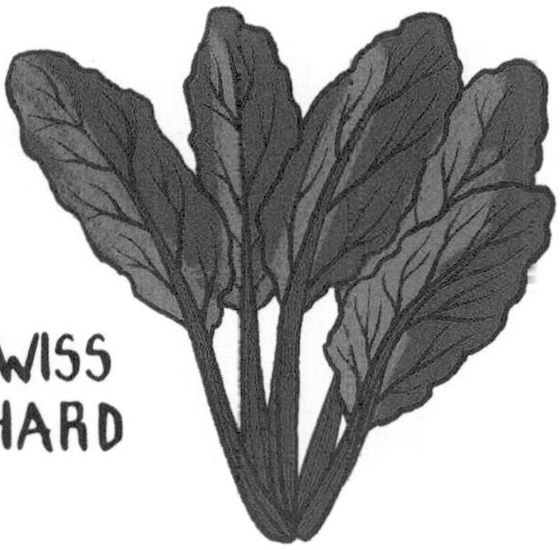

SWISS CHARD

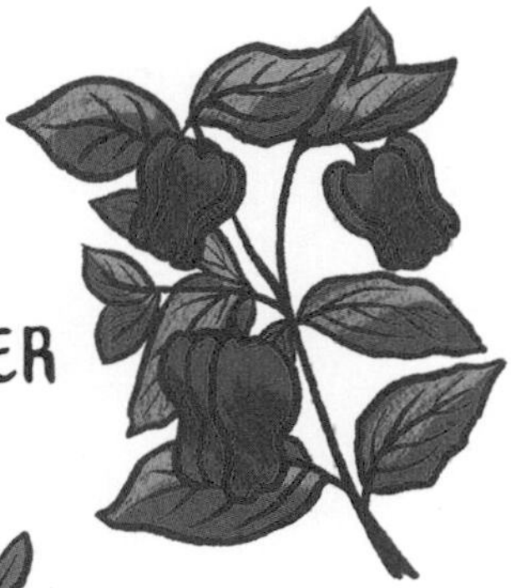

PEPPER

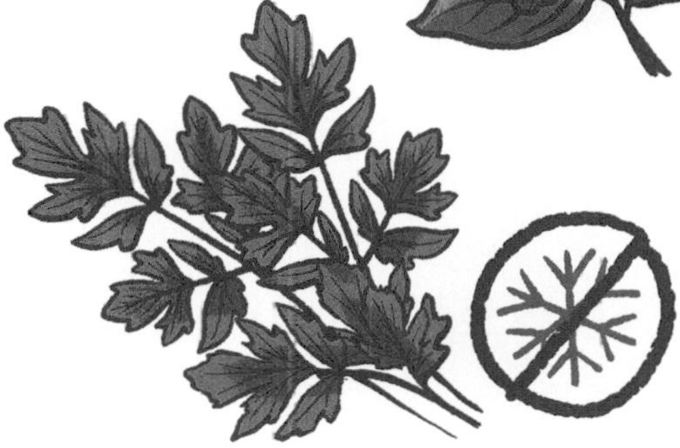

PARSLEY

GOES TO FLOWER AND STOPS PRODUCING LEAVES IF EXPOSED TO COLD TEMPERATURES. DON'T PLANT UNTIL AFTER YOUR LAST FROST.

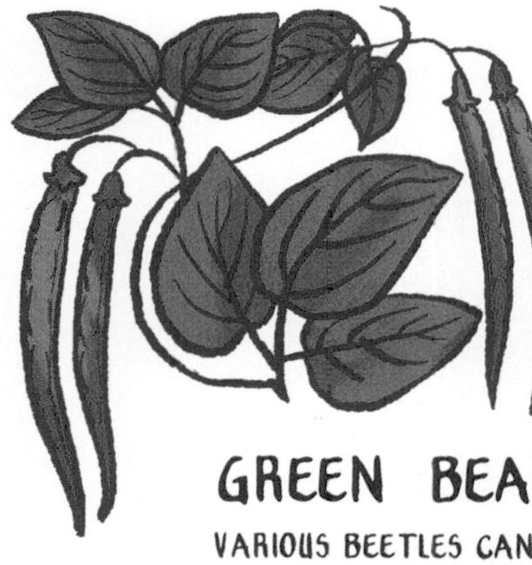

GREEN BEANS

VARIOUS BEETLES CAN EAT LEAVES, BUT GENERALLY NOT TOO SERIOUS.

ZINNIAS

WHITISH PATCHES ON LEAVES MEANS POWDERY MILDEW. UNSIGHTLY, BUT USUALLY NOT SERIOUS. JUST IGNORE IT.

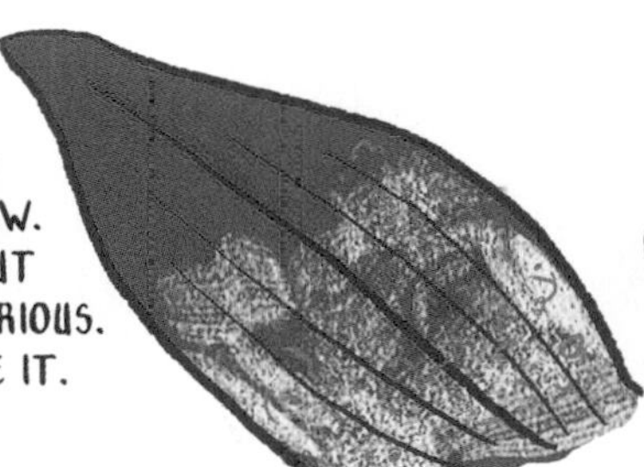

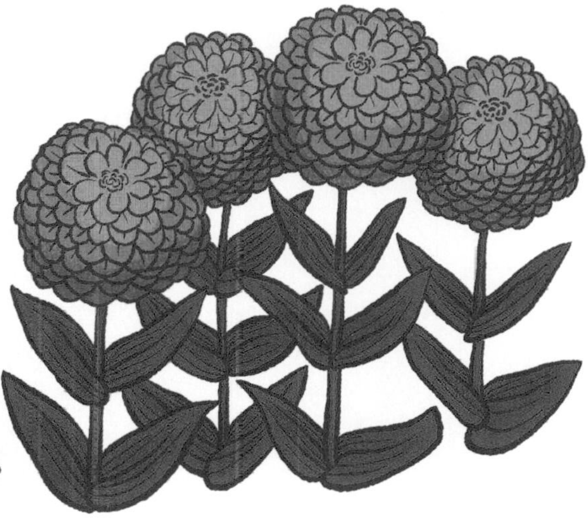

PLANT PROBLEMS

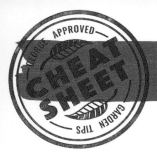

TOMATO

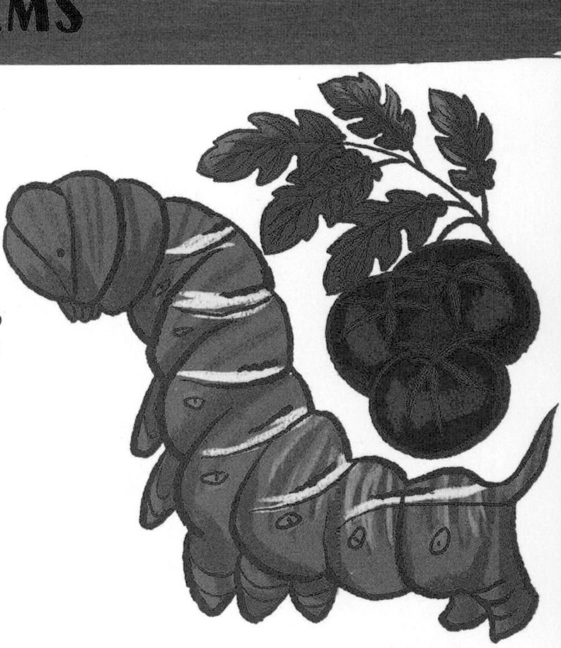

TOMATO HORNWORM.

LOOK FOR BIG GREEN CATERPILLARS WITH A VORACIOUS APPETITE. USUALLY THERE ARE JUST ONE OR TWO ON A PLANT, BUT THEY EAT A LOT. EASILY PICKED OFF AND SQUISHED OR DUNKED IN SOAPY WATER.

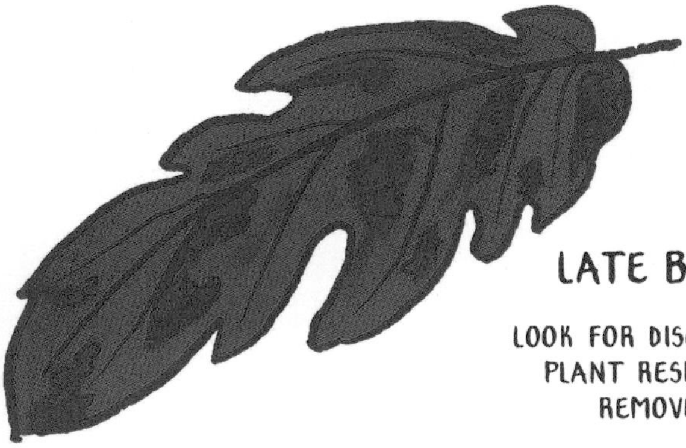

LATE BLIGHT AND OTHER FUNGAL DISEASES.

LOOK FOR DISCOLORATION ON LEAVES IN HUMID CLIMATES. NEXT YEAR, PLANT RESISTANT VARIETIES, AND IF YOU HAVE A LONG SUMMER, REMOVE AND REPLANT ONCE YOUR FIRST CROP DECLINES.

CUCUMBER

DOWNY MILDEW.

LOOK FOR YELLOW OR BROWN BLOTCHES ON THE LEAVES. AVOID GETTING THE LEAVES WET WHEN YOU WATER. IF DISEASE BECOMES BAD, REMOVE PLANTS AND REPLANT WITH A RESISTANT VARIETY.

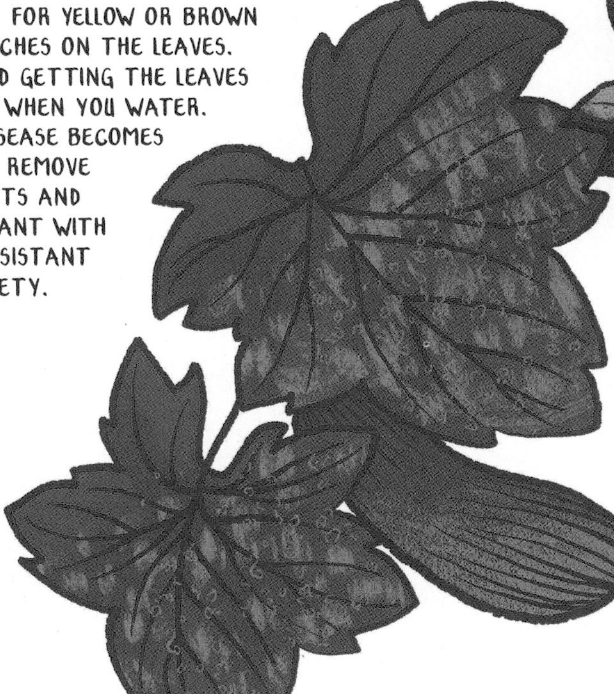

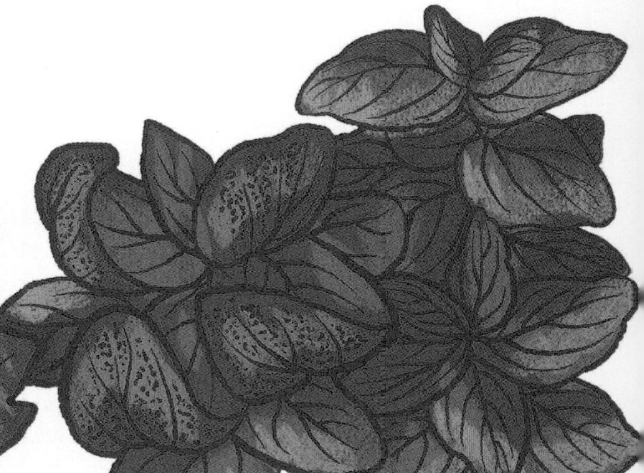

BASIL

DOWNY MILDEW.

LOOK FOR BROWN PATCHES ON UNDERSIDE OF LEAVES. HARVEST WHAT YOU CAN; NEXT YEAR ASK YOUR NURSERY ABOUT RESISTANT VARIETIES.

GEORGE APPROVED CHEAT SHEET GARDEN TIPS

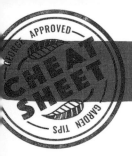

PLANT PROBLEMS

KALE

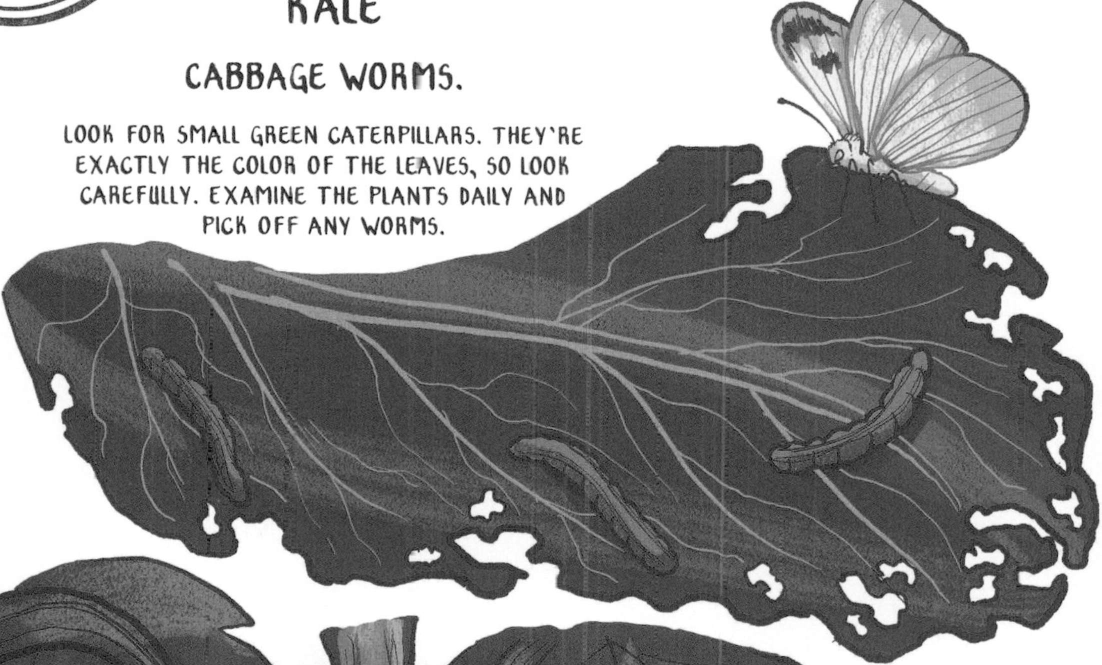

CABBAGE WORMS.

LOOK FOR SMALL GREEN CATERPILLARS. THEY'RE EXACTLY THE COLOR OF THE LEAVES, SO LOOK CAREFULLY. EXAMINE THE PLANTS DAILY AND PICK OFF ANY WORMS.

ZUCCHINI

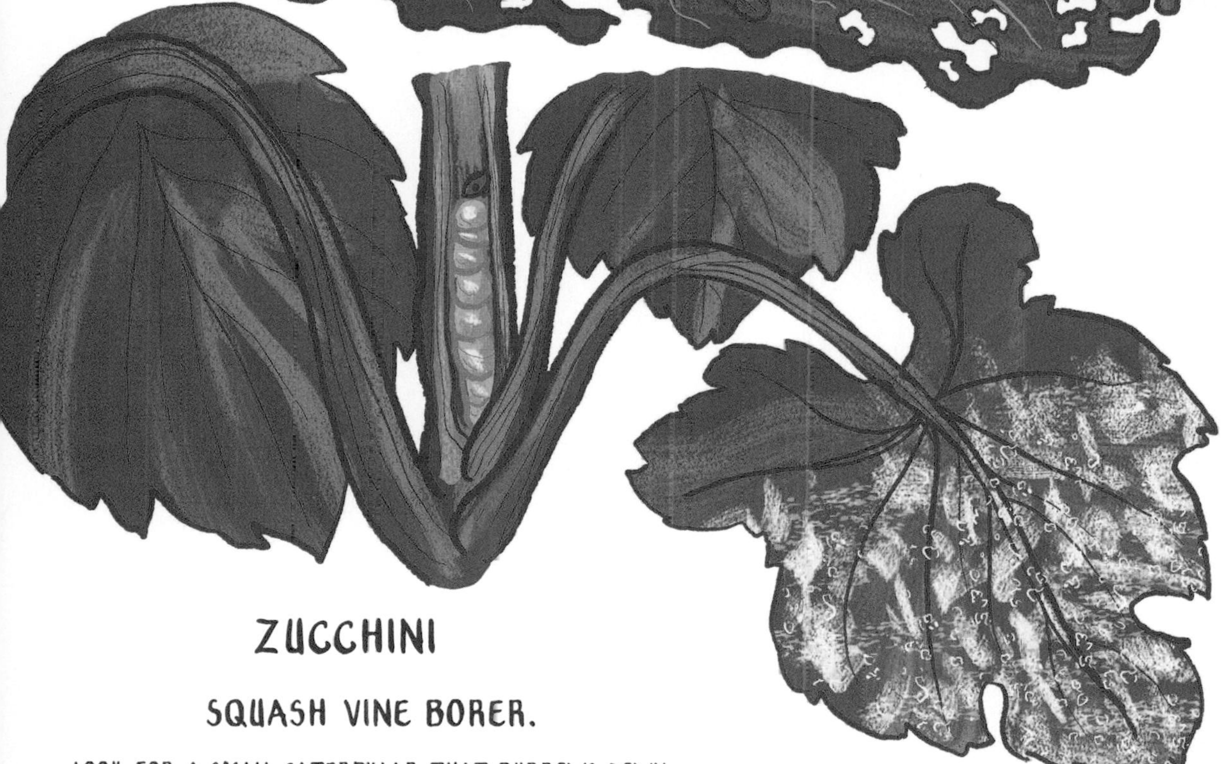

SQUASH VINE BORER.

LOOK FOR A SMALL CATERPILLAR THAT BURROWS DOWN INTO THE BASE OF THE PLANT STEM. WHAT YOU'LL SEE IS USUALLY THE GREEN OR BROWN FRASS (INSECT POOP) ON THE STEM, AND THE PLANT WILTING SUDDENLY. PULL UP AND DESTROY INFESTED PLANTS TO STOP THE BORER FROM BREEDING ANOTHER GENERATION. USUALLY YOU CAN GET A GOOD CROP BEFORE THE BORER ARRIVES. IF NOT, TRY THE CULTIVAR 'TROMBONCINO' NEXT YEAR, WHICH IS RESISTANT.

POWDERY MILDEW.

LOOK FOR WHITISH PATCHES ON THE LEAVES. UNSIGHTLY, BUT USUALLY NOT SERIOUS. JUST IGNORE IT.

NINE:
HARVESTING

HOW TO BRING IN THE GARDEN BOUNTY.

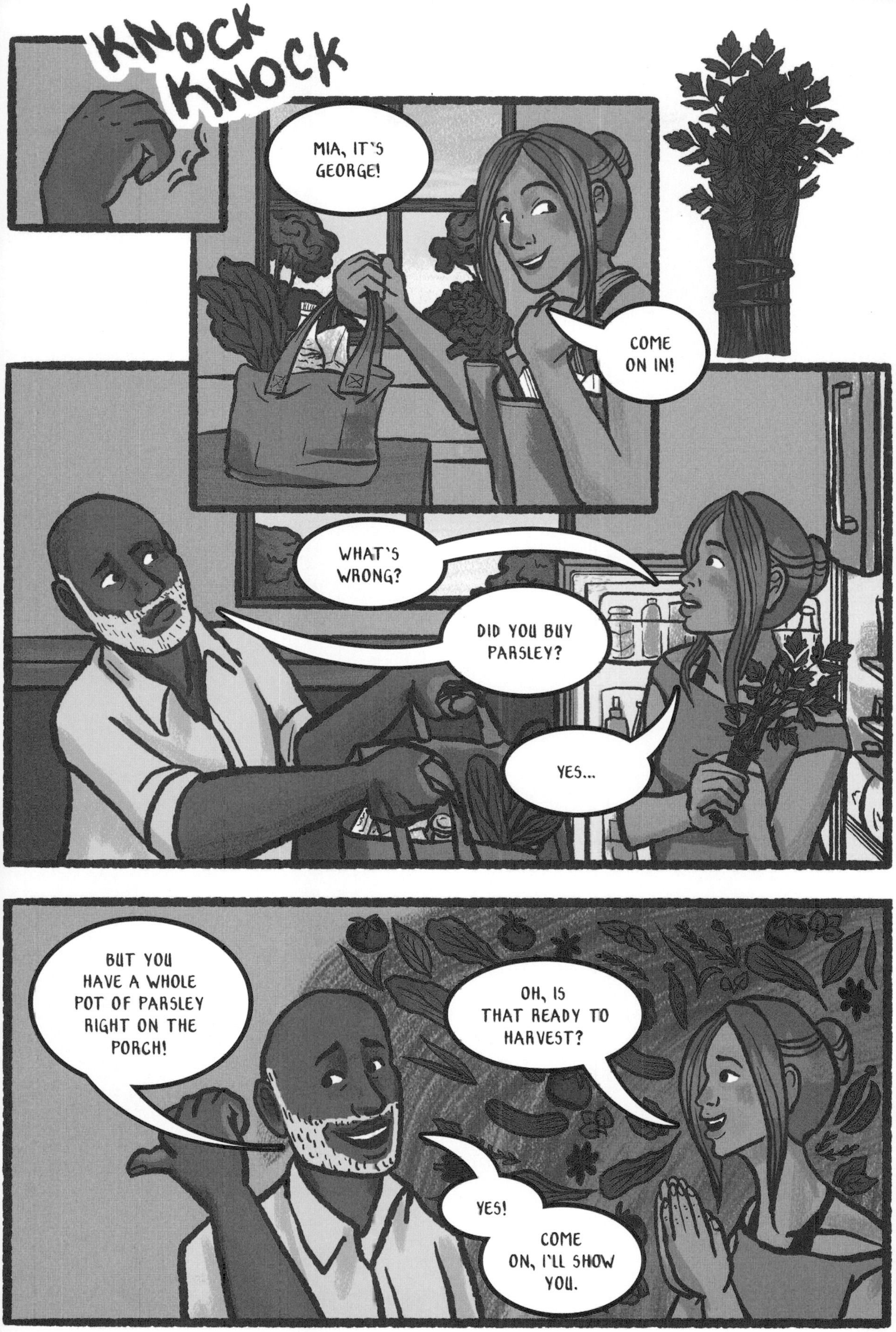
KNOCK KNOCK
MIA, IT'S GEORGE!
COME ON IN!
WHAT'S WRONG?
DID YOU BUY PARSLEY?
YES...
BUT YOU HAVE A WHOLE POT OF PARSLEY RIGHT ON THE PORCH!
OH, IS THAT READY TO HARVEST?
YES!
COME ON, I'LL SHOW YOU.

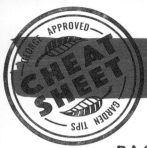

WHEN TO HARVEST

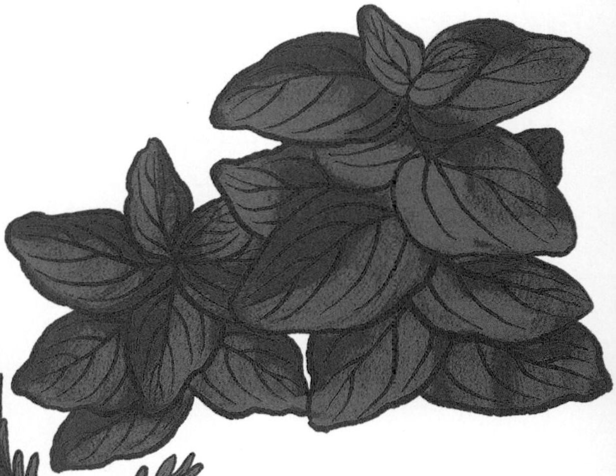

BASIL

ONCE THE PLANT REACHES ABOUT 8 INCHES TALL, PINCH OFF THE TOP OF EACH STEM WITH THE TOP TWO TO FOUR LEAVES ABOUT ONCE A WEEK. THESE NEWEST, YOUNGEST LEAVES HAVE THE BEST FLAVOR. IF FLOWER SPIKES BEGIN TO FORM, CUT THEM OFF AND THROW AWAY TO ENCOURAGE MORE LEAFY GROWTH.

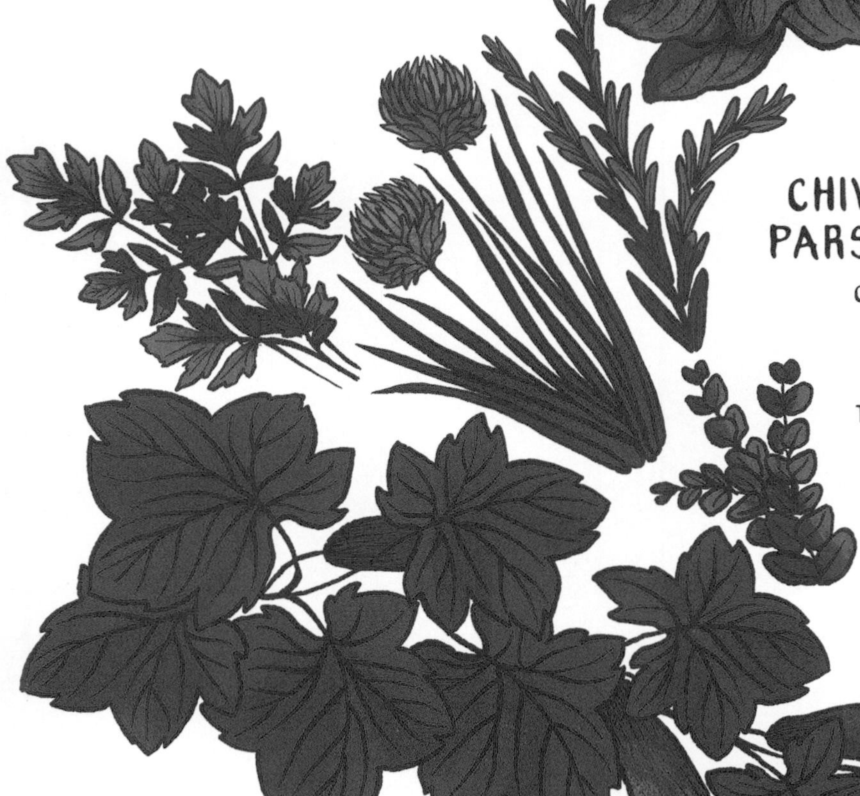

CHIVES, OREGANO, PARSLEY, ROSEMARY

CUT LEAVES AND STEMS AS NEEDED ONCE THE PLANT REACHES ABOUT 6 INCHES TALL. DO NOT CUT MORE THAN HALF THE PLANT AT ONE TIME, AND LET THE PLANT REGROW BEFORE HARVESTING AGAIN.

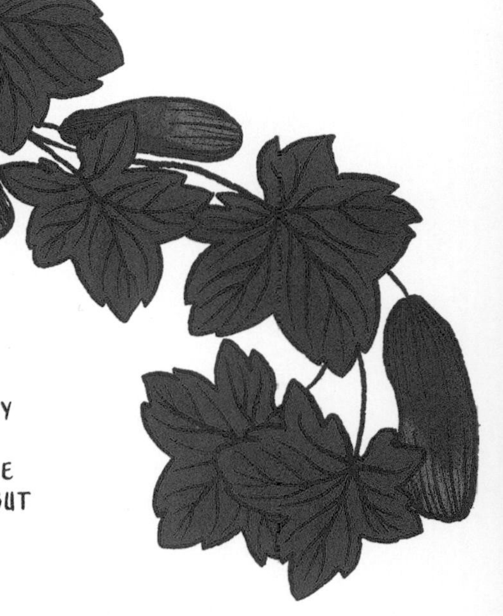

CUCUMBER

PICK WHEN FRUIT HAS FILLED OUT, BUT BEFORE IT BEGINS TO HARDEN AND GREEN ONES TURN YELLOW. HARVEST NEARLY DAILY WHEN IN PEAK PRODUCTION. IF YOU MISS ONE AND IT GETS TOO BIG, PICK AND COMPOST IT TO ENCOURAGE MORE CUCUMBERS TO DEVELOP. PLANTS CAN PRODUCE ALL SUMMER, BUT SOMETIMES ARE KILLED BY DISEASE LATE IN THE SUMMER.

APPROVED CHEAT SHEET GARDEN TIPS

WHEN TO HARVEST

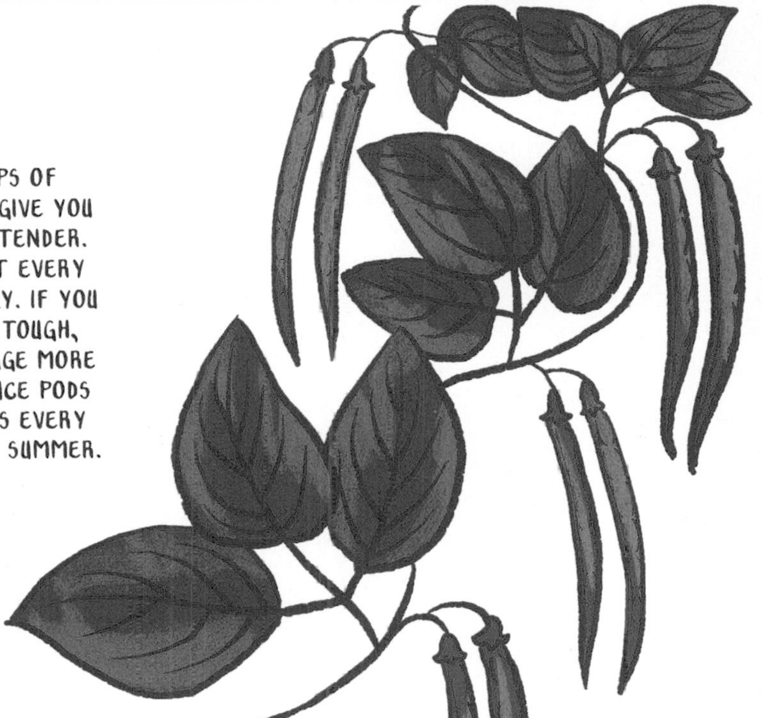

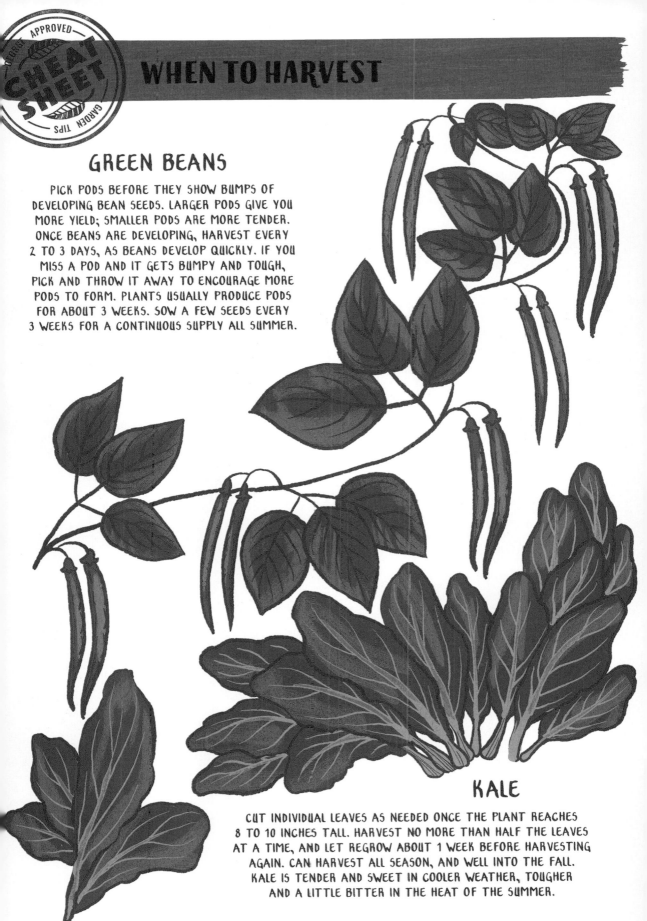

GREEN BEANS

PICK PODS BEFORE THEY SHOW BUMPS OF DEVELOPING BEAN SEEDS. LARGER PODS GIVE YOU MORE YIELD; SMALLER PODS ARE MORE TENDER. ONCE BEANS ARE DEVELOPING, HARVEST EVERY 2 TO 3 DAYS, AS BEANS DEVELOP QUICKLY. IF YOU MISS A POD AND IT GETS BUMPY AND TOUGH, PICK AND THROW IT AWAY TO ENCOURAGE MORE PODS TO FORM. PLANTS USUALLY PRODUCE PODS FOR ABOUT 3 WEEKS. SOW A FEW SEEDS EVERY 3 WEEKS FOR A CONTINUOUS SUPPLY ALL SUMMER.

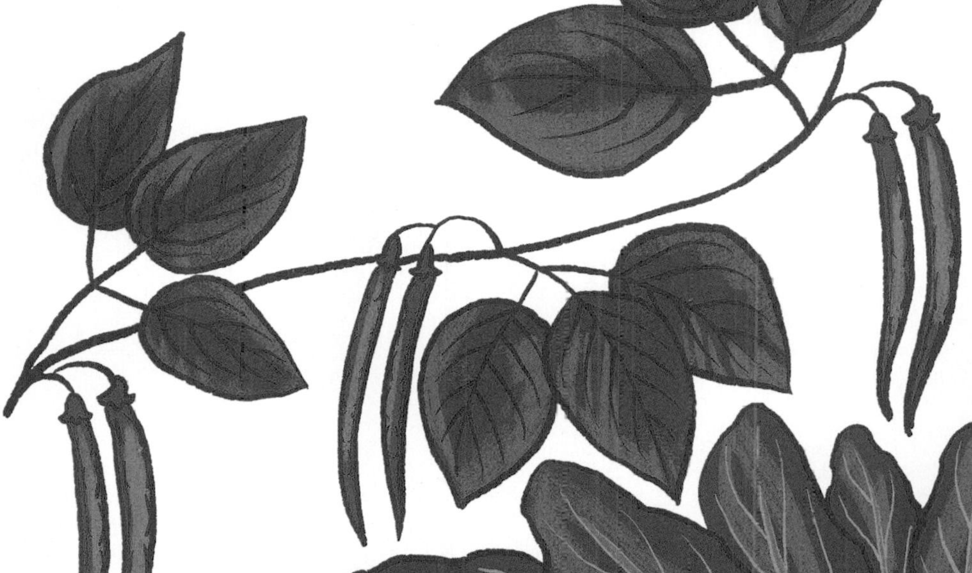

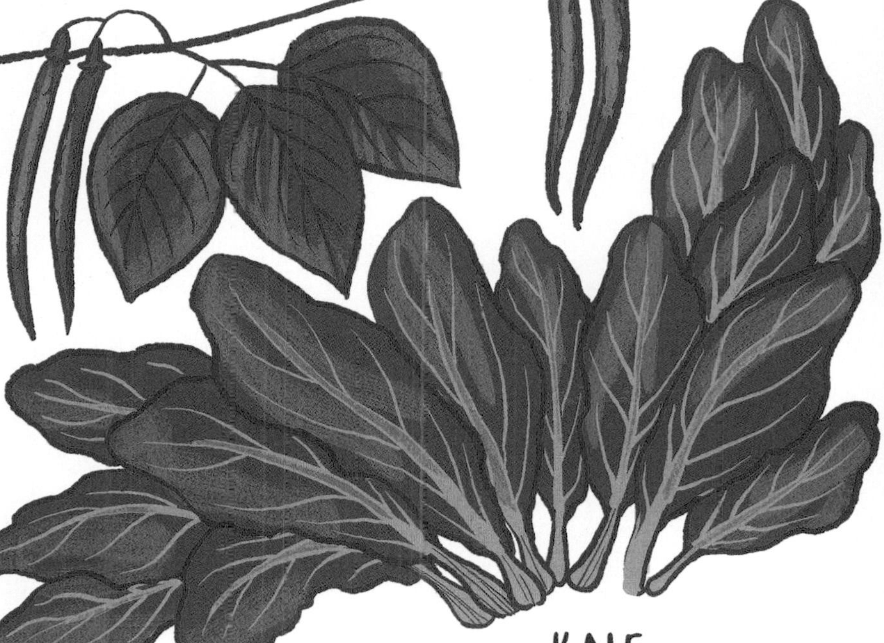

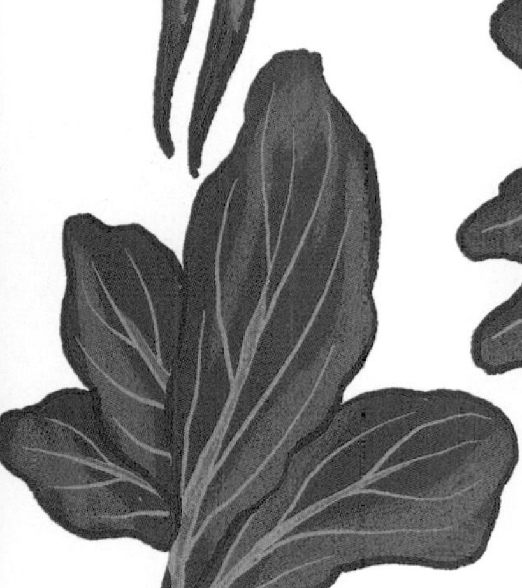

KALE

CUT INDIVIDUAL LEAVES AS NEEDED ONCE THE PLANT REACHES 8 TO 10 INCHES TALL. HARVEST NO MORE THAN HALF THE LEAVES AT A TIME, AND LET REGROW ABOUT 1 WEEK BEFORE HARVESTING AGAIN. CAN HARVEST ALL SEASON, AND WELL INTO THE FALL. KALE IS TENDER AND SWEET IN COOLER WEATHER, TOUGHER AND A LITTLE BITTER IN THE HEAT OF THE SUMMER.

CHEAT SHEET
GEORGE APPROVED GARDEN TIPS

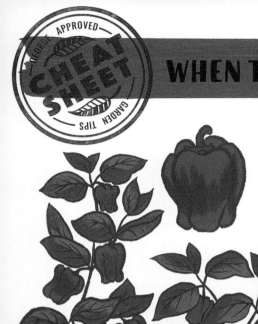

WHEN TO HARVEST

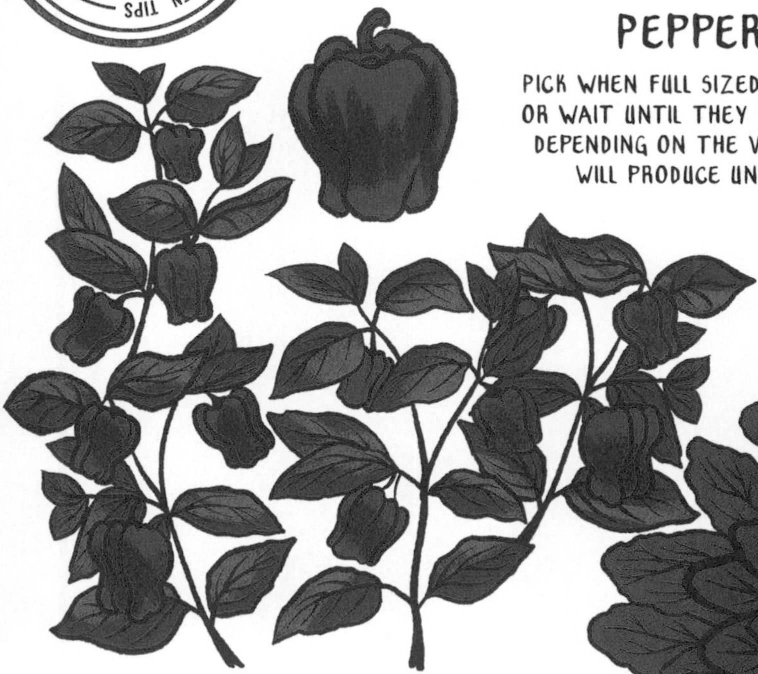

PEPPER

PICK WHEN FULL SIZED, BUT GREEN, FOR GREEN PEPPERS, OR WAIT UNTIL THEY TURN RED (OR ORANGE OR YELLOW, DEPENDING ON THE VARIETY) FOR A SWEETER PEPPER. WILL PRODUCE UNTIL THE FIRST FROST OF FALL.

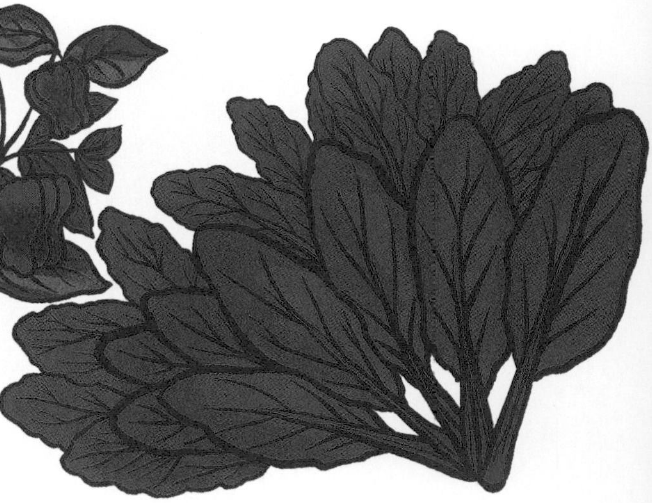

SWISS CHARD

CUT INDIVIDUAL LEAVES AS NEEDED ONCE THE PLANT IS 8 TO 10 INCHES TALL. HARVEST NO MORE THAN HALF THE LEAVES AT A TIME, AND LET REGROW ABOUT 1 WEEK BEFORE HARVESTING AGAIN. CAN HARVEST ALL SEASON AND WELL INTO THE FALL.

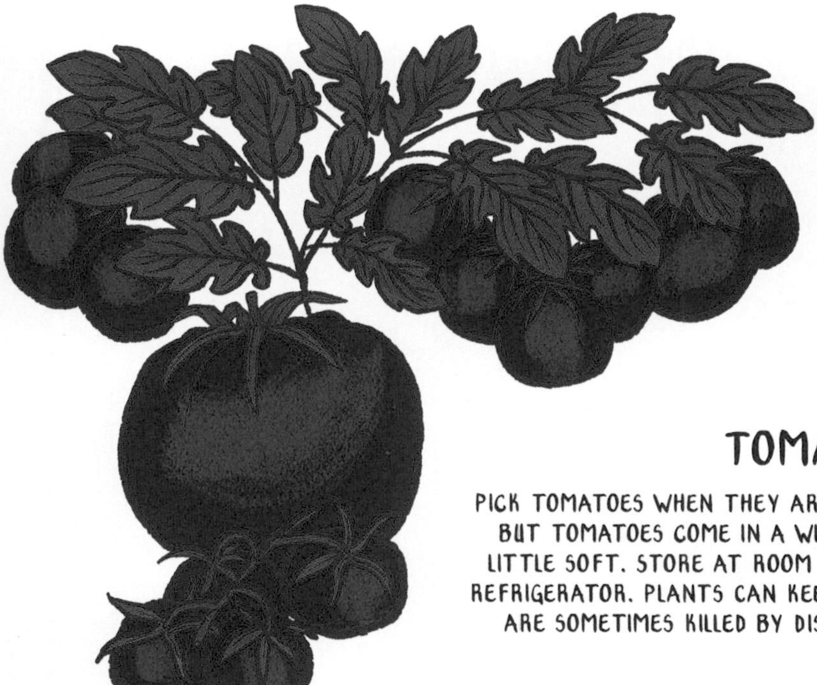

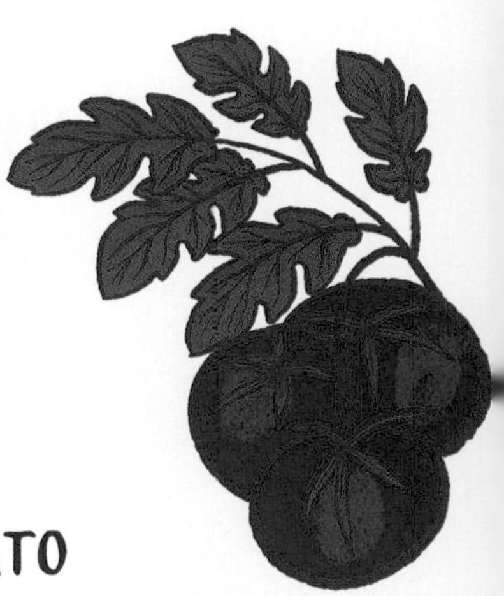

TOMATO

PICK TOMATOES WHEN THEY ARE FULLY COLORED (USUALLY RED, BUT TOMATOES COME IN A WIDE RANGE OF COLORS) AND A LITTLE SOFT. STORE AT ROOM TEMPERATURE, NEVER IN THE REFRIGERATOR. PLANTS CAN KEEP PRODUCING ALL SUMMER, BUT ARE SOMETIMES KILLED BY DISEASE LATER IN THE SEASON.

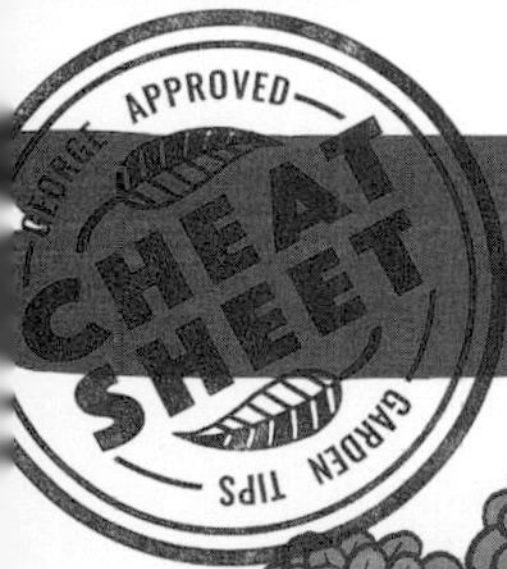
GEORGE APPROVED
CHEAT SHEET
GARDEN TIPS

WHEN TO HARVEST

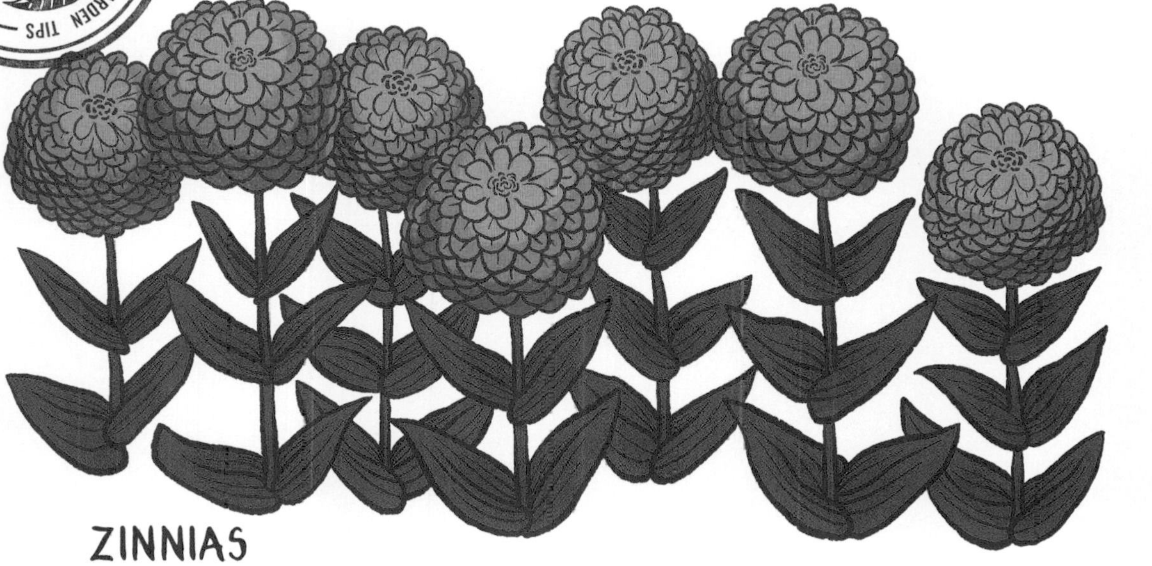

ZINNIAS

CUT FLOWERS WHEN THE FIRST ROW OF PETALS HAS UNFOLDED. TRIM OFF THE LEAVES AND PLACE IN A VASE OF WATER. FOR LONGEST FLOWER LIFE, CHANGE THE WATER EVERY COUPLE OF DAYS AND ADD 1/2 TEASPOON BLEACH, 2 TABLESPOONS LEMON JUICE, AND 1 TABLESPOON SUGAR PER QUART OF WATER. IF YOU LEAVE FLOWERS ON THE PLANT, CUT THEM OFF ONCE THEY BEGIN TO BROWN, TO ENCOURAGE MORE FLOWERS TO DEVELOP.

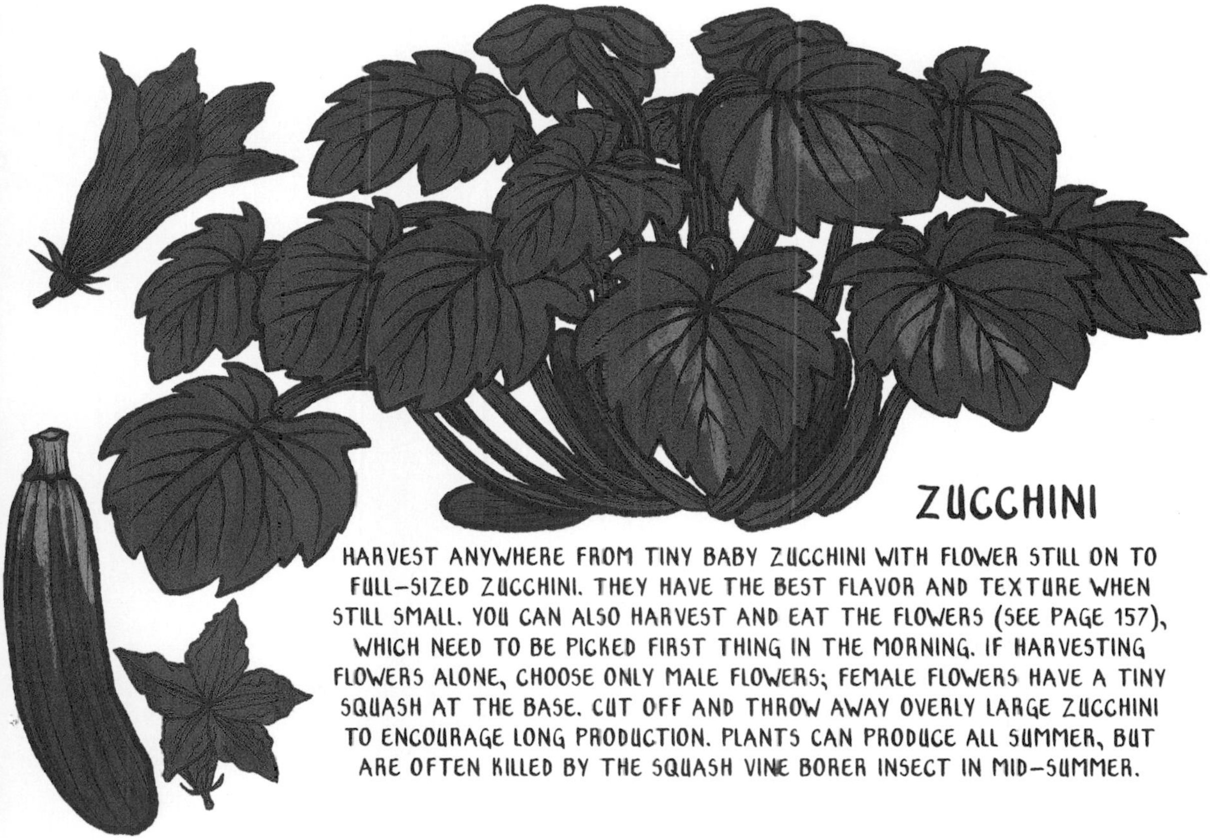

ZUCCHINI

HARVEST ANYWHERE FROM TINY BABY ZUCCHINI WITH FLOWER STILL ON TO FULL-SIZED ZUCCHINI. THEY HAVE THE BEST FLAVOR AND TEXTURE WHEN STILL SMALL. YOU CAN ALSO HARVEST AND EAT THE FLOWERS (SEE PAGE 157), WHICH NEED TO BE PICKED FIRST THING IN THE MORNING. IF HARVESTING FLOWERS ALONE, CHOOSE ONLY MALE FLOWERS; FEMALE FLOWERS HAVE A TINY SQUASH AT THE BASE. CUT OFF AND THROW AWAY OVERLY LARGE ZUCCHINI TO ENCOURAGE LONG PRODUCTION. PLANTS CAN PRODUCE ALL SUMMER, BUT ARE OFTEN KILLED BY THE SQUASH VINE BORER INSECT IN MID-SUMMER.

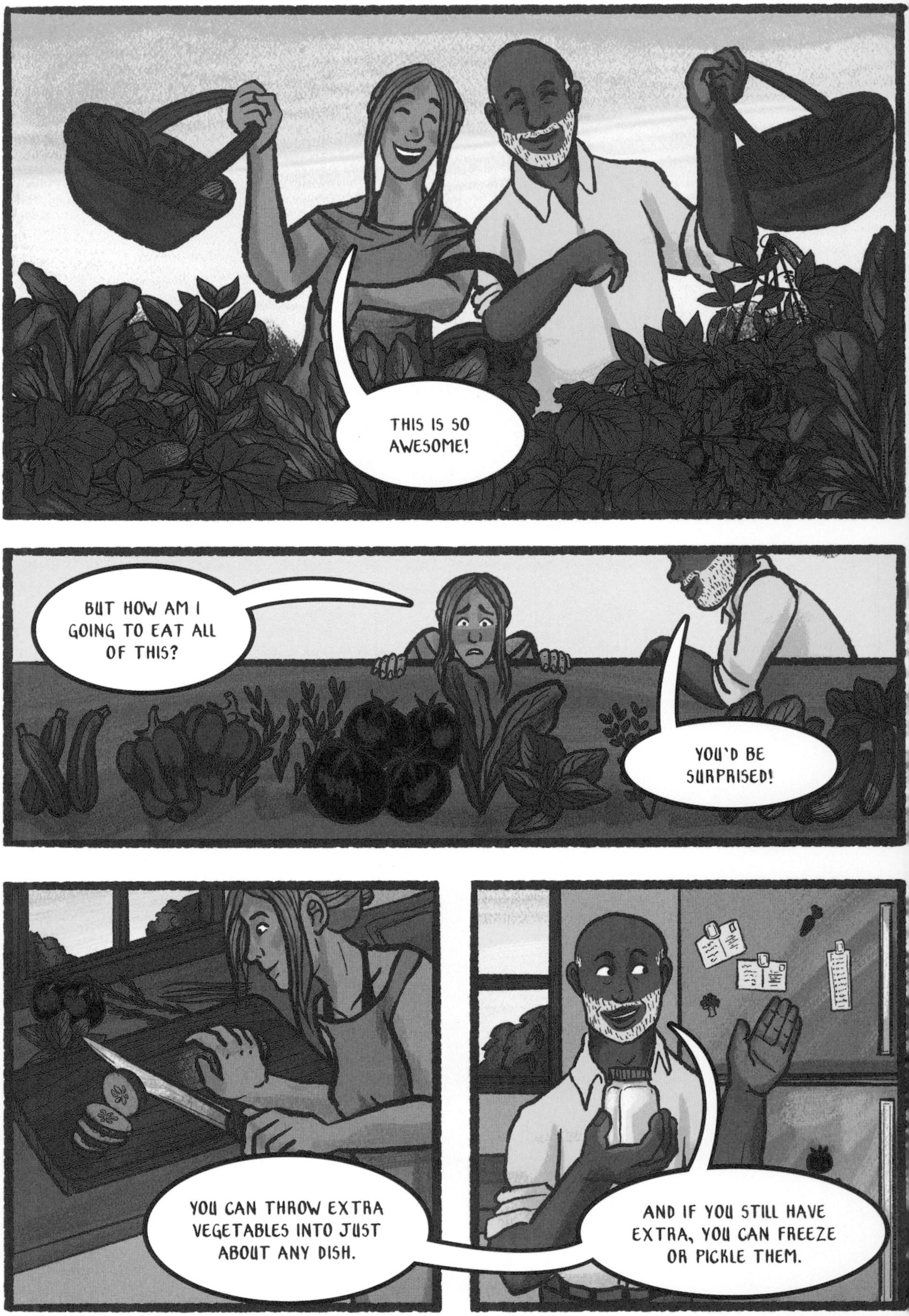
THIS IS SO AWESOME!
BUT HOW AM I GOING TO EAT ALL OF THIS?
YOU'D BE SURPRISED!
YOU CAN THROW EXTRA VEGETABLES INTO JUST ABOUT ANY DISH.
AND IF YOU STILL HAVE EXTRA, YOU CAN FREEZE OR PICKLE THEM.

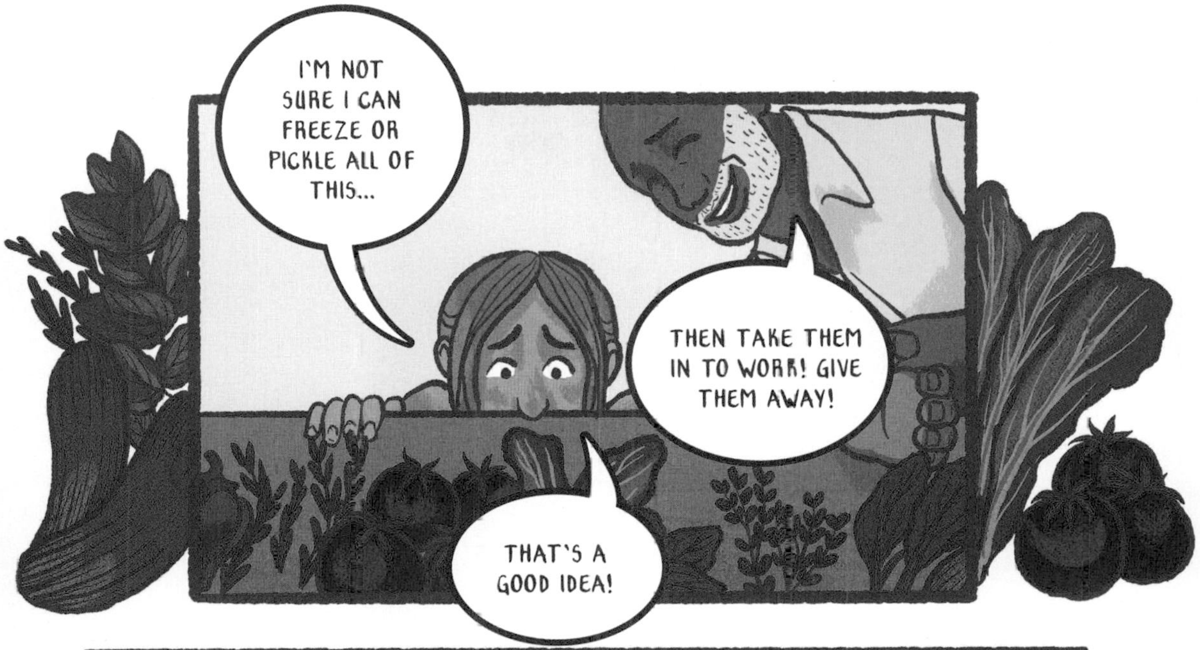
I'M NOT SURE I CAN FREEZE OR PICKLE ALL OF THIS...
THEN TAKE THEM IN TO WORK! GIVE THEM AWAY!
THAT'S A GOOD IDEA!

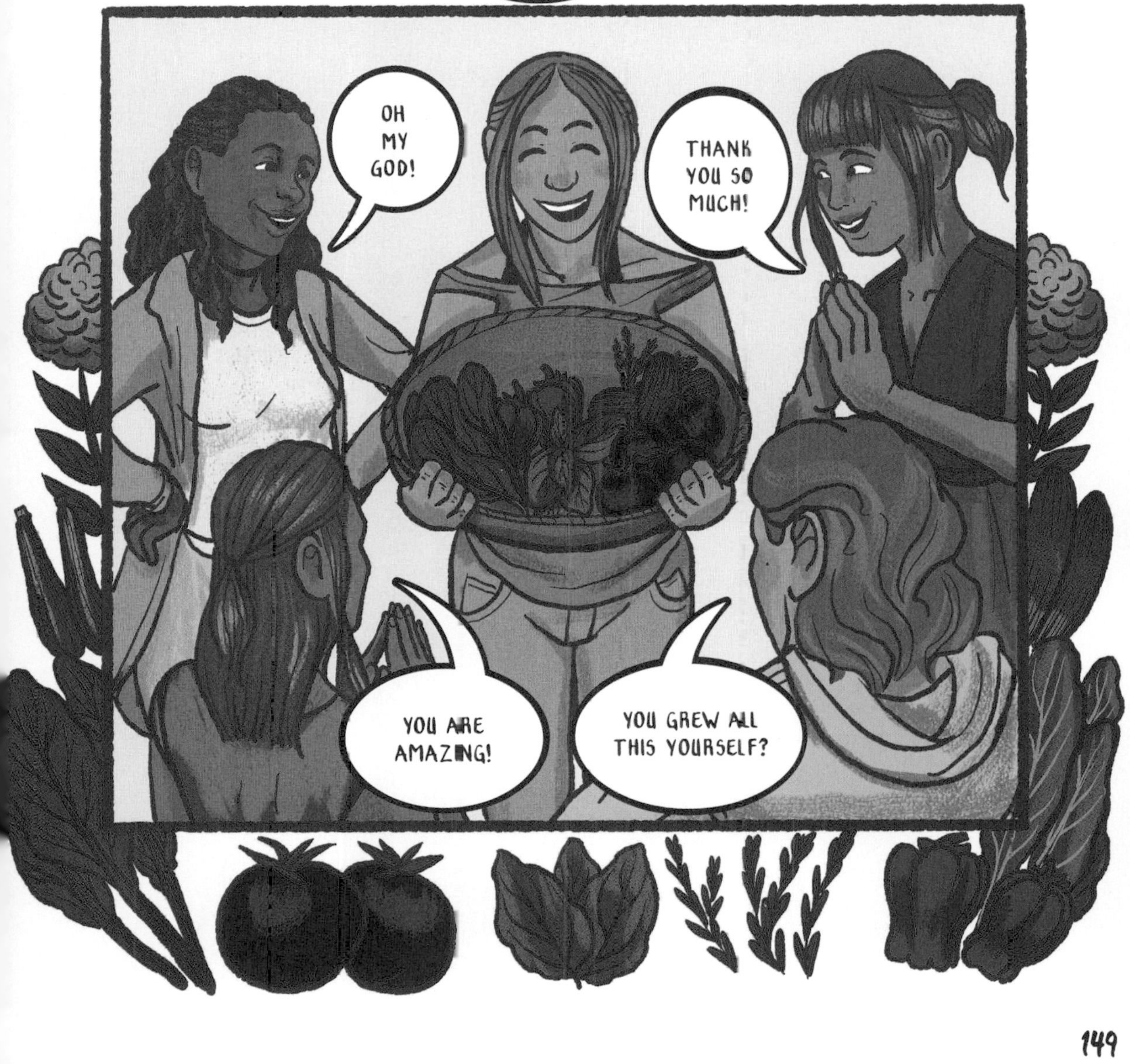
OH MY GOD!
THANK YOU SO MUCH!
YOU ARE AMAZING!
YOU GREW ALL THIS YOURSELF?

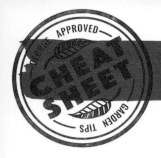

USING UP EXTRA PRODUCE

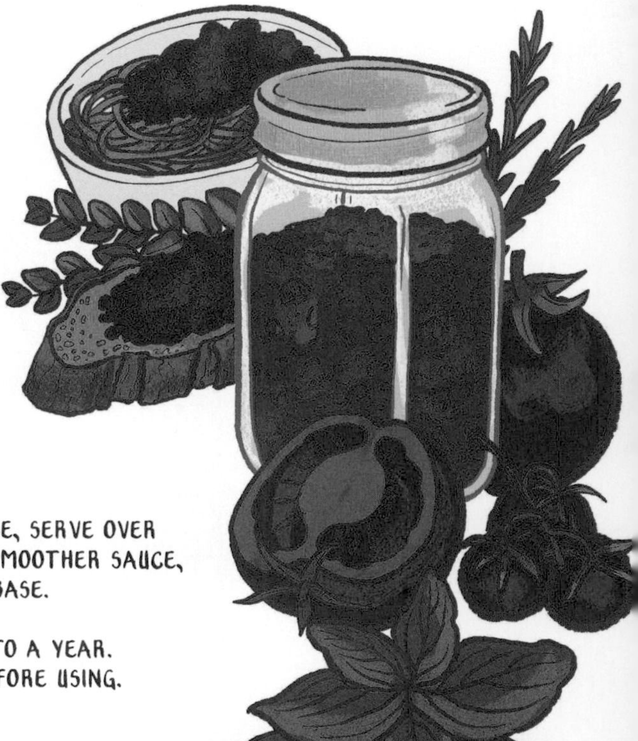

TOMATO GLUT SAUCE

PREHEAT THE OVEN TO 400°F.
ROUGHLY CHOP ABOUT 5 POUNDS OF TOMATOES
PLACE IN A 9 BY 13-INCH GLASS BAKING PAN.
SEASON WITH SALT, PEPPER, A DRIZZLE
OF OLIVE OIL, AND FRESH HERBS.

THROW IN CHOPPED ONIONS, GARLIC, PEPPERS,
AND/OR ZUCCHINI IF YOU HAVE THEM ON
HAND AND IF YOU FEEL INSPIRED TO.
ROAST FOR 45 MINUTES.

EAT WITH CRUSTY BREAD AND GOOD CHEESE, SERVE OVER
PASTA, PULSE IN A FOOD PROCESSOR FOR A SMOOTHER SAUCE,
OR PUREE FOR A TOMATO SOUP BASE.

EXTRA GOES IN THE FREEZER FOR UP TO A YEAR.
DEFROST IN YOUR FRIDGE OVERNIGHT BEFORE USING.

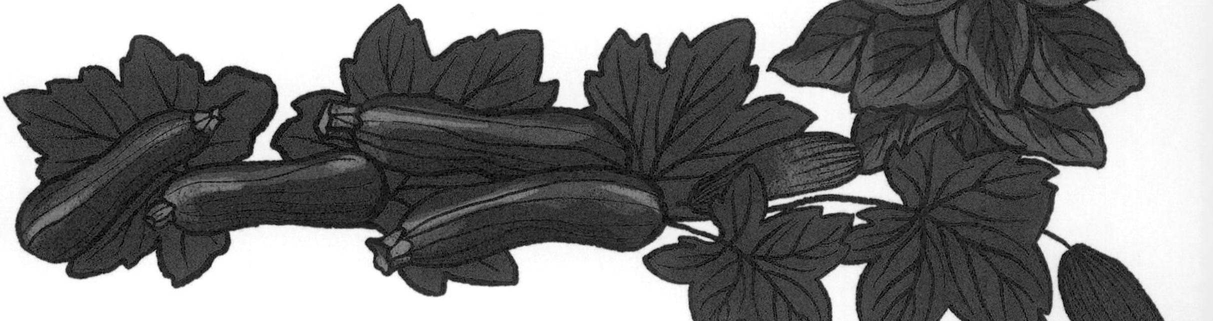

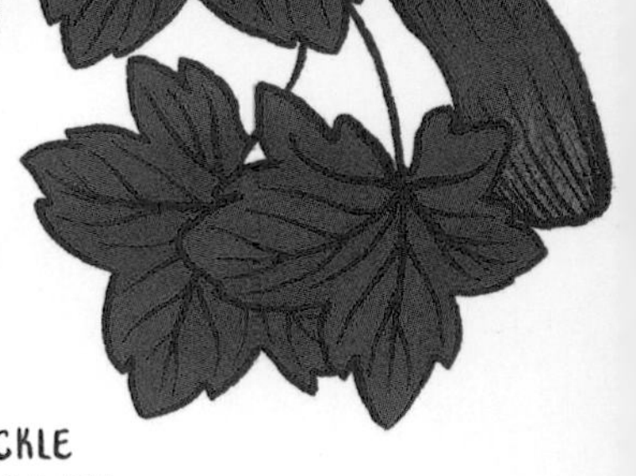

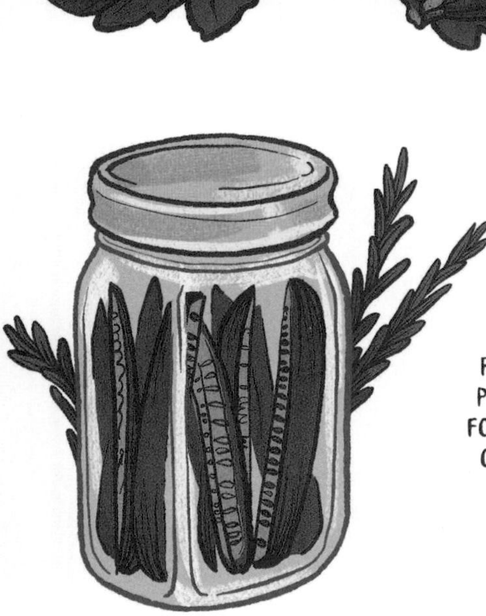

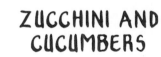

ZUCCHINI AND CUCUMBERS

PICKLE THEM! ANY CUCUMBER PICKLE
RECIPE WILL WORK WITH ZUCCHINI AS WELL.
PICK THEM WHEN JUST A FEW INCHES LONG
FOR MINI-ZUCCHINI PICKLES, OR SLICE LARGER
ONES TO ALLOW THE BRINE TO PENETRATE.

USING UP EXTRA PRODUCE

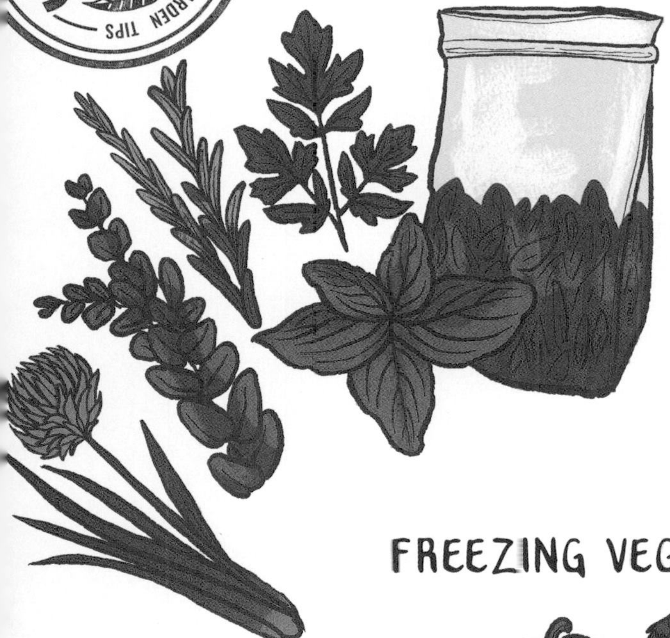

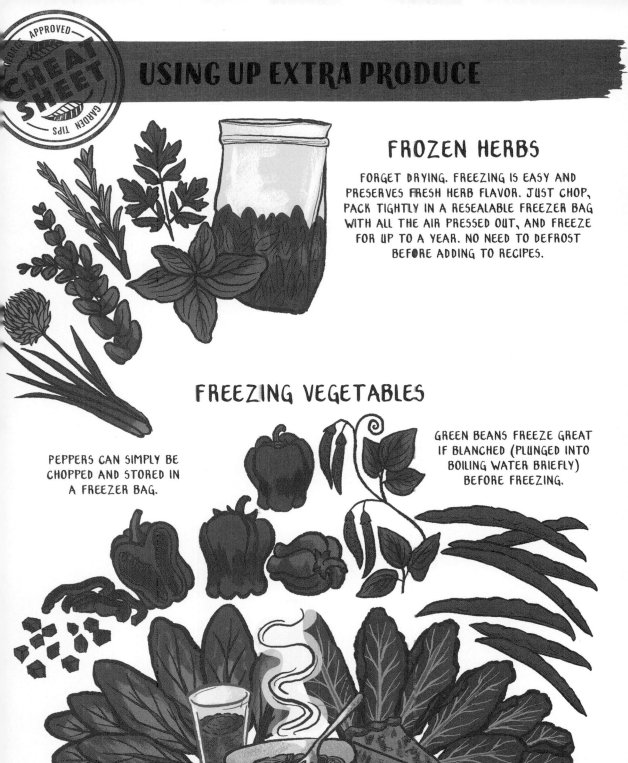

FROZEN HERBS

FORGET DRYING. FREEZING IS EASY AND PRESERVES FRESH HERB FLAVOR. JUST CHOP, PACK TIGHTLY IN A RESEALABLE FREEZER BAG WITH ALL THE AIR PRESSED OUT, AND FREEZE FOR UP TO A YEAR. NO NEED TO DEFROST BEFORE ADDING TO RECIPES.

FREEZING VEGETABLES

PEPPERS CAN SIMPLY BE CHOPPED AND STORED IN A FREEZER BAG.

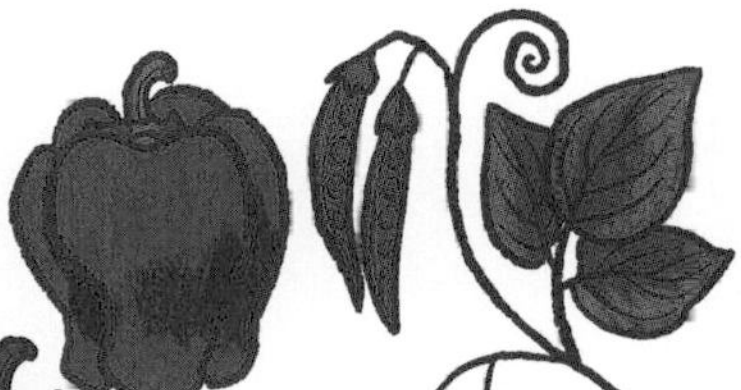

GREEN BEANS FREEZE GREAT IF BLANCHED (PLUNGED INTO BOILING WATER BRIEFLY) BEFORE FREEZING.

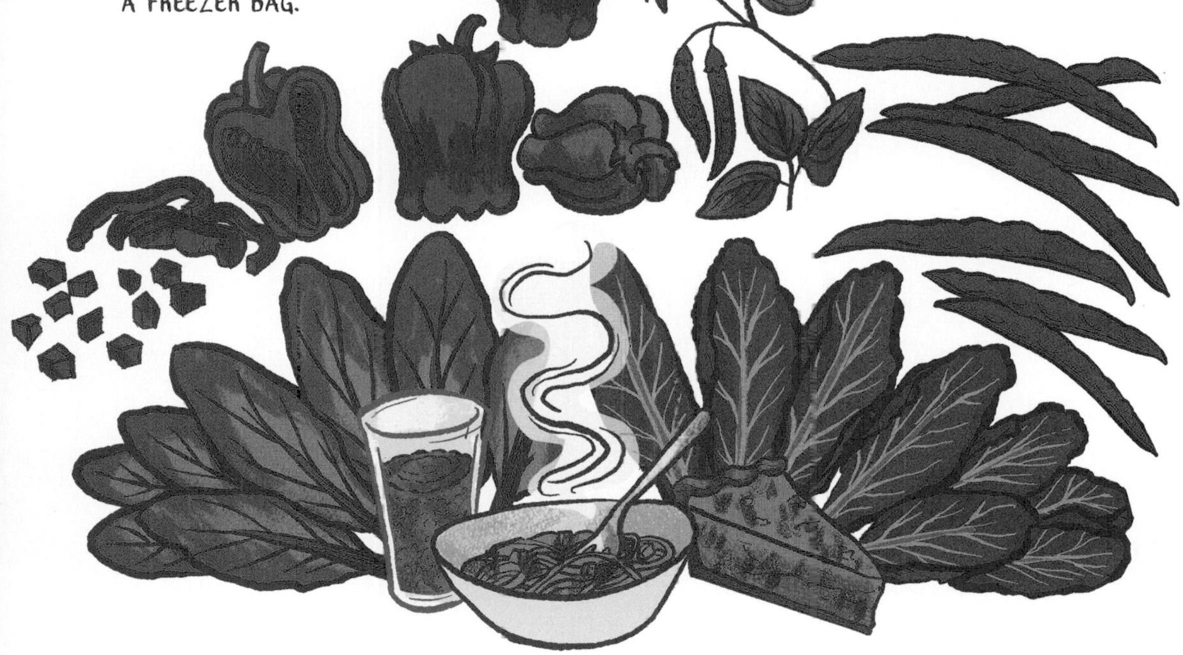

KALE AND SWISS CHARD WILL TURN TO MUSH IF FROZEN, WHICH IS FINE IF YOU'LL LATER BE USING THEM IN SMOOTHIES OR COOKED FOOD LIKE SOUP, PASTA SAUCE, OR QUICHE. YOU CAN FREEZE VEGETABLES FOR UP TO A YEAR, AND DEFROST IN THE FRIDGE OVERNIGHT BEFORE USING. OTHERWISE, EAT THEM FRESH, AND IF YOU HAVE TOO MUCH, SHARE WITH FRIENDS.

TEN:
CELEBRATION

**ENJOYING THE GARDEN'S
PRODUCE WITH FRIENDS.**

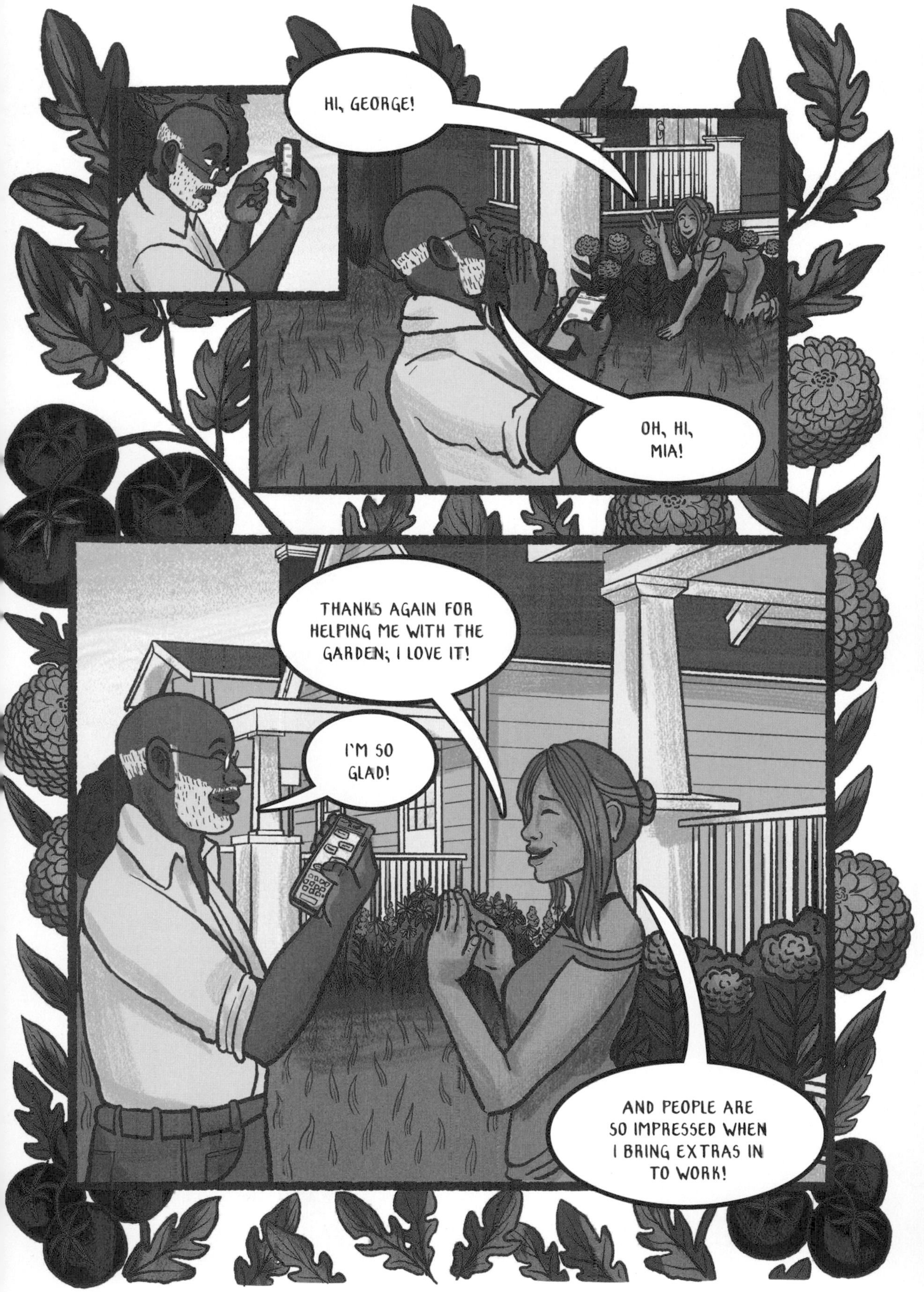
HI, GEORGE!
OH, HI, MIA!
THANKS AGAIN FOR HELPING ME WITH THE GARDEN; I LOVE IT!
I'M SO GLAD!
AND PEOPLE ARE SO IMPRESSED WHEN I BRING EXTRAS IN TO WORK!

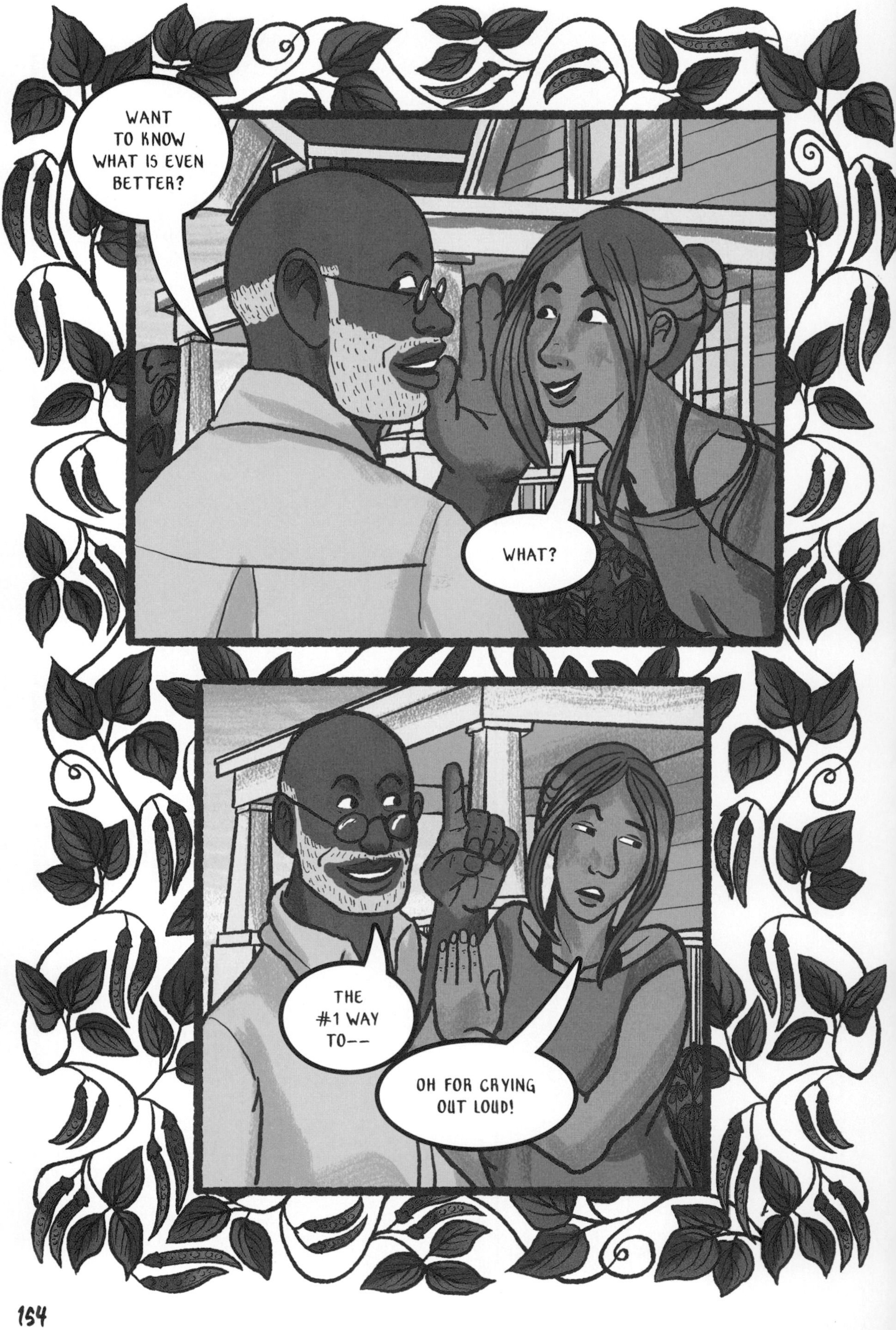
WANT TO KNOW WHAT IS EVEN BETTER?
WHAT?
THE #1 WAY TO--
OH FOR CRYING OUT LOUD!

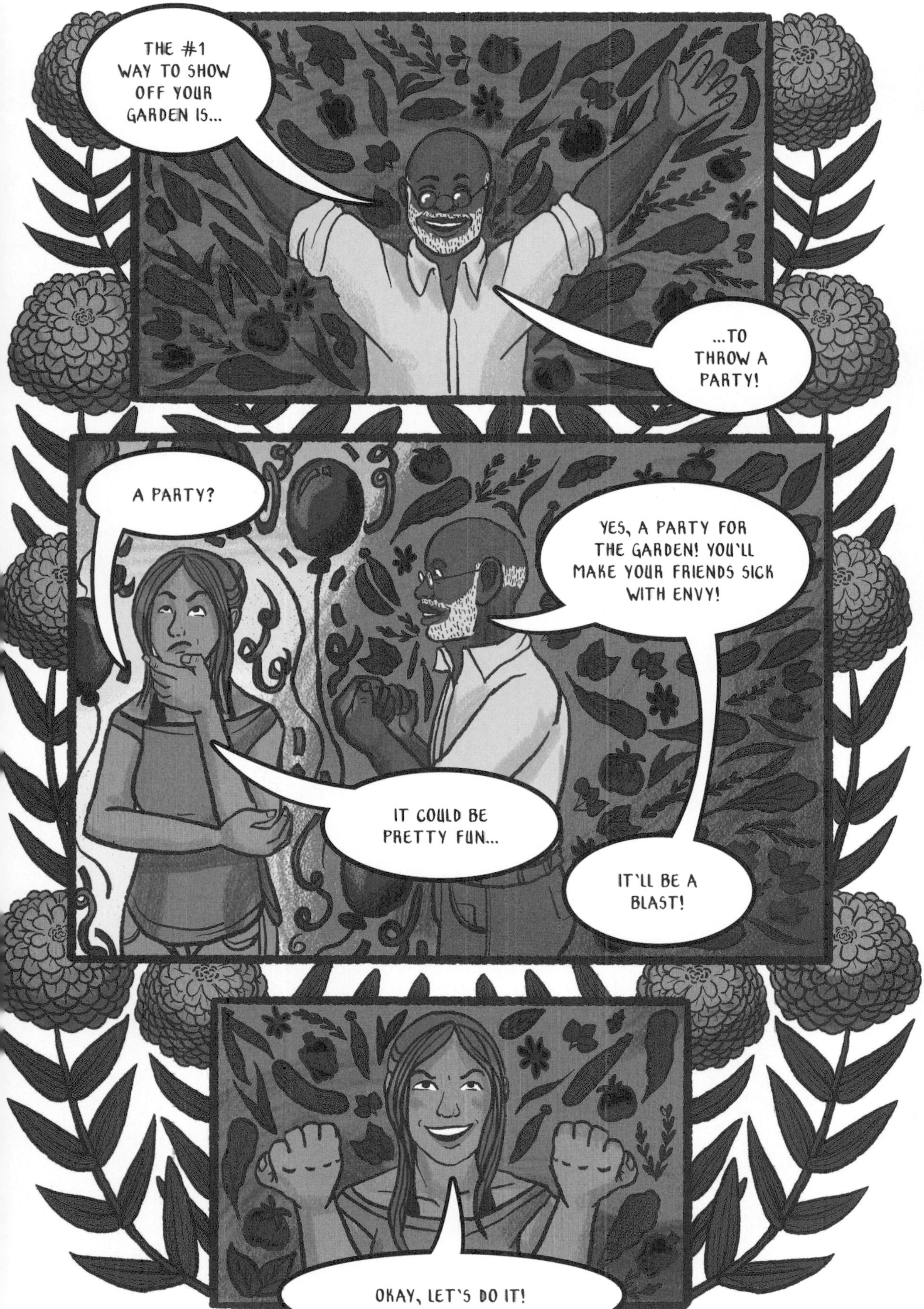
THE #1 WAY TO SHOW OFF YOUR GARDEN IS...
...TO THROW A PARTY!
A PARTY?
YES, A PARTY FOR THE GARDEN! YOU'LL MAKE YOUR FRIENDS SICK WITH ENVY!
IT COULD BE PRETTY FUN...
IT'LL BE A BLAST!
OKAY, LET'S DO IT!

GARDEN PARTY SNACKS

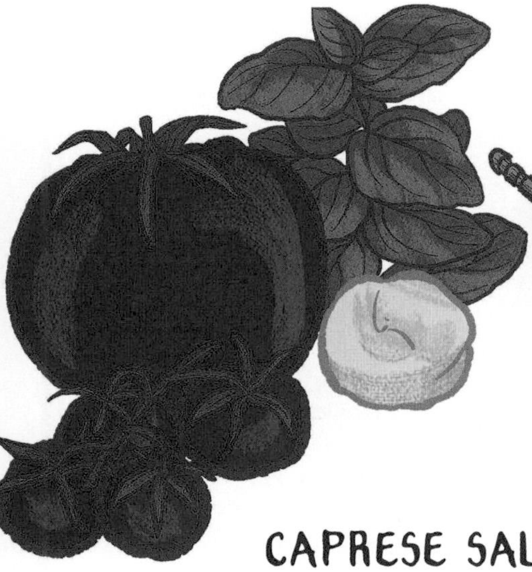

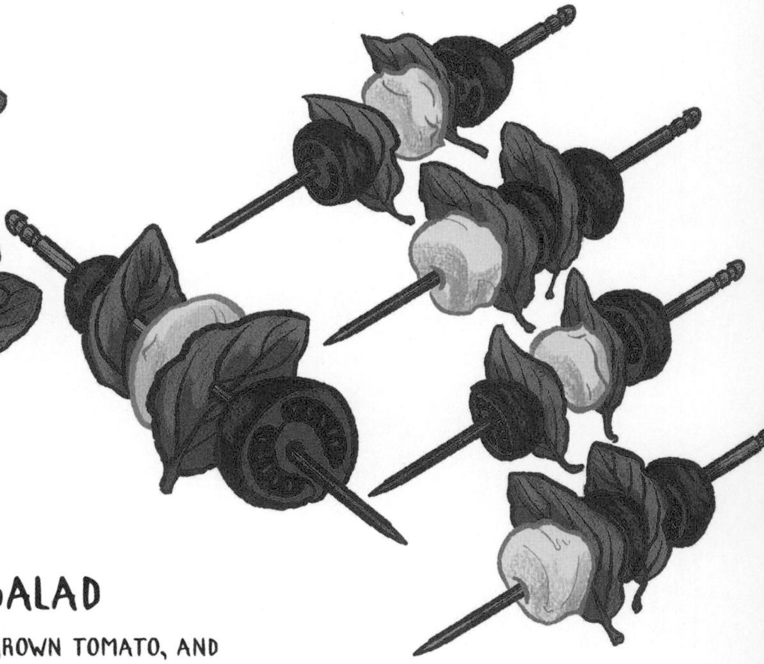

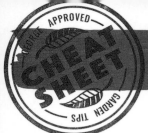

CAPRESE SALAD

BUFFALO MOZZARELLA, HOMEGROWN TOMATO, AND FRESH BASIL, SERVED BITE-SIZE ON TOOTHPICKS.

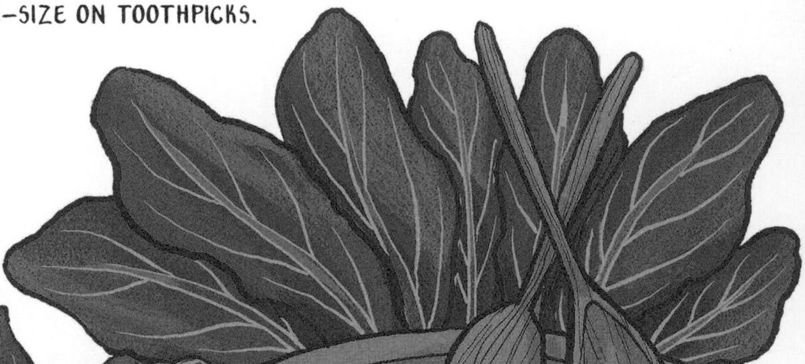

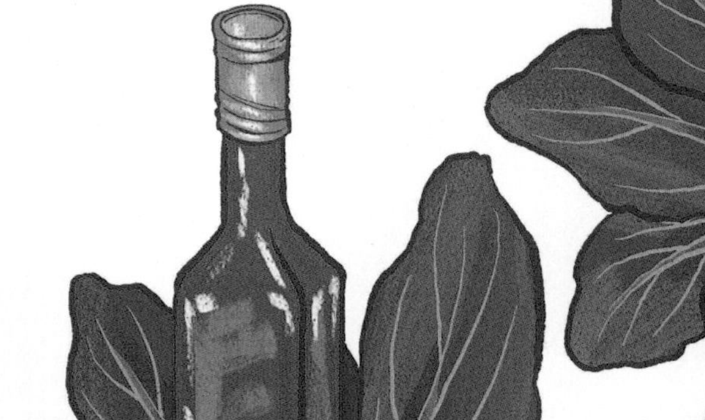

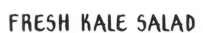

FRESH KALE SALAD

TORN KALE DRESSED WITH LEMON JUICE, OLIVE OIL, CRUSHED GARLIC, AND FETA OR PARMESAN CHEESE.

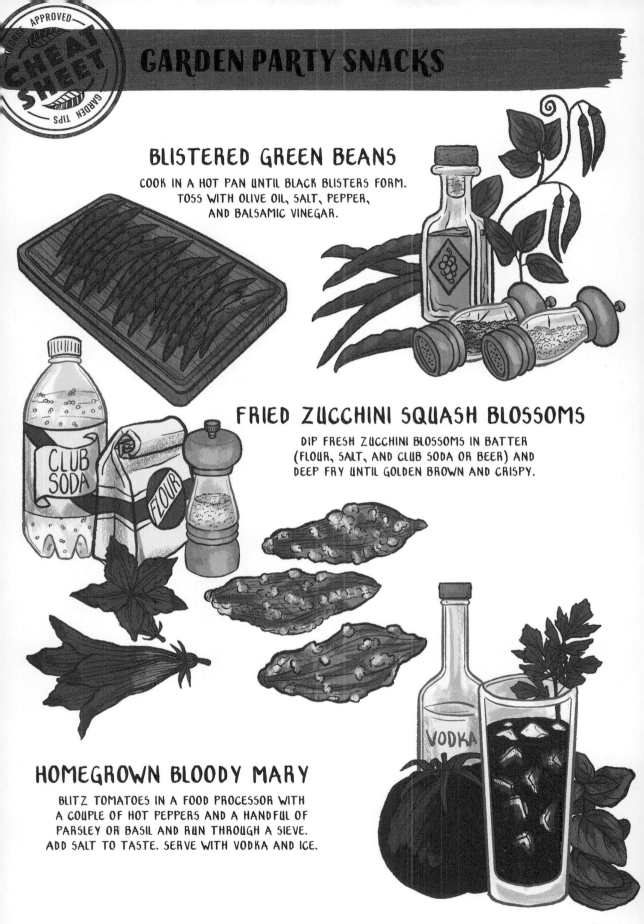

APPROVED
CHEAT SHEET
GARDEN TIPS

GARDEN PARTY SNACKS

BLISTERED GREEN BEANS

COOK IN A HOT PAN UNTIL BLACK BLISTERS FORM. TOSS WITH OLIVE OIL, SALT, PEPPER, AND BALSAMIC VINEGAR.

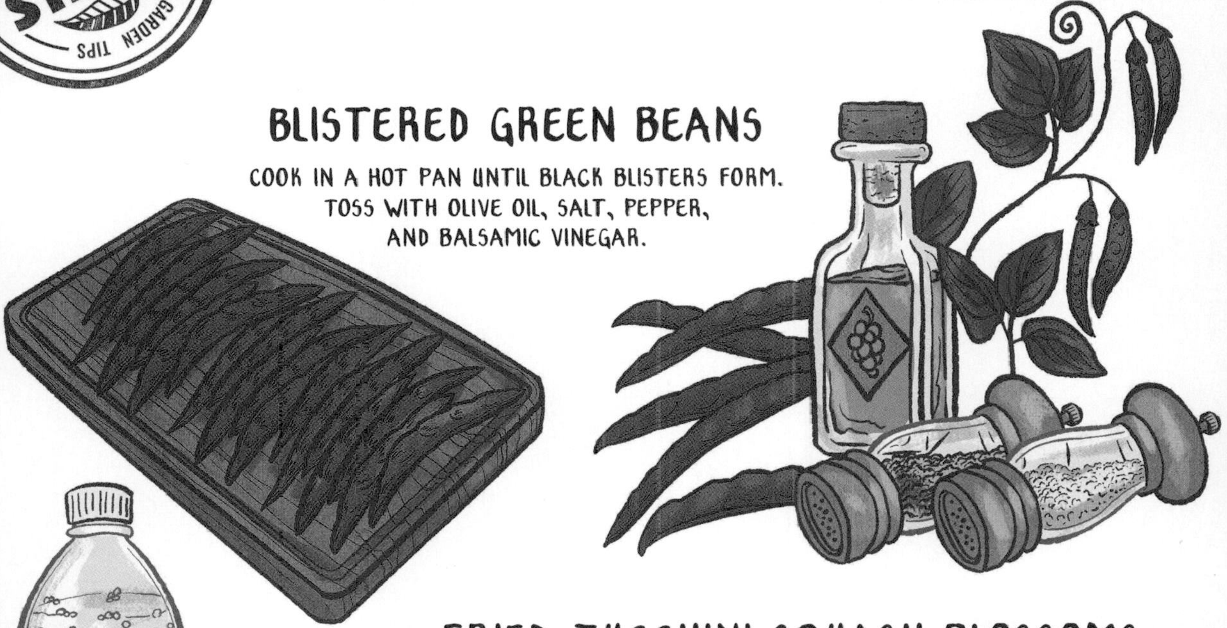

FRIED ZUCCHINI SQUASH BLOSSOMS

DIP FRESH ZUCCHINI BLOSSOMS IN BATTER (FLOUR, SALT, AND CLUB SODA OR BEER) AND DEEP FRY UNTIL GOLDEN BROWN AND CRISPY.

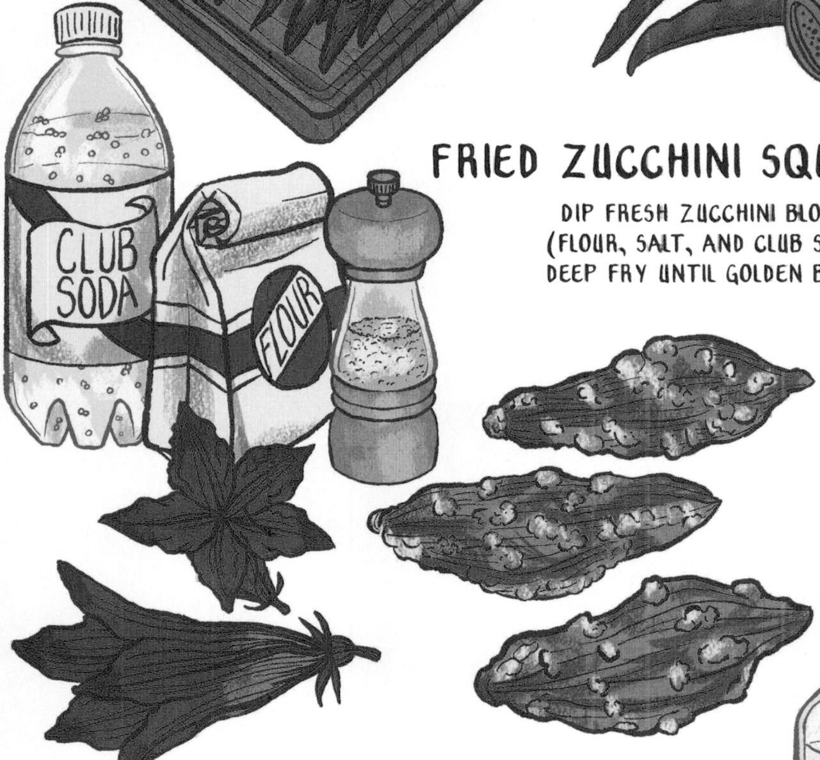
CLUB SODA
FLOUR

HOMEGROWN BLOODY MARY

BLITZ TOMATOES IN A FOOD PROCESSOR WITH A COUPLE OF HOT PEPPERS AND A HANDFUL OF PARSLEY OR BASIL AND RUN THROUGH A SIEVE. ADD SALT TO TASTE. SERVE WITH VODKA AND ICE.

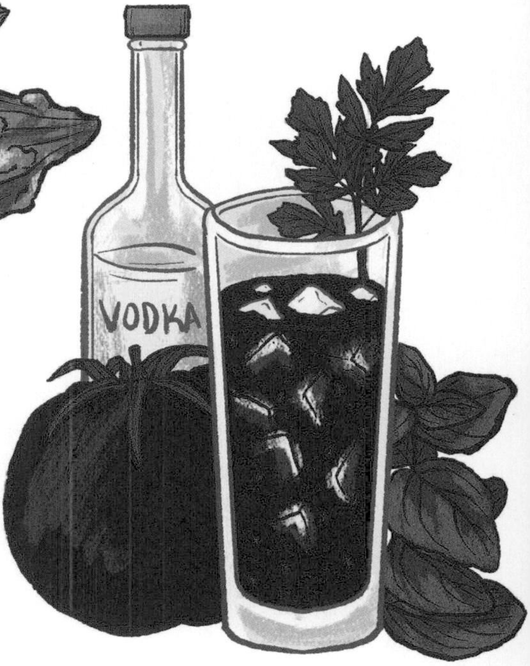
VODKA

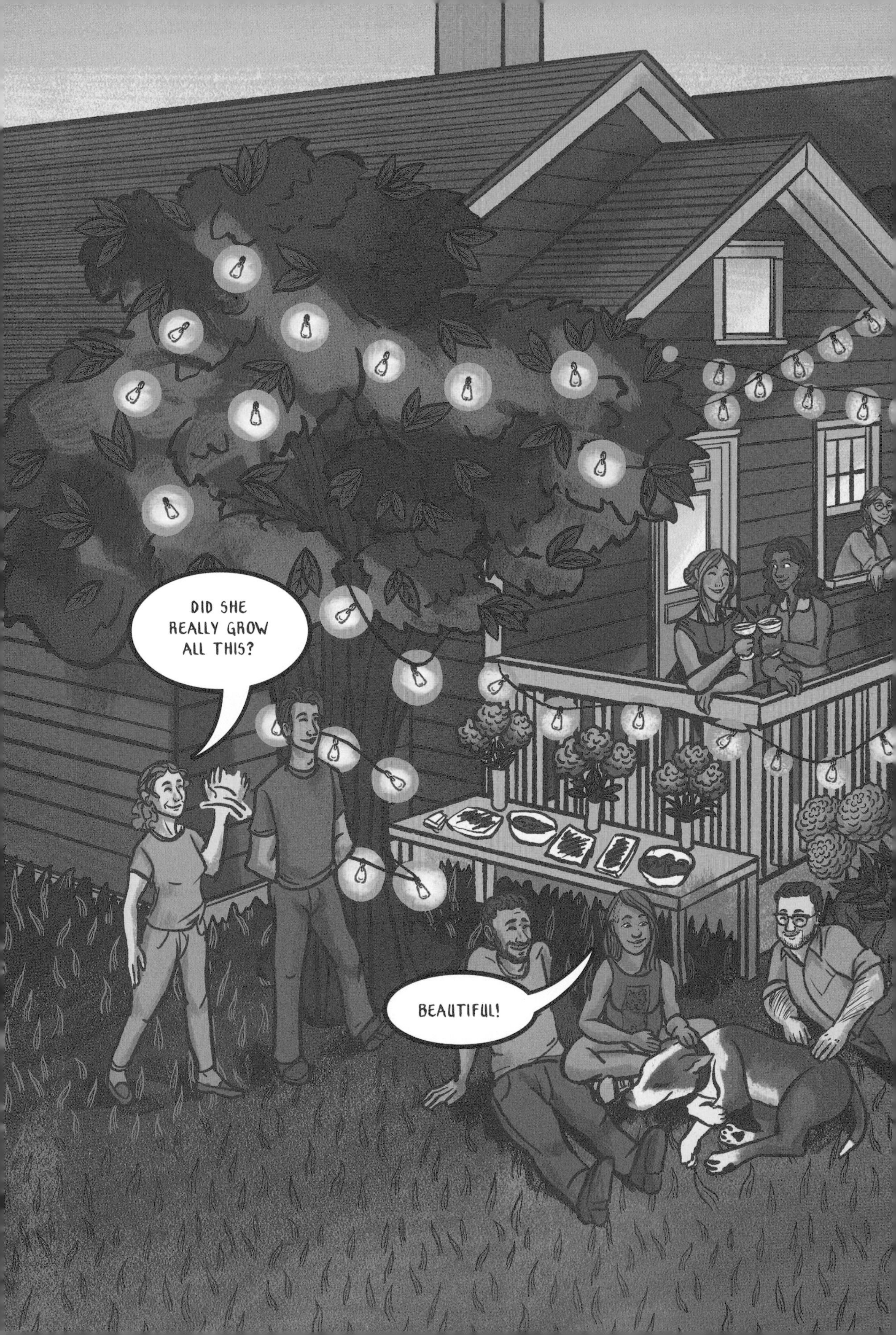
DID SHE REALLY GROW ALL THIS?
BEAUTIFUL!

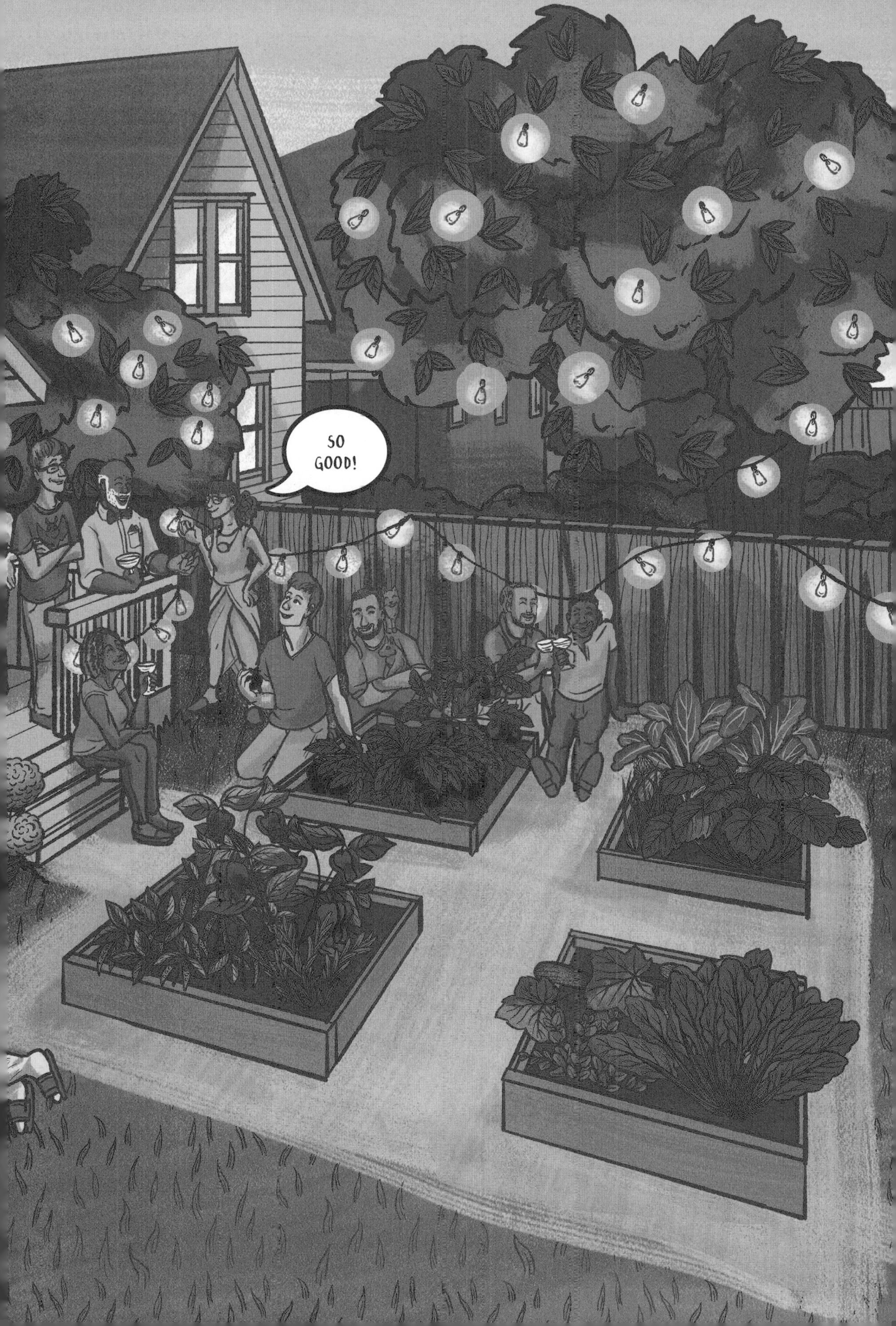
SO GOOD!

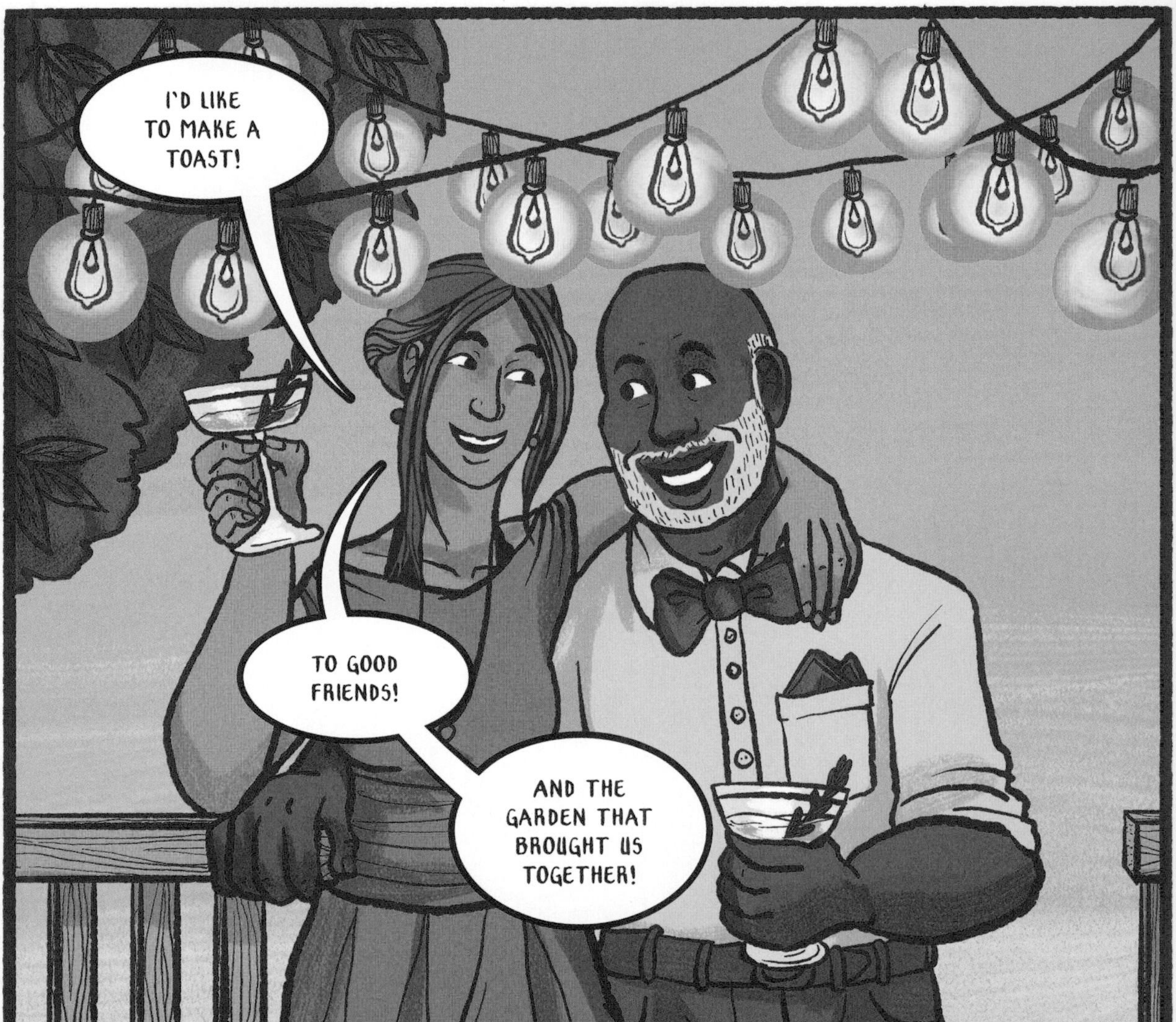
I'D LIKE TO MAKE A TOAST!
TO GOOD FRIENDS!
AND THE GARDEN THAT BROUGHT US TOGETHER!

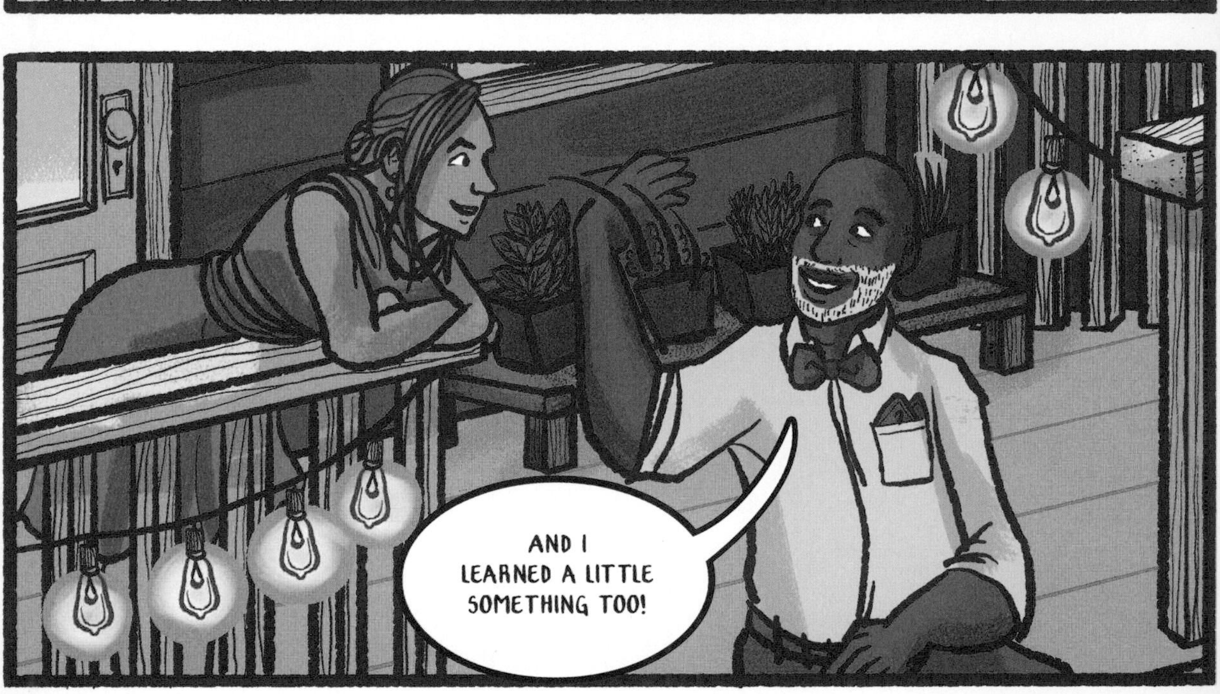
AND I LEARNED A LITTLE SOMETHING TOO!

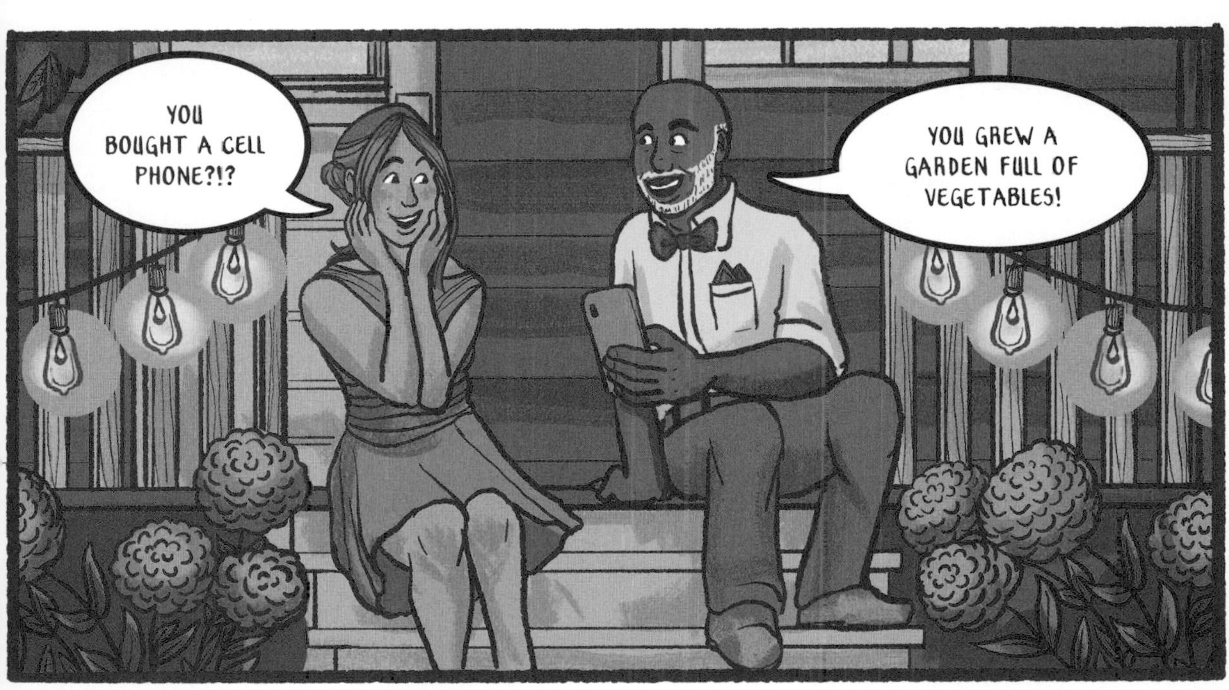
YOU BOUGHT A CELL PHONE?!?
YOU GREW A GARDEN FULL OF VEGETABLES!

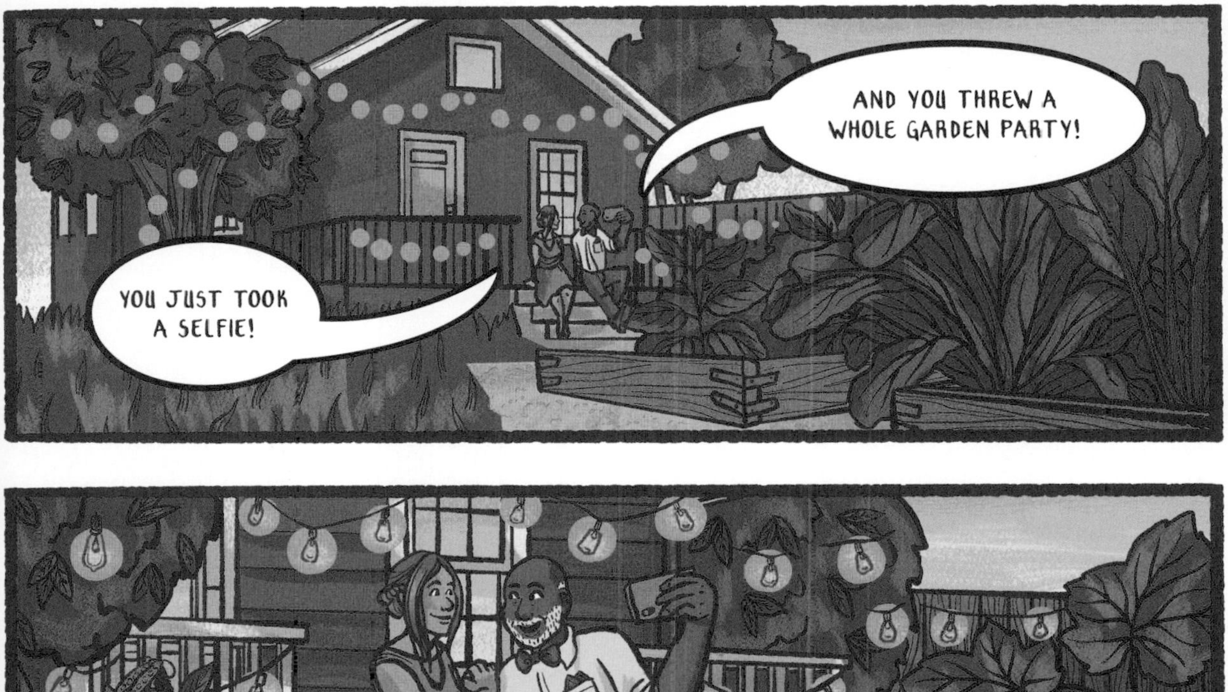
AND YOU THREW A WHOLE GARDEN PARTY!
YOU JUST TOOK A SELFIE!

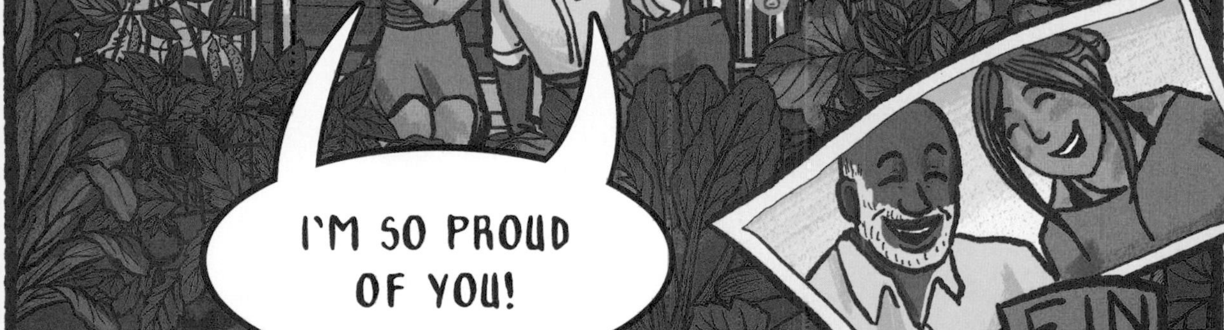
I'M SO PROUD OF YOU!
FIN

THE CHEAT SHEET OF CHEAT SHEETS

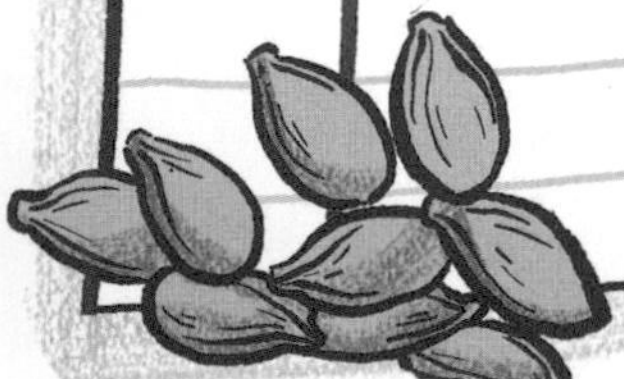

THE CHEAT SHEET OF CHEAT SHEETS

FURTHER READING AND RESOURCES

GEORGE'S READING LIST FOR GARDENERS WHO HAD FUN AND WANT MORE

WANT MORE VEGETABLES?

THE EDIBLE FRONT YARD BY IVETTE SOLER. LEARN TO GROW VEGETABLES THAT ARE PRODUCTIVE AND PART OF A BEAUTIFUL LANDSCAPE THAT WON'T UPSET YOUR HOA.

EPIC TOMATOES BY CRAIG LEHOULLIER. EVERYTHING YOU COULD WANT TO KNOW ABOUT THE WORLD'S FAVORITE VEGETABLE.

MASTERING THE ART OF VEGETABLE GARDENING BY MATT MATTUS. TAKE YOUR VEGETABLE GROWING TO THE NEXT LEVEL AND GROW PICTURE-PERFECT PRODUCE.

THE POSTAGE STAMP VEGETABLE GARDEN BY KAREN NEWCOMB. GROW VEGETABLES EVEN IF YOU DON'T HAVE MUCH SPACE.

VEGGIE GARDEN REMIX BY NIKI JABBOUR. IF YOU WANT TO GO BEYOND FAMILIAR VEGGIES, READ THIS FOR OUTSIDE-THE-BOX IDEAS.

THE YEAR-ROUND VEGETABLE GARDENER BY NIKI JABBOUR. EXTEND THE GARDENING SEASON RIGHT THROUGH THE WINTER, EVEN IN COLD CLIMATES.

WANT TO MOVE PAST VEGGIES TO THE WIDER WORLD OF GARDENING?

GOOD BUG, BAD BUG BY JESSICA WALLISER. LEARN THE INSECTS IN YOUR GARDEN—— HOW TO LOVE THE GOOD ONES AND MANAGE THE ONES THAT CAUSE PROBLEMS.

A WAY TO GARDEN BY MARGARET ROACH. A COMPLETE GUIDE TO EVERY ASPECT OF GARDENING IN EVERY SEASON.

THE WELL-TENDED PERENNIAL GARDEN BY TRACY DISABATO-AUST. A CLASSIC WORK ON CARING FOR YOUR FLOWERS.

YARDS BY BILLY GOODNICK. A SIMPLE GUIDE TO DESIGNING A LANDSCAPE THAT WORKS FOR YOU.

SOIL TESTING LABS

A & L LABORATORIES: AL-LABS-WEST.COM

LOGAN LABS: LOGANLABS.COM

YOUR STATE'S EXTENSION OFFICE: SEARCH FOR [THE NAME OF YOUR STATE] COOPERATIVE EXTENSION

GREAT WEBSITES

GOOD GARDENING VIDEOS: GOODGARDENINGVIDEOS.ORG
A WEBSITE THAT VETS GARDENING VIDEOS ONLINE FOR ACCURATE, EVIDENCE-BASED INFORMATION. START HERE RATHER THAN YOUTUBE FOR MORE RELIABLE INFORMATION.

A WAY TO GARDEN: AWAYTOGARDEN.COM
MARGARET ROACH'S WEBSITE IS FULL OF USEFUL INFORMATION, INTERVIEWS WITH GARDENING EXPERTS, AND A MONTHLY GARDEN CHORE LIST.

YOUR STATE'S EXTENSION OFFICE: SEARCH FOR [THE NAME OF YOUR STATE] COOPERATIVE EXTENSION
EACH STATE'S EXTENSION OFFICE IS TASKED WITH SHARING RESEARCH-BASED INFORMATION WITH HOME GARDENERS AND FARMERS. MOST STATES' WEBSITES WILL HAVE ARTICLES, SOIL TESTING SERVICES, INFOMATION ABOUT MASTER GARDENER TRAINING CLASSES, AND OTHER RESOURCES SPECIFIC TO YOUR STATE AND CLIMATE.

GEORGE'S FAVORITE SEED SOURCES

BAKER CREEK HEIRLOOM SEEDS: RARESEEDS.COM
PROBABLY THE MOST DIVERSE AND UNUSUAL CATALOG OF VEGETABLE SEEDS OUT THERE, CARRYING TRADITIONAL VARIETIES FROM AROUND THE WORLD.

JOHNNY'S SELECTED SEEDS: JOHNNYSEEDS.COM
A GREAT SEED COMPANY THAT PERFORMS EXTENSIVE TRIALING TO ENSURE THEY OFFER THE VERY BEST VARIETIES. BASED IN MAINE, SO IT'S A PARTICULARLY GOOD SOURCE FOR GARDENERS IN COLD, NORTHERN CLIMATES.

PINETREE GARDEN SEEDS: SUPERSEEDS.COM
A HUGE, VERY DIVERSE LISTING OF SEEDS. PACKETS ARE SMALLER AND CHEAPER THAN MOST OTHER SOURCES.

SEED SAVERS EXCHANGE: SEEDSAVERS.ORG
NONPROFIT FOCUSED ON SAVING A DIVERSITY OF HEIRLOOM PLANT VARIETIES. THEY HAVE A RETAIL CATALOG WITH SOME VARIETIES, AND IF YOU JOIN, YOU HAVE ACCESS TO AN ABSURDLY ENORMOUS LIST OF SEEDS FROM OTHER MEMBERS.

SELECT SEEDS: SELECTSEEDS.COM
FOCUSED ON HEIRLOOM FLOWER VARIETIES. A GREAT SOURCE IF YOU WANT TO ADD MORE FLOWERS TO YOUR GARDEN.

SOUTHERN EXPOSURE SEED EXCHANGE: SOUTHERNEXPOSURE.COM
FOCUSING ON HEIRLOOM SEEDS, ESPECIALLY—-BUT NOT EXCLUSIVELY—-THOSE FOR WARM SOUTHERN CLIMATES.

TERRITORIAL SEED COMPANY: TERRITORIALSEED.COM
HUGE SELECTION, WITH A PARTICULAR FOCUS ON VARIETIES WELL SUITED TO THE PACIFIC NORTHWEST.

ACKNOWLEDGMENTS

MANY THANKS TO LIZ FOR BRINGING MY WORDS SO BEAUTIFULLY TO LIFE; MY EDITOR, LISA REGUL, FOR HER INSIGHTFUL FEEDBACK AND COLLABORATION THROUGH EVERY STAGE OF THIS PROJECT; AND MY HUSBAND FOR BEING AN INSPIRATION, SOUNDING BOARD, AND ALL-AROUND INCREDIBLE LIFE PARTNER. OH, AND TO MY CAT MOCHAN FOR VERY HELPFULLY WALKING ACROSS MY KEYBOARD WHENEVER HE FELT IT WAS TIME FOR ME TO TAKE A BREAK AND SCRATCH HIS HEAD.

--JOSEPH

THANK YOU TO MY FAMILY NEAR AND FAR FOR ALWAYS SUPPORTING ME DESPITE MY MEANDERING PATH--TO NATEENE, NORA, AND CHRIS FOR CARRYING ME ALONG, AND TO BIN, WHO IS ALWAYS MY BACKBONE AND BETTER SENSE. LASTLY, THANK YOU TO PROFESSOR MANDRAKE, NÉE LYNDA BARRY, FOR BRINGING ME BACK TO COMICS. WE DO SOME PRETTY COOL THINGS ALL BECAUSE WE DRAW SOME PICTURES.

--LIZ

ABOUT THE AUTHORS

JOSEPH TYCHONIEVICH

HAS BEEN GARDENING MOST OF HIS LIFE AND GROWS WAY TOO MANY PLANTS. HE IS THE AUTHOR OF *PLANT BREEDING FOR THE HOME GARDENER* AND *ROCK GARDENING: REIMAGINING A CLASSIC STYLE*, AND THE EDITOR OF *THE ROCK GARDEN QUARTERLY*. JOSEPH LIVES AND GARDENS WITH HIS HUSBAND AND TWO ADORABLE BLACK CATS IN EASTERN VIRGINIA. VISIT HIM AT JOSEPHGARDENS.COM.

LIZ ANNA KOZIK

IS AN ILLUSTRATOR AND SCIENCE COMMUNICATOR WHO SHARES STORIES ABOUT THE ENVIRONMENT, ITS HISTORY, AND THE PEOPLE WHO LOVE IT. SHE WORKS WITH SCIENTISTS, GARDENERS, AND HISTORIANS TO CAPTURE THE JOY AND WONDER OF THE NATURAL WORLD, ESPECIALLY PRAIRIES. YOU CAN SEE MORE OF HER WORK AT LIZ.KOZIK.NET AND ON SOCIAL MEDIA @CHASE_PRAIRIE.

INDEX

PUBLISHED IN THE UNITED STATES BY TEN SPEED PRESS,
AN IMPRINT OF RANDOM HOUSE, A DIVISION OF
PENGUIN RANDOM HOUSE LLC, NEW YORK.
WWW.TENSPEED.COM

LIBRARY OF CONGRESS CONTROL NUMBER: 2020942488

TRADE PAPERBACK ISBN: 978-1-9848-5726-2
EBOOK ISBN: 978-1-9848-5727-9

PRINTED IN CHINA

EDITOR: LISA REGUL
DESIGNER: CHLOE RAWLINS
PRODUCTION MANAGER: DAN MYERS
COPYEDITOR: KRISTI HEIN
PROOFREADER: JEAN BLOMQUIST
INDEXER: KEN DELLAPENTA
PUBLICIST: LAUREN KRETZSCHMAR
MARKETER: MONICA STANTON

10 9 8 7 6 5 4 3 2 1

FIRST EDITION

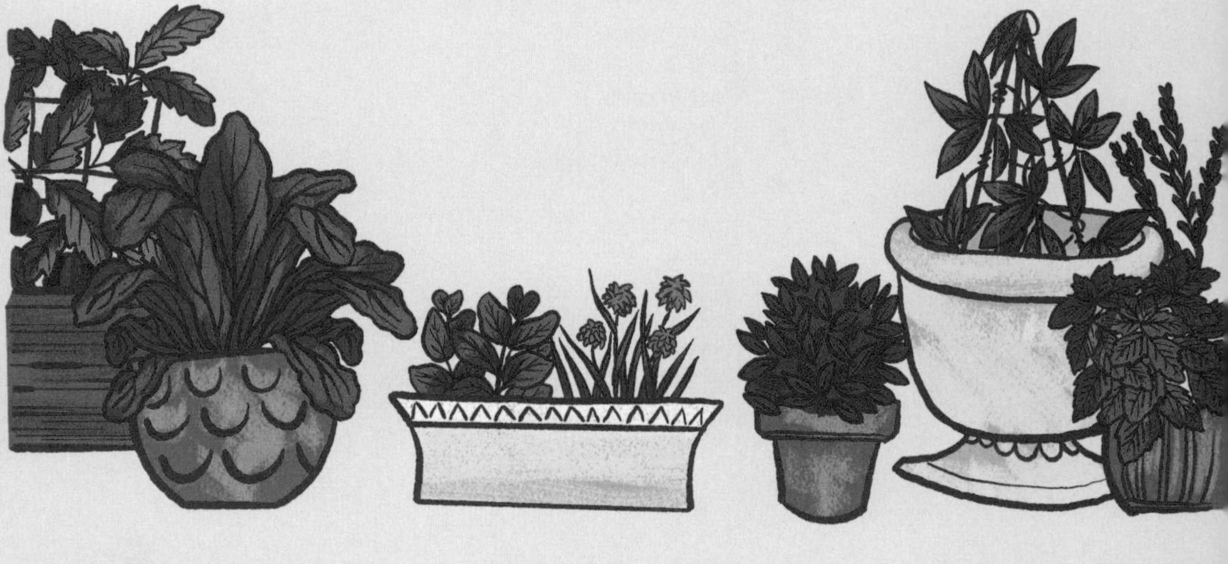